Liquefied natural gas

LNG export facility (completed)

LNG export facility (planned)

Major LNG shipping lanes

Major pipelines

Completed

Planned

Cancelled (NS2)

© Arnold Platon, 2022

Yamal LNG

Vostok

Norilsk

Vankor

Srednebotuobinskoye

Power of Siberia

Power of Siberia 2

Yamal-Europe

Moscow

Brotherhood

Sakhalin

Kyiv

Soyuz

Astana

Sakhalin LNG

Odesa

Kashagan

Tengiz

hwedt

Tbilisi

Central Asia China

Beijing

ofia

Baku

West-East Pipeline

Seoul

N.Burgas

Blue Stream

Ashgabat

Tokyo

İstanbul

Trans-Anatolian

sab

New Delhi

Qatar LNG

Karachi

Riyadh

Doha

Vadinar

Khartoum

Singapore

Cabo Delgado LNG

Gorgon LNG

Australia Pacific LNG

ECONOMIC WAR

NEW PERSPECTIVES ON EASTERN EUROPE AND EURASIA

The states of Eastern Europe and Eurasia are once again at the centre of global attention, particularly following Russia's 2022 full-scale invasion of Ukraine. But media coverage can only do so much in providing the necessary context to make sense of fast-moving developments. The books in this series provide original, engaging and timely perspectives on Eastern Europe and Eurasia for a general readership. Written by experts on—and from—these states, the books in the series cover an eclectic range of cutting-edge topics relating to politics, history, culture, economics and society. The series is originated by Hurst, with titles co-published or distributed in North America by Oxford University Press, New York.

Series editor: Dr Ben Noble—Associate Professor of Russian Politics at University College London and Associate Fellow at Chatham House.

MAXIMILIAN HESS

Economic War

Ukraine and the Global Conflict between Russia and the West

HURST & COMPANY, LONDON

First published in the United Kingdom in 2023 by
C. Hurst & Co. (Publishers) Ltd.,
New Wing, Somerset House, Strand, London, WC2R 1LA
© Maximilian Hess, 2023

Distributed in the United States, Canada and Latin America
by Oxford University Press, 198 Madison Avenue, New York,
NY 10016, United States of America.

A Cataloguing-in-Publication data record for this book
is available from the British Library.

ISBN: 9781787389564

www.hurstpublishers.com

Printed in Great Britain by Bell & Bain Ltd, Glasgow

How Far We Have Come,
Yet How Close We Remain

CONTENTS

INTRODUCTION

Ukraine has been beset by war since February 2014, when Russian President Vladimir Putin ordered his forces to seize Crimea. He subsequently fomented a conflict in Ukraine's eastern Donbas region. After eight years of conflict in Ukraine and growing tensions, Russia launched an all-out invasion on 24 February 2022, not only sparking the largest war in Europe since 1945 but also transforming Russian and Western tensions into an economic war—the impacts of which would be felt around the globe.

This book is about that economic war. It aims to explain why the conflict between Russia and the West escalated and why Russia's invasion of Ukraine triggered economic disruption on a global scale. Led by the West, the initial sanctions aimed to decrease Russia's linkages to the US-dominated international economic order. Russia, long convinced that it should be treated as a great power, responded by attempting to exacerbate intra-European tensions to weaken the efficacy of the initial sanctions and mitigate against the risk of further sanctions. Acting as a would-be great power, Russia has sought to build new linkages across the globe, as well as partnering with other states opposed to US influence over the international order.

Russia's initial invasion was prompted by Ukraine's 2014 Euromaidan Revolution, which forced the then Ukrainian President Viktor Yanukovych to flee the country. The revolution undoubtedly had an economic component, the first protests having been ignited by Yanukovych's decision to reject a trade agreement with the European Union. But its underlying cause was the Yanukovych government's deep corruption, which many protesters saw as intertwined with his pro-Russian agenda. Ahead of the revolution, Putin argued that closer links between Ukraine and the West, as envisaged in the association agreement, would threaten his own economic agenda and his vision for the future of Eurasia.[1]

1

Russia's annexation of Crimea shaped relations between Russia and the West in the ensuing years. Western sanctions dented Moscow's ability to seek financing in the West and made Putin's inner circle *personae non gratae*. Although most of Russia's biggest businesses and their economic linkages to the West were largely unaffected, the sanctions nonetheless prompted a visceral response from the Kremlin, which asserted firmer control over Russia's economy and increasingly sought to undermine the West's influence both at home and abroad. Russia also became increasingly active in seeking to foment the West's internal tensions, perhaps the most infamous example of which is the debate around Russia's role in Donald Trump's 2016 election as US president.

Although Russia's annexation of Crimea played a key role in the deterioration of Russian–US relations during this period, the book aims to contextualise the tensions between Russia and the West against the backdrop of developments occurring outside Ukraine. These are the focus of Part I, which begins with an examination of the genesis of the Russian and Western economic war in conjunction with Ukraine's Euromaidan Revolution and Putin's annexation of Crimea in 2014. It then examines how the West chose to fight back with sanctions, which is followed by a detailed analysis of their impact on Russia in Chapters 2 and 3. Chapter 4 argues that Europe's failure to adopt a unified approach to Russia's aggression offered the Kremlin key benefits in mitigating the initial sanctions and led it to hope it could avoid further sanctions in the future. As we will also see, many key regional players were able to take advantage of this situation to further their own interests, and how Turkey did so is the focus of Chapter 5. The book then returns to Eurasia in Chapter 6, as the region has traditionally been the site of the fiercest Russian–Western competition. Chapters 7 to 9, however, aim to show that some of the most important developments occurred farther afield, in Africa, Latin America, and Asia. Finally, Chapters 10 and 11 focus on China and key Middle Eastern countries that played a crucial role in escalating tensions.

Part I ends on the eve of Putin's decision to expand his war against Ukraine in February 2022. Launching a *blitzkrieg* towards Kyiv and bombing runs across the country, Putin not only sought to topple Ukraine's government and annex wide swathes of its territory but to restore Russia to great power status. Yet he failed to account for many crucial factors in making his decision to attack—least of all the Ukrainian people's willingness to resist, at significant cost. He also misjudged the West's unity and its ability and willingness to strike back, although the United States in particular made no secret of the fact that it planned to impose crippling sanctions on the Kremlin if it did undertake such an attack in the months leading up to the invasion.

But the question remains why the two parties were willing to escalate the conflict to the level that they did.

One line of argument consists of geographic determinism. In 1904, Halford Mackinder argued in his 'heartland theory' that '[w]ho rules East Europe commands the Heartland; who rules the Heartland commands the World-Island; who rules the World-Island commands the world'.[2] Mackinder focused on the balance of resources and state power and concluded that Eurasia's mass meant that whoever controlled its centre would dominate global politics. Applied to the war in Ukraine, Mackinderism holds that the reason a full-scale war in Ukraine led to an economic war was because Ukraine's ultimate orientation would have global repercussions.

Geography has indeed been a factor in the conflict. The proximity of Russian gas to European consumers, Russian conglomerates to European banks, and Russian oligarchs to glamourous European resorts has helped foster economic interdependency between Russia and the West even as their politics radically diverged following Putin's return to the presidency from his prime ministerial waiting post in 2012. But even Mackinder's theory proves sorely lacking as an explanation for how the conflict over Ukraine turned into an economic war.

Indeed, the fate of Ukraine's northern neighbour, Belarus, casts further doubt on Mackinder's hypothesis. In 2020, its strongman leader Alexander Lukashenko quashed protests after a blatantly rigged election. Belarusian opposition leader Sviatlana Tsikhanouskaya fled into exile and declared herself the rightful president, gaining vocal but not material support in the West. The economic fallout was minimal.

Putin prioritised Ukraine, and the wider Eurasian region, in a way that the West did not, seeing its closer affiliation with Europe after the Euromaidan Revolution as an indication that the West was seeking to encroach into Russia's 'near abroad'—the term for the region comprising former Soviet republics that Russia believes should be within its orbit.[3] Russia's desire to limit Western encroachment on its borders had already prompted it to go to war with Georgia in 2008. Tbilisi's government was openly seeking NATO membership at the time and had adopted a Western-backed free market agenda in the years after its pro-democracy Rose Revolution in 2004. The 2008 Russo-Georgian war was an attempt to deter the expansion of what Russia sees as the United States' NATO empire. Russia effectively occupied Georgia's Abkhazia and South Ossetia regions in the aftermath, making it all-but-impossible for Georgia's NATO membership aspirations to be realised. Russia's dominance of these regions and annexation of Crimea after 2014 served to lay the groundwork for his own rival empire. Though Kyiv was no closer to membership than it had been in 2008, Putin again used the NATO canard to justify his 2022 attack on Ukraine. But whereas the 2008 war had almost no international economic impact—US proposals for sanctions over Russia's actions went nowhere—and did not set the groundwork for major geo-economic competition between Russia and the West, Russia's 2014 attack on Ukraine did.

This book will return to how Russia's response unfolded in later chapters, but a key turning point was the passage of the United States' 2012 Magnitsky Act, the first sanctions legislation targeting Russia since the Soviet era. The bill consisted of a series of visa bans and asset freezes on Russian officials who were accused of involvement in the murder of lawyer Sergei Magnitsky. Magnitsky died in a Moscow jail cell. He had found himself imprisoned as an act of revenge for his work defending the interests of Bill Browder, an investment fund manager barred from returning to Russia in 2005 and declared a threat to national security after reversing his earlier support for Putin's anti-oligarch agenda. In preventing Browder from returning to Russia, the Kremlin effectively endorsed the seizure of Browder's wealth and barred him from business in the country that had generated it. Browder lobbied Congress to hold those responsible to account. The Obama administration initially opposed doing so and watered the bill down, but Congress included the Magnitsky Act in a bill meant to normalise trade with Russia.

The act did not threaten wider trade with Russia, nor was it an abuse of US power in the international economic order. Instead, it effectively meted out the same punishment to those who had pursued Browder as the Kremlin had imposed on him. The Russians targeted were barred from investing in and moving their money to the West, just as Browder had been barred from Russia. Nevertheless, Putin took this as a personal affront to his power and saw it as the very definition of US hypocrisy—declaring 'if they slap our face, we have to retaliate. Otherwise they'll go on slapping us for ever.'[4]

Putin thus saw the incident as evidence of the West's double standards, claiming that the United States had 'plenty of problems of that kind [referring to Magnitsky's mistreatment]. Abu Ghraib—or Guantanamo, where people are kept jailed years without being charged … they are up to the ears in shitty stuff, they're drowning in it, and they still insist on criticising us.'[5]

When the West responded to Russia's 2014 annexation of Crimea with more strident sanctions, Putin argued that he was only following the precedent that the West had set in recognising Kosovo's independence from Serbia, an argument he had also employed in the recognition of Abkhazia and South Ossetia six years earlier.[6] He also pointed to how the 2003 US-led invasion of Iraq had breached the same rules of the so-called 'international rules-based order' that Russia was now being penalised for breaking over its actions in Ukraine.

The difference between Russia and the United States is that the West has been able to take action over Russia's violations, whereas the West is impervious. There is no 'rules-based international order'—but there is an international economic order, and understanding the West's privileged position in it is key to understanding what would come to be at stake in the economic war.

The international economic order consists of the structures and networks that underpin both international trade and finance, from formal institutions such as the International Monetary Fund (IMF) to investment dispute mechanisms and arbitration courts. It is undoubtedly a Western-led order. The IMF and World Bank are formally sister agencies of the United Nations, but unlike the UN they are headquartered in Washington D.C. The United States has an effective veto over their management and directors. The order has a core European component as well. Interstate debts have historically been renegotiated at the Paris Club. English law is the preferred form of international commercial contracts and London is home to the world's largest trade finance and international credit insurance markets, even if relatively little of this is financed in pounds sterling. At the core of these institutions—and in turn the international economic order—is the US dollar, which serves as the ultimate reserve currency around the world, from the vaults of central banks to individual savers. Whereas the world once depended on gold to regulate international finance and commerce, today it depends on dollars. This grants the United States a form of economic power known as 'exorbitant privilege'. While the United States is not alone in its ability to bail out its banks and businesses in times of crisis—other countries with internationally traded currencies can also do so, as can some with closed markets, such as China—the difference is that the United States can shrug off concerns over the impact of such actions on its government balance sheet. The dollar is in such sufficient demand internationally that other countries effectively finance its growing deficits, which have little impact on the value of its currency.

This exorbitant privilege also sits at the core of US geopolitical strength—enabling it to insist on the enforcement of sanctions abroad, to shape allies' and adversaries' futures by determining their access to dollars, and to pursue activist foreign policies other countries can only dream of. And because even its rivals need dollars, it can do all of this with relative impunity, including with regard to acts of economic warfare.

The modern era is the first in which one country—the United States—enjoys such singular influence over international trade and finance. Economic globalisation and the resulting interdependence of major global economies have further strengthened the US position, as the dollar became the global reserve currency. After the Second World War, the United States was the only country left operating a gold standard, and it agreed to allow other countries to access gold through its currency—but it abrogated this policy in 1971, leaving countries reliant on the dollar as the reserve monetary instrument instead of gold.[7] Some 60 per cent of global foreign exchange reserves are denominated in dollars as of 2021.[8] The dollar is also the primary means of global exchange and financing: roughly 60 per cent of bank claims and liabilities globally are in dollars, while the number is closer to 79 per cent for trade invoices, a figure that would be even higher if the euro were not so dominant in Europe.[9] The dollar's role as the pre-eminent currency is at the heart of the United States' ability to police global financial and trade markets, as well as to impose sanctions—its key tools in the economic war. No other country has this ability.

Other countries can still engage in economic competition with one another, at least in the form of trade wars. The Trump administration initiated a trade war between the United States and China that has continued ever since, with Beijing fighting back with its own tariffs in response to US measures, with real impacts for the US economy. But while the United States can use sanctions as a tool of geopolitical power, Beijing cannot do so in a similar manner. It could seek to fight back by dumping its US Treasury assets, an idea that has often been floated, but China's dependency on the dollar means such a move would devastate its economy as well. Russia lacked the ability to effectively use financial instruments as a tool to pressure the West and the United States as well, albeit not for lack of trying. The Kremlin also had other tools that it could, and would, seek to use to undermine the United States' privileged position in the international economic order.

That the United States has a form of geo-economic power for which the Kremlin and other powers have no match provides the answer for why it was so willing to engage in the fight with Russia. Ukraine may have become an increasingly important feature of the political debate in Washington in the years between 2014 and 2022, but even were the Kremlin to conquer Kyiv, it would not in and of itself affect the United States' power in any significant way.

Washington was so committed to the conflict because it viewed Russia as a genuine threat to its leadership of the international economic order. Although it is far smaller in GDP terms, Russia's control over crucial commodities makes it a genuine threat to the West's economic stability—left unchecked, this could pose a real threat to the United States' leading position in the international economic order. The Kremlin made no secret that it was actively seeking to build up an alternative order together with countries such as China and India and increasingly over the post-2014 period even with countries that had more traditionally fallen into the Western orbit, such as Saudi Arabia and Turkey. And if Russia's actions were not dealt with, Russia's 2022 invasion of Ukraine even posed the risk of Europe becoming subservient to the Kremlin. If Russia had succeeded in its war on Ukraine, it would thus potentially enable Putin to realise his vision of an alternative economic order, one in which the United States was no longer so dominant. That was a risk Washington could not accept.

Part II of the book examines how Russia and the West's economic war has unfolded in the period since Russia's invasion of Ukraine in February 2022. Chapter 12 begins in Ukraine itself, examining how the West marshalled support for Kyiv as Russia's conflict recast its economy and politics. Chapter 13 then turns to how the West chose to respond with the most strident sanctions regime imposed by one major economic power on another since the lead-up to the Second World War. The book then examines the impact this had on Russia in Chapter 14. The following chapter outlines how Russia began to fight back, with Chapter 16 looking at how Europe in particular was affected by the economic war to a far greater extent than the United States, which has remained largely unscathed. Chapters 17 and 18 examine the global impact of the conflict and how Russia's strategy sought to undermine international macro-economic stability. The conclusion turns to the state of the conflict at the end of its first year, for while the economic war is not over—and will not be until Putin withdraws from Ukraine and sues for peace—there are clear lessons to be learned from how the conflict unfolded and escalated, including for avoiding a potentially even graver economic war between the West and China.

But to return to the narrative—while Putin saw the Magnitsky sanctions as the first step in the conflict, something the West considered a relatively minor issue at the time—Russia's first major salvo against the international economic order came while Yanukovych was still in power in Ukraine, struggling to hold on to office as the protests against him put Ukraine on the precipice of revolution in late 2013. For the West, the story of the economic war begins there.

PART I

2013–21

BOND OF WAR

Pavlo Mazurenko was one of the hundreds of thousands of Ukrainians who descended upon Kyiv's central Maidan Nezalezhnosti, Independence Square, in the winter of 2013. On 21 November, Mustafa Nayyem—an Afghanistan-born Ukrainian journalist—had taken to Facebook to urge his fellow citizens to come out and protest against President Viktor Yanukovych's decision to abandon talks on signing an Association Agreement with the European Union.[1]

Born in 1971 in Ukraine's western Zhytomyr region, Mazurenko's family subsequently moved to Crimea.[2] He went on to Kyiv to study engineering, graduating in 1995 and building a career as an IT engineer and programmer in the capital.[3] His life was unexceptional until the evening of 18 December 2013.[4]

The protests sparked by Nayyem's call led to a major political crisis. Independence Square had turned into a battlefield, with protesters setting up barricades to separate them from police and counter protesters encamped uphill from the square around Ukraine's presidential palace. Yanukovych's security services had sought to disperse the demonstrations, but they had rapidly spread nationwide. Tents on the square carried signs representing all of Ukraine's regions, including predominantly Russophone Crimea and Donetsk. A group of dedicated activists formed the 'Automaidan' movement that sought to disrupt police crackdowns and use car rallies to take the protest out of the square and to Yanukovych's allies' homes.

Mazurenko was not a protest leader. However, given the tense environment, the police were questioning anyone found walking around Kyiv at night outside of the security that the protesters occupying the Maidan provided. According to Mazurenko's wife, when police challenged him, and he produced documentation that showed he was not registered as living in Kyiv, they beat him to a pulp.[5] Mazurenko succumbed to his wounds, including a punctured lung, four days later.[6]

Despite the escalating violence in Kyiv, Yanukovych was still seeking to keep Ukraine in hock to Moscow. Although this path was the very thing that had prompted the protests, Yanukovych doubled-down because his own wealth and hold on power depended on partnering with a regime that would turn a blind eye to, and even enable, his corruption.[7]

The day before the assault on Mazurenko, Yanukovych was in Moscow. He was no stranger to Ukraine's revolutionary tumult, having initially been declared the winner of the November 2004 presidential runoff against Viktor Yushchenko before Ukraine's Supreme Court declared that result invalid. Yushchenko—who had run on a pro-Western reform platform—was poisoned during the campaign with dioxin, one of the key ingredients in 'Agent Orange', used as a chemical weapon by the US military during the Vietnam war.[8] Mass protests had broken out over the rigging of the election and Yushchenko's poisoning. Yanukovych would lose to Yushchenko when the election was re-run that December. It was dubbed the Orange Revolution.

Yanukovych's December 2013 trip to Moscow was an effort to save his government from crisis. The protests' intensity was approaching that of the Orange Revolution, but Russia had made clear that it saw Ukraine as having no future outside its orbit. In the months before Yanukovych abandoned the EU Association Agreement, the Kremlin had heavily pressured Ukraine's economy, introducing random customs checks at the border and barring various imports—from chocolates to steel pipes.[9] The Kremlin cited an array of excuses for the moves. But Putin was publicly adamant that Ukraine's planned Association Agreement with the EU was a 'great threat' to Russia's own economy[10] and demanded that Ukraine join his nascent Eurasian Economic Union, a rival bloc seeking to turn the post-Soviet space into a unified trade and customs zone. The trade spat with Russia strained Ukraine's economy, which had already fallen into recession in 2012, and thus the Ukrainian government's balance sheet. This prompted credit rating agencies to judge Ukraine at very high risk of default by September 2013.[11]

When Yanukovych met with Putin in the Kremlin, Yanukovych agreed to Putin's terms for a bailout. Russia's National Welfare Fund, a sovereign wealth fund collecting excess energy revenues, would spend $15 billion buying new Ukrainian government bonds.[12] Protesters in Kyiv were outraged at Yanukovych's decision to abandon their EU aspirations and to turn to Moscow instead. Tensions flared as they seized several buildings around Independence Square over the coming weeks. Yanukovych's crack-down would only escalate, with special forces opening fire on demonstrators in February 2014.

One hundred and five more Ukrainians were killed as Yanukovych sought to hold on to power before he fled the Ukrainian capital on 21 February 2014. They would ultimately be enshrined on Ukraine's list of national heroes known as the Heavenly Hundred, as would Mazurenko.[13] Yanukovych, however, became a national outcast—after fleeing Kyiv, he went to Crimea, and from there to Moscow.[14] But Russia's invasion had already begun.[15] Russian soldiers cartoonishly camouflaged as unaffiliated 'little green men' quickly began seizing key positions in Crimea. The Kremlin issued perfunctory denials of involvement, dubbing the soldiers 'polite people', though Putin ultimately admitted responsibility on 17 April.[16]

Putin had already laid the groundwork for using the conflict in Ukraine to challenge the international economic order. Three billion dollars of the bonds Yanukovych had agreed to sell the Kremlin had already changed hands. The sale revealed how Russia's actions in Ukraine were part of a wider agenda to weaken the West's advantages in the international economic order.

Bonds are an instrument for enabling loans from one party to another. What differentiates bonds from other loans is that they are exchangeable. Interest and principal repayments flow not to the original issuer of the bond but to their holder when these payments come due. Such debts have sat at the core of state finance for centuries. Venice transformed itself from a city-state into a mercantile and military power on the back of the first ever such debt, the *prestiti*, beginning in the twelfth century.[17] Today, bonds form the backbone of capital markets, and governments use their own sovereign bonds to finance their expenditure and underpin their banks.

There are two primary forms of sovereign bonds, domestic-issued bonds in a country's own currency and those issued in foreign currency, predominantly in a form known as Eurobonds. This moniker can be misleading, as most Eurobond issuance is in dollars. Such debts are almost entirely written under English law or New York law, granting creditors and debtors the security of established legal systems but also granting outsize influence to the United States and the UK in these markets. That developing countries in the modern era cannot borrow abroad in their domestic currency, but must do so in established currencies, has come to be known as 'original sin', as developing countries are in an unprivileged position in financial markets compared to developed ones that have currencies that are accepted abroad.[18] These currencies are referred to as 'hard currencies' and consist of the major international currencies such as the dollar and euro that constitute most reserves.

Eurobonds address this deficiency but pose a structural risk to borrowers—a country cannot print foreign currency, whereas it is free to print its own. However, there are many advantages to accepting this risk. Issuing hard currency Eurobonds enables developing countries to invest for their long-term future and to establish a yield curve—the difference in the value between receiving cash today and receiving it at various points in the future—for borrowing in those currencies. This in turn creates a base rate for lending to companies in those markets and ensuring they have access to hard currencies with which they can trade internationally.

The power of debt should not be underappreciated. Borrowing enables the moving of money over time. The power of this effect enables most real estate transactions, where buyers use a mortgage to borrow a multiple of their down-payment to afford a home. In addition to this power over individual lives and economic fortunes, borrowing can also have a macro-economic impact when such loans grow large enough to be considered systemic risks. This was epitomised by the 2008 global financial crisis, as the collapse of the mortgage-backed security market—i.e. bonds backed by home loans—swept across the globe and prompted banks to curtail lending (a so-called credit crunch). The ensuing Great Recession was only constrained by the extraordinary response of central banks buying up trillions of dollars of debts, a process known as quantitative easing.

As the Great Recession demonstrated, credit markets can have historic ramifications. Sovereign Eurobonds are arguably even more important than the mortgage markets that precipitated that crisis: they underpin the very central banks that manage the mortgage market and are therefore significant in relation to the power of the state. Sovereign Eurobonds are the primary instrument for states to raise money and for private creditors to invest in their growth. They also serve as a benchmark for the issuing state's creditworthiness in relation to other borrowers. They are inherently political.

To understand the importance of Russia's Eurobond strategy in Ukraine, it is therefore important to understand the power structures of international debt markets.

No country parallels the power that the United States has over global debt markets, at least over the last fifty years. President Richard Nixon withdrew the United States from the gold standard—ending the free conversion of dollars into gold at a fixed rate—in 1971. At the time, the world was still dominated by capital controls, restrictions on moving currencies and savings across borders. This was because of the prevailing economic orthodoxy on the so-called 'economic trilemma'—the idea that countries can choose to have sovereignty over only two of three policy choices: allowing capital to flow freely, maintaining a fixed currency exchange rate, and being able to independently set interest rates. At the time, the prevailing consensus was that nations should choose options two and three and maintain capital controls.

Nixon's move collapsed the post-Second World War Bretton Woods settlement in which countries would rely on the dollar to access gold. Although his move was intended to weaken, not strengthen, the dollar, its ultimate effect was to solidify the dollar's role as the global reserve currency—in effect making dollars the new gold. The key factor in enabling this transformation, however, was that Nixon's actions incentivised foreign bankers to circumvent capital controls. The Eurobond was invented as a tool to facilitate this circumvention. [19]

Eurobonds would render capital controls effectively meaningless, and throughout the 1970s and 1980s the world adjusted to a new stance on the trilemma. The preferred settlement abandoned fixed exchange rates for free-flowing capital and allowing markets to determine exchange rates. Even the Soviet Union got in on the game, issuing its first Eurobond in August 1986.[20]

The complex market mechanics of such loans are significant to this story. It is important to note that Eurobonds are an instrument for states to borrow from private markets. When news headlines announce that a country has fallen into default, that is, failed to meet its financial obligations, they typically refer to failures to meet the contracted terms of its Eurobonds. States can be sued for such breaches in English and New York courts—and they frequently are.

Russia's decision to bail out the Yanukovych regime with Eurobonds was unprecedented. States have their own intergovernmental debt structures—governed by international financial institutions, most prominently the IMF—whereas Eurobonds are used by private investors to loan to governments. Interstate loans, unlike Eurobonds, are typically not tradable, or fungible, and are often offered at concessional rates—which has led to an established consensus that they be renegotiated separately from private sovereign debts such as Eurobonds. Russia's move to use Eurobonds to loan to Ukraine blurred the lines between intergovernmental and private debt markets, essentially seeking to make both categories of Ukraine's debt stock a political battlefield. It also threatened to cause major challenges for Western countries seeking to lend to a subsequent Ukrainian government as doing so would push it into a dispute with its private creditors in the event of a restructuring.

The move initially received little attention. One of the first to ring the alarm bells was sovereign debt scholar Mitu Gulati, who identified an extraordinary clause pledging Ukraine not to exceed a 60 per cent debt-to-GDP ratio.[21] If Ukraine's debts exceeded that level, Russia could demand repayment and push Ukraine into default on its Eurobonds.

The Eurobonds that Yanukovych sold to Russia also contained a clause seemingly designed to protect Russia's leverage over natural gas, one of its key economic tools for shaping relations with Ukraine. If Ukraine missed a payment on the Eurobond, it would enable the bondholder to order immediate repayment of any other debts owed 'to any entity controlled or majority owned by the Noteholder'—and Ukraine was already $3 billion in arrears to Russia's state-owned gas giant Gazprom.[22] Including such a specific provision in a sovereign Eurobond was also unprecedented.

The world of sovereign Eurobonds is governed by stability and the fungibility of similar debts for one another. The slightest change in the wording of their contracts, or the interpretation thereof, can have dramatic impacts. For example, in 2012 Argentina fell into default over a novel interpretation of the Latin phrase *pari passu* in its bond contracts—a phrase translating roughly as 'on an equal footing'—by a New York court.[23] The discovery of the few altered sentences in the Eurobonds sold by Yanukovych to Russia was a shocking revelation to the small coterie of sovereign debt scholars who pick over such markets and recognised the Eurobond's potential as a tool to keep Kyiv in hock to Moscow. The Eurobond also spread the tentacles of Russia's war on Ukraine into international capital markets as its soldiers spread across Crimea.

Russia also attacked Ukraine in a more traditional sense. Following Yanukovych's ouster, Ukraine was in a chaotic state. Putin dispatched Russian troops to seize control of Crimea; Ukrainian commanders who refused to join Russia were forced to stand down at gunpoint, but the chaos in Kyiv meant there was little chance of putting up an effective resistance. Putin also deployed special forces to eastern Ukraine and fomented once-fringe Russian nationalist political movements there. Russia announced the annexation of Crimea on 18 March, twenty-five days after Yanukovych fled Kyiv.

On 6 April 2014, Putin's attacks spread to Donetsk and Luhansk, the capitals of the two eponymous regions that make up Ukraine's Donbas. Employing similar tactics to those used in Crimea, the armed men who seized government buildings in the region denied any links to the Kremlin, though some identified themselves as members of Yanukovych's Berkut special forces, which had been blamed for most of the killings during the Euromaidan Revolution in Kyiv.[24] Despite its denials, Moscow's involvement was obvious—social media reports from the families of fallen Russian soldiers provided ample evidence.[25]

On 7 April, Ukraine declared it would fight back, launching an 'anti-terrorist' operation in the Donbas. Ukraine simultaneously made clear that it blamed Moscow for the seizures of state institutions, revealing that an officer from the Main Directorate of the General Staff of the Russian Armed Forces, commonly known as the GRU, had been arrested for coordinating the unrest.[26] Putin had brought war to Ukraine's industrial heartland.

While Yanukovych was still in power, Putin argued that were Ukraine to join the EU, it would pose a threat to the Russian economy and that Ukraine needed to integrate economically with Russia's Eurasian Economic Union instead.[27] Russia's decision to attack Ukraine after it turned towards the West thus made it clear that the Eurasian Economic Union project was simply an imperial venture seeking to lock Ukraine into Russia's orbit and under its dominance. As Russian arms poured in, many of Ukraine's most economically significant assets came under threat. On 13 April, pro-Russian forces seized the city councils of Mariupol and Yenakiieve. Mariupol was home to two giant steel plants, Azovstal and Illyich Steel, and Yenakiieve housed a third, the Yenakiieve Iron and Steel Works.[28]

All three steel factories were owned by Rinat Akhmetov, one of Ukraine's most powerful businessmen, through his holding company SCM Holdings' majority stake in the company Metinvest.[29] Many of the Donbas' largest coal mines also belonged to Akhmetov, through his firm DTEK. Metinvest and DTEK formed the bulk of Akhmetov's assets, alongside extensive media holdings and the football club Shakhtar Donetsk, which had become a serious European competitor thanks to Akhmetov's largesse, winning the UEFA Cup in 2009.

Akhmetov's wealth had long made him one of the most influential people in Ukrainian politics. The Maidan protesters in Kyiv saw him as the man behind the Yanukovych regime. A model court displayed on the Maidan during the protests listed Akhmetov as due for execution alongside Yanukovych and Viktor Medvedchuk, another oligarch-cum-politician (in)famous for naming Putin guest-of-honour at his 2003 wedding and having Putin baptise his daughter the following year.[30] When Yanukovych flew to Moscow for the meeting with Putin to agree the bailout-cum-bond sale, he did so on Akhmetov's plane.[31]

Oligarchs in the post-Soviet space are seen as political actors, but there is a stark difference in the role they play in Ukraine compared to Russia, where Putin spent years neutering their political influence.[32] David Dalton, an expert on the politics of Ukrainian oligarchy, explained that 'whereas Russia's oligarchs were defeated and subordinated by the state, in Ukraine, neither the politicians nor any of the big oligarchs and their originally region-based networks have ever been able to get the upper hand for long'.[33] Ukrainian oligarchs have both clashed and collaborated with Ukraine's various post-independence governments—and many have risen to Ukraine's top political posts. In effect, pre-Euromaidan Ukraine was very much an oligarchic state—one in which businessmen had sway over the distribution of spoils—in contrast to the kleptocratic state Putin built up, in which he claimed exclusive remit over the distribution of spoils to a narrow elite. Putin had enforced a transition from oligarchy to kleptocracy by curtailing the power of the businessmen who dominated Russia in the 1990s and transferring that power to his allies from St Petersburg and his pre-presidential career in the security services. In Ukraine, the oligarchs still dominated.

Russia's invasion threatened to overturn Ukraine's oligarchic order. Putin had few qualms with this order when he used it to Russia's advantage, as he had throughout the 2000s, for example, with companies connected to the businessman Dmytro Firtash positioned as middlemen in dealings between Russia's and Ukraine's state gas companies.[34] Firtash's position in the trade was diminished after Ukraine's nominally pro-Western Prime Minister Yulia Tymoshenko signed a new contract with Gazprom in 2009. Putin had labelled Tymoshenko as someone he could 'do business with'—a nod to her own lucrative background in the energy trade, which had earned her the moniker 'Gas Princess'.[35] But the shifting political allegiances of Ukraine's oligarchic class around the Maidan Revolution had proven they could be a threat to Putin's agenda, as could Western actions—Firtash was arrested on US corruption charges in Austria shortly after the revolution.[36] Putin's 2014 attack was in part intended to put Ukraine's oligarchs in their place and to re-assert Russia's dominance. The conflict put their assets in the firing line, and Putin hoped the oligarchs would rally for peace on the Kremlin's terms or create conditions for oligarchs more amenable to the Kremlin to return to the fore. But it had the opposite effect.

Akhmetov had already sought to distance himself from Yanukovych during the Maidan crackdown, albeit unsuccessfully. However, in one of the most decisive moments in the initial conflict, Akhmetov inveighed against Russian-backed separatist forces, calling on workers from his steelworks to take back control from the separatists. Mariupol was swiftly returned to Ukrainian control, with Akhmetov in an awkward symbiosis with Ukraine's new interim government.[37]

Some of Akhmetov's assets were also located in the territory that was ultimately seized by the proxy statelets Moscow forged in eastern Ukraine, the 'people's republics' of Donetsk and Luhansk. Those assets fared far worse than those remaining in Ukrainian-held territory. Yenakiieve Steel Works' production plummeted—and it was ultimately seized by the Russian-backed separatists.[38] Many assets in the occupied territory would be handed to another oligarch, Sergei Kurchenko, a member of Yanukovych's inner circle before the revolution.[39]

The revolution and subsequent conflict recast the networks of Ukraine's politicians and oligarchs, though it failed to break the system that enabled them to rotate in and out of business and politics. Petro Poroshenko—a former member of Yanukovych's cabinet known as the 'Chocolate King' in homage to his confectionary conglomerate Roshen—was elected president in May as fighting raged in the Donbas. Another major oligarch, Ihor Kolomoisky, who led Privat Group and controlled Ukraine's largest bank, also became a key figure, funding militias supporting Ukrainian sovereignty.[40] Poroshenko appointed him governor of Ukraine's Dnipropetrovsk region, from which many of his fighters were recruited and where he controlled extensive assets, to support the effort.

Kolomoisky soon fell out with Poroshenko's government over control of the oil firm Ukrnafta. The Ukrainian government held a majority stake, but Kolomoisky had previously been able to control the company's board with a 42 per cent stake and corporate governance laws designed to favour him. In 2015, Poroshenko was pursuing reforms to Ukraine's state assets, having pledged to do so in exchange for financial support from the West and to stem the financial bleeding by oligarchic interests. In an attempt to retain control, Kolomoisky allegedly brought in members of the militia he funded to resist Russia's attacks in Eastern Ukraine and to surround Ukrnafta's Kyiv offices that March in an effort to force Poroshenko to halt reforms that would undermine his control of the business.[41] Kolomoisky was sacked shortly thereafter. Poroshenko and Kolomoisky had fallen out over the distribution of Ukraine's spoils, but Putin no longer had a say in these matters.

Kolomoisky described the shifting alliances of Ukrainian oligarchs amid the conflict in a December 2015 interview with Politico. Explaining why he and former rival Akhmetov had entered into an alliance in support of Ukraine's sovereignty while simultaneously fighting with Poroshenko, Kolomoisky retorted:

> You know the joke about the dying Armenian? He surrounds himself with all his children and relatives, and he tells them to take care of the Jews. They ask him why. 'Because if they aren't there,' he says, 'they will come after us next.' Akhmetov and I need to take care of each other, because if he goes, they'll come after me. And if I go, they will come after him.[42]

Kolomoisky's explanation may have been off-colour, but he correctly identified that Russia's war had recast Ukraine's economy and its internal balance of power. Kolomoisky would ultimately be among the biggest losers of this process when he was stripped of control of Privat Bank in 2016 after the Ukrainian government claimed he had siphoned off funds to other areas of his business empire—but whereas in the past Ukrainian oligarchs could seek to make deals with the Kremlin for support in such circumstances, Putin's attacks on Ukraine meant this was no longer an option.

Privat Bank's nationalisation cost Ukraine some $5.6 billion.[43] That Kyiv even had the funds to take over the bank was the result of the West's fight back against Russia's economic war on the country via a series of emergency loans and aid from the EU, the United States, and the IMF.[44] However, this aid was not enough to alleviate all the devastation that Russia's war had wrought on the economy. Kyiv's new authorities needed another source of funds to sustain the country. US-born Finance Minister Natalie Jaresko was tasked with leading the effort of restructuring Ukraine's debts and sustaining its finances.[45]

The United States stepped in to help keep Kyiv afloat, with the Obama administration agreeing to $3 billion in guarantees for Ukrainian Eurobonds between May 2014 and June 2016.[46] These guarantees enabled Kyiv to borrow from the market at a far lower rate than would otherwise have been the case, as the guarantee meant if Ukraine failed to pay, Washington would pick up the bill. The European Union provided a €1 billion loan as well, and both Brussels and Washington offered humanitarian and non-lethal military supplies. The IMF and World Bank also stepped in to support Ukraine with billions of dollars of new loans. But these required restructuring Ukraine's debts, which Putin's invasion and ensuing ravaging of Eastern Ukraine had made unsustainable. Ukraine's private and public creditors would have to take losses in the principal of loans.

The Eurobond that Yanukovych had sold to Russia in 2013 threatened to disrupt these efforts. Russia would seek to use the the Eurobond as leverage in both Ukraine's private and official, i.e. interstate, sovereign debt restructuring processes.

The Kremlin initially argued that the Eurobond was only a private debt, refusing to include it in its list of claims at the Paris Club, the forum where Western countries agree to restructure interstate loans. The Kremlin did not oppose a February 2015 IMF programme for Ukraine, and Kyiv continued to pay contracted interest payments on the Eurobond.[47]

Russia would wait until Ukraine began negotiations with its private bondholders to use the Eurobond's unique terms to its advantage. It sought to complicate the process by saying that if it were to agree to a restructuring, it would demand far better terms than those offered to other creditors.[48] Ukraine refused but continued to make interest payments on the Russian-held Eurobond. When it ultimately agreed to a restructuring with its other Eurobond holders, it excluded the one held by Russia. Russian Finance Minister Anton Siluanov subsequently announced that Russia considered the bond as official debt.[49] If the Kremlin could not frustrate Ukraine's private debt restructuring, it would seek to complicate support for Kyiv from international financial institutions.

The Kremlin had a clear reason for doing so. At the time, the IMF had a rule that countries in dispute with other states over their official debts could not receive a bailout. By claiming the bond was official debt, Moscow threatened to pull the rug out from under the IMF regarding its support for Ukraine. But the IMF acted to prevent such a catastrophe.

On 10 December 2015, ten days before the Eurobond was set to mature, which would have required Kyiv to pay the Kremlin $3.15 billion, the IMF changed its rules on lending to countries behind on their payments to other sovereigns. The adjustment allowed the IMF to lend to countries in arrears to official creditors. Though the IMF has steadfastly denied that the move was political, it did explain the decision by citing a policy paper arguing that the old policy risked allowing 'an official bilateral creditor to block IMF assistance to a debtor country by refusing to participate in a restructuring'.[50] The announcement was also published in just two languages, English and Russian, an indication of the intended audience.[51]

Russia vociferously denounced the IMF's policy change. Then-Prime Minister Dmitry Medvedev blamed the United States for the move, saying it had used its influence to push the IMF to take action hostile to Russia, while ignoring his own country's weaponisation of Ukraine's debt. He compared the move to the opening of Pandora's, warning of grave ramifications for the international economic order.[52]

The Eurobond saga showed that Russia's attempts to weaken and subjugate Ukraine while undermining the Western-led institutions of the global economy were fully intertwined. Russia had used the loan to try to undermine the international economic order from within. But much as Russia's seizure of Crimea and fomenting of conflict in the Donbas had inadvertently weakened its influence over Ukraine's oligarchic class, this move also proved to have unintended consequences. Western influence over the institutions of the global economy was resilient to Russia's legal manoeuvres. This same influence gave it far greater tools for the fightback against Putin's agenda as well.

2

THE WEST FIGHTS BACK

While geo-economic competition extends far beyond the realm of sanctions, sanctions are increasingly the preferred tool for Western countries, and in particular the United States, to leverage their economic influence.[1] Less than a week after the annexation of Crimea, the US Treasury took its first major action.

On 20 March 2014, the Office of Foreign Assets Control (OFAC), the branch of the Treasury that wields the United States' most significant sanctions tools, announced it was blacklisting sixteen members of Putin's inner circle and one financial institution, Bank Rossiya.

Credit cards issued by Bank Rossiya had become something of a status symbol for the Russian elite. The American Express 'black card' is famous as a marker that its holder can spend upwards of a quarter-of-a-million dollars annually; Bank Rossiya cards signified something far less quantifiable but potentially even more lucrative: proximity to the Kremlin. They stopped working within twenty-four hours of OFAC's action.

Whereas Russia's two largest state-owned banks, VTB and Sberbank, had become established players internationally, with offices in London, New York, and Berlin, Bank Rossiya had no such presence. What attention the bank had attracted was from observers of Putin's background and his rise from the Soviet KGB to the Russian presidency. Bank Rossiya was founded in the dying months of the Soviet Union by local Communist Party insiders in St Petersburg. By the end of 1991, however, it was under the control of the city's new mayor, Anatoly Sobchak, and his deputy, Vladimir Putin.[2] Putin quickly rose from his role as Sobchak's link to the KGB to become his right-hand man, helping shape the city's economic future.[3]

By 2014, Bank Rossiya was controlled by Yuri Kovalchuk, whom OFAC dubbed the 'personal banker for senior officials of the Russian Federation including Putin' when blacklisting him in 2014.[4] Many of the businessmen and politicians connected to the bank had worked alongside Putin in his early St Petersburg political career, and many had gone on to amass great wealth.[5] Nevertheless, eight years later, this network could still be linked to billions of dollars' worth of assets across Russia, regardless of the waves of further sanctions against those close to Putin.[6]

Alongside Kovalchuk and Bank Rossiya, twelve senior Kremlin officials and three further members of Putin's inner circle, brothers Boris and Arkady Rotenberg and businessman Gennady Timchenko, were blacklisted by OFAC in March 2014.[7] Timchenko's blacklisting threatened to have a far larger global impact than the sanctions on Bank Rossiya.

Timchenko co-founded the commodities trading firm Gunvor, which had become the world's fourth largest commodities trader in the fourteen years since its establishment.[8] OFAC asserted that this overlap with Putin's presidency was no coincidence, alleging that 'Putin has investments in Gunvor and may have access to Gunvor funds.'[9] Within hours, Gunvor announced that Timchenko had sold his share to his Swedish business partner, Torbjörn Törnqvist, the previous day.[10] According to Törnqvist, they had been tipped off about the coming sanctions by the firm's lobbyists in Washington.[11]

It later turned out that Törnqvist lacked the funds for the purchase at the time, with a special $1 billion dividend from Gunvor in 2016 used to settle his debts to Timchenko, who remained unsanctioned in the European Union until 2022.[12] Since buying out Timchenko, Törnqvist has publicly sought to distance himself from Russia and diversified Gunvor's business away from its previous reliance on Russia. The sanctions may not have been perfect, but they appear to have removed Putin's alleged influence over the firm. The Kremlin's state capacity was being targeted.

Sanctions come in many forms. The blacklisting of Timchenko, Bank Rossiya, and Kovalchuk are examples of the most powerful tool in the United States' sanctions armoury: the specially designated nationals (SDN) list. Inclusion on the SDN list bars all interactions between the individual targeted and the US financial system. As Washington considers the latter to include any user of dollars, US sanctions have near-global extraterritoriality.

Russia's 2014 invasion of Ukraine also prompted Washington to develop new economic weapons. Though these were more narrowly targeted than the SDN restrictions, they would have a far larger impact on Russia's position in the global economy.

VTB and Sberbank may have had international offices, but they were not systemically significant to the wider world economy or even that of the European countries where they had established branches. Russia's state gas and oil giants, Gazprom and Rosneft, however, very much were. In 2013, Gazprom supplied 28 per cent of the European Union's natural gas.[13] As early as 2007, the Kremlin had declared its intention to make Gazprom the first trillion-dollar company. Rosneft was of a similarly significant size, producing around 5 per cent of global oil.[14]

The hydrocarbons boom Russia was able to capitalise on in the years after Putin came to power not only enabled significant headline growth. Russia's GDP in 2013 was nearing $4 trillion, up from $2 trillion in 1999, in part fuelled by access to European credit. By the time Putin invaded Crimea, Rosneft and Gazprom were two of the largest developing market firms borrowing in the Western financial system, collectively owing more than $60 billion.[15]

The same day as Kovalchuk's, Bank Rossiya's, and Timchenko's blacklisting, President Barack Obama signed Executive Order 13662. The order threatened sanctions on Russian 'financial services, energy, metals and mining industries, engineering, and defense and related materiel'. However, Obama announced that he would refrain from implementing the sanctions, which would instead be triggered if the Kremlin escalated further. He warned 'these sanctions would not only have a significant impact on the Russian economy, but could also be disruptive to the global economy'.[16]

The warning went unheeded. Over the next three months, Russian arms and special forces poured into Eastern Ukraine, arranging 'independence' referendums and the Potemkin facades of separatist states, essentially repeating the Crimea playbook. And as

Ukraine fought back in its east, Russian forces became ever more directly involved.

On 16 July 2014, the United States announced it would proceed with sectoral sanctions, creating a new designation, the sectoral sanctions identifications (SSI) list.[17] Companies could be affected by one or more of four OFAC directives under the programme. The directives targeted debt financing, new equity issuances, certain accounts for financial institutions, and Russian shale, deep-water, and Arctic hydrocarbon projects. The initial financial industry targets were VEB and Gazprombank, two banks for state investment. The first energy sector targets were Rosneft and Novatek, Russia's second largest gas producer after Gazprom. Controlled by Timchenko and Leonid Mikhelson, who remained unsanctioned, Novatek had since 2010 been developing Russia's first liquefied natural gas (LNG) export terminal on the Yamal Peninsula in the Arctic.

The sectoral sanctions drew a clear line between how business had been done with Russia previously and how the White House wanted it to be done thereafter. Russian energy was no longer going to be the engine of growth that it had been, and businesses seen as connected to the Kremlin would no longer be able to finance themselves with Western credit. But the Obama administration was proceeding alone, with European leaders hesitant to endorse similar sanctions.

A tragedy would change that. The day after the United States launched the sectoral sanctions, one of the war's deadliest incidents brought the conflict in Ukraine to the top of the global agenda. At 4:20 pm local time, a Russian 9M38 missile shot down Malaysian Airlines Flight MH17 in the skies over Donetsk;[18] 298 people were killed. Russia engaged in a disinformation campaign to try to deflect blame on to Kyiv, but the propaganda was so absurd that one of the longest-serving correspondents at the Russian state's English-language propaganda network, RT, quit in protest.[19] A Dutch-led international investigation would find that the missile's launcher was supplied by Russia, that the missile had been launched from territory controlled by Russian proxies, and that the launcher subsequently returned to Russia.[20]

Dutch Foreign Minister Frans Timmermans led the effort to bring Europe on board with the sectoral sanctions after the

MH17 disaster, lobbying recalcitrant European leaders by citing his personal ties to MH17 victims.[21] Persuading his European counterparts to go along with the move was no easy task—Europe was heavily divided over whether to pursue such sanctions. Many of the bloc's eastern members were fearful of Russia and saw its economic linkages as a tool of malign influence and as a result were in favour of sectoral sanctions. Leading politicians from many of the EU's western member states were more reticent, noting the potential impact on their own economies given their dependence on Russian energy supplies.

On 29 July, the European Union duly agreed to implement sectoral sanctions—but its internal divides and Russian energy dependency meant it only joined those that the United States imposed on Russia's financial sector and left the energy sector untouched. It also imposed an arms embargo on Russia and introduced restrictions on the export of dual-use goods, those with both military and non-military applications.

These dual-use and arms export restrictions directly targeted Russia's war-fighting capability. France scrapped a deal to sell Russia two helicopter gunships, which had been due to be the largest-ever Western arms sale to Russia.[22] But the impact of the restrictions was far more wide reaching, as demonstrated by the fate of Russia's efforts to develop new helicopters for its state civilian and military aircraft manufacturer, the uncreatively named Russian Helicopters.

Before Russia invaded Ukraine, the vehicles produced by Russian Helicopters had been powered primarily by engines from the Ukrainian firm Motor Sich. One of the world's largest military helicopter manufacturers, it claimed 56 per cent of the global market for heavy-lift helicopters in 2013.[23] But its forebears were developed during the Soviet period, when internal borders were of little importance to economic planners. After the collapse of the USSR, Russian helicopter production continued to rely on Motor Sich, which was happy to do business with Russia much as it had in the Soviet era, albeit far more profitably.

The firm was controlled by Vyacheslav Bohuslayev, an engineer who had taken over the company during the messy privatisations that followed the Soviet collapse. He became one of Ukraine's main businessmen-cum-politicians and was a member of Yanukovych's ruling Party of Regions before the 2014 revolution.[24] However, Motor Sich's ties to Russia were deeply affected by the Russian invasion—Ukraine's own sanctions on Russia barred it from doing business with the Kremlin. US and EU sectoral sanctions meant Russia was unable to import substitutes or seek Western expertise in developing its own engines, while corruption in its military and engineering industries further hampered the development of replacements.[25]

Corruption did, however, enable Russia to continue to receive some supplies from Motor Sich after Russia's 2014 revolution. Ukrainian media and open-source investigations would reveal that the firm sent more than $250 million worth of helicopter engine components to Russia between 2017 and 2019, via Bosnia and Herzegovina.[26]

There would be intense battles for control of Motor Sich in the years after 2014. China's Skyrizon Aviation agreed to buy control from Bohuslayev in 2017 but saw its shares frozen by a Ukrainian court on national security grounds.[27] The United States also decried Motor Sich's planned sale, and in January 2021 both Kyiv and Washington imposed sanctions on Skyrizon.[28] In March 2021, the Ukrainian government announced it would nationalise the firm, offering compensation to Skyrizon and its partners, who are still pursuing damages via arbitration.[29]

The fates of Bank Rossiya, Gunvor, and Motor Sich demonstrate how sanctions can work, as well as their limitations. Other examples will follow, but these stories reveal an underlying thread: sanctions are political restrictions and are therefore shaped by the geopolitical and domestic environment of the countries in which targeted entities operate.

The successful implementation of sanctions, and geo-economic policy more broadly, therefore requires careful and considered application by the countries issuing such sanctions. The November 2016 election of Donald Trump as president of the United States would threaten to throw the West's economic response to Russia's annexation of Crimea and attacks in Eastern Ukraine into disarray.

The story of the Kremlin's disinformation campaigns during the election campaign is well known. So too are Trump's positive comments about Putin. But the prevailing consensus in Washington was that sanctions must continue. Even before Trump was inaugurated, a bipartisan group of senior senators proposed legislation to enshrine the Obama-era sanctions—which Trump could have expunged with the stroke of a pen given they were enacted as Executive Orders over which the serving president has sole discretion—into legislation.[30]

By August 2017, the task had been accomplished: the Countering America's Adversaries Through Sanctions Act (CAATSA) passed 98–2 in the Senate and 419–3 in the House. Trump signed it 'for the sake of national unity', despite carping that the legislation 'encroaches on the executive branch's ability to negotiate'.[31]

CAATSA did not just enshrine the Obama-era sanctions but added new restrictions as well. Financial sectoral sanctions were tightened, new cyber sanctions were to be introduced, and the bill laid the groundwork for secondary sanctions—the blacklisting of entities caught circumventing US sanctions. These would come to play a major role in some of the subsequent sanctions' battles.

This was not the only time legislators in the United States would push for more sanctions. Issues far beyond Ukraine were driving pressure for more action against the Kremlin, including Russia's involvement in Syria, where in February 2018 Russian private military forces clashed with US Marines.[32] Later in 2018, a group of senators, including many of those who had drafted CAATSA, proposed another sanctions bill. One of the sponsors, Republican Senator Lindsey Graham, dubbed it the 'bill from hell'.[33] The bill called for further sanctions on Russia's financial sector and, most notably, a ban on Russian sovereign debt sales.

The trend was not confined to the United States. European Union politicians would squabble over the extent of sanctions. The most significant wave of new measures came after Russian military intelligence officers were revealed to have attempted to assassinate ex-spy Sergei Skripal and his daughter in Salisbury, England, with a nerve agent in March 2018. Detective Sergeant Nick Bailey, who responded to the incident, would also be hospitalised with symptoms of poisoning from the agent.

British Prime Minister Theresa May announced the expulsion of a host of Russian diplomats shortly thereafter, a move joined by almost all Western allies. She also announced increased customs checks and threatened to freeze Russian state assets.

As if to underline how underwhelming the new measures were, the same day Russian state-owned investment bank VTB Capital, which had an office in the heart of the city of London, sold €750 million in Gazprom bonds. Demand was so high they sold at a premium.[34] British MP Tom Tugendhat subsequently called for Russia to be barred from selling sovereign debt in the UK, the key foreign capital market for Moscow. He declared Britain should 'use sovereign debt here too, as a tool and a weapon, because we are being fought on every single level in a cross-spectrum battle'.[35] On both sides of the Atlantic, proposals for other financial services sanctions against Russia swirled again.

Under public pressure to act, the United States sanctioned a trio of prominent Russian oligarchs in April 2018. But the way the sanctions were announced prompted tumult in global markets. One of those blacklisted, Oleg Deripaska, controlled Rusal, the world's third largest aluminium producer. The Trump administration reacted with panic to the market tumult. It soon began talks with the firm's representatives about lifting the sanctions. Trump also insisted on simultaneously seeking diplomacy with Putin, announcing on 28 June that they would hold their first bilateral summit in Finland on 16 July. Trump's agenda granted those in the Western business community who saw Russia predominantly as a source of profits permission to criticise the sanctions regime. Bob Dudley, CEO of the British oil major BP, belittled Washington's issuance of sanctions on Russia as unconstructive, noting they 'get handed out like train tickets'.[36] The post-Skripal impetus for more sanctions was short lived.

On 10 July 2018, Dawn Sturgess, a local woman whose partner had found a discarded perfume bottle near Salisbury, died from similar side effects to those experienced by the Skripals and Bailey. Trump was unfazed, and his bilateral summit with Putin in Helsinki went ahead eight days later. Trump's own Russia advisor later dubbed the event a 'terrible spectacle' as Trump implied that he trusted Putin more than his own intelligence agencies.[37] The Organisation for the Prohibition of Chemical Weapons would find that the Skripals, Bailey, Sturgess, and her partner were poisoned with the Russian nerve agent Novichok.[38] Agents from Russia's GRU had smuggled it in the perfume bottle.[39] But the Rusal fallout and Trump's belief that his friendship with Putin was genuine meant his administration now had little appetite for further sanctions.

Europe was not going to lead in responding to the bungled assassination plot. In Helsinki, Trump pledged to pursue cooperation with Putin, who said they agreed to set up an economic cooperation council.[40] This was never followed up on. The Trump administration did ultimately tighten sanctions on Russia in August 2019 but only after missing several congressionally mandated deadlines and then choosing weaker options laid out in the Chemical and Biological Weapons Act that authorises sanctions in response to such incidents.[41]

The Salisbury affair did provoke an outpouring of European unity, even amid Britain's highly emotional Brexit negotiations, including expulsions of Russian diplomats suspected of working for intelligence agencies across the continent. However, cutting off Moscow entirely was a step Europe, Britain, and the Trump administration were unwilling to consider. Trump's allies in the Republican Congressional leadership sat on the 'bill from hell', and it failed to advance.

Washington would return to a policy of signalling to Russia what actions would warrant new sanctions after Joe Biden defeated Trump in the 2020 presidential election. But the Biden administration only announced a few relatively insignificant sanctions designations on 15 April 2021. However, they were accompanied by restrictions on US banks trading in future Russian debt issuances and by a new Executive Order that authorised the vast expansion of sanctions against any sector of the Russian economy if the Kremlin were to 'violate well-established principles of international law, including respect for the territorial integrity of states'.[42] The White House's announcement explicitly noted it was meant to 'send a signal',[43] with the debt sanctions intended as a warning that Washington was willing to cut Russia off from the international financial system if it did invade Ukraine.[44]

The Kremlin, on the other hand, saw the debt warning as an abuse of the dollar's influence. Russian Foreign Minister Sergei Lavrov noted 'we do not have comparable levers of influence on the US on such a scale' but threatened 'to impose painful measures on American businesses'.[45] Putin indicated that he saw one upside to the sanctions, claiming they would undermine the dollar's role as the international reserve currency. In June, he warned that US officials were 'sawing the branch on which they sit', a move that was to be welcomed because 'a plurality of reserve currencies is needed to guarantee the security and stability of the world economy and financial system'.[46] Putin's view also meant that sanctions were not going to deter him.

Though there was a small subsequent drawdown of Russian troops near the Ukrainian border following a summit meeting between Putin and Biden later that June, Putin was indeed undeterred. Russian troops began to mass on the Ukrainian border again from September—by 11 October, the head of the US military's Cyber Command was convinced Russia would invade.[47] Yet many US officials and allied leaders continued to believe that sanctions could be used as a deterrent. But as intelligence regarding an impending invasion continued to mount, Biden shifted the approach. The sanctions package that the United States and its allies began to consider in late 2021 was designed to 'maximi[s]e the impact on Russia and their ability to continue fighting the war' according to Biden's Deputy Treasury Secretary Wally Adeyemo.[48] But by then it was too late.

The sanctions that had been imposed on Russia after February 2014 reshaped the linkages between the Russian economy and the West. However, reticence from key Western European leaders and the Trump administration limited their extent. The Obama and Biden administrations on the other hand saw them primarily as a deterrent tool. Eight years after the first sanctions were introduced, the Kremlin did not expect the West to be sufficiently united to implement the most significant sanctions and believed that the United States was at risk of overstretching itself in politicising the dollar, which Putin argued would diminish its attractiveness as an international reserve and trade currency.[49] The realisation by Western policy makers that sanctions were primarily a tool to curtail Russia's state capacity came too late. Nevertheless, the pre-2022 sanctions did have a real impact on the Russian economy and its internal politics.

3

RUSSIA UNDER SANCTIONS

Although there were divisions over the imposition of sanctions and the sectors that would be targeted, the measures ultimately imposed in the wake of Russia's annexation of Crimea—particularly the sectoral sanctions regime—did have severe consequences for the Russian economy. State oil giant Rosneft, one of the four entities listed, faced an immediate crisis.

Just a year earlier, Rosneft had completed the purchase of TNK-BP. The firm was a 50–50 venture between the British oil giant BP and a holding company representing the interests of businessmen Mikhail Fridman, German Khan, Viktor Vekselberg, and Leonard Blavatnik.[1] TNK-BP was formed amid the early 2000s commodities boom, as BP, which had profitably charged into the former Soviet Union, sought to cement its position in Russia.

The partnership paid off handsomely—in March 2013, TNK-BP was sold to Rosneft.[2] The four oligarchs would split about $27.7 billion.[3] The sale process was by no means smooth, and the oligarchs reportedly leaned on the Kremlin to advance the sale. It was later reported that Bob Dudley, then CEO of TNK and future head of BP, fled the country amid the sale after poison was found in his blood.[4] BP was nevertheless keen to retain a sizable foothold in the Russian market that had proven so profitable. BP netted $12.48 billion but exchanged most of its stake for shares in Rosneft. Dudley took a seat on Rosneft's board.

The transaction resulted in BP owning 19.75 per cent of Rosneft but also saw Rosneft's ultimate parent Rosneftegaz receive $4.87 billion, though it was the effective purchaser. Rosneftegaz was, and still is, controlled by Igor Sechin, one of Putin's longest-serving aides. The fate of funds controlled by Rosneftegaz, which also holds nearly 11 per cent of Gazprom, has been repeatedly queried over the years. No suitable answer has emerged. BP's billions were swallowed up by Rosneftegaz, whose opacity earned it the moniker 'black hole' in the Russian press.[5] Rosneft's shareholding would be reshuffled three more times after 2014. But Sechin has always remained in charge.

However, Sechin's efforts to evade the pain of Rosneft's inclusion on the US sectoral sanctions list would have a major impact on the Russian economy—and on Russian internal politics, as Putin became ever more reliant on his trusted deputy amid the fallout.

Rosneft was in trouble after its US sectoral sanctions designation in July 2014 because it had borrowed heavily from a consortium of international banks to finance the purchase of TNK-BP. It was not the first time Sechin had turned to the Western financial community to underwrite his expanding control of the Russian oil industry. Sechin saw to it that the Western financial community would underwrite the largest expansion of the state's role in Russia's oil industry. Yukos was effectively handed to Rosneft and Sechin following the 2003 arrest of its main shareholder, Mikhail Khodorkovsky. Khodorkovsky had dared to challenge Putin's Kremlin, and Sechin himself reportedly led the charge to punish him.[6] Foreign investors were burned, but they did not lose their appetite for Russian investments. Just three years later, sixteen US and European banks supported Rosneft's London initial public offering (IPO), enabling international investors to purchase shares in the firm.[7] They split $120 million in fees for their efforts with a handful of Russian banks.[8] Many of the Western banks involved later eagerly supported Rosneft's TNK-BP buyout as well.

Sechin had been counting on these relationships continuing. The first significant loan repayment for the TNK-BP stake, $6.8 billion, was due to foreign banks in December 2014.[9] A further $19.5 billion was due in 2015. But the sectoral sanctions the Obama administration imposed barred any new long-term loans to Rosneft. No Western bank was willing to skirt this restriction, and Rosneft lacked the cash to make do on its loans without further financing.

Sechin turned to Russia's central bank. Rosneft's sectoral sanctions came just a year after Putin had named a new central bank head, Elvira Nabiullina. Unlike most of Putin's other senior appointees, Nabiullina did not have a longstanding link to Putin. She was widely seen as a competent manager and would go on to receive widespread praise in the Western press, including for easing the pain of the sanctions and maintaining international investors' access to the Russian market. This was a deep misunderstanding of her role.

The solution that Sechin and Nabiullina engineered for Rosneft's challenge was complex but ultimately amounted to a direct bailout by the state.[10] First, Rosneft issued a whopping 625 billion roubles of Russian bonds, worth nearly $11 billion at the time. The central bank then authorised it to use these notes as collateral for dollar loans, handing Rosneft the currency it needed to repay its foreign creditors. However, after the exchange was concluded, the rouble collapsed, experiencing its largest single-day fall since 1998.[11] Markets shuddered at the move as the central bank was handing billions of dollars to Rosneft while effectively allowing it to print promises to pay with roubles in return. To stem the pain, Nabiullina raised Russia's baseline interest rate from 10.5 to 17 per cent, an equally unprecedented hike.

The move may have bailed out Rosneft and shielded Sechin, but it impoverished millions of Russians. It also marked a turning point for the Russian economy. According to data compiled by the Bank of Finland's Institute for Emerging Economies, Russian's real income— defined by economists as an individual's purchasing power—never returned to the level witnessed before the Rosneft bailout.[12]

Central banks typically have a single or dual mandate. A single mandate refers to seeking to maintain stable prices, a dual mandate is to simultaneously seek to promote full employment. They are also supposed to be independent of their governments. Russia's central bank maintained this myth, but Rosneft's bailout proved that Nabiullina's sole mandate was for regime stability, as with all other state institutions and enterprises under Putin.

Nabiullina was, however, an exception among Putin's senior cadres in one notable way. Unlike Sechin, she did not have a link to Putin dating back to his time in the KGB or from his time working for Sobchak, St Petersburg's first post-Soviet mayor. Putin's KGB career has provided the basis for countless biographies and spy stories, typically more rumour than fact. But it was while working for Sobchak that Putin had learned how to manipulate the strings of the global economy.

When Putin returned from his KGB posting in Dresden as East Germany rushed out of the Soviet bloc and towards German reunification, the agency found him a posting as assistant vice-rector for international affairs at Leningrad State University. The post had long been a KGB sinecure to vet the university's international links, and Putin continued to receive a KGB salary.[13] But as market forces arrived under Mikhail Gorbachev's *perestroika* reforms, Putin's boss at the university, Yuri Molchanov, transformed the international affairs department into a facilitator for foreign businesses to the Russian market, even agreeing a joint venture with US consumer products giant Procter & Gamble.[14] Putin soon transferred to Sobchak's employ, working for him in his new role as head of the Leningrad soviet. According to Philip Short's biography *Putin: His Life and Times* (2022), Sobchak 'was desperate to find someone to liaise with [the security services] on his behalf ... Putin fitted the bill perfectly.'[15]

Putin's position under Sobchak saw him take an even more direct role in forging Leningrad's foreign economic links. He initially helped arrange barter exchanges in which businesses would sell commodities that were produced to increasingly meaningless Soviet economic plans. Putin and Bank of St Petersburg President Yuri Lvov set up the city's first foreign exchange bureau in 1991.[16] A year later, Putin would join the advisory board of the new St Petersburg Real Estate Holding Company (SPAG), as would another St Petersburg official—Herman Gref, under whose tutelage Nabiullina would later enter Putin's circles.[17] SPAG was founded by Vladimir Smirnov, who would later chair the infamous Ozero cooperative outside St Petersburg where Putin and many of his closest friends built dachas. Many of its members went on to earn vast riches under Putin's rule.[18]

SPAG went public in 1998, though the subsequent collapse of its share price would serve as a warning of the dangers of public company disclosures to Putin when it provoked a money-laundering probe.[19] When his German friend Franz Sedelmayer's St Petersburg residence was expropriated, Putin acknowledged that he was unable to help.[20] But it was an important lesson for the future president: he witnessed first-hand that the state could act in contravention of economic norms and take measures with relative impunity when targeting foreign business interests.

Putin also learned to manage the local underworld's business interests and about the importance of commodity exports. When Sobchak later fell out with rivals in Yeltsin's Kremlin, Putin arranged for him to be flown out of the country on a medical evacuation flight chartered by none other than Gunvor founder Gennady Timchenko.[21]

Putin's market education continued when he moved to Moscow in September 1996, taking along his trusted deputy Igor Sechin.[22] His first job in the Kremlin was to oversee state economic policy, with a brief to improve economic security.[23] Putin's performance in the role led to a swift promotion to head of the Federal Security Service (FSB), the KGB's domestic successor agency. Yeltsin was also impressed by Putin's loyalty to Sobchak, having risked his career only shortly after arriving in Moscow to save him.

By 2014, Putin's friends were established atop the heights of Russia's economy and politics. Gref would go on to head Sberbank, Russia's largest bank. Sechin, who 'served Putin with limpet-like devotion' as his aide in St Petersburg, was atop Rosneft.[24] Alexei Miller, who had also worked for Sobchak, was head of Gazprom. Sobchak's legal advisor, Dmitry Medvedev, was prime minister and had even been trusted with the presidency between 2008 and 2012 while Putin temporarily replaced him as prime minister. Nikolai Tokarev, who served with Putin in Dresden, was president of Transneft, Russia's state oil pipeline operator.[25] Even Putin's PhD advisor—who has been accused of ghost-writing Putin's dissertation—reaped rewards, becoming a billionaire on paper through his shares in fertiliser firm PhosAgro.[26]

Access to world markets made many in Putin's inner circle fabulously wealthy. Putin had demonstrated his skill at using market structures to eliminate political opponents: shortly after taking power, he used Gazprom's stake in media tycoon Seva Gusinsky's NTV station to oust him. Putin soon did the same with Boris Berezovsky, arguably the most influential oligarch of the Yeltsin era, pressuring him to sell his shares to Sibneft, which was controlled by the businessman Roman Abramovich.[27] Another oligarch, Vagit Alekperov, the largest shareholder in oil firm Lukoil, helped shut down another station Berezovsky controlled, TV6, through a technicality regarding the channel's authorised capital.[28] ORT was swiftly transformed into the Kremlin's main propaganda network, Channel One, and TV6 was shuttered. Next, Putin went after Khodorkovsky. Putin wanted a growing economy that could generate wealth but one that remained under his control.

Putin's circle's wealth linked them to the world, but this connection also left them vulnerable, as demonstrated by Timchenko's sanctioning and the Gunvor fire-sale. Putin's time in power before 2014 had shown the benefits of integration into the international economic order. But the introduction of sanctions revealed it posed greater risks. The Rosneft affair demonstrated how the Russian economy's integration into the international economic order left Putin's system of governance vulnerable, given the inseparable intertwining of politics and business among Putin's inner circle.

As Rosneft's bailout was tanking the rouble, the sanctions compounded the Kremlin's difficulties. Over the second half of 2014, benchmark global oil prices fell by 50 per cent as global supply outpaced demand and the Saudi-led Organisation of Petroleum Exporting Countries (OPEC) cartel refused to cut production in hopes of squeezing out higher-cost US shale production. Russia's benchmark for oil exports, known as Urals oil, earned an average of $107.88 per barrel in 2013 but just $61.07 in December 2014, according to Russian customs officials.[29] In the coming years, Putin would try to insulate Russia from such shocks, which he saw as the greater threat to Russia's economy than the sanctions agenda. Nonetheless, Putin remained confident. Three days after Rosneft's bailout, he pledged that Russia's 'economy will overcome the current situation', predicting that 'under the most unfavourable circumstances, I think it will take about two years'.[30]

While Rosneft was subject to US sectoral sanctions, Europe eschewed doing the same. Though European banks were unwilling to evade the US sanctions regime, Putin could take comfort in the fact that Gazprom had not been targeted by the sectoral sanctions. Brussels and most European capitals balked at the suggestion, given the importance of Russian gas to their economies. Sanctions had not yet come for Russia's crown jewel, but Putin turned to his statist inclinations to try and insulate the Russian state he had crafted in his image to protect against such threats in future.

The Kremlin responded to the sanctions by changing Russia's political economy, trying to insulate key sectors from future threats. One such effort was Russia's launch of its own National Card Payment System in 2014, subsequently rebranded MIR, which it instituted after card-processing giants Visa and Mastercard said they would stop processing payments in Crimea as a result of sanctions imposed by the United States.[31] However, MIR was almost entirely a domestic solution: by 2022, it was only operational in just eight countries— seven former Soviet republics and Turkey—and it did not offer a solution to the potential for sanctions on Russian banks' access to the SWIFT messaging system, necessary for executing international transfers in other currencies. Threats to sanction Russia's access to SWIFT had emerged as early as 2014, and Washington signalled it would take such action in the event of further major escalation in Ukraine.[32] While Russia did seek some efforts at a potential work-around, none of these made much progress.[33] Its proposal of an alternative System for Transmission of Financial Messages, known as SPFS, also launched in 2014, had even less take-up and failed to address one key feature of the international banking system over which the United States had significant influence, namely the network of banking connections known as correspondent accounts that is essential to moving dollars internationally.[34] Because of the United States' ability to issue secondary sanctions threats—the idea that it will apply sanctions to a foreign entity even if it engages in activity with no US nexus other than its use of dollars—a genuine workaround is all-but-impossible for the vast majority of international trade.[35] China did have an alternative to SWIFT, the Chinese Cross-Border Interbank Payment System (CIPS), which a number of Russian banks did join.[36] While it offered an alternative for trade with China, it was hardly an international competitor, with a 2020 analysis finding that it settled just 0.3 per cent of the international sanctions settled by the SWIFT system.[37] And because Putin reportedly kept the Russian central bank in the dark about his 2022 plans for a full-scale invasion of Ukraine, the former did not escalate plans for further integration with the system or develop other alternatives.[38]

Another move to mitigate the potential impact of Western action came in the form of Russia's own sanctions. Putin barred the importation of beef, pork, vegetable, fish, fruit, poultry, and dairy products from countries that had sanctioned Russia, which would pursue a strategy of import-substitution to replace Finnish yogurt, French cheese, German pork, and American poultry. These were industries that earned hundreds of millions of dollars annually exporting to Russia, but the overall economic impact was a pittance compared to the sanctions the West had imposed on Russia.

The aim of the policy was certainly to harm affected producers in Western countries, but it also had an important domestic policy impetus. To protect against potentially far more damaging sanctions—the banning of technology exports from the West to Russia, an idea that was regularly touted by Kremlin critics and foreign policy thinkers at the time—the Kremlin would pursue a strategy of import substitution. Russia's agriculture and farming industries would be the test ground.

The policy was initially viewed favourably in the press, with Russian newspapers and international media highlighting, for example, the development of Russian soft cheeses. However, the failings quickly became clear when shrimp purportedly from Belarus—almost certainly rebranded re-exports given that Belarus is landlocked—began appearing on Russian shelves.[39]

Yet there were some areas of real success. According to John Haskell, an American businessman who left the finance industry to become a cattle farmer in Russia, food import substitution was mainly 'focussed on wheat growing, where Russia had huge unrealised potential—and after 2014 a lot of that potential was realized, including through the better use of technology and fertilizer'.[40]

Putin aimed to use the programme of import substitution to turn Russia into a food exporter. In 2018, he ordered Russia's Agriculture Ministry to achieve $45 billion in agricultural exports by 2024, though by 2020 it acknowledged that the target had been moved to 2030.[41] Haskell decried it as 'absurd that Russia still imports roughly 40% of its beef—it should be a major beef exporter'.[42] In the face of Russia's own sanctions, Belarus became the major source of beef imports, and meat imports more broadly.[43] As with the 'Belarusian shrimp', these goods were likely disguised re-exports from 'sanctioned' markets.

In September 2022, the Kremlin had reportedly acknowledged that the import substitution programme had largely failed, noting its continued dependence on imports for pharmaceutical, machine-building, and even continued agricultural and livestock output.[44] Russia's import substitution faltered in no small part because it depended on the state, not on private industry. Russia's response to the 2014 sanctions was to increase the state's role in the economy, at the expense of private industry and even seemingly loyal oligarchs. Rosneft again serves as among the starkest examples: even as Sechin was arranging its bailout by the central bank, he was plotting his next expansion. Sanctions may have hurt the Russian economy and threatened Rosneft, but the response was to give him even further control over Russia's oil production.

In September 2014, a Russian court ordered the seizure of businessman Vladimir Yevtushenkov's majority stake in Bashneft, the regional oil producer in Russia's Bashkortostan region.[45] Yevtushenkov was one of many Russian businessmen who made fabulous wealth in the 1990s and retained it under Putin. Yevtushenkov had never challenged the Kremlin's exclusive remit over politics that Putin established by going after oligarchs like Khodorkovsky, Gusinsky, and Berezovsky. Russia was soon aflutter with rumours that the takeover had been ordered by none other than Sechin, which he fiercely denied.[46]

Yevtushenkov was detained, and then put under house arrest.[47] The courts had ruled that Bashneft's privatisation was illegal and corrupt, but it was clear that politics were at play. Yevtushenkov was subsequently freed, and Putin even told him that he was welcome to invest in another oil company.[48]

Rosneft would ultimately take control of Bashneft, purchasing a majority stake from the state in October 2016. But the story did not end there. The next month, Economic Development Minister Alexei Ulyukayev was arrested—he had allegedly demanded a $2 million bribe from Sechin to approve the deal, which Sechin had reportedly disguised under a gift of sausages from boars he had hunted.[49] Although Sechin was repeatedly called as a witness by Ulyukayev's defence, he remained silent throughout the trial. As if to emphasise Sechin's domineering influence, during the trial Yevtushenkov was again investigated over his earlier investment in Bashneft.[50] In December 2017, Ulyukayev was sentenced to eight years' imprisonment. Sechin would continue to gift other Russian businessmen boar sausages in the coming years, a move seen as a potential threat that one might be his next target.[51]

Despite the troubles Sechin's management of Rosneft had caused the Russian economy in 2014, he remained Putin's trusted consigliere. Although the sanctions aimed to target Russia's instruments of economic leverage, they also led Putin to believe he could only trust those with whom he had long surrounded himself, the very targets of sanctions.

The Bashneft affair would not be the last time sanctions had a major impact on the balance of power among Russia's economic and political elite.

In January 2018, the Trump administration released a list of Russian oligarchs. The list's publication was not Trump's choice but was mandated by CAATSA, the 2017 bill that had enshrined the sectoral sanctions in law.[52] But the Trump administration had clearly not taken the task seriously. Some of those included on the list had recently fled Russia after falling out with the Kremlin. Rather than order a forensic investigation of Russia's oligarchy and their connections to Putin, the Trump administration had, by its own admission, largely cribbed Russia's Forbes 'Rich List'.[53]

Trump's half-hearted compliance with the CAATSA requirement came in the context of a heated US political debate about Russia policy and an investigation led by Robert Mueller, a former FBI director tasked with probing any potential collusion between the Trump campaign and the Kremlin in the 2016 election, which was making daily headlines.

Trump continued to balk at imposing new sanctions but was under increasing pressure to do so after the attempted assassination of the Skripals in Salisbury that March. After all, Trump had repeatedly said he did not oppose sanctions but merely wanted to simultaneously continue diplomacy with Putin.

The administration's response was to sanction three influential Russian oligarchs, Suleiman Kerimov, Viktor Vekselberg, and Oleg Deripaska, just weeks after the Skripals' attempted assassination.[54] All three had substantial assets abroad, with Vekselberg in particular having invested in a number of Swiss companies that risked being affected as well, though a deal was quickly struck for him to partially divest.[55] One of the world's largest gold miners, Polyus Gold, was linked to Kerimov, who had once held sizable stakes in Western banks including Morgan Stanley, Goldman Sachs, and Deutsche Bank and had feted JP Morgan CEO Jamie Dimon and Goldman Sachs supremo Lloyd Blankfein in Moscow.[56] However, Polyus was unaffected, as Kerimov had transferred his stake to his son Said in 2015.[57] There was far more tumult over Deripaska's sanctioning, particularly as his firm EN+, through which he also held shares in Rusal and other key Russian companies, had gone public in London the previous year—the first major Russian IPO since Putin's 2014 invasion.

While Trump quickly pulled back from sanctions and launched talks with Deripaska's representatives, these sanctions prompted the Kremlin to realise that US restrictions could also encroach on Putin's exclusive remit over the distribution of spoils within Russia.

At the time Deripaska was blacklisted, he was publicly feuding with fellow oligarch Vladimir Potanin for control of Nornickel, the world's largest nickel producer.[58] Both held sizable stakes in the firm, with fellow oligarch Roman Abramovich holding the deciding vote. The ownership structure had been instituted after the Kremlin intervened in a previous Potanin–Deripaska dispute.[59] Deripaska's US designation, however, barred him from moving to take majority control of Nornickel. When Putin held his annual 'direct line' teleconference that June, he implored 'big Russian businessmen' to move assets back home and warned that dollar transactions would 'undermine the trust of businesses'.[60]

But after Trump met with Putin in Helsinki in July 2018, the mood music changed. Russian IPOs began to return to the London market in 2019 after the fallout from 2018 made additional major sanctions under Trump seem unlikely. Polyus, controlled by Kerimov's unsanctioned son Said, issued additional shares on the London Stock Exchange.[61] Even state-controlled rail shipping firm

Rustranscom filed paperwork for a potential London listing that April.[62] The Kremlin continued to sell sovereign bonds in London, armed with clauses that could see foreign holders forced to accept roubles rather than dollars or other established foreign currencies. The market demanded no premium.[63]

After the Trump Helsinki summit, the wind was taken out of the sanctions regime. The conflict in Ukraine faded from the global headlines. Democrats and a number of Republican senators continued to call for more sanctions on Russia, but the Senate leadership refused to advance them. Business as usual returned, especially after Trump struck a deal with Deripaska's representatives to lift the sanctions on Rusal and EN+. The deal was negotiated by Lord Barker, a former British government minister whom Deripaska appointed to EN+'s board, for which Barker reportedly received a $5.9 million bonus.[64] This would prove the crowning glory in the Anglo-Russian tradition dubbed 'Lords on Boards',[65] in which British elites export a sheen of legitimacy.

The deal saw Deripaska's EN+ shareholding adjusted and placed a Trump administration-approved director on its board— though Deripaska's stake combined with that of his charity, that of his ex-wife Polina Yumasheva, and that of her father Valentin Yumashev—Yeltsin's former chief-of-staff and son-in-law—still amounted to 53.95 per cent.[66] It marked the most significant surrender in the sanctions regime to date. As if to celebrate the victory, just weeks later Russian authorities arrested American investor Michael Calvey, co-founder of private equity firm Baring Vostok. The Trump administration did not complain. The sanctions regime appeared at risk of dying out, and Western businesses were eager to rush back in. BP CEO Dudley met Putin in Moscow that April openly lobbying for new deals, leaving Calvey's arrest unmentioned.[67] That December, Rusal announced a major new loan, whose sale was led by Dutch bank ING and France's Natixis, with support from Société Générale and Italy's Intesa Sanpaolo and Unicredit.[68]

Sanctions changed Russia's economy, and its politics. The sanctions against Deripaska and their impact on his tussle with Potanin for control of Nornickel also showed they could threaten Putin's monopoly on the distribution of spoils in Russia. But

Trump's erratic Russia policy stopped the sanctions regime from expanding. Meanwhile, the conflict in Ukraine had faded from Europe's agenda. Europe's attraction to Russian hydrocarbons and capital meant that Russia's economic levers over Europe were only increasing. Putin saw this division between Europe and the United States as something he could exploit to contain the risk of further sanctions.

4

GASEOUS INTERDEPENDENCE

Whereas Russia's 2014 attack on Ukraine prompted a sea change in Washington's approach to Europe, in Europe's most important capitals there was great resistance to change. Many European states wanted business to continue as normal—key Western European states believed that continuing with their pre-Crimea strategy of seeking economic interdependence with Russia could reduce tensions and prevent further conflict, and some Eastern European states were swayed by economic inducements offered by the Kremlin, even as others warned of future Russian hostility. The Kremlin recognised Europe's divides and sought to exploit them to enhance its influence and attempt to blunt potential sanctions and economic competition from other energy suppliers.

Sechin arrived in Berlin on 20 June 2014—two months after being added to the United States' SDN sanctions blacklist. He was feted by a troupe of many of Germany's most prominent business leaders, who gathered in the hall of a villa in Berlin's poshest suburb, Schwanenwerder, to hear the Rosneft boss explain how Russian–German relations and economic ties could continue to flourish.

Sechin brought along many of his key deputies—future targets of the sanctions regime—and put on a magisterial display of confidence and braggadocio, vowing to personally push for new opportunities for German and Russian business cooperation. Rosneft was not yet under sectoral sanctions, and Sechin eagerly took questions from many of the attendees, including my own, though I was undoubtedly the least notable figure in the room.

As questions were asked, Sechin—with the airs of a Russian Napoleon—would wave his hands, sending Rosneft executives rushing over to point out additional documents in the multiple folders of briefing materials distributed to help resolve queries. Most audaciously, Sechin put forward proposals well outside his remit as Rosneft's boss. The most stunning of these was a suggestion that Germany and Russia work together to build a nuclear powerplant in Kaliningrad, the Russian exclave sandwiched between Poland and Lithuania. The city was the former Prussian capital, named Königsberg, until Russia annexed it after the Second World War. Sechin suggested that such a project was perfectly suited to lead German–Russian relations to new heights.

Some details of the meeting were subsequently published in the German press: one attendee was keen to emphasise that Sechin had 'overshot the target a little' with his nuclear power proposal.[1] The nuclear suggestion caused more opprobrium than the idea that Germany should still do business with US-sanctioned Kremlin appointees: then-Chancellor Angela Merkel had announced the phaseout of nuclear power in Germany in 2011, the culmination of the Western world's most politically influential anti-nuclear movement.[2]

Otherwise, the meeting's tone was genuinely cooperative—there was no rebuttal to Sechin's invocation against further sanctions, warning that 'if the energy sector becomes the target of sanctions, then millions of people who are not involved in the conflict will be drawn into it'.[3]

Discouraging Europe from pursuing such sanctions was a core aim of Sechin's visit. Throughout Putin's presidency, Russia had developed deep economic linkages with Europe and continued to pursue these ties after Crimea's annexation. German business appeared to agree: just a week after Putin formalised the Crimean takeover, the CEO of German industrial giant Siemens, Joe Kaeser, visited Russia and met with Putin.[4] Kaeser dismissed Russia's invasion of Ukraine and the West's initial sanctions as 'short-term turbulence' that would not feature in Siemens' business planning.[5]

There is a long history of Germany seeking to deepen economic links with Russia. West Germany pushed for deepening trade with Russia in the Soviet era, including on developing oil and gas links. Its 1970s-era *Ostpolitik*, the policy of seeking to reduce tensions and collaborate with the Soviet Union and the Warsaw Pact countries, was built on a series of initial trade exchanges, dubbed 'pipes for gas' arrangements. Under these arrangements, the West German government provided loans and steel piping to the Soviet Union in exchange for gas supply contracts.[6] Germany believed economic interdependence was a path to peace on the continent long before Putin arrived in the Kremlin.

But Putin exploited that belief. What is remarkable is that faith in interdependence faded hardly at all among much of Europe's business community and among many leading politicians in the fourteen years after Putin came to power. By 2014, there were no credible illusions that Russia had been turned towards the West as a result of its increased integration into the international economic system. Putin said so himself as early as 2007, when, speaking at the annual Munich Security Conference, he lambasted the US-led 'unipolar' world. Putin decried the system as 'pernicious' and one in which the United States was the only true 'sovereign'. He also declared that the system was unstable and bound to change.[7]

In the same speech, Putin pointed to Russia's integration with the West, noting that some '26 percent of the oil extraction in Russia is done by foreign capital'.[8] While he said that he would continue to support such investment, the speech also contained clear economic threats, including a warning that if Russia and Ukraine failed to agree on transhipments of gas to Europe, 'then all European consumers would sit there with no gas. Would you like to see this happen? I don't think so.'[9] He continued by making an explicit link between building a 'fairer system of global economic relations' and international security. As for the existing system, Putin declared 'this balance is clearly destroyed'.[10]

History would go on to show that Putin himself aimed to be the driving force behind the changes he outlined. He had turned extremely hostile towards NATO, Russia's traditional opponent in the Soviet era that Putin increasingly claimed was a threat, particularly after the former Soviet republics of Estonia, Latvia, and Lithuania were admitted as members in 2004.

At the time of the Munich Security Conference, NATO was considering 'membership action plans' (MAPs) for Georgia and Ukraine to join the alliance. Berlin and Paris were opposed to offering the MAPs to the two countries, largely because of Russia's warnings. In April 2008, NATO settled on a middle ground, in which it expressed its ambition for the two states to join but withheld MAPs.[11] That August, Putin sent his forces into Georgia. After negotiations mediated by France brought an end to the conflict, Putin announced he was recognising the breakaway regions of South Ossetia and Abkhazia—some 20 per cent of Georgia's territory—as independent, while building up bases of Russian troops in both. This scuppered any potential offer of NATO membership for Tbilisi as NATO could not accept a member with Russian troops occupying part of its claimed territory—doing so would risk bringing NATO and Russia into direct conflict.

Putin's drawing of a link between economic ties and international security was by no means novel. But it stood in stark contrast to the liberal internationalist dogma that held that globalisation would trend towards peace, as encapsulated by Thomas Friedman's famous 'Golden Arches Theory of Peace', according to which 'no two countries that both have a McDonald's have ever fought a war against each other'.[12] Friedman softened his stance in 2005, revising it to focus on integrated supply chains, but that too has subsequently been disproven, not least by Putin's wars against Ukraine.

Rather than economic liberalism, Putin was effectively invoking the idea of geo-economics. The concept was first promulgated by political economist Edward Luttwak in a 1990 essay, in which he argued 'the methods of commerce are displacing military methods—with disposable capital in lieu of firepower, civilian innovation in lieu of military-technical advancement and market penetration in lieu of garrisons and bases'.[13] Luttwak's writing was prompted by the end of the Cold War, which had sparked great hope for the subsequent era of liberal free trade driving globalisation. While geo-economics was highly incongruous with such thinking, it fit neatly with a worldview based on neo-mercantilism, the 'belief in the need for strategic trade protectionism and other forms of government economic activism to promote state wealth and power'.[14]

Neo-mercantilist thought experienced a resurgence in Russia after the Soviet collapse, which continued through Putin's presidency.[15] But Putin's focus was not on building state wealth via protectionism but rather building state power through economic activism.

Whereas many in Europe saw economic interdependence as a way to pacify Russia, Putin saw it as a means to limit the West's ability to stand up to his vision for re-ordering the world. Energy, corruption, and commodities would become key levers for the Kremlin to dissuade Europe from taking hostile action. As Sechin pointed out in Berlin, if they did take such steps, millions risked being caught up in the negative repercussions.

Russia had long shown a willingness to use economic weapons against its own neighbours. Russia used such threats in the 1990s to cajole other ex-Soviet republics into joining the Commonwealth of Independent States (CIS), a regional, Russian-dominated intergovernmental organisation formed after the Soviet collapse, and extract other key concessions.[16] This escalated under Putin. In March 2006, Russia had imposed a ban on Georgian wine, a key export to Russia, to pressure Tbilisi's pro-Western government, acting similarly in Moldova as well. Even before that, Europe was forewarned of a potential gas crisis: Putin had halted gas supplies to Ukraine in January 2006 amid tensions over Ukraine's geopolitical direction as the Orange Revolution a year earlier had prompted talk of Kyiv seeking to join NATO. The halt prompted sharp declines in onward deliveries to the rest of Europe.

Even after Putin invaded Georgia, Western politicians did not believe the Kremlin would turn these economic weapons against them—nor did the markets.[17] The Kremlin, however, saw that it could use European politicians to advance its economic and political interests.

The same day that Georgia and Russia signed a ceasefire, 15 August 2008, it was reported that Moscow had hired ex-Finnish Prime Minister Paavo Lipponen to lobby for its plans to build a gas pipeline linking Russia to Germany, known as Nord Stream.[18]

The 2008 Russian–Georgian war came amid a flurry of fighting over Europe's future gas supplies, and Russia again briefly cut off Ukraine's gas that winter. Some European politicians had started to wake up to the threat posed by Russia's dominance in European energy markets in the preceding years, as Russia engaged in repeated gas spats with Ukraine. However, a clear divide was emerging between those who did and those who did not see Gazprom as a geo-economic threat.

Lipponen was just one of a number of ex-European officials whom the Kremlin brought on board to advocate for Nord Stream, which Gazprom and German energy firms E.ON and BASF had agreed to build in September 2005. Just weeks later, Gerhard Schröder stepped down as chancellor of Germany after losing out to the opposition Christian Democrats, led by Angela Merkel. Almost immediately, Putin offered Schröder chairmanship of Nord Stream's shareholder committee—Schröder swiftly accepted.[19]

Poland's then-Foreign Minister Radosław Sikorski was perhaps Nord Stream's most prominent opponent. In 2006, prompting criticism from Moscow, Brussels, and Berlin, he compared the project to the Molotov–Ribbentrop Pact, under which Adolf Hitler and Josef Stalin had divided Eastern Europe at the beginning of the Second World War.[20]

These opposing views of Gazprom and the Kremlin's reliability as an energy partner were being fiercely debated in Brussels when the Russo-Georgian war began. The previous September, the European Commission—the executive branch of the European Union, as far as there is one—had proposed new legislation on the bloc's internal gas and energy markets. However, the European Parliament had yet to pass it.

The proposal, known as the Third Energy Package, was very much in the European spirit of compromise and market liberalisation. It set the framework for unifying Europe's energy and electricity markets and enabling cross-border access. However, it also sought to blunt Gazprom's influence, in response to demands from Sikorski, by limiting vertical integration in energy networks as it mandated the separation of energy generators and suppliers from pipeline operators.[21] This aimed to contain Gazprom's influence by, at least in theory, barring it from controlling how Russian gas was distributed within Europe.

Europe had also begun to realise that it needed to diversify its resources. In November 2008, the European Commission came out in favour of the development of an alternative 'southern gas corridor' to seek imports from as far afield as Azerbaijan, Turkmenistan, Iraq, and potentially even Iran and Uzbekistan.[22] The European Parliament approved the Third Energy Package in April 2009, though the commission still held ambitions to negotiate a deeper relationship with Russia, even as it acknowledged that linking these efforts to other trade liberalisation efforts with Russia was failing.[23]

The Kremlin had its own rival plans for the southern gas corridor, aiming to undermine its potential as an alternative to its gas. Together with Italian energy firm Eni, Gazprom proposed a pipeline that would link Russia with Europe via the Black Sea, dubbed South Stream.[24] Like Nord Stream, it conveniently circumvented Ukraine.

The 2008 Russian–Georgian war directly threatened the viability of Europe's alternatives. Its plans to import gas from Azerbaijan and beyond were dependent on the South Caucasus Pipeline, which carried Azeri gas to Turkey through Georgia. Russian attacks in the conflict had briefly forced it offline, and, following the ceasefire, Russian forces within eyesight of the pipeline manned the de facto border of Russia's newly recognised ally, the Georgian breakaway statelet of South Ossetia.

At the time, a consortium of European energy companies was seeking to realise the southern gas corridor via the Nabucco pipeline project, which would stretch all the way from Turkey to Austria. In addition to linking to the South Caucasus Pipeline, it envisaged importing Turkmen gas via Iran or through a link under the Caspian Sea to Azerbaijan. Schröder repeatedly denigrated the project, even mocking the negotiating skills of his own former foreign minister, Joschka Fischer, who backed Nabucco.[25]

The substantial geopolitical challenges, and proposed costs, repeatedly delayed progress. The pipeline was no closer to being realised in 2014 when Russia invaded Ukraine than it was when Russia invaded Georgia in 2008. Russia had successfully capitalised on European divisions to hinder threats to its economic influence, a strategy it would continue to employ in subsequent years.

As Nabucco faltered, Azerbaijan pushed ahead with an alternative plan: proposing the Trans-Anatolian Pipeline (TANAP), taking Azerbaijani gas across Georgia and Turkey to the EU border with Greece and Bulgaria and the Trans-Adriatic Pipeline (TAP) to carry it from Greece via Albania to Italy. Both pipelines also received support from the European Union in the aftermath of the Russian–Georgian War but were lesser cousins to Nabucco's ambitions, with a smaller planned capacity. Azerbaijan, Turkey, and Georgia sped up their efforts to finance the pipelines in the aftermath of Russia's 2014 attack on Ukraine.

Funding from Europe and the West, however, continued to be delayed. The European Union did at least recognise after a second Russian invasion in Europe in six years that it had to act to kill Russia's South Stream project, though Moscow had close backers in Bulgaria, where it was due to come onshore.

Bulgaria was led at the time by Plamen Oresharski. His coalition held 120 of the legislature's 240 seats—eighty-four were held by the Socialist Party and thirty-six by the Movement for Rights and Freedoms (MRF), a party backed by Bulgaria's sizable ethnic Turkish minority. They had only formed a government the previous year, thanks to the far-right pro-Russian Ataka party abstaining from a confidence vote.

Moscow had long had substantial influence in Bulgaria, dating back to the Communist era when it was often seen as the Soviet Union's most loyal ally. But Bulgaria joined the European Union without much opposition from the Kremlin in 2007.

One of the main areas of Russian influence in Bulgaria was energy dependency, in the form of the oil refinery in Burgas that dominates the country's domestic market. Russia's Lukoil purchased a majority stake in the refinery in 1999.[26] The refinery would nonetheless become a tool of significant political leverage. It reported losses almost every year, meaning it owed no income tax.[27] In recent years, it has faced allegations of corrupt ties to all of Bulgaria's major political parties—including the Socialists and their main rival, GERB, led by Boyko Borissov, as well as the MRF.[28]

Following the annexation of Crimea, Russia sped up plans for South Stream, trying to get it over the line before it could be targeted with sanctions. In June 2014, Russia accelerated shipments of steel pipes for work to begin.[29] However, the MRF had announced that it would now oppose the project, pulling support from the government. Oresharski suspended work and called a new vote.[30]

The election was won by Borissov's GERB. Borissov said he would restart work on South Stream. The United States threatened sanctions and pressured Brussels to act, and Borissov's support wavered. However, it was Putin who announced the project's cancellation in December 2014—stating that Russia would pursue an alternative via Turkey instead.[31]

Another alternative soon emerged as well. In September 2015, Gazprom announced it had reached an agreement to build a second Nord Stream pipeline.[32] Nord Stream 2 would double the capacity of the route from 55 to 110 billion cubic metres per annum, roughly a third of the EU's annual imports at the time. European energy firms E.ON, BASF/Wintershall, OMV, ENGIE, and Shell would take 10 per cent stakes in the new project, with the remainder going to Gazprom, a structure designed to signal compliance with the EU's Third Energy Package.

Merkel's government repeatedly deflected concerns about the project's political impact, describing it as a private project—though when questioned, she emphasised that 'in general, we welcome the construction of new infrastructure'.[33]

While Russia used parties across Germany's and Bulgaria's political spectrum to advance its geo-economic interests, the situation was inverse in Poland. Polish politics are fractious, and the divide between the two main parties, Law and Justice (PiS) and the Civic Platform, is as fierce as the Republican–Democrat divide in the United States in the post-Trump era. Their one area of agreement is opposition to Putin's Russia, particularly its geo-economic agenda.

Sikorski and the Civic Platform had supported alternatives to Russian gas even as Nord Stream 1 was being built. In 2011, they set in motion plans to build an LNG terminal in Świnoujście, which aimed to reduce Warsaw's own Russian gas dependency. Shortly before construction finished in 2015, the PiS would win a majority in parliament, vowing an ever more assertive line against Russia and its energy politics.

There seemed to be little that Poland could do to compel the European gas giants backing Gazprom to halt Nord Stream 2. Warsaw's appeals repeatedly fell on deaf ears among Western European politicians, and the PiS had adopted a Eurosceptic tone in its campaign that left it with few friends in Brussels. European Council President Donald Tusk, a former Civic Platform prime minister, did oppose the project—but there was little hope for coordination given that PiS had called for probes into his time in office earlier that year.

Despite these barriers, the very structure that Gazprom and its partners had agreed for Nord Stream 2 provided an opening. In December 2015, Poland's Office of Competition and Consumer Protection (UOKiK) announced it was investigating the Nord Stream 2 consortium.[34] Although Nord Stream 2 did not go through Polish territory, Poland threatened to fine the firms involved, who did have other Polish operations, if they proceeded with the project.

Gazprom's partners, however, did not get cold feet—even as political opposition in Eastern Europe mounted. In 2015 and 2016, the leaders of Croatia, Czechia, Estonia, Hungary, Latvia, Poland, Slovakia, Lithuania, and Romania signed a letter opposing the project.[35] In December, Poland's UOKiK officially ruled against it, and the Nord Stream 2 consortium withdrew their application for approval.[36] This was merely an effort to buy time as they pursued a workaround. On 24 April, Gazprom's partners announced that rather than take a 50 per cent stake in the project, they would provide loans amounting to 50 per cent of its forecast cost—€950 million each.[37] Gazprom would be Nord Stream 2's sole shareholder.

The structure, on its face, appeared to violate Europe's Third Energy Package. But as the pipeline ran directly to a non-EU country, its proponents argued the rules against vertical integration between pipeline owner and supplier did not apply. Nord Stream 2 would bring Russian gas through a loophole directly to Germany.

The issue would continue to be among the most contentious in Europe over the ensuing years, with calls for barring it repeatedly proposed whenever the debate over Russian sanctions returned to the fore. But the near-unanimous opposition voiced by the EU's eastern members in March 2016 was under threat. Russia was seeking to use other tools of economic influence to build ties with Hungary, led by populist premier Viktor Orbán who clashed with Brussels even more regularly than Poland's PiS government and had long proven himself open to Russian entreaties.

That much was clear when Hungary announced in January 2014 that it would work with Russia's state nuclear company Rosatom to expand Hungary's Soviet-built Paks nuclear power plant, which already provided half of the country's electricity. Moscow was willing to offer a €10 billion loan below market rates for the project.[38]

Hungarian officials quieted talk of the project in the aftermath of the annexation of Crimea, as the opposition ramped up criticism ahead of the April 2014 election. But Orbán's Fidesz party retained its supermajority in the vote, and the government said it would separate Paks from Ukrainian affairs. In July 2014, Orbán announced his intention to ensure that 'the new state that we are building is an illiberal state', listing Putin's Russia among the models he wished to emulate.[39]

Orbán's open illiberalism was accompanied by increasingly vocal Euroscepticism, even as Hungary remained one of the largest net recipients of the EU's Cohesion Fund, through which budgetary support is provided to member states with below EU-average income levels. Tensions with Brussels came to a head in 2015, when Orbán announced a series of crackdowns on refugees from Syria amid that country's civil war. Relations with Germany in particular soured after Merkel announced she would welcome refugees to the country in August 2015. Orbán, on the other hand, instituted policies that the European Court of Justice later ruled made it 'virtually impossible' for refugees to claim asylum in Hungary.[40]

Germany was, and has remained, Hungary's leading export market and source of foreign direct investment. But Orbán saw Russia as an alternative source of cheap money. Rosatom had been awarded the Paks project without a tender. But nuclear projects are never quick and easy, and Paks' expansion was further hindered by opposition from some factions within Orbán's government.[41]

Nevertheless, Orbán continued to strengthen Hungary's financial ties to Russia. In 2015, he led Hungary back into the Russian-based International Investment Bank (IIB). The USSR had set up the bank in 1970 as a Moscow-led effort to challenge Western international lenders like the European Bank for Reconstruction and Development (EBRD) and the Asian Development Bank. Hungary left in 2000, when the bank, by its own admission, was inactive and untransparent.[42] Putin had prioritised reinvigorating the institution in light of the sectoral sanctions, part of a wider strategy of fostering non-Western state development banks. Orbán also agreed the IIB should re-locate its headquarters to Budapest.

While Orbán sought to shift Hungary towards Moscow, it was European disunity and Russian influence that enabled it.

In November 2015, the European Commission announced it would investigate Budapest's award of the Paks II contract to Rosatom yet ultimately approved it on a technicality sixteen months later.[43] The project's approval would uncover further uncomfortable details about the extent to which Russia was using business networks across Europe as tools of influence.

It had been reported that European Commissioner Günther Oettinger, who oversaw the energy portfolio when Paks' Russian financing was agreed, had accepted a flight to Budapest on the private jet of Klaus Mangold, a lobbyist for both Gazprom and Orbán's government.[44] Mangold, dubbed 'Mr Russia' by the German press, was known for his advocacy for German–Russian business ties.[45] Oettinger, a political ally of Merkel's, denied they had discussed Paks' expansion.[46]

And while Berlin was willing to clash with Orbán over its treatment of migrants, it clearly did not see Russian energy as a threat, given its ongoing support of Nord Stream 2. It was also somewhat flippant in enforcing the EU's own sanctions, including those barring economic support for Russia's takeover of Crimea.

In June 2017, the Kremlin inadvertently revealed that it was planning to install power turbines made in Germany in a pair of new powerplants in occupied Crimea.[47] A month later, Siemens announced it would stop delivering power plant equipment to Russia, but only after it had been revealed that not two but four such turbines had been shipped to the occupied peninsula. The company's denials of complicity were hardly credible—Russia's main business newspaper, *Vedomosti*, had publicly disclosed the plan to ship the turbines to Crimea two years earlier.[48] Berlin called for sanctions against Siemens' Russian business partners but no action against the firm itself. Shortly thereafter, Rosneft announced it was naming ex-Chancellor Schröder to its board of directors. Upon his election, he was immediately named chairman—Sechin declared that Schröder 'entered history as the most loyal German leader to Russia'.[49]

Russia soon also assuaged Hungary's concerns around Nord Stream 2. These concerns primarily derived from the fact that

Budapest had become increasingly dependent on gas piped via Ukraine. Following two visits by Putin to Budapest in six months, in October 2017 Hungary announced that Gazprom agreed to deposit significant additional gas in the country's storage facilities and that they would enter a new long-term agreement when their current deal expired.[50]

Orbán felt free to continue his drift towards Moscow, not only straining European ties but American ones as well. In 2018, he extradited a pair of Russian arms dealers to Moscow rather than the United States, although they had originally been arrested as part of a joint US–Hungarian operation. They were quickly freed. Washington subsequently leaked to the *New York Times* that not only was the IIB's chairman the son of a pair of Russian spies including the former KGB chief in Budapest but that it believed he himself had served in Russian intelligence.[51] Orbán nonetheless pushed ahead with plans for the IIB to move to Budapest. Its new headquarters opened in the city in February 2021.[52]

Both Hungary and Germany represent Europe's failings in mitigating the risk of Russian economic influence, as well as Russia's success in deepening such ties even amid sanctions. Despite vocal bipartisan opposition from Washington against Nord Stream 2's construction, Merkel's government literally laughed off their concerns. Construction was completed in September 2021.

Europe's deepening economic interdependence in the aftermath of Russia's initial invasion of Ukraine would sharpen Russia's economic leverage. The examples discussed here are only a few of the most prominent. Similar examples can be found across Europe. They were so widespread that in 2017 Austrian far-right leader Heinz-Christian Strache was surreptitiously recorded openly discussing what he believed to be Russian state support for his party's election campaign. In exchange, he agreed to steer state contracts towards Russian-linked entities. Strache would become vice-chancellor after the vote and nominated Karin Kneissl as foreign minister. She would invite Putin to her wedding the subsequent year, where, in a move laden with symbolism, she curtsied to him before they waltzed together. Although the leaking of the recording in 2019 would prompt the Austrian government's downfall, and end Strache's career, Vienna took no meaningful action to mitigate the risk of Russia continuing to expand its influence in the country. Kneissl would go on to work for RT and join Schröder on Rosneft's board.[53]

It was not just in Europe that Moscow sought to deepen economic linkages. When Putin announced the cancellation of the South Stream pipeline in 2014, it was not just Nord Stream 2 that he pointed to as an alternative. His announcement came during a state visit to Turkey, where he also announced additional gas supplies for Turkey—at a discount. Ankara simultaneously granted approval for Rosatom to build a nuclear power plant in Akkuyu with an even larger capacity than planned for Paks. And Gazprom and Turkey's state pipeline corporation BOTAŞ also signed a memorandum of understanding to build a new gas pipeline under the Black Sea.

Germany's pursuit of economic interdependence failed because Putin did not oversee a democracy or have to answer to economic pressures from his own business community, which had been weakened or placed under greater state control as seen in the previous chapter. Europe was focused on Russia's role in providing its energy security, failing to recognise that it was in fact fostering insecurity. Putin's approach also focused on ensuring alternatives were not available on the European periphery—and Russia's geo-economic approach to Ankara would prove among its most successful efforts.

5

THE ERDOĞAN FACTOR

Turkey's President Recep Tayyip Erdoğan publicly condemned the 2014 annexation of Crimea but never joined the sanctions regime. Ankara's alliance with the United States became increasingly strained over the subsequent years, amid the fallout from a coup attempt in Turkey in 2016, tensions over Syria, and mutual mistrust. The Kremlin actively offered Ankara economic inducements as part of its efforts to take advantage of these tensions and increase its influence over European energy politics. The West used sanctions and sanctions threats to try and keep Turkey in its camp. In the subsequent years, Turkey's position between Russia and the West was more contested than at any point since before the Cold War. Although his controversial economic policies drove Turkish inflation consistently higher, Erdoğan managed to reap benefits from this position between the two sides.

One parable for how Turkish business found itself impacted by the growing geo-economic competition between Russia and the West is found in a surprising place—Netflix's *Selling Sunset*, a 'docusoap' reality show about picturesque and picaresque real estate agents and their multi-million-dollar California listings.

The show's second season, which aired in May 2020, introduces one of its longest-running subplots—the travails of broker Davina Potratz in her efforts to sell a Beverly Hills property belonging to Turkish-Danish businessman Adnan Şen, son of Ali Şen, a Turkish magnate with longstanding links to Russia's defence industry.[1] Adnan insists she agree to list the property at $75 million and not a penny less. Despite scepticism that such a price is achievable, Potratz's bosses reluctantly agree. By the time the programme's

63

fifth season aired in April 2022, however, the property remained unsold, though Şen still features, agreeing to allow Potratz to list another of his properties instead, albeit merely a rental.

According to his website, Adnan Şen has extensive business interests in the real estate, construction, and energy sectors.[2] While Şen was seeking a career as a reality television and real estate developer in the United States, he also had significant business links to Russia.

Şen is also the founder of Bosphorus Gaz, 'the second largest natural gas importer' in Turkey.[3] It buys some 2.5 billion cubic metres of gas annually from Gazprom, which held a majority stake in the firm until selling it to its junior partner, the Şen Group, in 2019.[4] In October 2020, Turkish media reported that Bosphorus Gaz's deputy general manager Emel Öztürk and five others had been arrested on espionage charges relating to Turkey's energy imports 'benefiting a foreign energy giant', later named as Gazprom.[5] They allegedly acquired information from Turkey's state gas firm and passed it to Gazprom.[6]

Turkey may have one foot firmly planted in the West, but the other has in recent years been increasingly moving towards Moscow.

Turkey is a NATO member, and its military is the alliance's second largest, but it frequently clashes with other members of the alliance. The closest the alliance has come to a war among its members came in 1974, when Turkey invaded Cyprus following a coup that aimed to unite the island with Greece. Cyprus has been divided ever since, and related issues remain a thorn in the side of the alliance's unity. Yet far older history also plays a role in Turkey's approach to the Russian–Ukrainian conflict.

Erdoğan was initially relatively quiet on Ukrainian matters when Russian forces began seizing Crimea in February 2014, but he could not ignore the issue entirely. The peninsula had been part of the Ottoman Empire, from which Turkey emerged in the aftermath of the First World War, but that was lost following the Russian–Turkish War of 1768–74. Russian Empress Catherine the Great formally annexed the peninsula nine years later. Throughout these changes, Crimea retained its indigenous Turkic population, the Crimean Tatars.

The Crimean Tatars suffered greatly under Russian and Soviet control. The population was almost entirely deported from the peninsula by Stalin in 1944. He alleged they had colluded with the Nazis and could no longer be trusted. Even after Stalin's successor, Nikita Khrushchev, allowed other deported populations to return to their ancestral lands, Crimean Tatars were not permitted to do so until 1989.

Russia's 2014 annexation of Crimea was accompanied by fears for the future of the Crimean Tatar population, and activists from the community who opposed Russia's annexation began to disappear. Others were forced into exile, including Mustafa Dzhemilev, arguably the community's most prominent leader. This prompted increasingly vocal denunciations from Ankara—Erdoğan was attempting to position himself as a 'neo-Ottoman' leader at the time, transforming Turkey from a parliamentary government to a presidential one and seeking to win the top post in the presidential elections of August 2014. The historical and cultural links between the Crimean Tatars and Turks meant that continued silence was not an option. Erdoğan hosted Dzhemilev a month after the annexation, awarding him Turkey's highest state honour.[7]

But Erdoğan refrained from the denunciations of Putin himself that rang out in the West. The Kremlin was actively seeking to position itself as a partner for Erdoğan's government, noting Erdoğan's comments that Turkey would not join the sanctions regime, which it had good reason to believe. At the time of Crimea's annexation, Erdoğan was already facing a scandal over alleged evasion of US sanctions on Iran.

In December 2013, the Istanbul Security Directorate detained a large number of officials—including the sons of three of Erdoğan's ministers—on suspicion of bribery and involvement in a gold trading operation in which Turkish gold was allegedly funnelled to Iran in exchange for natural gas and oil deliveries.[8] The trades were allegedly facilitated by an Iranian-Azeri-Turkish businessman, Reza Zarrab, and Mehmet Hakan Atilla, an employee of Turkey's state-owned Halkbank.[9] Both would be found guilty of sanctions evasions charges in the United States in 2018, but in January 2014, Erdoğan labelled the probe a 'judicial coup' and sacked many of those who had investigated it.[10] *The Atlantic* dubbed the case 'the biggest sanctions-evasion scheme in recent history'.

Turkey and Iran have a complicated and often acrimonious relationship. The case was more representative of the general intertwining of state and business interests in Turkey under Erdoğan,[11] already in power for ten years at that point, but it also highlighted growing tensions between Washington and Ankara that led Erdoğan to increasingly flout the rules the United States attempted to impose on the international economic order. Erdoğan publicly blamed the probe on Fethullah Gülen, an Islamist cleric and former ally, whom he has repeatedly and unsuccessfully sought to have extradited from the United States.[12]

Both the Halkbank scandal and Gülen's fate became sticking points in US–Turkish relations in subsequent years. Zarrab was arrested on a trip to Florida's Disney World in March 2016, incensing Erdoğan. Relations would reach a nadir that July after the failed coup attempt that was allegedly linked to Gülen. Erdoğan later publicly implied that the United States was at least complicit, if not responsible. Related tensions would continue under the Trump administration, although Trump's initial choice for national security advisor, Michael Flynn, would be implicated in a scandal over alleged lobbying on behalf of the Erdoğan government.[13] In September 2017, Turkey arrested a US consulate worker, claiming he had worked for Gülen, leading to another spat. Soon thereafter, Zarrab began cooperating with US prosecutors and testified in the trial against Atilla that Erdoğan had approved the scheme.[14] After Atilla was released and deported from the United States following his sentencing in 2019, Erdoğan's son-in-law and then-finance minister Berat Albayrak announced Atilla had been appointed to head the Istanbul Stock Exchange.[15]

Tensions with Washington over the Atilla and Gülen cases, the coup attempt, and increasingly antagonistic positions on the conflicts in Syria and Libya would push Erdoğan to seek to deepen ties with Russia. In these efforts too, he would be willing to risk serious US sanctions violations.

Putin's 2014 announcement that he would seek to build a new natural gas pipeline across the Black Sea via Turkey rather than Bulgaria was the latest step in strengthening energy and financial links between the two countries that had slowly built up in Erdoğan's and Putin's first decade in power. The Blue Stream pipeline, launched in the 1990s, served as the first gas link between the two countries when it opened in 2005. Russian tourists would become mainstays on Turkish beaches as their incomes rose in the early 2000s and package tours became wildly popular. Although there were plenty of issues on which Russia and Turkey did not agree, Erdoğan's government initially pursued a strategy of 'no problems with neighbours' that sought to avert tensions affecting the development of the Turkish economy and Erdoğan's popularity.

That would change drastically in 2011, when the Arab Spring rocked the Middle East and Erdoğan emerged as one of the most vocal backers of the Muslim Brotherhood-aligned government that emerged in Egypt. He also endorsed other protest movements, including in neighbouring Syria. But the attempted revolution against the Assad regime in Damascus quickly spiralled into a brutal civil war. Erdoğan backed some of the rebels, while Moscow backed Assad. However, in December 2014, neither Moscow nor Ankara had overtly intervened in the conflict. Erdoğan was already engaged in a dispute with Brussels over migration, with well over a million Syrians estimated to have become refugees in Turkey. At the time, Syria's troubles appeared not to be a challenge to Putin's plans to disrupt the EU's Southern Gas Corridor strategy. The new pipeline, dubbed TurkStream, aimed to triple the amount of Russian gas that could be delivered to Turkey annually.

However, Russia's decision to enter the Syrian Civil War on behalf of the Assad regime in September 2015 put an immediate chill on relations with Turkey. Russian troops would now be fighting against Turkish-backed forces. Matters turned from bad to worse that November, when a Turkish F-16 fighter shot down a Russian Su-24 attack plane that had violated Turkish airspace while crossing over the Syrian border.[16] Talks on TurkStream were suspended.[17] It seemed the project was dead in the water before it could even begin.

Although the incident was the first direct clash between NATO and Russian or Soviet airpower in sixty years, it came as Ankara's ties with the alliance were strained. The United States and Europe supported Kurdish forces in northern Syria that Erdoğan saw as terrorists. When he triggered Article 4 of the NATO Treaty in July 2015 to trigger alliance-wide discussions over terror concerns, the alliance's response was muted. NATO even withdrew its Patriot missile defence systems from Turkey just weeks before the Su-24 shootdown.[18] They had initially been deployed in 2013, following the shootdown of a Turkish airplane by the Assad regime, which had provoked an earlier Article 4 consultation.[19] Erdoğan did not trigger Article 4 again.

Relations with NATO allies, in particular the United States, went from bad to worse after the 2016 coup attempt, which nearly removed Erdoğan from power and left at least 270 people dead.[20] Erdoğan felt that he was strongly in need of an alternative ally and turned to Russia, which could supply him with gas and arms and was unlikely to criticise his increasingly illiberal tendencies.

Russian state media inveighed against the coup, blaming it on Washington even before Erdoğan had made similar insinuations. Putin called him the day after the event and offered his condolences.[21] Less than a month later, after jailing thousands of suspected Gülenists and alleged coup sympathisers, Erdoğan took his first post-coup trip abroad—to Moscow.[22]

In October 2016, Putin in turn visited Erdoğan in Istanbul, where they had reached a new agreement on TurkStream.[23] This time, Ankara reportedly secured a gas price discount, building on the discount Putin had initially offered in 2014.[24] Although both sides noted that there remained key differences over Syria, the topic of Ukraine was apparently not on the agenda. The deal would mark a watershed in Russian–Turkish relations.

Ankara would turn to Moscow to address one of the other major sticking points in Turkish–US relations. Ankara had long sought to buy its own missile defence systems. The 2016 withdrawal of the NATO Patriots convinced Erdoğan that the alliance could not be relied on.[25] While Russia and Turkey remained on opposite lines of the Syrian conflict, Erdoğan felt comfortable dealing with Putin, whereas in Washington the ebbs and flows of US politics meant positions on the Syrian conflict could change rapidly. Trump had, after all, won that year's presidential election in part on campaign pledges to halt US involvement in overseas wars like the Syria conflict, while also threatening to ban Muslims from entering the country. What direction the bombastic new president would actually take the country in, however, remained unclear. In contrast to his pledge, one of the first actions Trump took in office was to order a raid in Yemen, which would quickly be revealed to have been bungled.[26] The tumult of Trump's initial days in office—including firing Flynn, who had published a pro-Erdoğan op-ed a day before the 2016 election—only made Washington more vexing to deal with.[27]

While it had repeatedly turned to NATO for missile defence support when tensions in the Middle East flared up, Turkey now signalled that it was willing to consider alternatives even before the escalation of the Syria conflict and relations with Washington grew cold.[28] Erdoğan had repeatedly sought to drive a hard bargain with the United States, seeking substantial technology transfers and to drive down the price of the state-of-the-art Patriot missile defence system. Such technologies are carefully protected by the US national security establishment, and they are frequently used as carrots when seeking concessions from other allies. For example, the deployment and sale of the same Patriot system has been a key point of negotiations between Saudi Arabia and the United States for years. Erdoğan was willing to play hardball and in 2013 even announced plans to buy an alternative Chinese missile defence system. That deal, however, was quickly dropped when talks around the Patriot sale subsequently resumed.

When no progress had been made by 2017, Putin proposed an alternative solution. Moscow was willing to sell Ankara its latest missile defence system, the S-400, and would do so at a lower price than the Patriot system. Erdoğan quickly agreed to the deal, signing an agreement in July of that year.

Many in Washington were aghast—not only did the deal mean that Turkey would have to invite in Russian military specialists to train its forces on the equipment but the S-400 would ultimately be sat alongside NATO's state-of-the-art equipment that Turkey had purchased or was stationed at NATO bases in the country. The risks of industrial espionage were grave. Even more shockingly, Ankara signed the deal after the CAATSA legislation that enshrined and expanded the Obama-era sanctions was introduced to Congress but before it had passed, though there was little doubt that it would. The bill made clear that countries buying Russian defence equipment would be subject to secondary sanctions.

Erdoğan had shown himself willing to work around the sanctions in the Halkbank-Iran affair, but this represented an even more egregious potential violation—Ankara was undercutting US sanctions policy as it was still being developed, and in a deal with direct military implications, including for the NATO alliance no less.

After CAATSA passed in September 2017, there were calls for Turkey to be sanctioned if the S-400 deal went ahead, and Washington and Ankara grew further apart, as we have already seen. Erdoğan was unfazed and appeared confident that Turkey was too important to the alliance, despite its occasional tensions, for the threat to be acted upon. Washington's opposition to TurkStream had proven futile—construction had begun that May. It was equally ineffective in halting the S-400 sales. Russia delivered the first components in July 2019.[29]

Initially, Trump resisted enacting sanctions under CAATSA, which he repeatedly claimed violated his executive authority. Instead, the United States announced it would suspend Turkish participation in the programme to develop the F-35 fifth-generation fighter jet. Trump was still willing to seek a better relationship with Ankara despite all the tensions and described it as 'not a fair situation'.[30] Meanwhile, voices in Congress insisted on action. Erdoğan in turn only grew more incensed, particularly as Congress had passed resolutions calling for waivers for India and Vietnam over their planned purchases of the same system.

Erdoğan pushed ahead with other efforts to build ties with Moscow. The TurkStream pipeline was inaugurated in January 2020. Work on Rosatom's Akkuyu nuclear power plant project began to pick up pace, and construction of reactor sites began that year. Putin and Erdoğan also moved to discuss extending TurkStream into the Balkans, prompting the US Congress to swiftly pass legislation threatening to sanction the firms involved.[31] Nevertheless, an extension was built through Bulgaria, enabling Russia to bypass Ukraine for Balkan deliveries as the Trump administration failed to act on the threat.[32]

Although there were still tensions between Russia and Turkey over Syria, and increasingly Libya as well, where Russia was overtly supporting the efforts of Khalifa Haftar, who clashed with the UNrecognised government that Ankara backed, Erdoğan and Putin's relationship continued to blossom. Despite their differences, they had established a trusting working relationship.

This was evident in September 2020 when Ankara and Moscow once again found themselves on opposing sides of the conflict that Azeri President Ilham Aliyev launched to retake the disputed Nagorno-Karabakh territory from neighbouring Armenia. Erdoğan provided direct military support to Aliyev's regime, including the provision of Bayraktar drones, which proved critical in rapidly turning the fight into a rout.[33] On the other side, Armenia was allied to Russia through the Collective Security Treaty Organisation (CSTO), the mutual defence pact that had been formed in the aftermath of the Soviet collapse. Although Russia refused an Armenian request under the alliance's treaty to intervene, citing the technicality that Nagorno-Karabakh was de jure Azerbaijani, Putin did ultimately step in to broker a ceasefire in November 2020 that handed most of the Armenian-controlled territory in Azerbaijan back to Baku. Even though Ankara had acted in what Russia considers its own backyard, the conflict did not meaningfully affect Russia's bilateral relations with Turkey.

The Trump administration would ultimately follow through with the CAATSA-mandated sanctions over Turkey's S-400 acquisition but only in December 2020 as policymaking descended into a free-for-all amid Trump's attempts to hold on to office, refusing to recognise his loss in the previous month's presidential election. The sanctions included a ban on US export licences for the Turkish Defence Industry Agency and an asset freeze and visa ban for a handful of officials involved in the deal. Turkey–US relations hit a new nadir. Russia had successfully developed its partnership with Turkey to increase its energy leverage over Europe through the TurkStream pipeline, and the West's sanctions had failed to halt closer Russian–Turkish cooperation. That would be a problem for the Biden administration to deal with, as would the fallout from the Armenia–Azerbaijan war, which remained unsettled despite the November peace deal.

6

EURASIAN ECONOMIC DISUNION

Economic competition between Russia and the West has been a dominant feature of the post-Soviet space throughout and before Putin's time in power. While Russia was in an extremely weak economic position in the early 1990s, it nevertheless employed the threat of trade restrictions to pressure countries to join the CIS and to secure other political concessions.[1]

During this period, and much as was also the case in Russia itself, Western investors were eager to invest in the former Soviet republics as they emerged as independent states. Nowhere was this more evident than in Azerbaijan, despite getting off to a belated start as a result of its war with Armenia over the Nagorno-Karabakh region—which the Soviet Union had established as an autonomous region within Azerbaijan despite its Armenian majority—that began even before the USSR's collapse and raged until 1994.

The conflict had left Azerbaijan in turmoil during its initial years of independence, with three presidents in three years. The fighting only ended after Heydar Aliyev—Azerbaijan's former Communist Party chief—rose to power and signed a ceasefire with Armenian forces in May 1994. Though this resulted in Armenian forces consolidating control over the disputed Nagorno-Karabakh territory and occupying some 9 per cent of Azerbaijan's territory outside it, the agreement set the stage for Azerbaijan to begin profiting from its oil reserves, which birthed the international oil industry in the late nineteenth and early twentieth century and helped fuel the engines of the Soviet economy and war machine thereafter.

In 1994, Baku struck a deal with BP to restore and expand upon pre-war levels of production. The 'contract of the century', as those involved dubbed it, also saw BP pledge to undertake a programme to build a new pipeline carrying Azeri oil to international markets.[2] Azerbaijan's sole existing export route ran only to Batumi in Georgia's Adjara region. The pipeline was originally laid by Alfred Nobel in 1906—though launched twenty years earlier,[3] it was regularly disrupted, including by strikes in 1904 led by Josef Dzhugashvili, the future Stalin.[4] Georgia was again wracked by conflict in the early 1990s, and the local strongman Aslan Abashidze had carved out Batumi and the surrounding Adjara region as his own personal fiefdom. In 1996, construction began of a new pipeline from Baku to Georgia's Supsa terminal, just north of Abashidze's Adjara.[5] However, Aliyev and BP had set their sights far beyond, planning to vastly increase Azerbaijan's oil production at fields whose development had lagged under Soviet rule and carrying it west to ports from which it could be traded around the world.

Construction began on the new route, dubbed the Baku–Tbilisi–Ceyhan pipeline, in 2002. The pipeline transverses Azerbaijan and Georgia en route to the Turkish port of Ceyhan, where Azeri fuel is loaded on to tankers that ship it around the world.[6] BP and Baku were aware that Russia saw the ex-Soviet countries as an area in which it deserved particular influence. Rather than exclude Russian firms from the project, Russia's privately held Lukoil, whose controlling owner Vagit Alekperov was close to the Kremlin and an ethnic Azeri, was brought into the consortium that underpinned the 'contract of the century', with a 10 per cent stake.[7]

Russia also sought to keep a foothold over Kazakhstan's hydrocarbon resources after the Soviet collapse, although it took a more active role than in Azerbaijan. A series of backroom deals enabled the Western oil majors Chevron and Shell to strike a deal with Kazakh President Nursultan Nazarbayev to lead a consortium exploiting the massive Tengiz field in 1992. Moscow responded to its exclusion from the deal by cutting off Kazakhstan's access to its refineries and pipeline network.[8] The strategy worked, and Nazarbayev approved Russia's inclusion.

Kazakhstan adopted a strategy that Nazarbayev labelled a 'multi-vectoral foreign policy' and Azerbaijan followed a similar approach. Economic ties would lead to diplomatic relations with the West and successfully mitigate most criticism over their own kleptocracy, nepotism, and human rights records, which were just as poor as those in Putin's Russia. Political opponents would be hounded into exile or jailed, and most of those who found their way to wealth and influence came from the circles around Aliyev and Nazarbayev. Despite their developing relationships with the West, Kazakhstan and Azerbaijan recognised that they also needed to retain a close relationship with Russia.

After the 2008 Russo-Georgian war, Azerbaijan invited Moscow to expand its energy investments. Even as it rushed to get the TANAP and TAP gas pipelines approved after the 2014 Russian annexation of Crimea, it never opposed Russia's own planned routes. Baku also bought more arms from Russia as it built up an arsenal to tip the balance of power with Armenia firmly in its favour. The flow was significant—Baku had adopted a policy of matching its annual defence budget to the entire national budget of Armenia. Yet it also retained its key economic linkages with the West: in September 2017, it extended the 'contract of the century' with BP until 2050.[9]

Kazakhstan's experience was similar. Despite the Tengiz tumult, Nazarbayev had little issue with Russian investments in other crucial sectors of the economy, including mining and mineral production. There were also significant personal and political links between the Kazakh and Russian governments, as highlighted by the 2011 appointment of Kazakh billionaire and Nazarbayev's son-in-law Timur Kulibayev to Gazprom's board of directors in 2011. Kulibayev would represent the continued expansion of Russian–Kazakh economic links in the years after Crimea's annexation, including his 2018 purchase of Russia's Baimskaya copper project from Russia's Roman Abramovich.[10]

Nazarbayev was also an enthusiastic backer of the Eurasian Economic Union project. He had initially suggested a similar proposal in the early 1990s, and Russian media were keen to highlight him as the 'father' of the effort when speaking to international audiences, so as to make it appear less like a neo-imperial project pushed by Putin. Nazarbayev claimed that the project, which created a unified customs zone, could help Kazakhstan diversify its economy and lessen its dependence on commodities exports. However, in the years after its 2014 launch, he would become increasingly disillusioned. Customs issues remained frequent at the Russian–

Kazakh border, and the project caused challenges for deepening trade links with China.

In 2017, Nazarbayev launched a new economic initiative that aimed to provide another basis for the country's growth. Kazakhstan's capital would host the 'Astana International Finance Centre', to give multinational, that is, Western, businesses a new place to base themselves in the heart of Eurasia. With Russia under sanctions and Moscow an increasingly controversial place for them to do business, Nazarbayev believed Astana would serve as a good substitute. It would adopt English law for a local arbitration court so that Western businesses would feel at home, at least in terms of business practices, in the windswept city in the middle of the steppe.

Putin never seriously criticised the Western business links fostered by Nazarbayev or the regime of Azeri President Ilham Aliyev—Heydar's son who assumed the presidency after Heydar's death in 2003—as the two kleptocratic regimes refrained from turning their economic ties into political ones. Putin would, however, bitterly criticise Western investment in Georgia, where the Kremlin had initially sought to retain political leverage in the years after its 2004 Rose Revolution, which called for a more openly Western orientation and led to the resignation of Eduard Shevardnadze, a former Soviet foreign minister who came to power in Georgia after a series of civil wars in the aftermath of the Soviet collapse. The subsequent rise to power of Mikheil Saakashvili and his United National Movement was initially unopposed by Putin, but Saakashvili and his allies soon become bugbears of the Kremlin when he secured an agreement to close Russia's bases in the country and moved to develop security ties with the West. While Saakashvili's NATO aspirations were a breaking point in relations, Putin had complained about Georgia's 'leeching' from the Russian economy shortly after assuming the presidency.[11] In a phone call to US President Bill Clinton at the end of 2000, Putin stated that 'Georgia exists mainly, if not totally, at the expense of our energy' and claimed it should follow Russia's policy suggestions because of Georgia's indebtedness to it, the large Georgian population living in Russia, and because Russia should be respected 'as a big power'.[12]

There was no denying the two states had long and deep ties. The American novelist John Steinbeck described his impression of

Russians' view of the country while on a trip to the Soviet Union after the Second World War, writing 'they spoke of the country in the Caucasus and around the Black Sea as a kind of second heaven. Indeed, we began to believe that most Russians hope that if they live very good and virtuous lives, they will go not to heaven, but to Georgia when they die.'[13]

That relationship would be shattered by Putin in the subsequent years. After coming to power, Saakashvili began to limit Russia's role in crucial sectors of Georgia's economy. In the aftermath of the 2008 war, however, ties would be severed. Russia's recognition of the breakaway regions of South Ossetia and Abkhazia would prompt a complete curtailing of bilateral relations. And though it would slowly cement its military control over both breakaway regions, neither would receive substantial economic investment. Georgia was painted as public enemy number one in Russian media for years thereafter. In late 2012, the Kremlin broadcast a propaganda film that portrayed Saakashvili ally Givi Targamadze as having fomented clashes ahead of a protest against Putin's return to the presidency.[14]

By that time, a new word had entered the Georgian lexicon. Georgians long had a term for those seen as influenced by Moscow, dating from the annexation of modern Georgia, then broken up into a series of small kingdoms, at the beginning of the nineteenth century: *tergdaleulebi*. It translates as 'those who drink from the Terek River', which runs down the Caucasus Mountains from northern Georgia through Russia's North Caucasus. Saakashvili and many of the generation around him would instead come to be known as the *potomakdaleulebi*, those who drink from the Potomac River, which runs through the heart of Washington, DC. These *potomakdaleulebi* reshaped Georgia along the lines of the neo-liberal orthodoxy that they had learned there, none more so than the libertarian policy advisor and investor Kakha Bendukidze. They ushered in an economic overhaul that made Georgia the darling of the West, and in particular the United States. In 2010, *Foreign Policy* dubbed US policymakers who had succumbed to the country's immeasurable charms as afflicted with 'Georgia syndrome'.[15] Putin's 2008 war with Georgia was intended to send the message that such deep entanglement between a former Soviet republic and the West would carry significant costs.

Georgia's economic ties with Washington would nevertheless be cemented after the 2008 war with Russia. Washington authorised a $1 billion aid package, some 10 per cent of Georgia's pre-war GDP.[16] While significant, Georgia remained wrought by the economics of its loss in the Russian conflict. The *potomakdaleulebi*'s neo-liberal reforms may have opened Georgia up to international capital, but individual incomes remained the lowest in the South Caucasus.[17]

In the run-up to its 2012 parliamentary elections, Georgian politics were shaken to the core. Many of Saakashvili's erstwhile allies had accused him of becoming increasingly strong handed in his governance, and some sought reconciliation with Russia to counter his influence. His UNM party was initially expected to win the vote, but, two weeks before the election, a series of videos recorded at the country's Gldani prison leaked online, revealing a pattern of extreme abuse of detainees, including sodomy. Their mistreatment was an affront to Georgia's 'traditional values' and the liberal aspirations of the *potomakdaleulebi*. Saakashvili's UNM was defeated by the Georgian Dream coalition, which had been put together by the billionaire Bidzina Ivanishvili. Although he too at one point had been aligned with Saakashvili, the UNM had spent the campaign casting him as representative of the old *tergdaleulebi*.

Ivanishvili, whose net-worth has been estimated at half of Georgia's GDP, made his fortune in Russia in the 1990s.[18] However, he sold off his Russian assets in the run-up to the campaign. Such a move was seen as only possible with Putin's backing—but it also made him immensely cash rich. Ivanishvili had long treated his hometown of Chorvila to substantial largesse, and there were hopes that he would put his funds to use elsewhere in the country.[19] Shortly after being named prime minister, he announced plans for a major investment fund to make good on his promise.

However, in the subsequent years Ivanishvili and the governments of his Georgian Dream party came under increasing criticism from the West over his investments and in particular his stance on Russia. Relations between the Georgian government and Ukraine also grew tense after many former Saakashvili allies joined the government of President Petro Poroshenko to transfer their experiences in overhauling Georgia's police force and other corrupt institutions to help liberalise Ukraine. Saakashvili himself was named governor of Ukraine's Odesa region in May 2015.[20] However, he was sacked in November after falling out with Poroshenko following a series of public outbursts over the pace of reform. Saakashvili was an imperfect vehicle for fostering the same kind of cooperation between Ukraine and the West as he had been in Georgia—he ended up making international headlines again when he was arrested twice in the same week in Kyiv a year later.[21]

The prominence of UNM officials in the Ukrainian government poisoned Georgian–Ukrainian relations. Ivanishvili, who left the prime ministership at the end of 2013 but was still seen as the key decision-maker in the years to come, took little heed. Georgia's domestic disputes took priority, and Saakashvili was wanted in Georgia on charges of abuse of office. The West's relationship with Ivanishvili's governments became increasingly strained.

At the same time, Ivanishvili's Georgian Dream had cooled tensions with Russia. Moscow agreed to lift its ban on imports of Georgian wine and its famed mineral waters in February 2013. Ivanishvili, as pledged, increased his own investments in Georgia, a not entirely altruistic effort that also generated criticism as the government's actions served his personal interests and helped him consolidate control. The most notorious example domestically was the Tbilisi Panorama project, the capital city's largest real estate development. It emerged that the land had been transferred to a company linked to Ivanishvili for 1 lari, just $0.40.[22]

International observers became increasingly critical of the conduct of elections under Georgian Dream's rule. The party was seen as beholden to Ivanishvili as allies departed, and it repeatedly reshuffled cabinets with an opaque decision-making process indicating that the party was more beholden to Ivanishvili's whims than to Georgian voters, further fuelling Western suspicions. However, Ivanishvili did not overtly move to expand relations with Russia, and, while trade recovered, the domestic political environment meant that no progress was made on restoring diplomatic relations between the two.[23] The Georgian Dream governments managed to avoid escalating situations involving the Russian-backed breakaway states of Abkhazia and South Ossetia, including a handful of shooting incidents and incidents relating to the politically sensitive Inguri Dam on the border with Abkhazia, the sole remaining major economic link between the Abkhaz and Georgians.

Just downstream from the Inguri Dam was another project that would again raise questions over the Georgian Dream government's agenda, and in particular its approach to Russia and the West. The project, to build a deep seaport, was initially launched by Saakashvili's government but was revived in 2015 under Ivanishvili. Ivanishvili simply substituted a new name—Lazika became Anaklia—but otherwise it retained the same overarching aim and location. The project was undoubtedly geopolitical, given Georgia's strategic location between Central Eurasia and the Black Sea. Anaklia also abuts the de facto border between Georgia and Abkhazia. The project was launched at the height of China's Belt and Road Initiative, and Chinese investment into Georgia was growing steadily. The two major bidders for the project were, respectively, Chinese and American, but the latter won out—Washington had made clear it saw the project as a strategic priority. A Chinese win risked doing more damage to Georgian–US relations than Ivanishvili's democratic backsliding. The winning US firm, Conti International, partnered with one of Georgia's most successful businessmen, Mamuka Khazaradze, who had attended Harvard alongside Conti's founder.[24]

Initially, all proceeded smoothly, and international funding was lined up to back the project. The United States offered to help finance Anaklia, and it also received consideration from international agencies such as the Asian Development Bank. But, in late 2018, the scheme ran into major difficulties just as Georgia's relations with Washington soured, with Tbilisi refusing to accept a career State Department official as US ambassador, claiming she was too close to Saakashvili.[25]

The Georgian government launched a probe into Khazaradze and his main business partner, Badri Japaridze, over a series of transactions they had undertaken in the aftermath of the 2008 global financial crisis. It was clear that the charges were politically motivated. But Washington continued to see the project as strategic—in June 2019, then-US Secretary of State Mike Pompeo personally lobbied Georgia's prime minister to back Anaklia.[26] Instead, Japaridze and Khazaradze were charged with money laundering. The contract ground to a halt; Tbilisi formally cancelled its deal with the consortium the following January, and its investors launched an arbitration dispute.

Georgia's formal reason for exiting the project at this late stage was that it was unwilling to risk its balance sheet by offering a sovereign guarantee for the project, as its international financiers sought.[27] Instead, Georgian Dream backed an expansion of the existing port at Poti further down the Black Sea coast, despite criticism that its capacity would be far lower than Anaklia's could have been.[28] It was rumoured that Mosscow may have sought to lean on Ivanishvili to cancel the project, but the explanation may be more straightforward. In 2021, the Pandora Papers leak of offshore financial entities revealed that a company allegedly linked to Ivanishvili had a sizable stake in the Poti port.[29]

Russia did not always feel the need to take a hands-on role in pursuing its geo-economic agenda: often, it relied on local business interests to do so on its behalf. In Armenia, this strategy helped it sustain influence and limit Armenian efforts to develop political ties with the West.

At the time of Ukraine's Euromaidan Revolution, Yerevan was also holding discussions with Russia and the European Union about its trade future. The situation in many ways mirrored that in Kyiv: Armenia was headed by President Serzh Sargsyan, who, like Yanukovych, had less than perfect democratic credentials and had repeatedly faced election-related protests. The country's youth also saw their future increasingly tied to the West. However, unlike Ukraine, Armenia was already embroiled in a frozen conflict with Azerbaijan over the Nagorno-Karabakh region. The dispute was still the main feature of Armenian politics nineteen years after the 1994 ceasefire, and Sargsyan and his allies' legacy as heroes of the conflict helped cement their grip on power.

Armenia saw Russia as its key security guarantor: it was a member of the CSTO and had a bilateral security treaty with Russia. Sargsyan may have held talks for months with various Brussels functionaries to explore an association and trade agreement with the EU similar to the one Ukraine had negotiated, but as Putin ramped up his rhetoric about the promised future of his rival Eurasian Economic Union, it was clear where Yerevan would end up.

In September 2013, Sargsyan duly signed up to join the Eurasian Economic Union. Protests that had simmered since his re-election earlier that year were re-kindled but never reached a mass nearing the scale of those in Kyiv. As Ukraine's Euromaidan ramped up in December, Putin stopped off in Yerevan and Gyumri, Armenia's second city. Gyumri is home to Russia's 102nd Military Base, at the time its largest by personnel outside of Russia, with an estimated 4–5,000 soldiers.[30] In a speech in the city, Putin praised the benefits of Sargsyan's decision and implied it was only logical. He ended with an invocation of the famous Russian war march 'Proshchanie Slavyanki' and vowed 'Russia will never leave' the South Caucasus.[31]

Putin had put Russia's business interests at work to ensure this was the case. During his preceding stop-off in Yerevan, he was accompanied by Gazprom CEO Alexei Miller. They signed a new long-term gas agreement with Yerevan that was set to lock in prices for five years. Armenia was and still is dependent on Russian gas piped in via Georgia. It would soon transpire, however, that the deal was accompanied by an agreement for Armenia to transfer the 20 per cent stake it still held in the country's gas distribution network to Gazprom, in exchange for a previously undisclosed debt of $300 million.[32] Although originally set up as a joint venture in which neither Moscow nor Yerevan held a majority, Moscow had gradually increased its stake and would now take full control of the gas network.

The Armenian economy remained troubled over the coming years, and public ire at the widespread corruption of the regime mounted. Major protests broke out again in 2015, led largely by pro-Western activists. The unity inspired by the role of Sargsyan and other members of the elite in the Nagorno-Karabakh conflict faded as well, and other veterans' groups threatened violence. One such group, Sasna Tsrer, stormed a Yerevan police station in July 2016 to demand Sargsyan's resignation. They took a number of hostages, including the deputy chief of the Armenian police. The crisis ended thirteen days later when the group surrendered after a police officer was killed by sniper fire, though Sasna Tsrer denied responsibility.[33] The crisis, however, only sparked more protests against Sargsyan's regime.

Sargsyan reacted by reshuffling his government, bringing in a supposed technocrat, Karen Karapetyan, as prime minister. However, Karapetyan's purported managerial expertise came from a role at Gazprom, where he had previously headed an Armenian joint venture before serving as deputy CEO of its Russian distribution network. There was little doubt Karapetyan's economic agenda would remain committed to Russia.

Karapetyan's appointment was not the only sign of growing Russian influence and investment. In the preceding years, one businessman in particular, Samvel Karapetyan, was responsible for many of Armenia's largest investments. Of no relation to Karen Karapetyan, Samvel Karapetyan had earned billions in Russia through close ties to Gazprom and in the Moscow real estate sector.[34] In particular, he invested in Armenia's electricity and power distribution sector and, by 2017, had control over their key networks.[35]

Both Karapetyans proved dutiful backers of Sargsyan's agenda. Although the country's economic outlook remained poor, Sargsyan was hard at work on consolidating his political power. In 2015, Sargsyan had called a referendum on changing the constitution. While nominally aimed at moving from a presidential to a parliamentary system of government, critics saw a clear attempt to enable Sargsyan to remain in power after his second presidential term expired in April 2018, conveniently when key changes would come into force.

When the time came, Sargsyan surprised no one by announcing that he would indeed transfer to the prime ministership.[36] Once again, protesters descended on central Yerevan in response.[37] But Sargsyan's allies controlled the parliament, and it initially appeared the demonstrations would be no more successful than earlier iterations.

That changed, however, on 31 March 2018, when ex-journalist and opposition figure Nikol Pashinyan launched a march from Gyumri across the country towards the capital.[38] It quickly gathered support, demonstrating it was not just the urbanites in Yerevan who were outraged at Sargsyan's alleged corruption and consolidation of power.

Shortly after Pashinyan's march reached Yerevan, Sargsyan was elected prime minister.[39] However, the march drove support for Pashinyan, and acts of civil disobedience soon paralysed the country. Pashinyan was arrested on 22 April, which only led to further demonstrations.[40] Sargsyan quickly backtracked, ordered Pashinyan's release, and agreed to a meeting. While the encounter ended in another impasse, the demonstrations grew in intensity. Members of the armed forces, long Sargsyan's power base, began to join the protests. The following morning, he resigned.

Sargsyan's Republican Party named Karen Kareptyan, who had stepped down from the role to make way for Sargsyan, as acting prime minister. But the tide had clearly turned for good. Members of Sargsyan's Republican Party acknowledged as much, and on 8 May enough voted with the opposition to name Pashinyan prime minister, the culmination of what would become known as Armenia's Velvet Revolution.[41]

Brussels and Washington welcomed the change in power. *The Economist* subsequently named Armenia its 'country of the year' to honour its non-violent revolution. Rather than intervene aggressively as he had done in Ukraine, Putin acquiesced to the change, confident that Russia's security and economic linkages meant that the potential for Yerevan to move out of Russia's orbit was limited.

Pashinyan had a reputation as Western-leaning based on his former roles as a protest leader and maverick journalist against corruption. Unlike other leaders of 'colour revolutions' in the post-Soviet space, he had been circumspect in any criticism of the Kremlin during his protest campaign. Moscow's security role in Armenia would have made it deeply unwise to alienate Russia. And although Pashinyan had previously criticised the Eurasian Economic Union when on the opposition benches in 2017, he quickly signalled to Putin that he would remain loyal to the bloc.[42] Within a week of being named prime minister, he travelled to Sochi for a Eurasian Economic Union meeting. Pashinyan said he wanted to 'stress that Armenia is ready to support the approval of all documents agreed' and endorsed Moldova's participation in the meeting as the bloc's first observer state, offering a more ringing endorsement than even Belarusian President Alexander Lukashenko.[43] Russia's influence over Armenia meant that despite Pashinyan's previous inclination, he would have to kowtow to Moscow and its agenda.

Nevertheless, as Pashinyan embarked on his reforms, Moscow used economic pressure to ensure that he continued to operate within approved bounds. Gazprom and its Armenian subsidiary proved, unsurprisingly, to be the mechanisms through which the Kremlin achieved this. On 31 December 2018, Gazprom announced it was increasing the price for gas delivered to Armenia by 10 per cent.[44] The move was a serious blow to Pashinyan's new government, which had openly spoken of negotiating with Moscow for lower gas prices.[45] The move came as Pashinyan's government was seeking to hold members of the old regime to account. In a sign of Moscow's displeasure at the process, Putin had sent a public birthday greeting to ex-President Robert Kocharyan, in jail at the time on abuse of office charges.[46]

Gazprom's price increase would set off a string of negotiations that would continue throughout the coming years. The Kremlin refused to budge on the price, even during the COVID-19 pandemic when international market prices for gas sank well below those paid by Yerevan. Pashinyan did flirt with seeking alternative supplies from Tehran, but this was never a realistic possibility—in 2015, Gazprom had taken control of the small pipeline linking Armenia and Iran.[47] Putin was confident Yerevan had few other choices but to look towards Moscow—EU and US diplomatic responses to the conflict were either ineffective or absent. Most of the main figures from Armenia's previous regimes would be acquitted or have their cases dropped thereafter. At the end of 2021, Yerevan and Moscow agreed to lock in prices for ten years, albeit at the higher 2018 price, as compensation for another set of previously undisclosed debts.[48]

Security politics may have been the main factor in Russia retaining its dominant political role in Armenia after its 2018 revolution, but Russia's economic threats limited Yerevan's ability to seek alternative security arrangements.

At the same time, Moscow could be acquiescent elsewhere in its 'near abroad' to changing regimes seeking a new economic agenda, so long as their political agenda did not follow suit. The case in point is Uzbekistan, which experienced its own significant transformations after the 2016 death of longstanding ruler Islam Karimov.

A colourful and megalomaniacal president, Karimov had pursued an isolationist policy since the late 1990s. Whereas Kazakhstan's Nazarbayev pursued a 'multi-vectoral' foreign policy, Karimov's could be fairly described as 'non-vectoral'. He clashed with almost every major regional and international power. By the time of his death, he had cut Uzbekistan off from the rest of the world. His regime was highly kleptocratic and corrupt, as the only business ties foreign firms could pursue were those that ran through Karimov or his family.

Two of the largest ever global fines for bribery—related to alleged bribes paid by Russian telecoms firm MTS, controlled by the same Vladimir Yevtushenkov from whom Sechin seized control of Bashneft, and by its Swedish rival Telia—were handed down in relation to such corruption. Telia agreed to pay total restitution to Swedish and European authorities of just over $1 billion,[49] and MTS agreed to pay the US Securities and Exchange Commission $850 million.[50] Both were accused of funnelling the bribes to Karimov's daughter, Gulnara Karimova.

Karimova had served as a diplomat at the UN in Geneva and designer at New York Fashion Week, as well as dabbling as a pop star, recording a famously awful duet with French icon Gérard Depardieu.[51] Her extravagance had made her controversial, but she was already on her way out of power by the time Karimov passed, having been placed under house arrest in September 2014.[52] The machinations of the move have never been suitably explained, but at the time rumours were already swirling about Karimov's health and the potential power vacuum that could emerge when he did die. However, his hermetic rule meant these were little observed, and even less understood, in the West.

When Karimov's death was announced in 2016, his constitutionally designated successor, Speaker of Parliament Nigmatilla Yuldashev, quickly made way for Prime Minister Shavkat Mirziyoyev to assume the presidency instead.[53] Mirziyoyev had long served under Karimov and was not expected to rock the boat. The early days of his presidency were also accompanied by open talk of a ruling triumvirate together with Finance Minister Rustam Azimov and Rustam Inoyatov, head of the feared State Security Service.

Azimov was initially seen as the most Western-friendly of the three, having once called for market reforms.[54] Inoyatov, on the other hand, was known for his close cooperation with Moscow on intelligence matters, at least when it came to targeting suspected dissidents.[55] Mirziyoyev was initially seen as the balance, but he rapidly began consolidating power, demoting Azimov the following June.[56] He also simultaneously launched a series of major economic reforms that saw Uzbekistan liberalise its economy. In September 2017, the much-hated currency controls were lifted, finally bringing the official exchange rate from its artificially inflated value of around 4,000 Uzbek som to the dollar to the market rate of 8,000 som.[57]

Mirziyoyev set about bringing in several Western-educated bankers and other elites to join his new government. At the same time, he retained close ties with Moscow, in large part mediated by the Uzbek-Russian businessman Alisher Usmanov.[58] The pair were related by marriage, and, in the early days of Mirziyoyev's presidency, when his grip on power was not so secure, Mirziyoyev had symbolically chosen to fly on one of Usmanov's jets to a UN summit in New York rather than an Uzbek state one, which were controlled by Inoyatov.[59]

By April 2018, Mirziyoyev felt secure enough to demote Inoyatov. Not only did Mirziyoyev subsequently overhaul the state security agency but he also assigned Inoyatov to oversee the country's fishing industry, an embarrassingly unimportant post in a doubly landlocked country that has seen its largest body of water, the Aral Sea, all but evaporate in the preceding decades.[60] Before Inoyatov's demotion, Mirziyoyev extended an olive branch to the Kremlin to highlight the move was not meant to affect bilateral relations, agreeing to the first joint military drills with Russia since 2005.[61]

Mirziyoyev subsequently doubled-down on his agenda of seeking Western finance, building relations with Western financial institutions and launching the country's first-ever sovereign Eurobond in February 2019.[62] That March, the United States would also remove the last sanction hanging over from the Karimov era, a ban on the import of Uzbek cotton, citing Mirziyoyev's reduction of child labour in the industry.[63]

Moscow remained wary, however, and increasingly sought to pressure Uzbekistan to join its Eurasian Union. During a speech in the Uzbek capital of Tashkent that October, Russian Federation Council Chairwoman Valentina Matviyenko declared that it was all but a sealed deal.[64] Mirziyoyev's government quickly distanced itself from such talk. The following March, Mirziyoyev announced his decision: Uzbekistan would only become an observer member of the bloc. But it was also around this time that he began to slow down talk of extending his economic reforms into political ones.[65]

The Kremlin apparently did not feel the need to intervene more assertively. With Usmanov's influence, and Uzbekistan's location at the heart of Central Asia, Russia saw little to fear from Mirziyoyev's opening-up of the economy to foreign capital. It was not the first time that Moscow had allowed such an economic shift in the region—neighbouring Turkmenistan had become a Chinese economic protectorate in all but name in the preceding years.

Turkmenistan is governed by the Berdymukhamedov family. Its current president, Serdar Berdymukhamedov, took over from his father Gurbanguly in March 2022, a long-managed transition.[66] Gurbanguly Berdymukhamedov remains head of the state's security council.[67] Exactly why the transition occurred remains subject to speculation, though there have long been more public rumours about the elder Berdymukhamedov's health than there were about Karimov's in his final years. Turkmenistan's isolation is also even more severe than Uzbekistan's was at the height of the Karimov era—the country is extremely reticent to hand out visas. When it does warrant a mention in the international press, it is often labelled a 'hermit kingdom' akin to North Korea.[68]

Turkmenistan is among the poorest and most poorly managed countries in the region. For a country whose territory is roughly 80 per cent desert, it loses an astounding $700 million to flooding each year, 2 per cent of its GDP.[69] The Berdymukhamedovs have had little incentive to modernise the economy, even as the population has increasingly suffered from frequent shortages and the same kinds of currency distortions that afflicted pre-Mirziyoyev Uzbekistan, for Turkmenistan is one of the world's most gas-rich nations.

As recently as 2008, Turkmenistan exported 40 billion cubic metres of gas to Russia annually.[70] A pipeline explosion the subsequent year—which Turkmenistan blamed on Moscow—ruptured ties.[71] The Turkmen regime, on the other hand, had already begun diversifying its export market, although this would ultimately result in trading one dependency for another. While talk of getting Turkmen gas to the European Union via the Southern Gas Corridor never went very far, Beijing was keen and willing to invest. In this case, Ashgabat also did not have to deal with the geopolitical challenge of getting Moscow's approval, whereas hopes for a pipeline to Azerbaijan were dashed by the still-disputed status of the Caspian Sea. Russia and the countries on the Caspian littoral had long been unable to make any progress on agreeing a new treaty for the body of water—and squabbled over the extent to which the sea was still governed by Soviet–Iranian agreements.

Talks on building a pipeline to China had begun under Gurbanguly Berdymukhamedov's own predecessor, Saparmurat Niyazov, who was even more isolationist and bizarre, having built a golden statue of himself that rotated to face the sun and renamed the months after his family. But when the elder Berdymukhamedov emerged as Niyazov's successor following his death in December 2006, there were hopes that Turkmenistan would now be ruled in a more rational way. During a trip to New York the following year, Berdymukhamedov was invited to Columbia University, where he spoke of reforms.[72] Although Berdymukhamedov replaced Niyazov's cult of personality, no serious economic reforms or political liberalisation would be forthcoming.

Berdymukhamedov was, however, serious about selling gas to China. In June 2007, Turkmenistan and China struck an agreement to rapidly speed up construction of the China–Central Asia pipeline. It opened two years later, just in time for Ashgabat's dispute with Moscow about the pipeline explosion. Supplies to Russia would never be the same, and by 2015, Turkmenistan was shipping some 30 billion cubic metres to China, Beijing's cheapest source of gas thanks to its financing of the pipeline's construction.[73] In contrast, Turkmenistan exported just 4·billion cubic metres to Russia.[74] In January 2015, Gazprom suspended imports entirely.[75] This was in part because of increasingly frequent spats between Moscow and Ashgabat, but also because Russia's increase in its own gas production meant it had little need for Turkmen gas, which it had historically re-exported to Europe. The last thing Russia wanted was a European gas glut.

Russian–Turkmen gas trade would eventually resume, in line with an upturn in bilateral relations at least in part fostered by a resolution to the Caspian Sea dispute.

In 2018, Gazprom announced it would resume talks with Turkmenistan about gas exports—two months after the Caspian Sea littoral states agreed to a new convention governing the sea's status and their respective rights.[76] Although Turkmenistan still had disputes with Azerbaijan over their sub-sea border, Ashgabat acquiesced to the pact, which included two notable gains for Moscow. Under the convention, foreign navies would be barred from ever accessing the sea. It also gave every state the right to veto trans-Caspian projects over environmental concerns. The Kremlin could continue to block a trans-Caspian pipeline. Russia did ultimately resume importing Turkmen gas the following April, albeit at a trickle. Exports recovered to 10 billion cubic metres annually, the same level as 2016, by 2021.[77]

While Eurasia was the traditional focus of political and economic competition between Russia and the West, the imposition of sanctions on Russia in 2014 prompted the Kremlin to expand its horizons. It began an effort to find new countries of opportunity, in hopes of securing partners to form the basis of a new sphere of international influence and alleviating the impact of Western restrictions. The Kremlin thus also applied many of the same tactics that it had originally honed in Eurasia much farther afield.

7

VISIONS OF GOLD AND AFRICA

Russian forces had been forced to retreat. At least ten of their number had been killed, and they were caught up in friendly fire with the army they were meant to be fighting alongside after they found themselves ambushed.[1] They had been poorly prepared and fed minimal intelligence and found themselves surrounded by hostile territory.[2] Such debacles were a common feature of Russia's attempt to strike deep into Ukraine in February 2022—but this fiasco actually took place two-and-a-half years earlier, more than 600 kilometres south of Ukraine in Mozambique's northernmost province, Cabo Delgado.

The true number of deaths remains unknown, though *The Guardian* reported at least five other Russian contractors were killed in the deployment.[3] They were not fighting for the Russian state—at least not officially—but had been hired by the Wagner private military company.[4]

Wagner has been the subject of significant controversy. Although separate from the state military, Wagner has publicly taken a leading role in Russia's war against Ukraine,[5] as well as in Syria and numerous other 'hot spots' around the world where the Kremlin has an interest. After a video leaked of the man long-reputed to be its key organiser, Yevgeny Prigozhin, recruiting prisoners to fight for the group in Ukraine, he finally admitted he was in fact in charge though he had spent years obfuscating control of Wagner through a network of offshore entities.[6] Despite years of denials—and lawsuits against researchers and journalists who uncovered his role—Prigozhin has used his leadership of Wagner to become a major player in Putin's Kremlin.[7] Putin's symbiosis of promoting loyalists, handing them lucrative contracts, and Russia's experience of using international corporate structures, a key feature of the international economic order for companies and individuals seeking to minimise or evade tax, enabled Prigozhin's rise.

Known as 'Putin's chef', Prigozhin had enriched himself as an organiser of catering to the Kremlin, beginning shortly after Putin came to power.[8] The two have long been alleged to be close, and Prigozhin's other business interests often served the state as well—his Internet Research Agency was identified as having played a key role in spreading disinformation during the 2016 US presidential election.[9] As with Wagner, Prigozhin initially denied involvement but later admitted to founding the agency.[10]

Wagner's intervention in Mozambique was deeply political. A month before Wagner forces arrived, in August 2019, Mozambican President Filipe Nyusi visited Russia for the Africa Forum in Sochi. He met with Putin, and the pair agreed to expand their relations. According to Nyusi, this included writing off 90 per cent of Mozambique's debt to Russia, most of which had been incurred for previous arms purchases.[11] Putin described the deal as a debt-for-development swap.[12]

The agreement came at a particularly sensitive time for Nyusi: he was facing re-election that October and had just signed a peace deal with Mozambique's main opposition-cum-insurgent group, RENAMO.[13] The country was also in default on its international debts, which it had no realistic means of repaying. The economic crisis was largely a result of government corruption, aided by Western finance. It had been tipped into default in January 2017 after a deal involving a group of alleged arms dealers, Credit Suisse bankers in London, and Mozambican officials went awry. The sale of Eurobonds relating to a host of publicly owned companies—including one ostensibly intended to develop a tuna-fishing fleet—had been diverted to the pockets of many of the participants.[14] Although a trickle of restitution was later paid, and Credit Suisse fined, some of those accused of involvement were still closely tied to Nyusi's government.

Ahead of Nyusi and Putin's meeting, Mozambique had begun making progress in talks to restructure its defaulted debts. Nyusi's government had identified a carrot to offer them to bring them to the bargaining table—the promise of wealth from its newfound hydrocarbon reserves. A deal was struck that September to repay bondholders, who accepted a delay in exchange for higher interest payments from 2023, when the first of the country's LNG export terminals was due to come online.[15]

But Mozambique's dream of becoming a major gas exporter faced a significant challenge. An insurgency had emerged in the preceding years in its far northern Cabo Delgado province, where the terminals were being built. The insurgency was initially fuelled by local concerns that the Muslim-majority region would be cut out of the benefits of the project, but it quickly took on an Islamist bent. Some of the insurgents declared themselves aligned with the Islamic State, though the extent to which the group was involved in driving the ongoing insurgency has been disputed.[16]

Wagner's involvement was clearly not intended to clear the field for the Western oil companies that had already struck agreements to exploit Mozambique's offshore gas riches, ExxonMobil, Total, and Anadarko.[17]

During the Putin and Nyusi meeting, Putin's trusted ally and Rosneft boss Igor Sechin signed a cooperation agreement with Mozambique's National Petroleum Institute. The pact gave Rosneft the right to explore for hydrocarbons both on- and offshore in Mozambique.[18] Sechin had deep experience in the country, having served there as a military translator for the Soviet Union.[19] The combination of Russian debt write-offs and military aid was intended to secure a role for Rosneft in exploiting Mozambique's natural gas resources. Sechin has repeatedly tried to make Rosneft a player in the LNG market, and growing Russia's role in such production would increase its ability to use gas as a tool of geopolitical pressure even as markets become less dependent on pipeline infrastructure. In 2019, the global LNG market increased by over 50 billion cubic metres, adding 12 per cent to the previous year's output.[20]

Rosneft and ExxonMobil had already agreed to work together on one exploration effort in Mozambique in October 2018, another indication of the waning sanctions environment in Trump's Washington.[21] But the defeat of Wagner's forces in November 2019 clearly had a stinging impact. The apparent friendly-fire incident with the Mozambican military was a key source of tensions. Although Wagner's troops subsequently withdrew, as of December 2021 Russia reportedly still had some advisory forces in the country and again dangled the carrot of further aid.[22] Nevertheless, no new major agreements with Rosneft would be signed, and the firm has provided no update on the status of its exploration interest.

There has been significant debate about Wagner's role as a private military company directed by the state.[23] In the case of Mozambique, the timing of Wagner's involvement aligns neatly with other Russian geo-economic interests—as does its failure. However, Wagner would be far more actively involved in a range of other conflicts in Africa between 2014 and 2022, where it had far more success, at least in terms of becoming a key tool for various despotic regimes. However, the economic benefit these relationships brought to Russia were limited, although they did support its narrative of re-establishing itself as a global power.

Wagner's earliest military involvement in Africa is reported to have been in Sudan and the Central African Republic in 2015.[24] By 2021, it was involved in Mali as well, and allegations emerged the following January that it had been involved in a coup that month in Burkina Faso.[25] Its playbook in all these countries was broadly similar: the group offered its protection services to local rulers. It often took advantage of coups to gain a foothold, and it was commonly recompensed with natural resource extraction deals, particularly gold mines.[26] Much of this gold was then allegedly re-exported via the United Arab Emirates.[27]

Moscow did secure other returns for Wagner's involvement in African countries. They typically began to vote in line with Russia at the United Nations, and, in 2020, Russia even secured an agreement to build a naval base in Sudan—which would be only its second abroad—excluding occupied Ukraine—after that in Tartus, Syria. But some believed that gold could play an important part in Russia's attempts to weaken its dependence on the dollar system, by serving as an alternative reserve on which it could base its trade and reserves strategy and thus undercut the post-2014 sanctions regime.

Shortly after the imposition of sanctions against Russia following its annexation of Crimea, a flurry of articles appeared in the

Russian press advocating for a move away from the dollar.[28] Many of these focused on building up Russia's gold reserves—some even advocated for a move to a new 'gold rouble', effectively a return to the gold standard, in which its currency would be freely exchangeable for gold.

Advocacy for such a position is by no means limited to Russia. There are many critics of the post-Bretton Woods financial system in which the dollar essentially replaced gold as the world's reserve asset. For example, Kwasi Kwarteng, briefly British Chancellor of the Exchequer, published a book in which he laments the passing of the gold standard but concludes the market may be fated to effectively return to one.[29] However, after he tried to expand fiscal policy amid a tightening monetary policy environment, Kwarteng was sacked as the markets rucked his economic agenda. Kwarteng's thirty-eight-day tenor made him the shortest-serving Chancellor not to die in office but nonetheless reveals how influential so-called 'goldbugs' are in the West.

Some Western voices even cheered on Russian rhetoric criticising the dollar system.[30] But while officials in the Russian government often threatened major actions—in 2015, for example, the Russian legislature considered proposals for a gold-pegged rouble—most of its economic decision-makers were not particularly keen on the idea.[31] In 2010, one of Putin's longest-serving economic advisors, Alexei Kudrin, had declared that 'in the modern era it is impossible to peg a currency to any one metal, commodity or other resource'.[32]

However, after 2014 it became clear Russia's more orthodox economists were losing the argument. Putin's security elite was more closely aligned with those who criticised the dollar system and sought alternatives, no matter how heterodox. Signs soon emerged that they had Putin's ear.

In April 2017, Putin gifted his then-finance minister, Anton Siluanov, the collected works of Sergei Witte, the finance minister who placed the rouble on the gold standard in 1897.[33] Russian outlet Lenta interpreted this as a sign that Putin wanted the move away from the dollar to escalate.[34] Putin perhaps overlooked that Witte had also been an advocate of the benefits of foreign capital.[35]

Ever since 2013, the central bank had been buying up additional gold reserves while substantially decreasing its share of dollars.

Their share of Russia's foreign currency reserves rose from 9.6 per cent a year before the annexation of Crimea to 18.5 per cent by March 2019.[36] In 2019, the central bank even said it would consider a gold-backed cryptocurrency.[37]

But the finance ministry and central bank never took any concrete steps towards enabling gold to become a suitable basis for banks and state corporations to finance trade, let alone back a cryptocurrency. As Kudrin warned, doing so is just not feasible in the modern era—as well as the difficulties in transporting sufficient amounts of gold, it would also require Russia to maintain fixed exchange rates with other currencies and weaken its ability to manage monetary policy. Even Russian gold producers preferred to sell their gold abroad in exchange for hard currency.[38] But the Kremlin increasingly pursued an ideology focused on gold. By 2020, it appeared Siluanov, who had just a year earlier criticised gold's suitability as a reserve base given its liquidity issues, had gotten the message.[39] Siluanov unexpectedly announced that Russia's sovereign wealth fund would begin moving some of its currency reserves to gold. In January 2021, the central bank's share of reserves held in gold exceeded its share of dollar reserves for the first time.[40]

But by the end of 2021, voices in the Kremlin were signalling that the shift from dollar to gold reserves had still not gone far enough. Vyacheslav Volodin was one of Putin's few close advisors with whom he did not have an association predating his presidency. But he had proven his loyalty and even came up with the slogan 'No Putin, No Russia'.[41] Volodin was also reportedly friendly with another late entrant to Putin's cadre—central bank head Elvira Nabiullina, who expressed reservations about gold's suitability as a reserve.[42] In December 2021, Volodin openly denounced Nabiulina's central bank in the Duma, which he chaired, for not buying more gold.[43] The fate of Wagner's African plunder, and whether any of it had gone to the state's coffers, went unsurprisingly unmentioned.

The Kremlin used Africa as a staging ground for how its security elite could expand its influence. But the benefit for the Russian economy was limited, even if certain Kremlin-favoured actors like Prigozhin profited handsomely.[44] Even when their efforts failed—

as in the case of Sechin's and Prigozhin's attempt to secure a slice of Mozambique's gas potential—the Kremlin's security elites were the ones driving policy, their influence growing from the military sphere they traditionally dominated into the fundamentals of Russia's economic agenda.

8

RUSSIA'S CARACAS CACHE

Latin America would be another sphere in which the Kremlin sought to expand its economic influence after 2014. Eager to challenge the United States in its traditional backyard, opportunities in the region were relatively limited compared to Africa, but one country in particular became a petri-dish for its attempts to circumvent Western influence over energy and financial markets.

In December 2017, Rosneft's Igor Sechin touched down in Caracas, for a meeting with Venezuela's political leadership and key oil executives.[1]

As with his subsequent forays in Mozambique, Sechin already had significant experience in the country. Shortly after Putin assumed the presidency, Sechin was appointed deputy prime minister, with a portfolio that included Latin American affairs.[2] Putin also appointed him to lead the Russian–Venezuelan High Level Intergovernmental Council. He soon established close ties with revolutionary leftist leader Hugo Chávez, who declared during their first meeting that '[n]ow we are not alone in the battle against the American empire! Now we have Russia on our side!'[3]

Chávez proved an enthusiastic backer of some of Putin's foreign policy ventures, including recognising Georgia's breakaway Abkhazia and South Ossetia regions, reportedly in exchange for $1 billion in arms deals.[4] But the relationship was not primarily ideological or martial. Rosneft invested heavily in Venezuela over the years, taking shares in a series of joint ventures that cumulatively gave it a sizable stake in the country's Orinoco oil belt and oil-processing industry.

After Chávez's death in 2013, however, Venezuela was steered by a far less charismatic leader, Nicolás Maduro. Following the global oil price collapse the subsequent year, Venezuela's mismanagement and corruption exacerbated the pain of its collapsing energy industry, while Maduro's poor diplomatic skills left Venezuela with no real allies other than China, Russia, and the three other regional states whose leaders also had overtly anti-American agendas: Cuba, Nicaragua, and Bolivia.[5]

Western banks had been willing to fund Maduro until shortly before Sechin's visit, albeit at extortionate rates. But in May 2017, Harvard economist and former Venezuelan minister Ricardo Hausmann published an article labelling the practice of financing Venezuelan debt as akin to selling 'hunger bonds'.[6] It was an apt description—the average Venezuelan lost 11 kilogrammes (24 pounds) that year.[7] Days later, the *Wall Street Journal* reported that Goldman Sachs had engineered just such a deal on the eve of Hausmann's article, paying just $865 million for $2.8 billion in Venezuelan government debt.[8] Goldman had bought the bonds directly from Venezuela's central bank. The ensuing scandal killed interest in further such dealings on Wall Street.

Rosneft, however, remained a willing lender to Maduro's government. Sechin was betting that expanding the company's interests in the country could help turn his firm, and thus Russia, into a global 'energy superpower'.[9] Just before Sechin's visit, Russia announced that it would restructure Venezuela's interstate debts.[10]

The deal was yet another signal from Moscow that it was seeking to break away from the international financial infrastructure it saw as biased in favour of the West. As seen in the case of Ukraine's intergovernmental debts, the forum in which most countries work these out is the Paris Club. Russia is formally a member, China is not.

By re-structuring Venezuela's debts in this way, Moscow was signalling that it would break away from the Paris Club and potentially align itself with Beijing, whose Belt and Road programme included a vast expansion of its lending to other sovereigns and had become a source of competition with the West. While Russia is nowhere near China's size as a sovereign creditor, Russia leaving the Paris Club could enable it to loan to other countries in arrears to Western nations.

Sechin had more immediate aims in his December 2017 visit. He granted further loans to PDVSA, the beleaguered Venezuelan state oil company, but crucially also secured the rights to develop two Venezuelan offshore gas fields, Patao and Mejillones.[11] Creating an outpost for Russia to sell LNG in the Western hemisphere would go a long way towards underpinning Sechin's energy superpower aims, if it could be realised.

Things would not prove so simple.

Whereas the Trump administration was skittish in using geo-economic tools against Moscow, it was extremely aggressive in deploying them against Venezuela. In August 2017, Trump issued an Executive Order prohibiting the Venezuelan government and state corporations, such as PDVSA, from accessing US financial markets.[12] While Venezuelan debt was already trading at bargain basement prices, the move was all but guaranteed to tip Venezuela and PDVSA into default. Both would indeed fail to make payments on their Eurobonds by the end of the year.

A number of creditors, investors, and contractors who had been bilked by the Chávez and Maduro governments had brought cases in US courts and international arbitration forums. Washington—which had long had tensions with the Maduro government—was particularly concerned over the fate of PDVSA-owned CITGO, which owned a number of US refineries and domestic oil distribution pipelines. Rosneft had secured a lien over a 49.9 per cent stake in the company in November 2016 in exchange for an earlier loan to PDVSA.[13]

The Trump administration's approach was not motivated by a desire to blunt Russia's interest in Venezuela per se. Trump had identified Venezuela as a rallying point for his party and was in need of a foreign policy success. Increasing his anti-Maduro rhetoric was also seen as bringing potential electoral benefits among US Hispanic voters and shoring up Trump's position in the key swing state of Florida.

The Trump administration would double down on this approach after John Bolton became Trump's National Security Advisor in April 2018. Bolton was known for his particularly hawkish stance towards Caracas.[14] The following month, Trump issued yet another executive order, barring any transactions related to Venezuela's debt, including barring Rosneft from taking control of its stake in CITGO.[15]

Further restrictions would follow, including the addition of Venezuelan officials to the United States' SDN sanctions list for allegedly siphoning off vast sums through preferential access to foreign currency and sanctions evasion. In January 2019, it took its strongest step yet, sanctioning PDVSA itself and vastly limiting the ability of oil firms to operate in the country; limited exceptions were made for US oil firms in the country to continue operations.[16]

The restrictions further amplified the pain of Venezuela's oil industry, in turn impacting Rosneft. However, their primary aim was to engender support for the US-backed Venezuelan opposition, whose de facto leader, Juan Guaidó, had just declared himself acting president.

Guaidó was named president of the country's legislature earlier that January, but the Maduro government had largely ignored the chamber since the opposition took a majority in the 2015 parliamentary election. Guaidó claimed the 2018 presidential elections were illegitimate and that he was therefore also in charge of the executive branch. Anti-Maduro protests accompanied the declaration, and Washington soon announced that it recognised Guaidó as the country's rightful leader.

However, the protests soon fizzled out, following a crackdown by Maduro's security services. Guaidó then called for an uprising for the end of April.[17] During the protests, Bolton announced that Venezuela's defence minister and supreme court president had held talks with Guaidó about switching sides.[18] No such move materialised. Russia reportedly offered to evacuate Maduro, though it denies this.[19]

Bolton also accused the Kremlin of offering military support to Maduro. The Kremlin had made little secret of this: it sent two nuclear-capable supersonic TU-160 bombers to Caracas the previous December. By April 2019, Russia's military support reportedly extended to a number of fighter jets, tanks, and missile defence systems.[20] Guaidó's uprising failed, though a number of other Western countries also recognised his government. This resulted in a series of legal tussles around the world, including court processes in the United States and the UK for Guaidó to establish control over CITGO and Venezuela's gold reserves. But neither Guaido nor other figures in the Venezuelan opposition came close to seizing power.

With Russia's ally Maduro still in charge, Rosneft would step up efforts to help it mitigate the pain from the US sanctions. According to US officials, Rosneft Trading—a Switzerland-based subsidiary of the Russian oil giant—began to facilitate the export of Venezuelan oil around the world.[21] Rosneft claimed that it had pre-paid for Venezuela's oil through its loans, and that the deals therefore did not violate the sanctions, but Washington had little patience for this contention. In February 2020, Rosneft Trading was added to the US SDN list.[22]

This did not stop Rosneft's activity. Rosneft switched to using another Swiss corporate structure—one that it had inherited from the merger with TNK-BP—to continue to facilitate such exports. Less than a month later, Washington blacklisted this entity, TNK Trading, as well.[23]

By this point, it appeared Russia would be forced to cut its losses from Sechin's Venezuelan exploits. Years of investment and fostering of political ties had brought little actual benefit. US sanctions on the Maduro regime—far more stinging than those in place against Russia at the time—made it impossible for Sechin to realise his goal of developing LNG exports in the country as well. On 28 March 2020, Rosneft announced that it had sold all of its Venezuelan assets to the Russian government.[24] Media reports revealed they were taken over by a previously unknown entity, Roszarubezhneft.[25]

That the new firm had close ties to Rosneft was clear from its name—it merely had *zarubezh*, Russian for 'abroad', stuck in. It was quickly revealed that the firm was headed by a former colleague of Sechin's from his days as a Soviet interpreter in Africa.[26] And the financing of the deal—in which the Russian state bailed-out Sechin's Venezuelan misadventure to the tune of $3.78 billion— benefitted Sechin. The deal was structured as a swap of 9.6 per cent of state holding company Rosneftegaz's stake in Rosneft to the company itself, in which they could be held as treasury shares and still receive a dividend.[27] This meant that more of the dividends that Rosneft were supposed to return to the state—long a source of controversy for its alleged underpayment thereof—could instead remain with the firm.[28]

Russia tried plenty of other ways to assist the Maduro regime. Perhaps the most notable is its support for the 'El Petro' cryptocurrency scheme that Maduro announced shortly after Sechin's December 2017 visit.[29] This would prove not just a failure but a complete embarrassment.

In February 2018, Maduro called a press conference to announce the details of the cryptocurrency. He did little to hide that it was intended as a way to evade US sanctions, describing it as 'kryptonite' to the United States.[30] Sitting in the front row of the press conference were two Russian businessmen, Denis Druzhkov and Fyodor Bogorodsky, whom Maduro praised for their support.[31] Although neither was formally working for the Russian state, according to a *Time* magazine exposé of the affair, the effort was approved at the highest level of the Kremlin after Putin was informed that 'this is how to avoid sanctions'.[32]

The following month, the United States imposed sanctions on Venezuela's crypto-endeavours as well. Venezuela did indeed launch El Petro, but it soon became little more than a running joke, even in the cryptocurrency community where such offerings often go from boom-to-bust in the blink of an eye. Cryptography has been lauded as a potential way to enable monetary independence since well before the crypto-mania of the last decade. Dreams of cryptography leading to monetary sovereignty have yet to be realised, and the failure of the El Crypto experiment should go down as a warning.

More traditional Russian attempts to support Venezuela would also prove disastrous. In 2006, the two countries agreed to open a factory for Russia's famous Kalashnikov arms manufacturer in the country by 2009.[33] It was quickly mired in delays and allegations of underperformance by the Russian contractors. A pair of Russian officials would later be charged with embezzling millions from the project.[34] Despite repeated pledges that its opening is imminent, as of 2023, production has not begun.[35]

Venezuela was the primary crux in Latin America of Russia's efforts to expand its energy influence and undercut the strength of the dollar system in the years after its annexation of Crimea. It was not for a lack of trying elsewhere, however, and Moscow did secure other political alliances in the region.

Moscow remained active in Cuba, its old Cold War ally in the region. But the country's weak economy and US sanctions meant that there was little incentive for major efforts or investments that could play a role in its geo-economic conflict with the United States. Moscow did help where it could, for example announcing in 2017 that it would resume exporting Lada cars to Cuba in 2020 and announcing plans to support the modernisation of the Cuban port at Mariel three years later. However, these efforts were far more limited than economic cooperation had been during the Soviet era, highlighting how Russia's capacity to act as a global power had become constrained.

The Kremlin found a handful of other partners. In Nicaragua, Daniel Ortega—a Cold War-era ally who had lost power in 1990—returned to the presidency in 2007. He would take symbolic actions in support of Russia, such as recognising Abkhazia and South Ossetia, but economic ties remained limited outside of the arms sector. Moscow also found support from the government of Evo Morales in Bolivia. The most important project it engaged in there was related to Rosatom, which in 2017 agreed to build a nuclear research facility in El Alto, which offered a potential foothold to develop links to the region's energy and security networks. It was widely seen as a front for deepening intelligence contacts, and when Morales was ousted in 2019 it was quickly suspended.[36] Morales's ally Luis Arce, however, won the presidency the following year, and in July 2021 construction finally began.[37] Other efforts signed in Morales's time in office, including an agreement for Gazprom to develop LNG infrastructure in the country—a particularly bizarre plan considering Bolivia is landlocked and the global LNG market is based on seaborne trade—have yet to come to fruition.

In 2013, Sechin travelled to Venezuela for Chávez's funeral. He gave a eulogy glorifying his legacy and signed off with the famous Cuban revolutionary call, *¡Hasta la Victoria Siempre!*—ever onwards to victory.[38] But Russia's attempts to open up Latin America as a major new field in the geo-economic conflict with the West provided little but failure. Nevertheless, the Kremlin saw it as important to challenge the United States in its own proverbial 'backyard', even if the economic benefits were limited because it enabled it to further the narrative, if not the reality, of being a true global power.

9

PUTIN'S PIVOT TO ASIA

On 23 October 2014, Putin declared: 'Asia is playing an ever-greater role in the world, in the economy and in politics, and there is simply no way we can afford to overlook these developments.'[1] Not for the first time since thrusting west to seize Crimea seven months earlier, Putin signalled that Russia's future lay in the East. After all, Asian economies were growing at far higher rates than the West, and the United States was a less dominant player there than it was in Europe.

Putin attempted to pre-empt criticisms that the move was defensive, denying that it was driven by sanctions and insisting it was 'a policy that we have been following for a good many years now'.[2] But it was not a turn away from the geo-economic sparring with the West—Russia was 'pivoting to Asia', just as the Obama administration was three years into its effort to do the same.[3] Competition would be fierce—for the Kremlin, reorienting Russian policy towards the East was a strategic imperative, guided by Putin's agenda of expanding Russia's influence in order to re-establish it as a great power and mitigate the US-led economic containment efforts.

Moscow had been seeking to build closer relations with Beijing since the beginning of Putin's tenure, but Putin's speech marked the beginning of a flurry of efforts to expand economic and political links across wider Asia. Moscow's pivot also provoked plenty of discussion of 'Eurasianism', including declarations that it would come to reshape the international order.[4] Chapter 6 has already examined how the Eurasian heartland very much remained a contested space. So too were South and East Asia, where Russia's geo-economic strategy would find some of its greatest successes in finding new markets and partners, as well as its biggest failures. For the West, it would reveal the limits of sanctions.

Arguably the most significant strategic success for Moscow was the 2016 deal struck by Rosneft to purchase a stake in India's Essar Oil. Since renamed Nayara Energy, it controls India's second-largest refinery, in Gujarat's Vadinar, and over 6,500 fuel stations.

Nayara's $12.9 billion sale was structured as involving three partners: Rosneft, commodities trading giant Trafigura, and Moscow-based UCP Investments. Rosneft took a 49 per cent stake in Nayara, as did the joint-venture Kesani Partners Limited. Trafigura and UCP would take 49 per cent stakes in Kesani. The remaining 2 per cent of both Nayara and Kesani remained with India's Ruia family, founders of the Essar Group that controlled Essar Oil before the sale and its renaming to Nayar.[5]

The deal marked a major foreign foray for historically Russia-focused UCP, but not its first strategic investment that could be construed as linked to the state. In 2013, it bought up shares in the social network VKontakte while Putin was cracking down on internet freedoms and pressuring VKontakte to share users' personal data with the Kremlin.[6] UCP's founder, Ilya Sherbovich, had sat on the boards of Rosneft, Sberbank, and Transneft, three of the most strategically significant state corporations. A 2013 Bloomberg profile described Sherbovich as having 'helped craft deals for people close to Vladimir Putin throughout his career'.[7]

The structure meant that Rosneft would not technically have majority control even if UCP was found to be a related party or sanctioned, as it did not have a majority in Kesani either. Andrei Kostin, the head of Russia's state-run VTB Bank, could not resist bragging to Reuters that the structure was specifically designed to enable it to evade sanctions.[8] Nevertheless, the deal sailed through without open opposition from the Trump administration when it was completed the following year.

It was a strategic success. Vadinar offered capacity to refine 405,000 barrels per day, some 10 per cent of Rosneft's production. Rosneft and its partners then increased Vadinar's refining capacity to 515,000 barrels per day, turning on the spigot that would become the key success in Putin's pivot to Asia.[9]

This was not the only time India saw Washington take a soft stance towards its approach to Russia. Whereas the Trump administration ultimately did sanction the Turkish government for its purchase of Russia's S-400 missile defence system as mandated by CAATSA in the weeks before Trump left office, there was far less pressure to do so with regard to India's deal with Russia to buy the exact same weapon. Numerous constituencies in Congress, from across both parties, repeatedly pushed for India to be exempted given its strategic position in the United States' own pivot to Asia.[10]

India's geopolitical position as the main bulwark to China in Asia has made it an increasingly important partner for the United States. While during the Cold War India tended to lean towards Moscow—its key arms supplier—the era's geopolitical divides in Asia were often more muddled than in the West. That is still in many ways the case. Russia has remained India's key arms supplier, while Washington sees it as its key future partner in resisting China's influence. Meanwhile, Moscow has become increasingly close to Beijing, including through high-tech defence cooperation.[11]

Both the Obama and Trump administrations took it as accepted wisdom that China had displaced Russia as the primary threat to global stability, even if their approaches to Beijing differed vastly. But both were far less willing to use sanctions threats targeting Russian links against Asian countries they saw as potential allies in the struggle for influence with China. India was not alone.

One example of the relatively soft US approach to countries in the region is Vietnam. Although it is still governed by the same Communist Party that defeated the US military, Vietnam has become an increasingly important partner to the United States in the region. It has even been a beneficiary of US 'friend-shoring' efforts to move production away from China to other countries, a focus of Washington's geo-economic strategy on the China front. Hanoi has also not faced any major calls for CAATSA sanctions to be enacted against it, though it explored purchasing Russia's S-400 system and remains reliant on Russian arms.[12]

Russia and Vietnam have ties stretching back to the Soviet era, when Moscow was Hanoi's closest ally. A joint venture, Vietsovpetro, was established in 1981. Five years later, it began extracting crude from the offshore White Tiger field, a deposit originally discovered by US oil firm Mobil in 1975, just weeks before the Fall of Saigon.[13] Vietsovpetro managed to continue operations and even expand them slightly through the turmoil of the 1980s and 1990s. Russia was named Hanoi's strategic partner in 2003.[14] Arms sales in particular continued to flourish, and Gazprom and its Vietnamese partner PetroVietnam agreed a series of cross investments wherein the former invested in a new Vietnamese offshore gas project and the latter took stakes in a series of existing Russian fields.[15]

In November 2013, Moscow and Hanoi announced they would be deepening relations further. Until that point, the geopolitical ramifications of Russia and Vietnam's burgeoning energy cooperation were fairly limited, and Gazprom largely focused on the domestic market, where it also invested in a local pipeline and electricity generation projects. The 2013 deal, however, included agreements for Rosneft to enter the market as well.

Rosneft signed agreements with PetroVietnam that shadowed the structure of the PetroVietnam–Gazprom relationship.[16] Although there has often been a fierce rivalry between Rosneft and Gazprom—driven in particular by Sechin's attempts to make his firm a significant gas player, thus encroaching on Gazprom's turf— the structure had worked in the past and represented a template for successful partnership.

Things would not be so straightforward.

PetroVietnam and Rosneft agreed to create a joint venture to focus on the Pechora shelf in the Russian Arctic, while Rosneft was to develop a Vietnamese offshore field.[17] But the project took on new strategic significance after the imposition of the US sectoral sanctions on Rosneft in 2014. Directive 4 of these sanctions, which was applied to the Russian oil giant, barred Western energy firms from supporting Arctic, deep-offshore, or fracking projects in which it was involved—so long as they were in Russia. Those outside of Russia were not so proscribed.

Rosneft then sped up its partnership with PetroVietnam and, crucially, signed on a Japanese drilling firm to support the project, as well as Britain's Noble Corp.[18] When drilling began in March 2016, Rosneft hailed it as the first time it had operated a project in international waters.[19]

Although Rosneft had managed to thread a loophole in US sectoral sanctions, another problem remained: the project was in international waters—specifically, within the 'Nine Dash Line' of waters that Beijing claimed deep into the South China Sea. Chinese pressure soon began to ramp up for Rosneft to withdraw from the project. Although Moscow was Hanoi's strategic partner, with Vietnam seeking to use it as a counter to China's influence, Moscow prioritised its relationship with Beijing over that with Vietnam. In 2018, Beijing sent a survey vessel to the area around Rosneft's operations, and they were subsequently quietly halted.[20]

By August 2020, it was clear that Rosneft would not pursue the project further.[21] This clearly annoyed Vietnam: when Hanoi compensated other firms with whom it had cancelled projects as a result of Chinese pressure, it excluded Rosneft.[22] All of Rosneft's Vietnam assets were eventually sold off to Zarubezhneft, another Russian state oil company that managed Soviet legacy projects abroad, including the stake in Vietsovpetro.[23] Although Zarubezhneft's and Gazprom's cordial relations with Vietnam continued, the project also had other negative ramifications for Russian–Vietnamese bilateral ties, including encouraging Vietnam to be more compliant with US sanctions. Vietnam cancelled a project with Russia's Power Machines—the former partner with Siemens in the Crimean turbine affair, which had been sanctioned in January 2018.[24]

Rosneft also undertook an arguably even more disastrous attempt to expand its role in South East Asia. In October 2019, Sechin met with Philippine President Rodrigo Duterte, who invited the firm to explore in its own territories in the South China Sea that Beijing contested.[25] But just twelve days later, Duterte fired the head of the Philippine National Oil Company Exploration Corporation, allegedly over his dealings with Rosneft.[26] A presidential spokesperson later said that the firm had not followed through on bidding and vetting procedures for its dealing with Rosneft.[27] Manila did not explain the about-face further—though the deal clearly engendered opposition from both Beijing and Washington.

Other South East Asian states were important partners for Moscow as well, although many of its relationships focused primarily on arms sales. One such relationship, with the Myanmar military, was particularly important. In 2021, the military launched a coup against the democratically elected part of its government, led by Aung Sang Suu Kyi, who had long been beloved in the West but had recently courted controversy for refusing to stand up to the military's attempts to ethnically cleanse the Muslim Rohingya minority. The military had deepened relations with Russia in the run-up to the coup, even amid international condemnation of its genocide of the Muslim Rohingya population in the country's west. Moscow was the only one to stand by the military's side after the coup, with Russia's deputy defence minister the sole foreign official to attend its subsequent Armed Forces Day parade.[28] While this may open up an opportunity for Russia to again expand its regional energy influence, so far there has been little real benefit for Russia.

Russia's geo-economic agenda did, however, bear fruit with South Korea and Japan, despite the two countries being Washington's leading allies in Asia.

Tokyo imposed some sanctions on Moscow after the annexation of Crimea in 2014 but fell short even of the measures imposed by Europe. Then-Prime Minister Shinzo Abe found it important to remain in line with actions taken by other G7 states (Canada, France, Germany, Italy, the UK, and the United States) but also set a priority of negotiating an end to Japan's dispute with Russia over the Kuril Islands.[29] Moscow has controlled the southernmost islands—Iturup, Kunashir, Shikotan, and the Habomai islands—since the end of the Second World War, but Japan has never acknowledged the Kremlin's claim to sovereignty over them.

However, Putin was happy to continue meeting, as Tokyo was willing to engage in economic diplomacy to advance Abe's aim. Abe even appointed a cabinet-level minister for economic relations with Moscow.[30] The pair met at least twenty-seven times, but the negotiations never seriously progressed, despite Tokyo's willingness to expand energy ties in the post-Crimea environment.[31] Nothing could indicate a poorer reading of Putin's power politics than to think that he might be willing to cede territory that Russia claimed. Nevertheless, Moscow and Japan's ties did expand, at least in relation to the development of Russia's Sakhalin oil and gas development project.

Tokyo has long been a voracious importer of energy and commodities, which it lacks in significant quantities domestically.

Russia's plan to turn the Sakhalin Peninsula, just 700 kilometres from the disputed Kuril Islands, into a key Asian energy hub had therefore attracted investment and interest from Tokyo since it was first explored in the 1990s.

While Sakhalin had provided oil and gas exports to Japan well before the invasion of Ukraine, the project took on a newfound strategic significance after Tokyo announced the end of its nuclear industry in response to the 2011 Fukushima Daichi nuclear power plant disaster. In May 2016, Tokyo and Moscow signed an enhanced economic cooperation agreement that would also see Japan invest in Russia's Yamal LNG project, and then, three years later, into its Arctic LNG project as well.[32] But the most significant component came not from its equity stakes—ExxonMobil was still the key operator of Sakhalin II, despite US sanctions—but rather from the financing and technological support that Japanese firms provided, which Western firms were largely unwilling or unable to amid the US sanctions environment.

Tokyo was not alone in these efforts. South Korea did not even go as far as Abe's governments had in nominally imposing some sanctions on Russia after the annexation of Crimea. Until 2022, it refrained from sanctioning Russia entirely. And South Korean shipbuilders and engineering firms would go on to plug crucial needs for Moscow's efforts to develop the offshore energy sector targeted by US sectoral sanctions, in particular shipbuilding.[33]

Singaporean shipbuilders also increased their ties with Russia, and there was ample talk in the years between 2013 and 2022 that the city-state would become Moscow's 'new gateway' to Asia.[34] There was an uptick in the number of Russian businesses moving to Singapore and growth in brokering of Russian commodities through traders based there. Singaporean firms have also been used to evade dual-use technology sanctions on Russia.[35] In 2019, Singapore even announced a free trade agreement with the Russian-led Eurasian Union, though in December 2021 Singaporean media reported that the agreement had still not been finalised.[36]

Russia would source other technologies from Asia in the aftermath of the Crimean annexation and imposition of sanctions that proved to have a strategic significance, and that slipped through the Western sanctions regime. Micro-chips were sourced from

India, Malaysia, Indonesia, and Taiwan, which, like South Korea, did not join the sanctions regime until after Russia's 2022 invasion of Ukraine, though it was a close US ally.[37]

Putin's 'pivot to Asia' may have encountered its challenges, as seen in Vietnam and the Philippines. But Russia's ability to cultivate ties with Japanese and South Korean firms to replace some of the engineering, financial support, and investment from Western energy firms undoubtedly helped mitigate the pain of the post-Crimea sanctions. Its success in India not only gave it a foothold in a new refinery market but also increased its strategic position in a key regional power while showing that US sanctions could be evaded, at least in certain markets. And there may still be room for future involvement as the Myanmar military has brutally fended off the uprising that its 2021 coup spawned. While Taiwan, South Korea, and Japan ultimately did introduce or scale up their sanctions against Russia in 2022, the growth of the chip manufacturing industry in Indonesia and Malaysia remains a key vulnerability for technology restrictions on Russia going forward. China is increasingly a major chip power in its own right and could prove a panacea for the West's choke-off of chips to Russia.[38]

Russia's position in Asia is not just dependent on its geo-economic competition with the United States and wider West. It is undoubtedly largely shaped by China, which went from being Russia's main partner in 2014 to an indispensable ally by 2022. Or so Putin thought. While Putin saw China as a partner for Russia's agenda of seeking to challenge Washington, he failed to read how Moscow's divergence from the West was making Russia more dependent on China in an increasingly lopsided relationship.

10

BEIJING AS BIG BROTHER

Russia and China often describe each other as their closest allies, though the exact phrasing used to describe their relationship frequently changes. In 2013, China's President Xi Jinping made his first foreign visit to Russia, where he named Putin his 'old friend' and Putin spoke of the historic nature of their partnership.[1] By 2021, China was declaring that the two countries were 'better than allies'; Putin described the relationship as 'at its best in history'.[2]

But these declarations belie a complex relationship in which the two countries regularly partner to achieve their mutual aims but also face regular challenges in their choice of tactics and approach. That Russia's post-Crimea 'pivot to Asia' has made Moscow more reliant on Beijing is clear—but the development of Russia and China's relationship over that time also reveals fundamental tensions that may affect its long-term stability. Sanctions left Russia with increasingly few alternatives, while Putin's belief in Russia's great power status blinded him to the increasing imbalance in the relationship.

Xi's 2013 visit to Moscow laid the groundwork for a new era in Russian–Chinese economic relations, particularly on the energy front. Their agreements were underpinned by a new loan from Beijing for Rosneft, as well as plans for Gazprom to begin sending gas to China by 2018 and for the two sides to agree a thirty-year contract on the supplies it would deliver.[3]

Western sanctions introduced in response to the annexation of Crimea accelerated matters. In May 2014, Putin travelled to China, where he and Xi agreed a thirty-year gas supply agreement the Kremlin valued at $400 billion as well as a joint declaration on unspecified security and strategic cooperation.[4] Just four months later, the pair met again in Russia to launch a new gas pipeline, dubbed 'Power of Siberia'.[5] That Beijing was establishing itself as the dominant partner was underpinned by reports that Putin had agreed to substantial gas discounts to get the nearly 4,000 kilometre pipeline, with an annual capacity of 38 billion cubic metres of gas, over the line.[6]

Despite the rush to the agreement, the pipeline only opened in September 2019—later than Putin and Xi had originally envisaged in their 2013 meeting. The delay was not due to Western sanctions but rather to domestic developments in both countries.

On the Russian side, one key factor was the favouring of companies closely linked to the state. The project's initial contracts were won without a tender by Stroygazmontazh (SGM), linked to Putin's close associates Boris and Arkady Rotenberg. SGM was selected to lead construction of Russia's other flagship project at the time, the Crimean Bridge linking occupied Crimea and Russia's Rostov region over the Kerch Strait by road and rail.[7] The next stage was won by a company tied to Samvel Karapetyan, whose investments in Armenia had helped to expand the Kremlin's influence there. The choice of companies trusted by the Kremlin was no surprise but led to a crowding-out of Chinese firms, which typically took the lead on most international infrastructure projects that Beijing backed. This did not dissuade China from proceeding with the project, but it nevertheless highlights how the Kremlin's domestic governance challenges continued to limit its geo-economic agenda.

Similar challenges could be seen in one of the other flagship projects Putin and Xi agreed in 2015: the construction of the Amur Petrochemical Complex on the Russian–Chinese border. The project was structured as a joint venture between China's state energy firm Sinopec and Russian petrochemicals firm Sibur.

At the time, Putin's then son-in-law Kirill Shamalov was building a stake in Sibur, which he reportedly acquired at a significant discount.[8] As if this wasn't enough to prove its close links to the state, it has since been alleged on the basis of leaked emails that Sibur financed the construction of a villa for Putin's personal use.[9] In 2015, in a sign of how far Beijing's investments into Russia went in the aftermath of Crimea, Sinopec bought 10 per cent of Sibur.[10]

The next year, China provided over $10 billion in financing for the Yamal LNG project—in which its other key state energy firm, CNPC, held a 20 per cent stake.[11]

But the Amur Petrochemical Complex's main contractor was named as China's Gezhouba Group.[12] However, it was soon revealed that most of Gezhouba's work was subcontracted to the Russian firm Velesstroy, which Russian outlet RBC described as a long-favoured contractor of Transneft and Novatek, a Kremlin-linked private Russian energy firm.[13] Putin may have been seeking to open the taps to China, but not at the expense of Kremlin-linked entities.

Other challenges would emerge. Violent protests struck the adjacent Gazprom-owned gas processing plant in July 2020, reportedly over non-payment of wages to its employees, though Russian officials denied this was the case.[14] The biggest issue the project faced was raising sufficient financing. Beijing was willing to underwrite the expansion of Russian trade but not at any cost, or, seemingly, when it felt its firms were being excluded. A deal was finally struck in December 2021, with the notable support of German and Italian export credit agencies, whose backing may have been what finally got it over the line, again highlighting how the Kremlin was able to be benefit from continued differences in the US and European approach.[15]

Xi Jinping's crackdown on corruption in China was another factor in delaying Russian–Chinese energy cooperation.[16] Launched shortly after Xi took office, the ongoing effort targeted many in China's energy industry as well as significant political potentates.[17] However, this does not appear to have been a major factor in the Power of Siberia project. It would, however, prove disastrous for another attempted Russian–Chinese project, between Rosneft and a firm dubbed CEFC China Energy.

CEFC was founded and led by Ye Jianming, a purported billionaire who was linked to the People's Liberation Army, China's military.[18] It had blazed a path ahead of China's 'Belt and Road' programme, striking deals and forming political ties across the world, from the Czech Republic, where he was named an advisor to President Miloš Zeman in 2012, to the United Nations, where a non-governmental organisation that CEFC backed was awarded consultative status in 2011.[19]

Ye appeared to be the exact kind of Chinese partner that Russia wanted and, in 2016, an opportunity arose to build the kinds of ties that Rosneft and the Kremlin so desired: energy linkages to China that would further its move away from dependence on the European export market.

That April, Putin had ordered that Rosneft sell a 19.5 per cent stake in the firm.[20] The reason for doing so was stated as support for the Russian state budget, but the move may also have been Putin effectively demanding repayment for bailing out Rosneft at the end of 2014. Although extremely close, Putin and Sechin had squabbled before over the direction of the company.[21]

Sechin initially dragged his feet on the Rosneft sale, and there were few partners who wanted to pay the sums that he sought abroad, particularly as the sale intertwined with Sechin's take-over of Bashneft, which Putin reportedly only approved in exchange for Sechin proceeding with the partial privatisation of Rosneft.[22]

But Sechin did in the end find a willing pair of partners, the international commodities trading giant Glencore, and the Qatari state, which was also Glencore's largest investor.[23] However, the deal had proven controversial—Russia's shifting alliances in the Middle East would soon cause it to pivot away from Qatar and towards its arch-rival, Saudi Arabia. Less than a year after the purchase, Sechin announced that a deal had been struck for CEFC to buy 14.2 per cent of Rosneft off Glencore and Qatar.[24]

The deal appeared to make sense. CEFC would pay a slight premium to Qatar and Glencore, it fitted in with the Belt and Road agenda of securing commodity supplies for Beijing around the globe, and, in 2016, Russia had displaced Saudi Arabia as China's main oil supplier,[25] with Rosneft the largest source of these deliveries.[26] But eight months after the deal was announced, it collapsed.[27] No official explanation was given for the move, though it was soon revealed that Ye had disappeared, detained by the Chinese state, reportedly on the orders of Xi himself.[28]

In the months before his fall from grace, Ye had become ensnared in a corruption scandal in which a former home secretary of Hong Kong was charged in the United States for paying bribes to secure a series of oil deals across Africa.[29] It appears unlikely that this is what precipitated his fall, which was probably the result of infighting within the Chinese government. In October 2018, the former Communist Party secretary of China's Gansu province, Wang Sanyun, was charged by Beijing with accepting bribes from Ye.[30] Wang later pleaded guilty and received a twelve-year sentence.[31]

The deal's collapse, however, also showed that Beijing was not interested in going as far as Russia was in cementing their relationship. Chinese state companies bought up a number of CEFC's assets in the aftermath of Ye's arrest, as his company was effectively unwound. The Rosneft deal was left uncompleted, though CEFC had already made 224.8 million euros in payments towards the purchase.[32]

That the payment was made in euros, rather than dollars, highlights another area of Russian–Chinese cooperation that was ultimately more successful.

Moscow's efforts to undermine the dollar's geopolitical influence saw the Kremlin undertake an effort to move away from the currency for international commodity payments in the years between 2014 and 2022. However, successes were limited—for example, Rosneft began pricing its supply contracts in euros rather than dollars beginning in November 2019 but still sold its output in dollars.[33]

The risks of dealing in the Russian rouble, and China's own capital controls, meant that even for Beijing and Moscow there remained substantial barriers to dealing directly in each other's currencies. By 2020, they had increasingly moved to denominate their trade on a euro basis, with euros being the basis for more than 30 per cent of trade, largely due to Beijing shifting its dealing with Rosneft to the currency.[34]

China's support for the Kremlin still had its limits. Russia was never a major beneficiary of its Belt and Road programme, with Russia's debt to China as a share of GDP growing less than other countries, including its neighbours.[35] Moscow's hopes that China would become a major new source of financing were not quite realised.

This is seen in the history of the BRICS Bank, since renamed the New Development Bank (NDB). Like the IIB whose headquarters Moscow had arranged to shift to Budapest, it was another challenger to the Western-led institutional investment structure of development finance entities like the Asian Development Bank (ADB) and the EBRD. The NDB was launched in July 2014 at a summit in Brazil timed to line up with its hosting of the football World Cup.[36] Its initial constituent members were those that make up the BRICS moniker: Brazil, Russia, India, China, and South Africa. They agreed to authorise it with $100 billion in capital.[37] This meant it was a potential challenger not only to the ADB and EBRD but even the World Bank itself. However, it fell far short of its ambitions. By the end of 2019, it had agreed to only $12 billion in loans and disbursed just $1 billion, whereas the World Bank distributed $2.23 billion in its 2019 year of account alone.[38]

The subsequent COVID-19 pandemic saw it agree to issue a special $1 billion loan to Russia to fund its frontline response,[39] but other activity slowed. This may have been a crucial panacea to Moscow, which did not take similar loans from other international institutions that underwrote much of the response to the pandemic elsewhere. But the bank has failed to establish itself as a challenger to the global financial order. China has not focused on supporting the bank's development, instead preferring its own Asian Infrastructure Investment Bank (AIIB).[40]

Russian attempts to grow financial links with China have also had a decidedly mixed track record. In March 2017, Deripaska's Rusal became the first major Russian company to issue so-called 'panda bonds'.[41] These debts are a Chinese take on the Eurobond structure in that they are bonds issued by a foreign company, under Chinese law, on the Chinese market and in renminbi. But Rusal failed to follow through on plans for a renewed issuance of the debt when it came due two years later.[42] By the time Putin vastly expanded his invasion of Ukraine in February 2022, no other major Russian company had issued such debts.

Beijing has proved a disappointment to Russia as an alternative creditor. It has, however, proven to be a willing partner for trade. By 2021, Russian–Chinese bilateral trade stood at $146.9 billion, up from $89 billion in 2013.[43]

On the eve of Putin's 2022 onslaught, the two would agree to go even further—announcing a new thirty-year gas deal for yet another major gas pipeline, to be dubbed Power of Siberia 2, with related payments settled in euros.[44] The Kremlin aims for it to be able to deliver some 50 billion cubic metres of gas a year, meaning that together with the original Power of Siberia, Moscow would ultimately pump around 90 billion cubic metres of gas annually to China. That would amount to almost half its total exports outside the former Soviet space in 2021 and a vast expansion of the 10 billion cubic metres delivered to China in 2021.[45]

Putin pushed for the deal to go through before his 2022 invasion of Ukraine. At the time, he was still adamantly denying he was planning such an attack. The Kremlin did not want to find itself in the weak negotiating position it had been in when structuring the first contract in 2014. Russian forces, however, were already amassed at the Ukrainian border, so Beijing may well have had an inkling of what Moscow had planned. After Russia's attack, Beijing dragged its feet on progressing the pipeline.[46]

Russia sees China as its ally—and celebrated this in a joint statement in February 2022 on the eve of its full-scale invasion of Ukraine as friendship 'with no limits'.[47] But although Beijing echoed the wording, it remained wary of Putin's agenda. A hint at this can be found in a statement of Xi's celebrating their bilateral relationship in 2019, on the occasion of the anniversary of the establishment of Sino-Russian relations seventy years earlier. Xi said that their 'relationship in the new era should be built on mutual trust'—and that remains lacking.[48]

But the West had its own allies with whom trust was strained. Chapter 5 explored how Turkey was one such country, and how Moscow exploited this to its advantage. The next chapter examines how Moscow took advantage of similar mistrust in the Middle East, finding partners who would help increase its leverage over international energy markets.

11

MIDDLE EASTERN POWER PLAYS

The Middle East was a particularly fiercely contested area of geo-economic competition between Russia and the West in the period between 2014 and 2022. Russia secured what is perhaps its most important economic alliance in the region, while consecutive US administrations found themselves dealing with regional leaders increasingly willing to oppose Washington's agenda. The result was an insulation of Russia's status as an energy superpower that weakened the West's ability to contain it after the full-scale invasion of Ukraine. However, Putin was not in the driving seat either—the region's shifting geopolitics played to his advantage not because of diplomatic skill but because Russia's position as a hydrocarbons superpower offered tactical benefits to the strategic shifts underway in the region's halls of power. Nowhere was this more evident than in the fallout from Rosneft's partial 'privatisation'.

In December 2016, Putin publicly praised Sechin for finally complying with his demand to privatise a 19.5 per cent stake in Rosneft—labelling the sale to Qatar and Glencore 'a very good result'.[1] Sechin also praised his own deal-making, declaring 'the consortium participants hold equal stakes: 50% each. Payment to the state budget will be made both with our own resources and with a loan organised by one of Europe's largest banks.'

Putin pressed Sechin on the impact of the €10.5 billion in foreign currency that the sale was bringing into the budget and foreign currency markets. Putin noted 'we must devise a method that would preclude a negative impact on the market and prevent any hikes on the exchange market'.[2]

Their exchange was of course staged for the press—but an examination of Sechin's comments revealed that not all was so straightforward. The sale price was indeed in line with the Kremlin's targets—and, incidentally, roughly the equivalent of the loans the central bank had supported to bail out Rosneft in December 2014. However, Glencore had only actually taken a 0.54 per cent stake in Rosneft; the remainder would be held by the Qatar Investment Authority (QIA). The pair also only stumped up €2.8 billion for the sale, all but €300 million from the QIA.[3]

The rest of the money came from bank financing—including €2.2 billion in financing from Russian state banks, despite previous statements from Putin that they should not finance domestic privatisations.[4] The lion's share, €5.2 billion, was to be financed by Italy's Intesa Sanpaolo bank. It was one of the European entities that openly flouted the spirit, if not the letter, of the Western sanctions on Russia. The president of Intesa Sanpaolo's Russian operations, who was awarded Russia's 'Order of Friendship' by Putin for his role in the Rosneft privatisation, declared in October 2017 that 'sanctions are illegal', making clear his attitude to the US sectoral sanctions that had sought to restrict long-term financing for Rosneft.[5]

But Sechin managed to pay the roubles required into the Russian budget even before the deal closed, apparently helped by a major domestic bond issuance—some 600 billion roubles, the equivalent of €9.3 billion at the time.[6] However, the deal soon ran into numerous challenges.

The geopolitical situation in the Middle East was changing rapidly. US President Donald Trump had taken office in January and quickly embraced Saudi Arabia, including its ascendant then-deputy crown prince, Mohammed bin Salman (MBS). Even before Trump took office, MBS had openly acted as Saudi Arabia's heir apparent, leading the country into war against Yemen shortly after his father King Salman assumed the crown in January 2015. MBS viewed the Obama administration critically, partly because Washington favoured then-Crown Prince Mohammed bin Nayef (MBN) as King Salman's successor and partly because of the Obama administration's pursuit of diplomacy with Iran.[7] Trump set out to change this.

Putin, however, appeared early on to recognise that MBS held the keys to the kingdom's future. He had even invited MBS to make his first foreign trip to Moscow—something MBS had mentioned to the then-US ambassador to the royal court to secure his first visit to Washington in 2015.[8] Although he was nominally the junior on that trip alongside MBN, MBS made a clear display of all but ignoring MBN's authority.[9] Washington appeared not to get the message about the re-ordering of the Saudi elite. Days later, MBS went to Moscow to meet with Putin and hedge his bets.[10]

In June 2017, MBS launched a blockade and economic war against Qatar, bringing other leading Arab states into his coalition, including the United Arab Emirates (UAE).[11] He formally replaced MBN—long seen as Washington's closest ally in the royal court—as crown prince the same month.[12]

The Kremlin suddenly found itself on one side in a potential new conflict in the Middle East, between two of its major economic powers. That was a position Putin did not want to find himself in.

Meanwhile, Qatar also had reason to grow uncomfortable with the deal. During Sechin's entanglement with Ulyukayev, the economy minister who was ultimately jailed for resisting Sechin's takeover of Bashneft, it was revealed that Sechin had first sought to sell the Rosneft stake to the Japanese government and even initialled a deal to sell it to Mubadala, the investment arm of Abu Dhabi, the leading power in the UAE.[13] The FBI also leaked to the press that it believed Russian hackers were behind a slew of fake messages from the Qatari government that had fuelled the tensions preceding the crisis, though the Kremlin denied any involvement.[14] Additionally, Intesa Sanpaolo's cavalier attitude to the financing was not reciprocated by other Western banks, and its efforts to syndicate the loan failed.[15]

There was clearly a desire on behalf of all parties to get out of the deal, leading to the September 2017 announcement that 14.2 per cent of the Qatari–Glencore joint venture's stake would be sold on to CEFC China Energy. But, as the previous chapter detailed, that deal collapsed as well. Qatar did retain the stake that was to be financed by Intesa Sanpaolo, after Russia's VTB—the same bank that had financed Rosneft's sanctions side-step in the purchase of India's Essar Oil—took on the financing itself.[16]

Meanwhile, MBS was making his influence felt on both the domestic and international stage. MBS sought to consolidate power by going after a host of local rivals—infamously detaining dozens of princes and billionaires in the Ritz Carlton in Riyadh, just across from one of the royal court's many palaces, as his purges escalated in late 2017.[17] That November, MBS also forced Saad Hariri to step down as Lebanon's prime minister in a video broadcast from Saudi Arabia, an incident that astounded regional and international observers by demonstrating just how far-reaching MBS's attempts to consolidate power would be.[18]

Although the agreements that MBS struck in his 2015 meeting with Putin were not seen as significant, they had opened the door to a new partnership.[19] MBS's brazen displays of power and wealth were not missed by Moscow, particularly after he was reported to have made—and closed on—a €350 million offer to buy Russian billionaire Yuri Shefler's 134-metre superyacht *Serene* the day that he first saw it in the summer of 2014.[20]

That September, MBS and Putin met again on the sidelines of the G20 summit in Hangzhou, China. The Russian ruler described the Saudi aspirant as a 'very reliable partner with whom you can reach agreements and be certain those agreements will be honoured'.[21] Putin made the remarks in an interview with Bloomberg, ensuring they would have a global reach, exactly the kind of positive PR that MBS longed for.

The effort paid off. Both Russia and Saudi Arabia had a mutual interest in seeing oil prices rise, given how their economies had been strained over the preceding two years. That December, Russia for the first time ever announced that it would join a coordinated effort to cut oil production led by the Organization of Petroleum Exporting Countries (OPEC), the international oil-producing nations cartel that Saudi had long dominated and that Sechin had labelled effectively dead seven months earlier.[22] The new alliance was dubbed OPEC+.

Saudi Arabia moved closer to Russia than it had ever been before, but the arrival of US President Donald Trump in the White House in January threatened to upend matters. Although he had campaigned on a racist and xenophobic pledge promising a 'total and complete shutdown of Muslims entering the United States', Saudi's new potentate embraced him with open arms.[23] MBS and his coterie had been angered by the Obama administration's initial support for the Arab Spring, its deal with Iran on its nuclear weapons programme, and hesitancy to treat MBS as the heir apparent. Trump's administration was primarily focused on the security relationship with Riyadh, and Trump himself was fixated on little more than arms deals that he believed would restore the famously fractious US–Saudi alliance.

But though MBS was happy to entertain Trump while dealing directly with his son-in-law Jared Kushner to handle sensitive matters, he was simultaneously securing his new oil partnership with Moscow.[24] It proved far more geopolitically significant than any of the deals struck between Trump and MBS.

Trump had made his first foreign visit to Saudi Arabia in May 2017 and relished the royal treatment his hosts showed him. He triumphantly proclaimed that at least $110 billion in arms deals had been agreed. However, it quickly transpired that Trump was not being forthright—the agreements were all non-binding letters of intent, rather than signed contracts.[25] Trump hoped such deals would keep MBS in Washington's camp but was blind to the fact that the prince was on manoeuvres elsewhere that would have far greater long-term impacts as they would undermine the West's efforts to weaken Russia as a military and economic competitor. Immediately after the Saudis hosted Trump, MBS departed for Moscow, where he praised the two oil superpowers' newfound cooperation and pledged to strive for more.[26]

The Kremlin soon snagged a diplomatic coup in its tussle with Washington for influence in the Saudi royal court. Just five months after Trump's Riyadh summit, King Salman undertook the first-ever official trip by a Saudi monarch to Moscow.[27] MBS travelled alongside him. The deals that were struck were nominally worth only a small fraction of those announced between Trump and Riyadh. But as if to demonstrate the new swagger that accompanied MBS's consolidation of power, one of those announced was an agreement for Saudi Arabia to buy Russia's S-400 missile defence system. The CAATSA legislation threatening sanctions on just such sales had been passed by the US Congress only a month earlier.

In December 2018, Qatar announced that it was quitting OPEC, the organisation that had come to be dominated by Russia and Saudi Arabia's expanded OPEC+ partnership.[28] The Kremlin had sought to retain good ties with Doha despite spats over the Rosneft investment and accusations Russian-based hackers were involved in the dissemination of false statements attributed to Sheikh Tamim bin Hamad al Thani. In 2018, the Kremlin even offered to sell Doha the S-400 system as well, drawing opprobrium from Riyadh, though ultimately nothing came of the talks.[29] Putin may have found MBS a willing partner in cutting oil supplies, but Russia was a long way from turning its economic partnership with Saudi Arabia into a political alliance.

That much would become clear on 8 March 2020, when Riyadh unexpectedly announced a series of oil price cuts and Moscow in turn announced that it would ramp up production. Global oil demand had cratered in the preceding days as it became clear that the COVID-19 pandemic would crash demand across the world.[30] The two countries essentially went from partners in a global oil cartel to fierce rivals—and oil prices experienced their largest one-day decline in thirty years as a result.[31]

However, just a month later, Saudi Arabia and Russia agreed to lay down their swords and to instead cut oil production.[32] The dispute was brief, but intense. Yet the rapprochement initially did little to calm markets, with oil prices going negative for the first and, so far, only time ever later that month.[33] In May, Riyadh made unilateral cuts, aiming to 'encourage' other major oil producers to do the same—Russia agreed to further cuts the next month.[34] Russia had expanded its political ties with Saudi Arabia significantly, but MBS saw to it that the Russian tail would not wag the Saudi dog.

The Kremlin made little secret of seeing itself as an increasingly activist power in the Middle East in the years between 2014 and 2022. But it sought to balance its interests across the region's fractious actors. Its intervention in Syria on behalf of Bashar al-Assad's regime in 2015 had already deeply upset many of the Gulf powers, who also opposed its relationship with Tehran. But the geo-economic benefits of those two relationships for the Kremlin were relatively limited.

The Kremlin's experiences with Syria and Iran offered opportunities to practise how to mitigate the impact of sanctions through barter deals and by obfuscating ownership through complex corporate structures. But these efforts were insufficient to change the regional or strategic balance of economic power.[35] Syria also offered opportunities for groups such as Wagner and other Russian elites to profit, including through oil deals. However, these are primarily a way to cement the Kremlin's position in Syria and extract rents for the individuals involved rather than to shift the needle on international markets.[36]

Russia also sought ways to expand its geo-economic leverage through other interventions in the region. It resumed investment in Libya soon after Putin returned to the presidency in 2012, a move in part motivated by Putin's criticisms of the caretaker president he had installed following his second term, Dmitry Medvedev.[37] Although Russia has continued to expand its economic ties with the country in recent years, it has primarily focused on providing arms to the forces of General Khalifa Haftar as the country's on-and-off again civil wars continue to hamper investment in its once-sizable oil industry.

Some smaller deals, have, however managed to increase Moscow's strategic regional position. For example, the Kremlin managed to regain a stake in Iraq's flagship West Qurna oilfield that Saddam Hussein had cancelled after the 2003 US invasion.[38] As the United States wound down its presence in Iraq under President Obama, Russia expanded its position further, with Lukoil investing in the Qurna field and Russia's state-run Gazprom Neft entering the Iraqi Kurdistan region, a historical battleground for US and Russian influence in the Cold War.[39]

In 2017, Moscow made a further move to vastly expand its influence in Kurdistan. Rosneft agreed to provide billions in pre-payments needed to plug the Kurdish government's budget deficits amid its dispute with Baghdad over then-regional President Masoud Barzani's decision to hold an independence referendum.[40] It also agreed to spend $400 million investing in five new oil blocks in the region, necessary to help it meet future needs.

The investments came at a particularly risky moment— Kurdistan and Baghdad were on the verge of full-blown war. In 2014, Kurdish fighters took control of the city of Kirkuk and its oil-rich environs after the Iraqi Army collapsed in the face of Islamic State attacks on the city.[41] Barzani vowed that it would be part of a future independent Kurdistan.[42] But on 15 October, Iraqi forces advanced on the city and its environs and took control within five days. Iranian officials warned Kurdistan against any counter action.[43]

However, Rosneft was not ready to give up on its efforts. Instead, it doubled down. On 20 October, as the last Kurdish units withdrew from the Kirkuk region, Rosneft announced it would take a majority stake in a Kurdish-built spurt to the Kirkuk–Ceyhan pipeline, known as the KRG pipeline.[44] The sale meant that it would have significant leverage over Kurdish oil supplies to Turkey, as well as over future relations between Baghdad and the Kurdish government.

Moscow's success in enhancing its strategic position in Iraqi Kurdistan was far less geopolitically significant than the partnership it established with Saudi Arabia, but both were representative of the growing importance of the Middle East to its geo-economic agenda. As Russia vastly escalated its threats against Ukraine in 2021, including building up large numbers of forces on its border, Putin felt more secure that its energy flank was secure ahead of the all-out economic war that would ensue when its forces attacked.

PART II

2022

12

THE ECONOMIC WAR IN UKRAINE

On 24 February 2022, Russian President Vladimir Putin ordered his troops to launch an all-out attack on Ukraine. They began a rapid assault from the east around territory they already controlled in Donetsk and Luhansk oblasts, as well as across the Russian and Belarusian borders into Kyiv and Kharkiv, Ukraine's second-largest city. Putin dubbed it a 'special military operation'. In reality, it was an effort to decapitate the Ukrainian government. Russian forces also stormed north of occupied Crimea, entering the town of Henichesk, in Kherson oblast, that very day.[1]

Ukrainian forces and civilians resisted in Henichesk, as they did across the country.[2] The Ukrainian people demonstrated, and continue to demonstrate, remarkable valour in fighting off Russia's attacks. Without this resistance, the war could have rapidly resulted in a Russian victory. The invasion also put Ukraine's economy in Russia's crosshairs. From the moment the invasion began, Ukraine's fortunes and those of the world would never be the same. The story of Ukraine's valiant defence will certainly receive substantial attention, and economic considerations should never come above those of life and limb. Nonetheless, understanding the economic and financial aspects of Russia's physical war in Ukraine highlights just how hollow Putin's vision for the Ukrainian territory he has since sought to annex is and the extent to which he is willing to go to stop Ukraine's integration into the Western-led economic order.

As Russian troops crossed from Crimea into Henichesk, one of the first pieces of Ukraine's economy to fall victim was a wind plant.[3] The Syvash wind farm was struck by at least one rocket and quickly taken over by Russian forces.[4] Far larger and far more

133

economically significant infrastructure would be targeted in the days, weeks, and months to come, but the project has a symbolic significance in that it has come to represent Ukraine's transition and integration into the Western-led international economic order after its 2014 revolution.

The Syvash wind farm takes its name from the marshy lagoons that separate Crimea from the Ukrainian mainland. The bridge to Henichesk is the main route enabling transport over the Syvash between Crimea and Ukraine's Kherson region. The Syvash project was led by Norway's renewable energy firm NBT, since renamed Emergy, alongside France's TotalEnergies and Saudi Arabia's Al Gilhaz Group.[5] Its high-risk location meant that support from international institutional investors was crucial, with the EBRD providing €150 million of the initial €155 million funding.[6] The lead contractor was PowerChina, while further financing also came from the Black Sea Trade and Development Bank, in which NATO members hold a majority share—and in which Russia is also a capital-contributing member, a legacy of its own integration with the Western-led economic order in the 1990s.[7]

The Syvash wind farm could have been an example of the kind of international economic cooperation and support that holds out so much promise for Ukraine. Instead, the attack by Russian forces wrecked the project, as Putin aims to wreck that dream.

The project's backers put in a claim with the London political violence insurance market, which supported the investment.[8] It was the first of many of such claims to result from Putin's attack, leading to estimates that the cost to these markets will run into the billions.[9] In the first eight months of the war, 90 per cent of Ukraine's wind power was destroyed.[10] Putin's war has targeted not just the territory in the country's east and south that Putin believes should be part of Russia but the entire country.

Infrastructure has been at the heart of Putin's war in Ukraine—with key economic, and military, implications. The Crimea Bridge was Putin's flagship project following the peninsula's 2014 annexation. A rail bridge briefly linked Crimea with the Russian mainland during the Second World War, but it was destroyed by an ice floe in February 1945; independent Ukraine and Russia discussed building a new bridge after the USSR's collapse but made no serious progress.[11] Putin's realisation of the bridge became a centrepiece of the Kremlin's propaganda. The Kremlin even commissioned a romantic-comedy film about the bridge's construction in 2018.[12] The bridge was critical to consolidating Russian control of Crimea, allowing the regular supply of goods blockaded from the Ukrainian mainland. It also facilitated Putin's build-up of forces in the peninsula at the end of 2021.[13]

Putin awarded the contract for the Crimea Bridge to one of his most-favoured businessmen, Arkady Rotenberg, and his firm SGM, which had a history of winning crucial infrastructure contracts. Rotenberg told Russian television that profit was not the primary motivation—though he did note that such a result would be a 'sign of success'—but rather that the bridge was meant to 'mean something for future generations'.[14] After its completion, SGM said that it did not make a profit, though the firm was ultimately sold to Gazprom for $1.2 billion.[15]

That the bridge was completed at all can partly be attributed to failings in the West's economic statecraft against Russia. Although Europe and the United States had sanctioned any investment in Crimea or involvement with Kremlin-backed infrastructure projects there, enforcement was sorely lacking, as also seen in the Siemens case.

One of the Russian contractors who supported the project's development was the St Petersburg-based Mostovoye Bureau, which was responsible for some of the bridge's key engineering tasks.[16] Among these was the measurement of the bridge's support pylons. According to the firm's own website, in order to carry out this work it purchased measuring equipment from Dutch firm Allnamics.[17] Simply supplying such technology for a project in Crimea is a violation of the post-2014 sanctions regime as since July 2014, the European Union has implemented a ban on investment into infrastructure projects in the region's transportation sector and also banned key equipment from export there. Mostovoye Bureau's website, however, included not just photos of the equipment being delivered but pictures that appear to show Allnamics' staff training Mostovoye Bureau's employees on how to install the equipment on site.[18]

Despite reports of Allnamics' sale of the measuring equipment in the Dutch media and from RFE/RL, the US-government funded news service focused on the former Soviet space, no action was ever taken.[19] Dutch prosecutors claimed they lacked evidence of sanctions violations.[20] The affair was yet another example of how Europe's less stringent attitude undermined the Russian sanctions regime.

Far more egregious holes in the sanctions regime quickly became clear. Although the United States had imposed various restrictions on the export of microchips to Russia given their dual-use potential as missiles rained down across Ukraine, evidence was tragically found in the rubble that the missiles employed chips designed by US firms, although largely in Asia where compliance with US sanctions was relatively weak.[21] The chips would also be found in destroyed Russian air defence systems and attack helicopters.[22]

Russian rocket attacks caused some of the most devastating destruction of Ukrainian assets throughout the conflict. The list of assets destroyed is extensive and stretches across the country, from the war-ravaged Donetsk and Luhansk regions to Ukraine's westernmost Lviv and Zakarpattia regions. Seven months into the conflict, an advisor to Ukrainian President Volodymyr Zelensky estimated the total damage amounted to around $1 trillion dollars, while the Kyiv School of Economics put the infrastructure damage alone at $127 billion by the start of September.[23] And that was before Russian forces adopted a tactic of destroying Ukraine's energy infrastructure in October, after a large truck bomb on the Crimea Bridge on 8 October that burst the propaganda myth of Russian invulnerability and impacted Russia's ability to resupply Crimea and the southern front in the Zaporizhzhia and Kherson regions of Ukraine.[24]

The devastation wrought by Russia's attacks on Ukraine's economy can also be highlighted by the fate of some of the country's most important enterprises. As a post-Soviet country, Ukraine inherited a number of large industrial clusters and enterprises.[25] These included the Kharkiv Turbogenerator Plant, the Kharkiv Tractor Plant, the Zaporizhzhia Automobile Plant, the rocket manufacturer Pivdenmash in Dnipro, and the giant steel factories of Kryvorizhstal, Zaporizhstal, and Azovstal. All were targeted by

Russian forces. Russia's attacks were of course primarily aimed at devastating the Ukrainian economy and weakening its ability and will to fight, but they also raised the cost to the West of supporting Ukraine in the conflict, something the Kremlin hoped would lead to reduced support for Kyiv. The economic damage to Ukraine of Russia's initial invasion in 2014—and the subsequent looting of coal and industrial machinery from the occupied Donetsk and Luhansk regions—had already been severe, but the 2022 attacks proved devastating.[26]

This was epitomised by the fate of Mariupol. Its Azovstal factory became internationally renowned after Ukrainian soldiers made it their last redoubt in the key Donbas port for eighty days before surrendering to the Russian invasion force that besieged it.[27]

Azovstal and another nearby steel plant, Ilyichstal, had been Mariupol's lifeblood. I visited Mariupol in 2015 and 2016, interviewing a number of its residents. At the time, the vast majority stated that they felt Russian in nationality—Ukrainian was not widely spoken—but that their fate lay with Ukraine. For many, however, this was merely motivated by practical reasoning—if the war came to their city and destroyed the two plants that were its largest direct employers and around which the wider local economy was based, there would be little chance of seeing the plants rebuilt. In the Stalin era, when both plants were first established, the logic of markets was anathema to Soviet economic planning. No investor today would rebuild them, particularly given the threat of the silting up of Mariupol's port.[28] The decision to side with Ukraine had been made for Mariupol's residents when Rinat Akhmetov, the majority owner of Azovstal and Ilychstal's parent Metinvest, unexpectedly decided to side with Ukrainian forces in 2014. Putin's devastation of the city, however, belied his once-stated desire for Russian and Ukrainian economic integration and lost him the battle for hearts and minds across the area, likely for generations to come. After Mariupol's capture, Russian officials acknowledged they would not rebuild Azovstal and Illyich Steel.[29]

Although Akhmetov had once been close enough to Putin to fly Yanukovych to Moscow at the height of the Euromaidan protests, his assets across the country would be devastated in the fighting in 2022. Demonstrating the extent to which Putin's strategy destroyed

Russia's relations with Ukraine's oligarchic elite, Akhmetov launched a series of arbitration disputes and legal claims against Russia over its seizure and destruction of his assets.[30] Other than Metinvest, SCM's main holding is the Ukrainian energy company DTEK, which dominates the country's power production and whose plants were repeatedly targeted by Russian missiles. Putin's attacks could also be indiscriminate—DTEK's Kyiv headquarters in the city's flagship office tower were damaged by a Russian rocket strike on 10 October.[31] The same tower also housed the German consulate and an office of the Korean conglomerate Samsung.[32]

A decade earlier, Forbes ranked Akhmetov the world's thirty-ninth-richest person.[33] The 2014 war destroyed the stadium of his Shakhtar Donetsk football club and displaced the team and its owner from the city that birthed them—but it also highlighted the importance of his maintaining good relations with Western capital, with his companies having to repeatedly restructure their debts thereafter. The 2022 war destroyed the basis of Akhmetov's wealth in Ukraine, despite having been a major player on its political scene until just months before. Three months before Putin expanded his invasion into the heart of Ukraine, President Zelensky said Akhmetov 'was being drawn into a war against the Ukrainian state', implicating him in an alleged pro-Russian coup attempt.[34] Zelensky's detractors, however, initially saw such moves within the context of Ukraine's oligarchic tussles. Zelensky's campaign had been backed by Ihor Kolomoisky, on whose television channel Zelensky starred as Ukraine's president in the comedy series *Servant of the People*.[35] Zelensky was criticised for going after Akhmetov's television stations and media holdings while leaving Kolomoisky's untouched.[36]

The war changed all that.

Fifty-two days after Ukrainian forces in Azovstal laid down their arms, Akhmetov announced he was giving up his media empire and handing its licences back to the state.[37] Ten days later, reports emerged that Zelensky had approved a decree stripping Kolomoisky of his citizenship.[38] Kolomoisky had long flaunted his dual Israeli–Cypriot citizenship. When a journalist confronted him over the matter, Kolomoisky retorted: 'In the constitution it says dual citizenship is forbidden. But triple citizenship is not forbidden.'[39] The move appeared to signal Kolomoisky's fall from grace. While he denied that his citizenship had been stripped, the next time he was seen in Ukraine was when he was questioned by the National Anti-Corruption Bureau that November. His shares in the state oil company, Ukrnafta, were seized days later.[40] His investments and assets, including the Kryvyi Rih Iron Ore plant and a pair of ferroalloy plants in Zaporizhzhia and Nikopol, also suffered directly as a result of Russia's war, struck by long-range Russian strikes.[41] The economic impact of the war affected a number of his other assets as well, with the oil refinery he controlled in the central Ukrainian city of Kremenchuk being forced to halt production.[42]

While Russian forces' furthest advance still left them 170 kilometres from Kremenchuk, the city witnessed a particularly horrifying attack on 27 June when twenty people were killed and fifty-six injured in a pair of Russian missile strikes on and around the Amstor shopping mall. Moscow claimed it had targeted the nearby Kredmash plant, which produced asphalt mixing units, and alleged that Western-supplied ammunition supposedly stored there had exploded, thus damaging the mall.[43] However, a BBC investigation showed that while a second strike landed near the Kredmash plant, it was comparatively lightly damaged.[44] The investigation found no evidence of such Western materiel having been present.[45]

Amstor's owner is Vadim Novinsky, a billionaire co-investor in Akhmetov's Metinvest. Novinsky was also elected as an MP for Mariupol for the pro-Russian Opposition Bloc in 2019.[46] Originally Russian, and awarded Ukrainian citizenship only by a decree from then-President Yanukovych in 2012, Novinsky announced he was breaking with Moscow after the 2022 invasion.[47] He later resigned as an MP, claiming that he could better serve Ukraine's reconstruction by dedicating himself to business, though the move may have been pre-emptive given the Ukrainian legislature was stripping other former pro-Russian MPs of their mandates.[48]

Nevertheless, the loss of Novinsky's seat, Akhmetov surrendering his media influence, and Kolomoisky's purported loss of citizenship highlight how the war weakened oligarchic influence in Ukraine. This was something the West had long advocated for, and that Putin's war inadvertently helped achieve.

Other powerful Ukrainian oligarchs also saw Russia's invasion blow a hole in their fortunes—including Dmytro Firtash, who, despite facing extradition from Austria on US corruption charges for the preceding eight years, still controlled vast assets across Ukraine including the Azot ammonia plant in Severodonetsk.[49] The plant was heavily shelled and bombed when it became a holdout for Ukrainian forces defending the city before Russian forces seized it on 25 June 2022.[50] Many others saw their assets affected by the war, centred on southern and eastern Ukraine—the country's industrial heartland.

Some oligarchs suffered far more than a loss of assets or capital. Those who cooperated with the Kremlin were removed from the political scene.

Viktor Medvedchuk, the Putin associate who became the effective leader of a pro-Russian opposition party after Ukraine's 2019 election, initially attempted to flee Ukraine.[51] However, he was found in hiding and arrested and would later be swapped in a prisoner exchange with Moscow for 215 Ukrainian prisoners-of-war, including some of those who had led the defence of Azovstal.[52] Some have claimed that it was Zelensky's attempts to close down media outlets linked to Medvedchuk, much as he had with those linked to Akhmetov, that prompted Putin to decide an outright invasion of Ukraine was necessary for him to continue to dominate its politics.[53] If Putin hoped the war would restore oligarchs to power in Ukraine who were willing to aid him, it clearly failed. Vyacheslav Bohuslayev, the owner of the aviation firm Motor Sich who had been implicated in illegally exporting helicopter parts to Russia,[54] was also arrested on treason charges in October 2022.[55] Motor Sich was subsequently nationalised.[56]

Russia's missile strikes also targeted economic interests in Ukraine that it saw as a threat. On 31 July 2022, a missile landed some 50 metres from the home of Ukrainian grain magnate Oleksiy Vadatursky and his wife Raisa in the port city of Mykolaiv.[57] The city had been under severe threat from Russia's rapid advances at the beginning of the war. But by the end of July, Ukrainian forces had established defensive lines south and east of Mykolaiv while limiting Russia's ability to supply the front by targeting the two bridges it controlled over the Dnieper River in the cities of Kherson and

Nova Kakhovka.[58] This did not alleviate Russia's attacks on the city of Mykolaiv; if anything, the attacks intensified as Russian forces began employing long-range missiles.

Journalists from *Der Spiegel*, The Insider, and Bellingcat later revealed the mundanity of the life of Russia's Main Computational Staff as they targeted missiles to strike Ukrainian city centres— with members simultaneously bidding for collectibles online and haggling with sex-workers.[59] Despite such distractions, their strikes often landed with deadly precision, including in one attack that Ukrainian officials believe to have been a deliberate assassination.[60]

Minutes after the strike outside the Vadaturskys' home, a second missile came crashing through their roof, killing Oleksiy and Raisa.[61] Oleksiy had founded Nibulon, a company that had become the 'backbone of Ukraine's agricultural infrastructure', controlling a network of grain elevators, silos, and even an export fleet.[62] The firm's success had been seen as helping Ukraine build an independent economy, and it had repeatedly secured support from Western development banks.

The day before his death, Vadatursky visited a site in Izmail, just across the Danube from Romania and thus NATO territory.[63] The aim was to build a new grain terminal that would be protected from potential Russian attacks, according to a Bloomberg profile of his son and successor, Andriy.[64] The death of his parent did not stop the Vadatursky heir from pursuing his father's aims. He said that he was preparing to persuade Nibulon's bankers to continue to support the firm, including the EBRD that, the day before his profile was published, pledged to commit €3 billion to Ukraine between 2022 and 2023.[65]

The EBRD was not alone in offering support for Ukraine. The West would all but bankroll the Ukrainian government almost immediately after the war began, as Russia's attacks and the move to full mobilisation by the Ukrainian government in response to the invasion left the country without an economic base. By the onset of the winter of 2022, the European Union had pledged €12.3 billion in financial assistance, on top of billions more offered by the bloc's members directly, as well as the UK.[66] The United States offered more than $15 billion in such support, as well as $9.5 billion in humanitarian aid and $27.1 billion in security assistance between

24 February and 31 December 2022.[67] By the end of the year, legislation had been passed that would authorise a further $48.7 billion in such support.[68]

To prevent Ukraine's economy from collapsing, the Western-led Paris Club agreed to suspend its debt repayments in July 2022.[69] So too did private bondholders, and even the holders of so-called GDP warrants, instruments that were issued as part of the post-Crimea restructuring of Ukraine's debts.[70] The latter was particularly notable, as the payments were linked to Ukraine's GDP growth rates and their potential pay-outs were uncapped.[71] While Ukraine's GDP has been devastated by Putin's war, the eventual rebound could see rapid growth rates from a base driven to its nadir by the war and thus offer potential value to investors. Whether it was because they did not want to be seen as war profiteers, or a genuine desire to help Ukraine, the warrants' fate highlights how Western private capital moved to support Ukraine even at its own expense. Far more support would be martialled by Western governments in support of Kyiv's resistance, with the West granting 64 billion euros in concessional loans and grants throughout the year to support Ukraine's budget, of which 31 billion euros had been disbursed by year's end.[72] This is by a significant extent the largest amount of financial support the West has granted to a country in a single year and more than a third of the total support, adjusted for inflation, offered by the US Marshall plan to sixteen European countries after the Second World War.[73]

While the West was on the financial defensive in its support of Ukraine, it met Putin's invasion with a rapid and vast escalation of its own geo-economic attempts to constrain Russia. While Ukrainian forces fought to defend their homeland, the West fought to incapacitate the Russian economy in a bid to weaken Putin's state capacity and his ability to execute his martial madness in Ukraine.

13

THE WEST'S ECONOMIC WAR AGAINST RUSSIA

On 26 February 2022, the third day of Russia's expanded invasion of Ukraine, the West launched an economic war on Russia via a direct assault on its central bank. Although major sanctions were already imposed the day the war began, this marked a true escalation from attempting to restrain Russia to attempting to sever it from the international economic order.

While many sanctions are intended as a deterrent, the cutting-off of a country's central bank has a different effect. When the United States imposes such a measure, it effectively severs the affected country from the international financial system. While the United States had taken similar action against Iran and Venezuela, it was the first time the West was united behind such a measure and the first time it had done so against a major political power with a sizable economy and its own tools to fight back.

Speaking in Warsaw, Poland, one month after Russia's central bank was sanctioned, US President Joe Biden made clear these sanctions were different: 'These economic sanctions are a new kind of economic statecraft with the power to inflict damage that rivals military might.'[1] He vowed they would sap 'Russian strength … and its ability to project power.'[2]

Despite Biden's declaration and the United States' centrality in making the sanction so significant, the move was not solely a US decision. The step was agreed following whirlwind diplomatic discussions by those opposed to Russia's invasion, including the EU, UK, and other smaller powers.[3] The central bank sanctions were first formally proposed by the Canadian government.[4] As a senior EU official told the *Financial Times*, 'We have never had in the history of the European Union such close contacts with the Americans on a security issue.' Even Switzerland and Singapore—which resisted the post-Crimea sanctions—joined the move.

Nevertheless, it was the US role in blacklisting Russia's central bank that was at the core of the sanctions' extensive reach. It had the almost instantaneous impact of freezing the lion's share of Russia's international reserves, its holdings of other currencies and claims held with financial institutions in the Western countries that held them.

Given the dominance of the dollar in international trade, and US Treasury debts in international reserves, Washington has a superior economic weapon to any other country. This is further enhanced by the US definition of what comes under the purview of its sanctions regime being particularly broad—any transaction that so much as touches dollars falls within their remit. This effectively makes US sanctions extraterritorial.

This meant that Russian reserves beyond the largely digital deposit boxes of the West could not be accessed. Some $300 billion of Russia's $630 billion central bank war chest was frozen by the beginning of March.[5] By severing the central bank, the West had cut off the pipeline of financial flows between Moscow and much of the world. Combined with the wider array of sanctions introduced at the time, it also became incredibly difficult for the Kremlin to spend the dollars, euros, and other currencies it still had to hand.

Many of Russia's key banks were subject to new sanctions barring them from accessing SWIFT, the communications system employed across the globe for banks to facilitate transfers with one another.[6] This made moving money in and out of Russia a major challenge, and many of Russia's existing banking relationships ceased to function. So-called correspondent banking relationships, in which banks agree to facilitate transactions in other currencies abroad for one another, were cancelled. This also affected Russian banks' subsidiaries abroad, including in nominal Russian allies such as Kazakhstan.[7] Supplementary sanctions would target Russia's ability to counter these measures through its own MIR payment system, established after the 2014 invasion when SWIFT sanctions on Russia were first raised. Even Tajikistan, where the Kremlin has a sizable influence and much of the population was directly dependent on remittances from migrant labour in Russia, cut off MIR's access.[8]

In addition to depleting Russia's war chest and constraining its ability to spend, the financial sector sanctions had two cumulative impacts. The first was to significantly increase the difficulty in financing Russian trade and credit, and the second was to impose a discount on those dollars and other hard currencies to which Russia did have access. In effect, a dollar that had crossed the Russian frontier—digitally or physically—was worth less than any other dollar abroad. To use the term preferred by economists, they were no longer fungible. Russia would instead have to rely on financial alchemy to make them transmutable.

This also vastly decreased the convertibility of the Russian rouble, causing its value to plummet. Russia's financial services sector almost immediately collapsed, with the Russian stock market closing for a month after the war began.[9]

However, with institutions tied to the Russian state the only major players active in trading the rouble thereafter, the Kremlin was able to get the rouble back to its pre-war level, and even beyond.[10] The nominative strengthening of the Russian rouble was a setback to the West's economic war strategy, at least on paper, though how much this mattered would depend on ensuring that there was little demand for the Russian rouble abroad. This is where the sanctions strategy initially faced its biggest hurdle in the form of some of the Western allies' hesitancy to impose sanctions on the Russian energy sector.

When the first new sanctions were announced, energy transactions were explicitly carved out by the United States, at least for non-sanctioned institutions.[11] Some restrictions were imposed, however. For example, the United States did impose sectoral sanctions on financing for Russian energy firms, including targeting Russian gas giant Gazprom with the measure for the first time.[12] European states that had put up major resistance to such a move after the 2014 invasion no longer objected. The most notable exception to the financial restrictions was the US and EU decision to keep Gazprombank off their sanctions blacklist.[13] The bank played a crucial role in the oil and gas trade, something Russia would later exploit.

While Western sanctions had not yet homed in on Russian energy, they did target its commodity sector. The first relatively low-hanging fruit to be affected were Russian coal exports, which the European Union announced it would phase out less than two weeks after the war began.[14] However, even this was delayed amid concerns about market instability, only coming into effect in August 2022.

Initially, much more disruption would be wrought by the sanctioning of many of Russia's richest oligarchs. While the sanctions strategy pursued by the Obama and Biden administrations, as well as the US Congress during Trump's administration, focused on the expansion of individual sanctions from the inner circle around Putin to the second and third rungs of the concentric circles of influence in the system orbiting Putin, after the 24 February invasion there was a dramatic expansion of those targeted.

The sanctions targeted some of the world's richest men. The financial and economic ramifications were vast. The international impact was encapsulated by the sanctions' effect on London's then-premier football team, Chelsea Football Club, which had won the most important international club football competition, the Champions League, just nine months prior. Chelsea was barred from selling new tickets, as its owner, Roman Abramovich, was sanctioned by the British government. His team scrambled to strike a deal with Downing Street enabling him to sell the club. It was only approved after Abramovich agreed to forego the proceeds of the £4.25 billion sale and for them to be 'used for humanitarian purposes in Ukraine', which British authorities would oversee.[15] Pushing businessmen seen as linked to the Kremlin out of positions with soft-power potential, was, however, only the beginning.

The sanctions also prompted a reshuffling of the oligarchic hierarchy within Russia. By challenging the Kremlin's authority in this way, the West hoped that it would provoke push-back from Russia's oligarchic elite. But this would be unrealised, as the Kremlin had long decimated the oligarchs' political power. The few who went abroad, or remained there after the war, saw their assets in Russia come under threat. But most of their criticisms of the war merely came in the form of calling for an end to fighting and for peace—direct denunciations of Putin for launching the war were rare. The two most stark examples were Yury Milner and Oleg Tinkov. Milner, who had shifted his business interests to Israel and the United States in 1999, announced in October that his family had 'left Russia for good, after the Russian annexation of Crimea. And this summer, we officially completed the process of renouncing our Russian citizenship.' Tinkov, who had been undergoing leukaemia treatment while also fighting fraud charges in London, denounced the invasion in April, employing the wide array of expletives that the Russian language offers to criticise the Kremlin.[16] Within days, Tinkov said he was forced to sell his remaining stake in the bank that he founded to Russian oligarch Vladimir Potanin.[17] Tinkov also announced that he had gone into hiding as 'maybe now the Kremlin is going to kill me'.[18] Tinkov later renounced his Russian citizenship as well.[19]

Things were by no means easy for those who did not break with the Kremlin. Billions of dollars' worth of sanctioned individuals' assets were frozen, and their business relationships with the West shattered. Abramovich's steel giant, Evraz, narrowly avoided defaulting on its debts, while its main Russian rival, Severstal, did fall into default.[20] Severstal's principal owner, Alexei Mordashov, had been sanctioned by the EU four days after the 2022 invasion.[21] His efforts to shield his businesses failed.

Shifting assets to family members had proven a shield in the past, as seen with Trump's sanctions against Russian oligarchs Kerimov and Deripaska. This was no longer the case. The EU and the United States blacklisted Mordashov's wife after he transferred his shareholding in the European travel operator Tui and the Russian gold firm Nordgold to her.[22] A similar fate befell the Serbian-Croatian wife of coal and fertiliser magnate Andrei Melnichenko, after he shifted many of his key assets to her just before he too was sanctioned.[23]

One notable aspect of the West's strategy of targeting oligarchs was that there were considerable differences in the lists of individuals and entities blacklisted by Canada, the EU, the UK, and the United States. In certain cases, oligarchs were left off the US list for weeks after they were sanctioned on the other side of the Atlantic.[24] Abramovich was left off the US sanctions list, reportedly at Ukraine's request as he sought to recast himself as a mediator in the conflict.[25] In some cases, being left off the US list was intended as a signal to third parties and countries that financial affairs should be put in order before Washington acted, given that its sanctions bore the extra-territorial threat that Brussels', Ottawa's, and London's did not. For example, Melnichenko was sanctioned by the United States in August, five months after the EU and UK blacklisted him, though the US sanctions authority OFAC explicitly noted his fertiliser firm Eurochem was unaffected, due to his marital transfer of control.[26]

But EU and UK sanctions were powerful enough to affect businesses, even when targets were not designated by the United States. Eurochem and Melnichenko's coal firm SUEK fell into technical defaults on their debts after the EU sanctioned them. Mordashov's Severstal's default also came before he was sanctioned by the United States in June.[27]

The cost to Western financial markets was one Brussels, Washington, and London were willing to see them bear. Russian debts were not seen as a systemic risk, and as long as they remained frozen and claims could be fought—a process that historically has lasted well after sanctions have been lifted even in less drastic scenarios—there would be economic reasons for keeping Russian firms out of Western financial markets, in addition to the regulatory and legal hurdles the sanctions themselves imposed. Nevertheless, Washington remained willing to make certain carve-outs. For example, the US Treasury issued a licence explicitly stating that firms connected to the Russian-Uzbek businessman Alisher Usmanov were not affected, even if he held a majority stake, unless they were explicitly named on sanctions blacklists.[28] This limited the impact on his interests in Uzbekistan.[29]

Perhaps the most symbolic action to result from the sanctions was the freezing of oligarchs' yachts around the globe. Many dashed for shores outside the reaches of Western authorities, undertaking a maritime migration to safer shores such as South Africa, Turkey, and the UAE.[30] Nevertheless, Russia's oligarchic class had taken a significant hit as a result of the war.

The oligarchs also came under increasing criticism from Kremlin propaganda channels. While propaganda regularly denounced the oligarchs' influence over the country in the 1990s as part of Russia's efforts to legitimise Putin's strong-man rule, in the context of the war and sanctions, it became clear this was a call for them to actively support the war or risk losing it all as Tinkov had done.

In September 2022, Russian forces suffered a string of defeats and were forced to retreat from much of Ukraine's Kharkiv region. Vladimir Solovyov, among the most prominent television hosts in the Russian state's propaganda machine, did not take this very well. In a particularly frenzied tirade that month, he set his sights on the country's businessmen who he claimed were insufficiently supporting the war. Solovyov quipped, 'the combined tonnage of our oligarchs' yachts would be the envy of the Navy of any major power' but that the Russian military appeared to lack supplies.[31]

Unsurprisingly, Solovyov failed to mention that Putin had his own small fleet of yachts. Two weeks before the war, one yacht in which the US Treasury said Putin had an interest, the *Graceful*, fled Germany for Russia's Kaliningrad region.[32] The yacht was soon renamed the *Killer Whale*.[33] Another yacht linked to Putin, the *Scheherazade*, was impounded in Italy.[34] The superyacht—whose captain previously served on Wagner founder Prigozhin's yacht—was moored in the Italian Rivera town of Marina di Carrara when the war began.[35]

Solovyov also failed to note that Putin, not the West's sanctions, fostered the kleptocracy that enabled the flow of funds out of the state's coffers and into bank accounts and yachts abroad. Solovyov also left unsaid that it was Putin's kleptocracy that left the oligarchs with a reason to want their assets abroad—so they could not be seized by the Kremlin's capricious cronies.

The sanctions targeted two further Russian fleets. The first was Russian aviation. The West barred aircraft manufacturers from selling or leasing aircraft to Russia, as well as from providing repairs or other technical services, a move that struck some 85 per cent of all aircraft operated by Russia airliners.[36] Putin quickly responded by seizing hundreds of Western aircraft that Russian firms had leased, worth $12.4 billion.[37] The move kept Russian aircraft flying in the interim, while triggering billions in losses for the aviation lenders and their insurers.[38] But over the long term the problem poses a critical challenge for Russia, whose airplane construction industry is a shadow of its past, Soviet self. Putin appeared to have little thought for such long-term consequences—in his initial attacks on Kyiv, he also decimated Ukraine's Soviet-legacy Antonov aircraft manufacturer, which could have proven a key prize if captured.[39]

The other affected fleet was that of Russia's state shipping firm Sovcomflot, which was sanctioned in March.[40] As with many such designations, the sanctions included wind-down periods for firms to bring an end to their relationships with sanctioned entities. In Sovcomflot's case, the wind-down period ended on 15 May.[41] The firm had billions in loans from Western banks, and failure to restructure and repay those risked triggering a default and a scramble by creditors to secure the assets. While Russian oil fields had proven all but impossible for foreign creditors to seize long before even the 2014 sanctions, oil tankers are easier targets given it is the very nature of their operations to bring Russian crude to foreign markets. Between the broad international coalition behind the sanctions, and Western threats to target those who did not comply, this meant it would merely be a matter of time before defaulted creditors would be able to seize Sovcomflot's ships. The firm scrambled to sell as many ships as it could to pay off its debts before the grace period ended.

Twenty were sold by the deadline, one-sixth of its fleet.[42] It was one of the largest such fire sales of all time. But the Kremlin had little choice unless it wanted to risk losing more of its export capacity, which was under threat on other fronts as well.

Broad sanctions were, for example, imposed on other Russian oil cargoes. In May, the EU agreed that it would halt Russian crude oil purchases by the end of 2022.[43] The ability to send cargoes to new markets was more important for Russia than ever.

However, the West's sanctions response left a number of loopholes for Russian oil to keep flowing. For example, landlocked Hungary, Czechia, and Slovakia were excluded from the Russian oil phase-out.[44] And while restrictions were imposed on insuring Russian oil cargoes, they stopped short of banning European brokers from servicing them. Greek firms, responsible for the lion's share of the ship-broking market, continued to handle Russian cargoes as a result, even if they were now chartered outside of Europe rather than within it.[45] According to shipping industry publication *TradeWinds*, four of the ships that Sovcomflot sold were purchased by

Greek shipping and football magnate Evangelos Marinakis.[46] In July 2022, Marinakis defended continuing to service Russian exports and publicly accused European leaders of 'making a mistake' in pursuing sanctions, which he warned risked costing Europe more than the Kremlin.[47]

This gets to an important point in the West's sanctions strategy. A key thrust of the 2022 sanctions was to deny Russia hard currency and to decrease the value of its existing holdings of these currencies. Barring Russia's direct oil exports to Europe aimed to achieve this by pushing Russia into accepting discounts for its crude from countries that had established relationships with other suppliers.

In considering further sanctions on Russian oil, the West could achieve only two of three aims: constraining Russia's total oil exports, maintaining the supremacy of the dollar in international oil contracts, and maintaining international oil market stability. Oil prices did spike significantly in the aftermath of Putin's invasion but fell every month from June through December. By allowing Russian oil to flow while targeting its price and markets at the margins, Western policy markets were seeking to protect the dollar and oil market stability. As Russia produces 10 per cent of global oil,[48] targeting its total exports risked prompting a crisis akin to that experienced by the global economy following the 1973 Arab Oil Embargo, when Arab producers cut off countries that supported Israel in the Yom Kippur War. They sought to avoid a re-run.

Even when the G7 instated a $60 price cap on Russian crude exports—barring most shippers from dealing in Russian oil sold above the price—the aim was not for Russia to sell less oil, but to effectively lock in discounts for countries such as China and India that had picked up the supplies no longer flowing to the West.[49]

If the West had genuinely wanted to cut Russian oil off entirely, it would have imposed a US secondary sanctions threat—i.e. a warning that those caught buying sanctioned Russian oil would also be sanctioned—a move that Washington had taken against Iran's oil production. No such threat was forthcoming. Nevertheless, the wider sanctions package upturned both Russian oil and gas exports, which had even fewer direct sanctions.[50] The Paris-based International Energy Agency (IEA), founded in response to the 1973 embargo, declared the war prompted 'a profound re-orientation of international energy trade'—with 'no going back to the way things were'.[51]

Many of the sharpest sanctions targeting Russia were aimed outside the hydrocarbons sector. Even macroeconomically inconsequential sectors were targeted, like cryptocurrencies. While Russia's experience in Venezuela showed these were not fit for any kind of new monetary basis, they did enable money laundering; as a result, Washington blacklisted a piece of code for the first time ever, with its blacklisting of the virtual currency mixer Tornado Cash in August.[52] Measures such as the vast expansion of barred 'dual-use' goods that could not be shipped to Russia were far more significant. These targeted the computer chips and semi-processors that are vital to Russia's arms industry as well as its wider economy.

These restrictions on exports to Russia will have a major impact on the Russian economy for years to come. A report prepared by Russian officials for a closed-door Kremlin meeting on 30 August that quickly leaked to Bloomberg acknowledged as much, warning that the aviation sector was critically exposed, with no alternative in sight, and that even sectors like pharmaceuticals and dairy production could be crippled.[53] It also forecast that the pain would hit even relatively low-tech goods, with restrictions on SIM cards likely to leave the country's telecoms sector well behind that of other countries and noted a lack of capacity to replace the 70 per cent of machine tools that Russia imported.[54]

It was, however, the financial sector sanctions and their extraterritoriality that formed the brunt of the Western assault and made the other restrictions hard and extremely costly to evade. The West's tools in the economic war are of a calibre that the Kremlin is unable to counter and will serve to keep Russia out of the international economic order, except for where the West grants waivers to its restrictions, for the foreseeable future. The West's response also sought to greatly weaken Russia's own ability to exert economic influence against it. While the Kremlin fought back, it lacked the ability to effectively counter many of the West's most significant actions. Chapter 1 explored how Russia's 2014 invasion pushed Ukraine into default in 2014. The West's 2022 economic war against Russia returned the favour, pushing it into default in just four months.[55]

14

RUSSIA ADRIFT

Russia had spent the previous eight years preparing for economic war. From 2014 until Putin's 2022 invasion, the Kremlin had built up a 'fortress balance sheet'.[1] In addition to building up the central bank's war chest, it gradually reduced its foreign debts, which amounted to $59.4 billion at the beginning of the war, just $18.1 billion of which was in the form of Eurobonds.[2] Russia's government debt amounted to just 17 per cent of GDP. Russian reserves could, in theory, repay its debts many times over.[3]

In building up the reserve cushion that was then decimated by the US sanctions, Russia conserved valuable capital that could have been spent on development projects. The decline in debt issuance also left money on the table. As explored in Chapter 2, after the sanctions regime slowed under the Trump administration, there was still considerable appetite for Russian debt, with all its Eurobond sales oversubscribed, meaning there were more orders to buy the Eurobonds than there were bonds available for sale. This defensive posture led many of Russia's most esteemed economists to predict that it would be able to avoid default.[4]

The Kremlin had also undertaken groundwork to improve the fighting power of its debt. Russia had been tweaking its Eurobonds to its advantage, much as had been done with the Yanukovych Eurobonds discussed in Chapter 1. Since 2017, the Kremlin's sovereign Eurobonds had included 'alternative payment currency clauses', which enabled it to repay noteholders in roubles, rather than dollars.[5] Although this implicitly threatened investors with sizable losses on their investment if triggered—something that the bonds' language left up to the Kremlin's discretion—the market placed no premium on their risk.[6] In the end, however, this innovation provided little protection because the extent of the West's sanctions showed its governments had no concern for losses borne by investors in any class of Russian debt.

The value of Russia's Eurobonds plummeted in the aftermath of the February sanctions, with many trading at under 10 per cent of their principal value, although the Kremlin in theory had enough funds to repay them even after the freezing of the central bank's reserves.[7] The Kremlin vowed to repay all its debts in roubles, even those that did not contain the alternative payment currency clauses, but ultimately made the first payments due after the invasion in dollars. Russian Finance Minister Anton Siluanov said the Kremlin wanted to retain its reputation as a 'reliable borrower', although its target audience for these comments was more likely Beijing than Western creditors.[8]

Thus Russia did not fall into immediate default. However, it lost agency over the process. In the first weeks after the invasion, the US Treasury authorised Western banks to process repayments of the Eurobonds. But that changed once Russia showed no signs of curtailing its war after the attempted *blitzkrieg* to Kyiv became mired in disaster, leading to Russia's first major defeat with its withdrawal from Ukraine's Kyiv, Zhytomyr, and Chernihiv regions at the beginning of April.[9] In May, the US Treasury signalled it would no longer authorise repayments on Russia's Eurobonds, and Russia fell into default when it was unable to pay interest to Eurobond holders.[10]

To adapt a quote from the Russian economist and politician Viktor Chernomyrdin that had become a famous refrain of 1990s Russia, the Kremlin had 'wanted the best, but it turned out as always'.[11] Putin had long legitimised his rule with a promise of stability and prosperity, vowing that Russia would not return to the economic mayhem of the decade that preceded his presidency. But four months into his war on Ukraine, the default raised uncomfortable comparisons with the period whose nadir was Russia's 1998 debt default.

Russia's war chest strategy was the wrong way to prepare for the economic war. To borrow an analogy from political economist Benjamin Cohen, it had acted as a bodybuilder. The Kremlin's focus on increasing savings while reducing borrowing was akin to a bodybuilder focusing on developing a chiselled physique but not training fighting skills. Taking on the dollar system as Putin sought required a competent wrestler's practised skill, and Russia's efforts to create alternative payment systems were lacking. Russia's balance sheet projected a strong image but was in reality no match for the West given the US dollar's dominant influence over global financial networks. The Kremlin's failures in helping Venezuela escape the impact of US sanctions should have served as a bellwether of things to come.

Russia started from a disadvantaged position, seeking to take on the dollar system that underpinned the United States' superpower status. The Kremlin also failed to realise that in leaving its foreign debt levels so low, the West had little to risk from pushing Russia into default. Had Russia's debt been a systemic risk, it might have provoked a very different response. For example, although the 1917 Bolshevik Revolution prompted a deep geopolitical fissure between the new Communist state and Western European powers when Russia repudiated its debts at the beginning of 1918, both London and Paris initially sought to protect their bondholders and even made the first missed coupon payments on Russia's behalf.[12] The matter was particularly important for Paris, where Russian debts where the second-most widely held investment, with some 1.6 million French people owning Russian government bonds, amounting to 4.5 per cent of France's national wealth.[13] The default, arguably the largest sovereign bankruptcy of all time, took more than eighty years and the Soviet Union's ultimate dissolution to be resolved.[14]

Russia's 2022 default is likely to poison its interactions with international financial markets for a long time to come as well, even if sanctions on its central bank are one day lifted. While the sanctions on Russia's central bank already block it from tapping Western credit markets explicitly, the default will see it also have to deal with creditor claims. Although Russia sought to continue making payments on its defaulted Eurobonds in roubles, the Kremlin mandated that its approval would have to be sought for funds to be repatriated as long as sanctions remain.[15] The offer had little uptake. Russia's default will be further politicised, given the raft of calls for Russia to pay war reparations to Ukraine, with many also proposing that the Kremlin assume some or all of Ukraine's debts.[16] Russia's 2022 default will have ramifications for years to come.

Countries that have messy relations with international financial institutions can see their defaults and their costs extend for decades. The Soviet debt repudiation is but the most famous example. Another more recent example is Sudan, which was cut off from international capital markets for more than thirty years, until a 2021 agreement saw both private and public creditors settle their claims and the latter offer renewed support.[17] In an indication of the importance of geopolitics to these markets, support was suspended again the following year after the Sudanese military launched a coup.[18] In contrast, debt defaults can be resolved remarkably quickly when international institutions support them, as was Russia's experience with its second default in 1998.[19]

The problems caused by Russia's sovereign default will vex the Kremlin for many years to come, even if it petitions for peace in Ukraine. The West's response to Putin's escalation of his war on Ukraine has also precipitated many other more immediate challenges for the Russian economy.

Most major Western firms left the country in the months after the war, many selling their assets at substantial losses.[20] These ranged from oil companies halting activity to retailers dumping their Russian subsidiaries, though the significance of these varied widely.

Many of the Western companies' withdrawals were not an explicit result of sanctions, as was the case with many consumer brands. While sanctions on Russian banks made it more difficult to export foreign currency earnings, the Kremlin itself continuously placed greater restrictions on such withdrawals. Many companies simply chose to walk away from Russia due to their concerns over reputational risk, which left Russia without access to Western consumer brands on a scale not seen since the Gorbachev era. For example, Starbucks disposed of its Russian subsidiary, though it soon re-opened under the ownership of businessman Anton Pinsky and the rapper Timati—who once released a song titled 'My Best Friend Is Vladimir Putin'—under the name Stars Coffee.[21] McDonald's, whose arrival in Moscow was heralded as marking the end of the Cold War when thousands queued for its 1990 debut, shut down its operations.[22] It too was rebranded, with most

franchises now operating under the name 'Tasty. And That's It'.[23]
Some Western consumer brands did remain, however, for example
French retailer Auchan.[24] The Kremlin would ultimately force them
into a catch-22, requiring companies that did sell out their assets to
pay 10 per cent of the sale price to the Russian state, leaving them
in a position of either accepting the reputational risk of continuing
to operate in Russia or leaving themselves open to accusations that
their withdrawal indirectly funded the Kremlin's war effort.[25]

More stinging impacts came from the withdrawal of industrial
firms, including all of the Western car manufacturers with operations
in the country, from Mercedes-Benz to Nissan and Renault, which
had a cooperation agreement with Russia's Avtovaz. The firm was
the parent company of the Soviet Union's workaday Lada brand.
Although the Soviet Union had managed to develop Lada and its
other automotive brands independently, they were no longer self-
sufficient in Putin's Russia. When Nissan and Renault pulled out,
Lada could no longer supply basic parts for its cars. Lada had to
halt production of its Granta model, Russia's second-best selling
car, in March.[26] By the time production resumed in June, Grantas
no longer featured seat-belt retraction locks and other key safety
components, like airbags.[27] In addition to the brands fleeing Russia,
so too did many of Russia's best and brightest, including those with
high-tech jobs. Consumer spending almost immediately fell by
10 per cent.[28]

Russia's hopes of developing its own industry to replace
Western firms that withdrew were also affected by another set of
restrictions, namely the vast expansion of trade restrictions. The
United States took the lead via its Bureau of Industry and Security
(BIS), a department within the Department of Commerce,
which imposed vast additional controls on exports to Russia and
Belarus, whose territory the Kremlin had used to launch its 2022
invasion of Ukraine, though Washington was by no means alone,
with all twenty-seven EU members, as well as the UK, Australia,
Canada, South Korea, New Zealand, Switzerland, Liechtenstein,
Singapore, Iceland, Norway, and Singapore also imposing similar
restrictions.[29] They included requirements for licenses on oil
and gas refining equipment as well as a wide array of propulsion,
telecommunications, aviation, and computer technologies.

Washington announced a 'policy of denial', signalling to industry that in all but the rarest exceptions approval for such exports would be denied.[30] The extraterritorial reach of Washington's restrictions was also particularly important, because the rules applied not only to goods manufactured in the United States but any that included 'US-origin' technology and even software, a far more wide-reaching definition.[31] Violation of these rules bore not only the potential for significant fines but criminal penalties as well. While luxury goods were also placed under BIS restrictions in March 2022, the primary aim of these restrictions was not aimed at the Russian consumer but rather at the country's industrial potential—in relation to its industrial capacity, hydrocarbons production, and its military capacity.[32] The United States had previously imposed significant restrictions on many cutting-edge technology exports to the Chinese telecommunications firm Huawei, but the restrictions imposed on Russia were far wider ranging, targeting an entire economy rather than one firm.[33]

Russia did seek to find workarounds. In June 2022 the Kremlin legalized so-called parallel imports, the purchase of goods and technology without approval of its license holder—effectively authorising piracy.[34] Trade data subsequently revealed that a number of former Soviet countries and Turkey had vastly increased their imports of a host of goods containing restricted technologies.[35] Washington in turn placed alleged violators on the BIS Entity List, meaning they too would require licenses for any future exports, and placed diplomatic pressure on the countries in which they were based to boost compliance.

Export restrictions created new headaches for the Kremlin in securing the technology it needed to wage an effective war on Ukraine, but they did not sap Putin's will for the fight.

At the end of September, Putin initiated a conscription of Russian men to fight in the war, following a series of embarrassing defeats outside Kharkiv that saw Russian forces largely expelled from that region.[36] Some 300,000 conscripts were supposed to be called up in the process, which officially ended on 31 October, but the Russian authorities did not release final numbers.[37] The call-up did, however, accelerate the exodus of Russians from the country. As many as 370,000 were estimated to have fled in the two weeks after the conscription was announced.[38] This depopulation will undoubtedly have severe long-term effects, particularly as it has sapped Russia of those with IT, tech, and engineering skills.[39] Nonetheless, Putin continuously prioritised his increasingly unrealistic view that Russians and Ukrainians are one people— describing the conflict as a civil war and bemoaning that Russians and Ukrainians 'unfortunately … ended up in separate countries'— over the Russian economy and its citizens' futures.[40]

The hydrocarbons-dependent economic model that Putin had overseen in his previous twenty-one years in office was also impacted by the West's sanctions and withdrawals. BP announced it would sell its share in Rosneft, and all other Western oil majors also halted investment in new Russian oil projects. One of the most stinging was ExxonMobil's withdrawal from the Sakhalin-1 project that it operated, resulting in output falling by more than half.[41] The company had actively opposed sanctions on Russia's oil sector after 2014 under CEO Rex Tillerson, who would go on to become Trump's first secretary of state.[42] When it announced it would support sanctions following the 2022 invasion, Putin ultimately stripped the company of its role in the joint venture, an action that may well also ultimately end up in further claims being lodged in international courts against the Kremlin.[43]

Nevertheless, overall Russian oil production was rather resilient to the withdrawal of Western companies in the short term. Despite a 10 per cent decline in production in the weeks after the war began, it soon returned to pre-war levels.[44] However, without access to Western investment and, even more importantly, technology, forecasts for Russia's long-term oil production are bleak. Russian output is forecast to decline significantly over the long term, from 10.9 million barrels per day in 2021 to 8.8 million in 2030 according to IEA forecasts.[45] This is just 43 per cent of what the IEA expects the United States will be producing in 2030, and 59 per cent of its forecast 2030 output for Saudi Arabia.[46] The loss of most of Russia's European oil export market will be even more significant, reducing Russia's ability to leverage its supplies to pressure countries in the region while increasing dependency on China and India.

But the most severe consequence of the economic war was the loss of Russia's gas market in Europe. By September, Russian gas flows to Europe were one-quarter of their 2022 level. No Russian gas had flowed through the Nord Stream pipelines since the end of August, after Putin halted deliveries on Nord Stream 1 to demand that Nord Stream 2 be allowed to open. On 26 September, explosives critically damaged the pipelines in international waters off Denmark's Bornholm island.[47] Although Germany had suspended the Nord Stream 2 project two days before Putin's invasion of Ukraine—in response to Russia's recognition of the Donetsk and Luhansk people's republic puppet states—until the explosions Putin had made repeated demands for it to open.[48] Some German politicians had even suggested caving into Putin's demands, including Walter Kubicki, vice president of the Bundestag, Germany's lower house of parliament.[49]

Were both Nord Stream 1 and 2 to flow at full capacity, Russia would have the ability to send some 110 billion cubic metres of gas under the North Sea annually. Combined with its new TurkStream route and the Balkan Stream extension, this would have enabled Russia to basically cut gas transit via Ukraine to zero. Instead, within seven months of launching his war, Putin was dependent on routes via Ukraine and the Balkan Stream, which has a capacity of only 15 billion cubic metres annually, to pipe Russian gas to Europe.[50]

The disastrous decline in Russia's gas exports was almost entirely Putin's own doing—the result of his decision to put gas supplies at the forefront of his response to the West's economic war. The West did not impose direct sanctions on Russian gas and even increased LNG purchases from Moscow in the months after the war began.[51] As with the oil price cap discussed in the previous chapter, Western action was calibrated to try and contain global market fallout. But the blacklisting of Russia's central bank, SWIFT restrictions, and sanctions' designation targeting key Russian firms and numerous businessmen were aimed at lowering Russia's state capacity in terms of its ability to finance the war in Ukraine, continue its military production, and invest in future growth. Russia's swift plunge into default demonstrated just how far-reaching Western actions could be, and how little even a would-be major power like Russia could do to resist them. Nevertheless, the effectiveness of some restrictions is in doubt, particularly the trade restrictions given that the globalised nature of supply chains has enabled evasion compared to previous such regimes.[52] Another key difference in the economic war against Russia compared to the actions the United States led in the past against countries such as Yugoslavia, Iran, and Venezuela is that Russia had a far greater ability to fight back.

15

RUSSIA'S RIPOSTES AND COMMODITIES CLASHES

Commodities have been central to Putin's economic war strategy. One of Putin's first steps was to threaten supplies of Ukraine's grain to global markets. Much of the world's most fertile soil, known as *chernozem*, or black earth, sits in the regions of Ukraine that Putin sought to annex. Before the war, Ukraine was responsible for 12 per cent of global corn exports.[1] For barley, the figure was 17 per cent, rapeseed 20 per cent, and for sunflower meal, a whopping 54 per cent.[2] Ukraine's ports, the key to bringing the grain this soil produces to global markets, were bombarded by Russian missiles on the first day of the war.[3]

The attacks by no means stopped there. Ships in Odesa Harbour, Ukraine's largest, were also struck on 25 February, including a fuel tanker and a grain ship.[4] Mines were laid outside Ukraine's ports as well: an Estonian-flagged cargo ship was hit by a mine three days later, causing it to sink.[5] Kyiv warned that Russian amphibious landings were also planned in Odesa,[6] while Russia famously seized Snake Island, south of Odesa, at the beginning of the war—prompting the Ukrainian commanders there to issue their famous reply, 'Russian warship, go fuck yourself.' Other attacks had more immediately damaging impacts—including forcing a halt in operations at the TolyattiAzot pipeline that runs from Russia's Tolyatti to the Pivdenny port in Ukraine's Odesa region.[7] It is the world's largest pipeline for ammonia, a key ingredient in global fertiliser production.

As well as blockading Ukraine's ports, Russia also laid waste to Ukrainian production. The war caused a significant decline in Ukrainian grain production and output of related goods, such as ammonia supplies at the Azot plant in Severodonetsk. The factory was heavily damaged as Russian forces pushed Ukrainian troops out of the city in June, and Ukrainian authorities later accused Russia of dismantling the remaining equipment and transferring it to Russia.[8] In the territory Russia occupied in Southern and Eastern Ukraine, the Kremlin also arranged networks to systematically loot Ukrainian grain.[9] While such destruction is a tragic component of all major conflicts, by decreasing Ukraine's grain and fertiliser output, Russia also increased the relative importance of its own supplies of these commodities.

This activity not only deprived Ukraine of its resources and the earnings they could bring in but also ensured that the impact of the war would be felt globally, which the Kremlin appeared to hope would raise pressure on Kyiv to surrender. With many countries in the Middle East dependent on Russian and Ukrainian grain, the blockade of Ukraine's ports was a valuable lever for keeping them in line and dissuading them from heeding Western calls to overtly support Kyiv. In addition to mitigating the potential for those countries to join the Western-led sanctions regime, the crisis allowed Russia to prioritise supplies to countries in the so-called 'Global South' where it was seeking to build up support, with Putin employing anti-imperialist rhetoric towards the West that he hoped would find currency there despite waging an imperial war himself. While many countries did strike agreements to increase Russian grain imports, and allies such as Syria happily picked up looted Ukrainian grain, there were also many exceptions. Ghanaian President Nana Akufo-Addo, for example, told the United Nations in September that '[e]very bullet, every bomb, every shell that hits a target in Ukraine, hits our pockets and our economies in Africa'.[10]

Russia's attempts to disrupt global grain markets were curtailed by its own military failures. Ukrainian forces retook Snake Island on 30 June after the sinking of the Russian Black Sea flagship, the *Moskva*, made its defence untenable.[11] Three weeks later, Russia agreed to the UN- and Turkish-mediated Black Sea Grain Initiative, which enabled exports to flow again from the ports in Ukraine's Odesa region. Its strategy of threatening a global food crisis was meant to help push Ukraine to admit defeat, sapping it of a key foreign currency revenue while raising global pressure for a swift end to the war. This approach failed miserably. When Ukrainian forces carried out another attack on the Black Sea Fleet in Sevastopol Harbour at the end of October, the Kremlin threatened to withdraw from the initiative.[12] However, it subsequently agreed to the extension, though it continued to call for sanctions it argued were affecting its own agriculture industry to be eased and a resumption in the TolyattiAzot pipeline's exports, despite its own bombs being to blame for its closure.[13] But with the deal extended only on a short-term basis, the Kremlin sought to retain the potential to replay its cards over global agriculture markets at a later stage.

While Russia overplayed its hands in grain markets, its strategy in gas markets would prove even more disastrous. One of the Kremlin's first responses to the sanctions imposed on its banking sector was to demand payment for its piped natural gas exports to Europe in roubles—raising many questions about why it would seek to forego hard currency payments.[14] The answer was in fact relatively straightforward, for Putin ordered that these payments be made via Gazprombank, which was unaffected by the SWIFT ban. This meant that if European buyers complied—as many initially did—they would have to keep currency trading with the bank open. It was an attempt to mitigate the threat that rouble convertibility would be fully closed off, particularly as Western European banks were unwilling to hold roubles in reserve given the sanctions regime.

But some of the Eastern European countries who had long called for a harder line on Putin's energy politics refused to comply—most notably Poland.[15] Although dependent on Russian gas, Bulgaria also refused. Bulgaria's government at the time, led by Prime Minister Kirill Petkov, could afford to take a bold line thanks to the prospect of Azeri gas shipments and the July opening of a new gas interconnector with Greece that allowed it to be supplied via LNG import terminals there.[16] Russia responded by shuttering gas flows through the Yamal–Europe pipeline,[17] its major overland gas pipeline to Europe, whose construction in the 1990s had been a first effort to bypass Ukraine in delivering gas supplies to the market.[18] Yamal's closure immediately removed the pipeline's ability to supply Europe, taking offline around a third of Russia's piped gas supplies to its markets.

The Yamal pipeline's closure, however, failed to prompt a reversal from any European buyer. Instead, it opened up the pipeline's Polish section to reverse gas flows, enabling increased supplies from Europe's increasing LNG exports to flow into the country, reversing its normal flow from east-to-west to west-to-east. Poland had also heavily diversified its gas supplies in the previous years, building LNG terminals that had already seen the arrival of American LNG beginning in 2019 at its newly constructed Świnoujście terminal. The US Energy Secretary at the time, Rick Perry, was mocked for dubbing the deliveries 'freedom gas'.[19] But Poland also recognised the importance of LNG and had increased Świnoujście's regasification capacity to 6.2 billion cubic metres.[20] However, an intra-European project, the Baltic Pipe that linked Poland to Norwegian gas supplies, was even more significant in replacing Russia's supplies.[21] Gas flows began on the route at the beginning of October. Its annual 10 billion cubic metres ended Poland's dependency on Russian gas.[22]

The Baltic Pipe opened at a crucial time. The explosions on both the Nord Stream 1 and Nord Stream 2 pipelines had occurred five days earlier, cementing the closure of gas flows through the route that the Kremlin had ordered at the end of August.[23] Danish, Swedish, and German observers have yet to announce a formal declaration of responsibility. Russia has denied any responsibility, and the Russian Defence Ministry blamed Royal Navy personnel for 'directing' the attack, albeit without evidence.[24] The Kremlin supplied no evidence for its charge. And it had plenty of history engaging in attacks it denied responsibility for, such as the Kremenchug mall and MH17 atrocities.[25]

It is not the first time Putin's Kremlin has been accused of blowing up gas pipelines. In May 2009, Turkmenistan accused Russia of responsibility for an explosion on a Turkmen pipeline that was used to deliver gas to Russia and that in turn re-exported to Europe—an incident that occurred as the United States was calling for Turkmenistan to support building new pipelines that bypassed Russia.[26] German officials have indicated that a Ukrainian group may instead have been behind the Nord Stream blasts but also noted this could have been a false flag to blame Kyiv, and suspicions remain over Russian ships' activity in the area in the lead-up to the blasts as well.[27]

Russia had spent the weeks before the explosions decreasing flows on the Nord Stream 1 pipeline as part of its demands to have

Europe open Nord Stream 2. The European benchmark gas price jumped more than 10 per cent after the Nord Stream explosions, though they were still a third lower than the all-time highs they reached at the end of August when flows stopped on Nord Stream 1. It was the final Russian gas link to Europe that Putin abrogated, following the cut-off in flows through the Yamal pipeline in April and the decrease in flows via the older pipelines through Ukraine, including via the Soyuz pipeline that Ukraine shuttered in May after Russian forces took control of its entry point in the Luhansk region.[28] That same month, the EU had set a target of filling its gas storage by 80 per cent ahead of the winter, fearful of the Russian gas cut-off that eventually materialised. But while Russian gas was still available, it had been used to fill the stores—EU gas storage levels had risen from 29.95 per cent of capacity at the end of February to 80.44 per cent at the end of August.[29] Europe paid dearly for the Russian gas as prices consistently reached new all-time highs from February through the end of August.

After Nord Stream's cut-off, European countries scrambled to secure alternative supplies, including from Azerbaijan, Algeria, Qatar, and the United States. The biggest beneficiary, however, was within Europe—Norway's gas exports reached all-time highs, as did its trade surplus.[30] The scramble managed to contain Putin's gas threat. On 29 December, European gas prices fell below their 24 February price for the first time.[31] Putin's gas threat had been contained.

Russia sought to use its leverage over gas, oil, and grain markets to amplify the economic turbulence resulting from its invasion of Ukraine. In doing so, the Kremlin relied on many of the countries with which it had developed or deepened relations. But even many of the Kremlin's previously supportive allies and partners drew well short of support for overtly violating the Western sanctions regime. Russia did, however, use many of these networks to try to circumvent the sanctions.

This was encapsulated by the break-up of one such scheme by the US Department of Justice on 19 October. It announced that Artem Uss—the son of the governor of Russia's Krasnoyarsk Krai, Alexander Uss—had been arrested in Italy at its request, while his alleged key business partner, Yury Orekhov, was detained in

Germany.[32] The pair had allegedly led a network that brokered illicit oil exports from Venezuela's state oil firm PDVSA to Russian and Chinese purchasers and then laundered the funds into a German commodity and equipment firm that the pair owned, Nord-Deutsche Industrieanlagenbau GmbH.[33] The Department of Justice stated that the firm was in turn used to acquire dual-use technologies for Russia's defence industry, whose firms were barred from acquiring such technology directly. According to the charge, 'the same electronic components obtained through the criminal scheme [were] found in Russian weapons platforms seized on the battlefield in Ukraine'.[34] The report also noted that one of the beneficiaries of the oil transactions was an unnamed Russian aluminium company controlled by a sanctioned oligarch. Orekhov had also allegedly communicated to one of his indicted Venezuelan co-conspirators that they were acting on his behalf.[35] According to a Bloomberg report, the company referenced had potentially violated the 2019 agreement brokered by Lord Barker to have the sanctions on the firm lifted as it had pledged not to violate other sanctions.[36]

Though Uss was caught, he escaped responsibility. After an Italian court moved him to house arrest while awaiting hearings on extradition to the United States, he disappeared, surfacing in Russia twelve days later and thanking 'strong and reliable people' for their assistance.[37] The effort to circumvent sanctions that Uss allegedly led was reportedly operational for at least three years and his escape from justice highlights the lengths that the Kremlin is willing to go to protect the networks involved. It was just one of many schemes that the Kremlin engineered to try to mitigate the pain of sanctions and trade restrictions.

These ran the gamut of its exports, from the all-important oil industry to the toilet paper industry, whose soft fibres are produced from the pulp of birchwood, of which Russia is a major exporter.[38] The exports had not been hit by direct sanctions, though the Biden administration did raise tariffs on Russian birch imports from 10 per cent to 50 per cent.[39] Putin, however, had banned birch exports to Europe and the United States in March.[40] According to a report by the Environmental Investigation Agency, this did not stop their flow to the United States. It found that imports of birch from Vietnam surged more than 200 per cent in the two months after the war.[41] Vietnamese exporters reportedly adapted a network that they had begun operating in 2017 to circumvent US tariffs on China for Russian birch.[42] The Environmental Investigation Agency's investigators said that managers it interviewed admitted that the vast majority of the birch had come from Russia via China, an evasion that not only helped Russian firms continue exporting but also meant their proceeds were received outside the sanctioned Russian financial sector.[43]

Sanctions and trade restrictions evasion also flowed in the opposite direction, with Russia scrambling to find ways to import chips and the technologies that depend on them from third countries willing to overlook such action—particularly in relation to export controls introduced by the EU and the United States. Exports of consumer technologies that depend on chips that Russia could no longer directly acquire via Kazakhstan and Armenia, members of its Eurasian Union, spiked after the restrictions were imposed.[44] While some of these imports could be explained by consumer re-purchases, the route also offered the Kremlin's military industrial-complex a way to evade trade controls.[45] Allen Maggard, an expert on Russian technology and procurement at the Center for Advanced Defence Studies, also notes that Russia faces a major challenge in replacing imported precision machine tools, given that the 'productivity of the Russian defence industry is ultimately governed' by access to such technologies.[46] Maggard noted that on numerous occasions in 2022 a subsidiary of a major South Korean industrial conglomerate shipped machine tools to companies linked to Russia's defence industry.[47] In turn, the United States raised its barriers for exports to Russia, adding dozens of Russian and foreign firms to the BIS 'Entity List' for which special scrutiny is required, and for whom licences are unlikely to be granted.[48]

Russia's oil sector also adapted its sanctions evasion techniques. Almost immediately after Russia's invasion in February, Russian oil tankers began disappearing from ship tracking systems.[49] The tactic had been adopted previously in attempts to evade sanctions on Venezuelan oil.[50] International commodities firms continued to ship Russian oil nonetheless, while Russia also set up its own insurance structures to mitigate against international bans on supplying such services.[51] Many of its key commodity partners did divest their stakes in important projects such as Rosneft's flagship domestic development, Vostok Oil. But their stakes typically disappeared into newly established firms in sanctions-free third countries such as the UAE and Hong Kong, whose limited corporate disclosures also made it impossible to verify their new owners.[52] Yet the trade these firms engaged in was primarily routed to Russia and India, which were able to buy Russian oil at substantial discounts to international benchmarks throughout the year.[53] These sales helped the Kremlin continue to record surpluses for much of the year, combined with increased revenues from sky-high gas prices, but most of the gain was in fact from decreased imports.[54]

But the Kremlin's most significant means for maintaining its energy export industry came not via the evasion of sanctions and trade restrictions but rather by exploiting the loopholes that remained within them. These were often due to the internal divisions within the international alliance that had imposed sanctions on Russia. For example, Orbán's Hungary refused to reduce its Russian gas purchases, which it could still receive via the Turkish Stream and Balkan Stream route via Bulgaria and Serbia. As European gas prices reached their August highs, Budapest agreed to purchase up to 2.1 billion cubic metres of gas per annum from Gazprom, while it also subsequently agreed to receive the gas supplies it had been contracted to receive from Russia's other disrupted export routes via Turkey as well.[55] The Kremlin even sweetened the deal by allowing it to defer certain payments over three years.

Chapter 5 examined how Turkey became a significant partner for Putin after 2014—and in 2022 it sat not only at the heart of Russia's continued Western gas exports but was also crucial to its attempts to escape the impact of Western financial sanctions. Despite Turkey's NATO membership and at least stated EU membership desire, Erdoğan steadfastly refused to impose sanctions on Russia, or to wholly enforce Western restrictions placed on its financial sector, even after the full-scale invasion of Ukraine. Turkish banks did comply with some Western demands, such as restricting the use of Russia's MIR bank and card payment system, but repeatedly rebuffed pressure from its NATO allies to go further.[56]

Erdoğan's relationship with Putin was no more straightforward than his off-and-on-again attempts to normalise ties with allies. Erdoğan's government did denounce Russia's 'annexation' of parts of Ukraine and has supplied crucial drones to Ukraine throughout the war. Turkey's key drone manufacturer, Baykar, even vowed to move ahead with a plan to construct a manufacturing facility in Ukraine agreed on the eve of the 24 February attack.[57] Erdoğan thus put Turkey's interests first, whether he was dealing with Russia or Ukraine.

The West's sanctions had threatened the value of dollars held within Russia, and the Kremlin wanted to make sure that it still had markets with which it could exchange them, meaning that it had more reason than ever to try to get them out of the country and into projects that could advance its interests. Erdoğan saw an opening. Russia and Turkish interests were further aligned by the fact that while Russia had a surplus of dollars it wanted to ensure it could still spend, Turkey faced a dearth of hard currency. Erdoğan's insistence on lowering interest rates to fight inflation—the inverse of the economic orthodoxy—had caused foreign capital to flee Turkey in the preceding years, while the Turkish central bank had also burned through its own foreign currency reserves trying to fight inflation that had run rampant in Turkey in the preceding years.[58]

On 3 August 2022, Russia's Gazprombank, which was not on the US SDN list and remained excluded from the SWIFT restrictions imposed on other banks due to its importance in handling energy payments, signed an agreement to fund development of the Akkuyu nuclear reactor to the tune of $9.1 billion.[59] Putin and Erdoğan had initially agreed for Russia's nuclear energy giant Rosatom to build the plant at the end of 2014.[60] According to a draft of the agreement, the money transferred would, at least in part, be used for 'placement in deposits [and the] purchase of dollar bonds of the Ministry of Treasury and Finance of the Republic of Turkey'.[61] The final announcement of the agreement avoided such explicit language, instead stating that they would be placed in 'an account that will be pledged in favour of the lender'.[62] That language nevertheless indicated they would be available for Turkish bond purchases.

Ankara did not disclose where the money went, but the following month the Turkish central bank reported it could not account for

$5.5 billion in capital inflows, a monthly record, raising suspicions that much of it was due to Russian inflows. At the end of 2022, Turkey recorded a whopping $24.2 billion in inflows of capital of unknown origin, far more than it ever had before.[63] Russia's weaponisation of gas had made such funding even more important for Turkey, given the rise in the cost of Turkey's energy imports. Erdoğan nonetheless said he would continue to pursue gas cooperation with Russia, which he saw as in Turkey's national interest.[64] With control of Russian gas flows to Europe for the foreseeable future given their newfound dependency on TurkStream, Erdoğan increased Turkey's geostrategic position in relation to both Russia and Europe as both sides were left dependent on Ankara for continued flows. Even if Russian gas exports were not going to increase, Erdoğan had been seeking to develop Turkey's own offshore discoveries. He claimed a 2020 discovery in the Black Sea contained at least 540 billion cubic metres of gas and aimed to produce 15 billion cubic metres annually by 2027.[65] If accurate, Turkey may soon be able to replace Russian supplies.

Russia's influence over key commodities markets enabled it to fight back against the West's sanctions onslaught, and the Kremlin worked hard to find workarounds to these restrictions. But its success was limited, with its leverage over grain markets at best helping retain some nations' neutrality rather than winning it new allies. Those countries sufficiently independent and powerful to trade with Russia outside the restrictions placed by the West, namely China and India, saw far more benefit. While Russia did record substantial surpluses, the dominance of the US dollar system meant that it lacked the ability to freely spend its hard currency earnings—instead having to turn to countries like Turkey to make investments that were aimed at trying to secure political rather than economic returns, but with no guarantee they would pay off.

Russia's energy weaponisation weakened its strategic position. But it deeply impacted the many European economies. Chapter 4 examined how a number of European states had sought a strategy of interdependency with Russia even after the annexation of Crimea. This would cost them dearly after the full-scale invasion in February 2022.

16

EUROPE ADRIFT

Europe was, at least until 2022, substantially dependent on Russian energy, receiving the lion's share of its oil and gas imports from Moscow. This left it particularly exposed to the fall-out of the economic war, though almost all European Union members were advocates of a strong response to the Russian invasion. The bloc's leading members and the United Kingdom effectively traded short-term economic security for physical security, as Putin's full-scale invasion of Ukraine turned into the deadliest war in the continent since 2022. But the costs were severe.

Europe's economies stumbled through 2022, with growth barely above zero. Subsequent forecasts predicted substantial recessions across the continent and in the UK.[1] Putin's disruption of gas supplies was the key factor.

As the Kremlin drove gas market turbulence alongside its invasion of Ukraine and natural gas prices reached all-time highs, the impact on Europe's economies was severe. Natural gas was responsible for 27 per cent of Germany's primary energy mix at the time, with roughly one-third of its gas sourced from Russia in 2021.[2] This dependency had only increased over the preceding decade, following former Chancellor Angela Merkel's *Energiewende* (energy transition) announcement that Germany was ending nuclear power production in the aftermath of the 2011 Fukushima Daichi disaster in Japan.

Other European countries had a relatively healthier energy mix. France, the Eurozone's second-largest economy, was less dependent on Russia. Unlike Germany, it retained a core of nuclear power infrastructure that provided the lion's share of its production. Italy, its third largest, was even more dependent than Germany, with gas accounting for 42 per cent of its energy production powered by gas, more than 90 per cent of which it imported.[3] Gas was only a small sliver of the mix in the Nordic countries and the island state of Cyprus. Yet the economic impact on Germany in particular rumbled across the continent. Germany is Europe's economic engine, and in particular that of the Eurozone with the European Central Bank dependent on Berlin for its credit-worthiness, offering a cheaper euro versus a stand-alone Deutsche Mark in exchange. This is the bargain that underpins the European Union's political economy—Germany effectively underwrites European borrowing, receiving in exchange access to a single market for its exports, with the relative currency discount thanks to the worse credit of other Eurozone members. This helps keep Germany's industrial output attractive on the international market as well. But the euro was not the only driving force in Germany's energy industry: so too was cheap energy.

One of the stars of German industry is BASF, the world's largest chemicals company. Its main hub in Ludwigshafen sits as a city of its own on the Rhine just south-west of Frankfurt, with its own hospitals, fire, and health services. In 2021, it directly employed nearly 40,000 people—roughly one-third of the firm's global headcount.[4] It consumes as much energy annually as Denmark and as much gas as all of Switzerland.[5]

Ludwigshafen may not survive the economic war. Although by the end of September, the German government had agreed a €200 billion 'defensive shield' for industry, on top of €95 billion in previously announced support for the country's energy sector, gas shortages present a very real risk.[6] A spokesperson for BASF warned that if the firm receives 'permanently less than 50% of our maximum requirements, we would need to wind down the entire site'.[7] It was able to get through the winter of 2022 as Germany had built up record gas storage, but this was enabled by Russian gas purchases before September. This is unlikely to be an option in future winters as long as Putin remains in power.

The German government was willing to break long-term taboos about increasing borrowing to finance support for industry amid the crisis. But it was unwilling to reverse the ban on nuclear power.

Only through gritted teeth did Berlin announce a delay to its phase-out of the country's last three nuclear power plants in September 2022.[8] But their lease on life was short, with the three plants coming offline on 15 April 2023—meaning they will be unable to counter potential future energy shortages in coming winters, which, while diminished, Russia still has some ability to induce. This reticence towards nuclear power stretches across the German political system—including the current coalition of the centre-left Social Democrats, liberal Free Democrats (FDP) and Greens that replaced Merkel's centre-right Christian Democratic Union (CDU)-led governments after the September 2021 election. For the CDU, reversing the policy would jeopardise Merkel's legacy, which her Social Democratic coalition partners endorsed. The FDP was supportive, but it has always been the smallest party in any German coalition it has joined, limiting its influence. The Greens meanwhile owe their political birth to the country's Cold War-era anti-nuclear movement.

The German government's failure to consider factors of geopolitical risk in policymaking extends well beyond this issue alone. In 2022, the oil refinery in Schwedt, established by the Communist East German government in 1964 and still the largest in the wider Berlin region today, returned to German state control for the first time since its privatisation in 1991, amid German reunification.[9] It had welcomed its newest owner, Sechin's Rosneft, at the end of 2016, when, five years after its initial investment in the refinery, Rosneft took majority control.[10] Sanctions had not hindered an earlier share purchase in 2014, nor had the drumbeats of war in late 2021 when Rosneft raised its stake to 91.67 per cent by buying out Shell.[11]

The imposition of sanctions on Rosneft therefore risked a disaster for Schwedt. Around 4 per cent of its 31,000 inhabitants were directly employed by the factory; counting subcontractors and service providers on the refinery, the figure was 6.5 per cent.[12] Given its strategic importance in supplying fuel to Berlin, the German government's intervention therefore came as no surprise. It had already begun helping to broker replacement crude for Russian supplies—shipped in from the United States by tanker—in August.[13] But to ensure sufficient supplies in the future, the

German government agreed to spend 400 million euros to lay new pipeline infrastructure to Germany's Rostock port, replacing the connection to Russia's Druzhba pipeline.[14] Additional support may ultimately cost Berlin billions more.[15]

Such challenges were by no means exclusive to Germany. Russia's second largest oil company, Lukoil, owned the ISAB oil refinery on the Italian island of Sicily. It provides 22 per cent of the country's road fuels. Italian officials secured exemptions for the refinery from sanctions, but Lukoil refused to sell the asset or to supply alternative crude.[16] The plant's future remains unclear. Such dealings remain key avenues of future Russian influence in Europe. In October 2022, Italy welcomed a new government led by the far-right Brothers of Italy party. Although the new prime minister, Giorgia Meloni, had spent the preceding election campaign saying she would not deviate from NATO's support for Ukraine, to build a right-wing coalition she had to turn to allies who were far more sceptical. One of them was ex-Prime Minister Silvio Berlusconi, who had visited Crimea with Putin after its annexation.[17] Another was the firebrand Matteo Salvini, Meloni's deputy prime minister. Salvini had long praised Putin, wearing a shirt with his likeness on it during a 2017 visit to Moscow where he signed a cooperation agreement between his political party and Putin's United Russia.[18] He faced a major scandal two years later in which a recording leaked of his former spokesperson ostensibly soliciting party funding in Moscow.[19] Meloni's government did honour its pledges to arm Ukraine, but Lukoil was allowed to sell the ISAB refinery at the beginning of January 2023 to an Israeli-backed private equity group for €1.5 billion.[20]

Other European countries still failed to enforce the sanctions they agreed to even as the conflict rolled on. One such case involved the Cypriot business interests of Aleksandr Annenkov, the owner of Russian transport group AnRussTrans. Although Annenkov had taken control of a firm implicated in the ferrying of Russian soldiers to Crimea in Russia's initial 2014 invasion via a holding company in Cyprus—and other Cypriot entities he controlled continued to service Crimea after its annexation in violation of EU sanctions—no action was taken against him.[21] The situation did not change even after AnRussTrans' cargo ship *Fedor* was implicated in smuggling looted Ukrainian grain to Turkey.[22] Nor was action taken when Ankara rejected the shipments and the *Fedor* began turning off its ship transponders near Syria before returning unloaded to the Black Sea.[23] Cyprus has long been a haven for Russian money and a hub of such offshore entities, and this lax enforcement helped enable Putin's war.

There were numerous other political challenges that hindered Europe's ability to act in response to Russia's economic war. The starkest example was in the Netherlands, home to Europe's largest gas fields north of the city of Groningen.

Groningen once produced nearly 88 billion cubic metres of natural gas per annum but planned to produce less than 10 per cent of that in 2022. The Dutch government confirmed in April that it would come offline in 2023 or 2024, despite the crisis in gas markets triggered by Russia's war in Ukraine.[24] Groningen's demise was not a result of exhausted resources but rather because it had become a flashpoint issue in Dutch politics. In 2015, the government of Prime Minister Mark Rutte had finally admitted that gas extraction facilities in Groningen were responsible for causing relatively minor tremors in the region, and the issue of the earthquakes—and the damage they caused to residents' well-being and house prices—had come to dominate local politics in Groningen, a key swing area in Dutch elections and one well below the national average in terms of individual income.[25] It is the only region in the Netherlands where GDP per capita failed to recover from the level recorded before the 2008 global financial crisis.[26]

Although Rutte, in office since 2010, was Europe's longest-serving prime minister, he had never commanded more than a four-seat majority in the 150-seat House of Representatives. His government felt it could not afford to risk losing support in the region, and, as a result, some 450 billion cubic metres of natural gas will remain in the ground.[27] Rather than authorise additional drilling to increase gas supplies, which would have in turn driven down European gas prices, the Dutch government gave hundreds of euros of energy tax rebates to all households, including €1,300 for each low-income household, and spent a further €406.4 million in funding for gas imports on top of a €160 million state guarantee for state energy firm Gasunie to lease a floating LNG import facility.[28]

The problem was not just one of a lack of Dutch political will. The European Union never seriously considered supporting policies that could have mitigated the cost to Groningen's residents and enabled gas production to resume, though it did approve the use of state aid for the LNG imports.[29]

Whereas ramping up production in Groningen would have the potential to significantly replace Russian imports, it was through the LNG market that Russia hoped to retain a foothold in European gas markets. Between January and September 2022, European LNG imports from Russia amounted to 16.5 billion cubic metres, 46 per cent more than in the same period a year earlier—and at far greater cost.[30] Although there is little chance that LNG from Russia will make up for its lost piped gas exposures, the continued import of LNG gives Putin another lever to influence European markets and politics by introducing volatility with threats to curtail such supplies in the future.

Perhaps the most notable victim of Putin's energy weaponisation was Germany's Uniper. The firm was spun out of German electricity utility E.ON in 2016, to handle its so-called upstream assets. This referred to the fossil fuel investments that had become a drag on E.ON amid the crash in oil and gas prices over the previous two years. A 53 per cent stake was floated on the Frankfurt Stock Exchange that September. E.ON had valued it at nearly €12 billion, but investors did not agree: on the opening day of trading, E.ON's market capitalisation, the value placed on it by shareholders, was just €3.9 billion.[31]

Uniper's disappointing debut was at least in part due to its dependency on Russian gas resources. It was also one of the investors in the Nord Stream 2 pipeline that Washington opposed. But the recovery in oil and gas prices throughout 2017—fuelled by the formation of OPEC+—saw its value steadily rise. In January 2018, E.ON accepted an offer from Finnish power firm Fortum to buy out its remaining share, at a valuation of €8 billion. By August 2020, Fortum had acquired a 75 per cent stake, effectively making Uniper a subsidiary.[32] This would prove to be a disaster.

Uniper was slammed by the impact of Russia's gas weaponisation. Incompetent management only compounded this. The firm had been among the most eager to continue doing business with

EUROPE ADRIFT

Russia and was among the first to agree to Putin's April 2022 demand that it pay for gas in roubles, thus helping Putin to shield Gazprombank from being cut off as its other banks had been. At the time, Uniper's CEO, Klaus-Dieter Maubach, defended the firm's Russian operations and maintained its positive outlook in an interview with Germany's leading business newspaper, the *Frankfurter Allgemeine Zeitung*.[33] His forecast was the very definition of improvident.

By July, volatility in energy markets had wracked its operations and profitability, prompting the German government to provide €15 billion worth of credit for Uniper to meet its liquidity demands, having already offered it €2 billion in support.[34] Berlin also took a 30 per cent stake in the firm as part of the deal, paying just €267 million—leaving Uniper with an €890 million valuation.[35] That too was soon cut when the support proved to be insufficient to deal with the volatility of the summer of 2022. In September, Germany nationalised the firm, paying Fortum €480 million for its remaining shares.[36]

Two weeks earlier, Maubach had apologised for 'defend[ing] Gazprom as a reliable supplier after the war started', stating that it was 'a mistake to think that gas would not be used, it was wishful thinking'.[37] The firm was losing more than €100 million *per day* at the time. Berlin's bailout came with an €8 billion capital increase, bringing Uniper's total bill from Russia's gas weaponisation to €29 billion.[38]

That Germany could finance such an intervention highlights the imbalance of power between the West and the Russia in terms of credit and capital. The bailout of Uniper was just one of many costly responses to the economic war in Germany. The bailout of €29 billion is roughly 1.7 per cent of Russia's entire 2021 GDP and nearly 40 per cent of Russia's officially stated defence budget for 2022.[39] While Russia had been pushed into default within weeks of the onset of the sanctions, markets largely took the Uniper bailout in their stride, even when Germany warned a month afterward that the cost of its rescue could rise to €60 billion.

Chancellor Olaf Scholz announced Berlin would pursue a *Zeitenwende* (epochal transition) in terms of its energy and Russia policies three days after Putin's 24 February attacks across Ukraine.

179

The *Zeitenwende*—a term intended to invoke Merkel's earlier *Energiewende*—declaration was meant to herald a new, more activist foreign and security policy. But Scholz was nonetheless reluctant to undertake the drastic political and economic overhauls that Berlin had so long resisted.[40] Scholz had his own legacy to protect, having served as a senior minister in the Merkel governments that had approved the continued *Ostpolitik* strategy of seeking economic interdependence with Russia. Scholz had explicitly endorsed the approach of seeking expanded energy relations with Russia as a way to deter its aggression as recently as August 2021, when he was campaigning for the chancellorship ahead of Germany's elections that September. Yet after the invasion, he sought to claim that he had foreseen the threat of Putin weaponising energy supplies.[41] However, Scholz maintained a Merkel-like unwillingness to take a more assertive stance on leading the European response. Not only did he fail to hold anyone to account for the series of *Ostpolitik* policy disasters but he also failed to announce a major new German energy strategy for overcoming the gas deficiency, merely tackling challenges as they arose, with bailouts and sporadic bursts of targeted spending.

Germany was not alone among the governments across the continent that had to bail out and underwrite dozens of energy and electricity firms. The European think tank Bruegel calculated that the twenty-seven EU member states together with Norway and the United Kingdom had cumulatively allocated €768 billion to address the energy crisis by the end of 2022.[42] Switzerland also extended some $14.5 billion in credit to the energy sector.[43] But the crisis also highlighted the continued tensions within the continent. Brussels warned that its plans for a gas price cap could not proceed unless the UK and Switzerland were brought onboard—traders would simply sell energy wherever it was more profitable. Cooperation remained Europe's key challenge. Although the EU had agreed to issue common bonds to finance its response to COVID-19, Germany's Scholz refused to support similar debt issuances to mitigate the energy crisis. The economic war with Russia was costing Europe dearly, and it was broadly united in opposing Russia's war on Ukraine, but this unity did not extend to the fundamental tensions within the European Union.

But greater unity is exactly what Europe, and the broader West, need. Europe in particular will also require support from the United States, which has increasing natural gas export capacities and has benefitted from some of the industrial troubles that Europe faced from higher energy prices, with manufacturers such as the aforementioned BASF shifting production to the United States as a result.[44] Today, Germany has the capacity but lacks the will, and Europe will likely be forced to rely on the United States once again.[45] At the same time, Russia has used the geopolitical upheaval its energy war has caused to try to build an alliance of its own, even as the world suffered from the ramifications of its renewed attack on Ukraine.

17

OIL AND GAS WAR GOES GLOBAL

Although the West's sanctions were aimed at Russia, and the aims of Russia's economic war are centred on the West, the conflict has had global ramifications.

One of the first countries to be thrown into turmoil by the economic war was Pakistan, which had been a leader in preparing for a natural gas-powered future. Islamabad began importing LNG in 2015, and, within three years, such purchases were providing 19 per cent of the country's power generation and enabling the construction of a slew of new power plants.[1] It proved an adept player at negotiating gas contracts, playing suppliers against one another to secure advantageous long-term supply agreements.[2] However, these agreements would come back to bite as gas prices rose considerably, in tune with the drumbeats of war. Suppliers used cancellation agreements contained within their supply contracts to back out of pledged deliveries, agreeing to pay penalties because the market price for spot gas sales more than made up the difference.[3] While Pakistan made up for some lost deliveries through spot market purchases at the new higher prices, it quickly found itself in an economic crisis.

As shortages wracked Pakistan, it experienced an internal political crisis. Prime Minister Imran Khan, a charismatic former international cricket star and renowned playboy recast as an Islamist populist, won office as prime minister following the country's 2018 election. As with all electoral politics in Pakistan, the military was seen to have had a hand in shifting the vote in his favour.[4] However, relations between the prime minister and the military had grown strained. In April 2022, Khan was ousted after his parliamentary allies abandoned him, enabled by the apparent withdrawal of military support for his government.[5] Khan insisted that the military had abandoned him because he had rocked Pakistan's geopolitical posture, insinuating it was a US-backed coup.[6] No evidence of such a plot was forthcoming.[7] His government had already been employing anti-US rhetoric to build domestic support—the previous year, Khan's foreign minister had declared that 'under Prime Minister Imran Khan, there will be no American base on Pakistani soil', even when no such thing was on the table. Nevertheless, Pakistan has long been dependent on US support for its military to maintain the balance of power with neighbouring India. However, Khan's visit to Moscow on 24 February—and his public meeting with Putin just hours after the Russian president launched his full-scale invasion of Ukraine—showed Khan was deadly serious about a reorientation.

Whatever the military's reason for pushing Khan out, the political turnover did not alleviate Pakistan's economic crisis. In the weeks following Khan's ouster, Pakistan was plunged into darkness, forcing a temporary curtailment of the work week and even cuts in the government's budget for security personnel.[8] Pakistan simply could not compete with the increased international prices.[9] The country's electricity demand tapered somewhat in the summer months, but this was no panacea—the decline had been caused by a series of devastating floods. It had to turn to the IMF for support, receiving a $1.2 billion bailout package at the end of August, just as international gas prices were at their peak.[10] The new government recognised it could not again be so dependent on LNG supplies and launched a new gas strategy at the beginning of August to construct 14 gigawatts of power, a tenfold increase on its installed capacity in 2021.[11] But although it said 9 gigawatts would be prioritised for rapid development, it provided no concrete timeline for when this would be achieved. The impact of the economic war on Pakistan may last for some time, as Europe's vastly expanded demand for LNG will crowd out less-wealthy countries.

Pakistan's major political rival, India, was also affected by the gas price increases. New Delhi was an even larger importer of natural gas than its neighbour in terms of total volume. Natural gas was a smaller share of India's energy mix, at just 6 per cent in 2019, but it planned to increase this to 15 per cent by 2030.[12] India too paid record prices for LNG imports throughout 2022, but, by the fourth quarter of the year, it reduced overall purchases as many industrial customers balked at paying the new, higher prices.[13] New Delhi's longstanding relations with Moscow in the crucial arms sector meant that India was unwilling to criticise Russia's invasion of Ukraine outright, abstaining in UN votes to condemn the act.[14] Prime Minister Narendra Modi did obliquely note that 'today's era is not an era of war',[15] but his government saw to it that India would refrain from taking sides and still benefit from the conflict.

This benefit primarily came in the form of increased oil purchases, with Russian oil rising from just 0.2 per cent of India's oil imports in March 2022 to 23 per cent six months later.[16] By year's end, it stood at 25 per cent.[17] The West did not oppose this— even when enacting its oil price cap on Russia, the aim was not for Russian oil to stop flowing to international markets but rather to lock in discounts that Russia had been forced to offer to buyers.[18] Nevertheless, New Delhi came under significant media criticism in the West.

Indian diplomats steadfastly defended the purchases. In a November visit to Moscow, Foreign Minister Subrahmanyam Jaishankar claimed it was his government's 'fundamental obligation to ensure that the Indian consumer has the best possible access on the most advantageous terms to international markets … if [the India–Russia relationship] works to my advantage, I would like that to keep going'.[19] But Jaishankar also noted that India's relationship with Moscow had a crucial defensive aspect, blaming the West for refusing to provide sufficient arms and instead prioritising Pakistan.[20] The embarrassing performance of Russia's military hardware on the battlefield in Ukraine, and revelations that most of its hi-tech weaponry is dependent on Western chip technology that Russia has been barred from accessing, may cause New Delhi to revisit this dependency.

India was saving on its bills by importing discounted Russian oil, which was not inherently against Western interests. The Pakistani government claimed that Washington supported Pakistan seeking similar discounts.[21] US Treasury Secretary Janet Yellen would later explicitly call on developing markets to take advantage of cheap Russian oil exports.[22] Maintaining Russian oil flows was in the US interest, especially since Russia was selling at a discount, because if Russian oil exports collapsed entirely, it would likely cause global oil prices to skyrocket, in turn plunging the United States into recession. However, Washington faced a challenge in oil markets: throughout the conflict, MBS's Saudi Arabia had moved increasingly close to Russia, seeking to use the war to maintain high oil prices to fund his transformation of the Saudi economy as outlined in his vaunted 'Vision 2030', the agenda he had announced as he consolidated power in 2016 that envisaged repositioning Saudi Arabia as a tourism, industrial, and technology power rather than merely the world's leading petrostate.

Tensions between Washington and Riyadh came to a head in October, when Saudi Arabia agreed to large oil output cuts in conjunction with Russia through OPEC+.[23] The move enraged Washington, which was concerned that further upward pressure on prices would risk economic growth while simultaneously stimulating inflation. Although Biden had travelled to Saudi Arabia in August in an effort to improve ties and lobby against Saudi–Russian oil collusion, Riyadh took little heed of Biden's calls. There was precedent for such failings. Biden had vowed to hold MBS accountable for the 2018 murder of journalist Jamal Khashoggi during his 2020 election campaign, even labelling Saudi Arabia a 'pariah state', but ultimately only issued visa bans for lower-level officials despite declassifying an intelligence report that implicated MBS in the assassination.[24] The *Wall Street Journal* reported Saudi officials floated dumping US Treasury bonds if Biden retaliated.[25] Meanwhile, Biden's fellow Democrats were willing to criticise MBS but did not act on these denunciations, while many leading Republicans continued to lobby for strong ties with Riyadh.[26] Thus Biden's promised consequences never materialised. The economic war against Russia made Washington even less likely to take action against Saudi Arabia given the increased importance of its oil output to global markets amid the West's restrictions on Russian oil.

Saudi Arabia was not alone in the Middle East in seeking to turn the crisis to its advantage. Russia and Iran also simultaneously deepened their cooperation. Tehran supplied Russia with drones for its attacks against Ukraine, with Moscow reportedly providing Iran with much-needed cash and captured Western military technology in exchange.[27] But Russia also sought to partner with arguably the United States' premier Gulf ally, the UAE. The UAE—led by Abu Dhabi's emir and Emirati President Mohammed bin Zayed (MBZ)—offered some Russian business a sanctions-free haven through which to operate, and a market free from both restrictions and disclosure rules that helped disguise transactions ranging from those involving Wagner's gold to the fate of commodity traders' Russian investments. The UAE also openly welcomed sanctioned Russian oligarchs such as Andrei Melnichenko, who moved the trading arms of both his coal firm Suek and fertiliser firm Eurochem to the country.[28] By November, the UAE had also joined Saudi Arabia in offering Russia a new market for some of its hard-to-refine heavy crude.[29] Both countries produce plenty of their own crude and used Russian imports to free up more exports, increasing their leverage over Moscow.

But oil geopolitics are no longer as important as they once were. Thanks to growing US oil production, which the IEA forecasts to continue increasing over the coming decades despite the green agenda, Washington may find other ways to shape oil markets than relying on Saudi support. It will also find more oil to export to Europe, even after recording a 52.2 per cent increase in the first nine months of 2022.[30] Furthermore, following a series of landmark discoveries in 2015, Guyana, the world's newest major oil producer, also moved to ramp up production to target European markets and is set to increase exports at a rate unmatched by any other country.[31] The geopolitical tumult resulting from Russia's energy weaponisation also opens the potential for Venezuela to increase production as Washington reconsiders its approach, though the Middle East is still expected to retain its dominant role in the coming decades.[32]

The hydrocarbon resource that will shape the geopolitics of the future the most is LNG, not oil. The fuel has become more important due to the emissions produced by gas-powered energy being lower than coal power, and proponents argue that it is more cost competitive than coal and faster to get up-and-running than many renewables. The decline in Russian piped gas supplies to Europe has also dramatically increased European demand for LNG.

This shift will have significant impacts for the Middle East's balance of power. The move to LNG will only further accentuate Qatar's importance as the dominant global gas exporter. Riyadh, which had ended MBS's three-year feud and blockade of Doha only at the beginning of 2021, sought to build closer relations with its erstwhile rival. MBS even began exploring cross-investments that could build up interdependence between the two monarchies.[33]

Yet the growing importance of LNG also plays to US strengths. Though its consumption was so voracious that it only became a net exporter in 2017,[34] in the first six months of 2022 it displaced Qatar as the world's largest LNG exporter.[35] Other developments also worked in the West's favour—China's decision to continue COVID-19 lockdowns until December 2022 resulted in a significant decrease in its LNG imports.[36] That helped free up some Australian cargoes for the European markets via swaps.[37] Europe also recorded its first direct delivery of Australian LNG when the tanker *Attalos* arrived at Britain's Isle of Grain Terminal on 24 August.[38] Mozambique's gas resources, which Sechin and the Wagner group had tried and failed to secure an interest in for the Kremlin, also finally came online in November, with their first cargo bound, unsurprisingly, for Europe.[39] Western gas and assets led by Western companies such as those in Mozambique will play a far larger role in global gas markets than Russia's.

Moscow's pipeline gas exports were also troubled, even outside of Europe where it had tried to weaponise them. Turkey cooperated with Russia in continuing its own gas exports—and even repeatedly pushed for the construction of a gas hub with Moscow's backing. With the Nord Stream and Yamal routes to Europe offline, Turkey offered the only potential export route for Russian gas to Europe except those through Ukraine. Of particular importance is the Balkan Stream route via Bulgaria and Serbia to Hungary. However, Ankara was also sitting on its own large gas discoveries, which it aimed to develop, and hoped to become the export route for discoveries in the East Mediterranean basin. Ankara aimed to be the senior partner in the gas relationship with Moscow. Even Beijing recognised the weakened position Putin had put Russia in. Despite initially agreeing to Power of Siberia 2—which Moscow hopes will add another 50 billion cubic metres of export capacity and is openly touted as a Nord Stream replacement—China dragged out negotiations beyond 2022.[40]

That September, however, China finally began building the fourth line of its Central Asian gas pipeline network, which it had delayed for years. It will add another 15 billion cubic metres in annual capacity to its existing 55 billion cubic metre capacity after nearly six years of delays.[41] The route will carry gas from Turkmenistan to China through Tajikistan and Kyrgyzstan for the first time, thus bringing them the benefit of transhipment fees and further cementing Beijing as the dominant power in Russia's supposed Central Asian 'near abroad'.

This marked a drastic turnaround for Moscow, which in January 2022 appeared to have dramatically reasserted itself in Central Asia. Russian troops led an intervention into Kazakhstan that month at the request of Kazakh President Kassym-Jomart Tokayev, helping to restore order in the face of protests that were subsequently hijacked by disaffected regime insiders. Tokayev—who was hand-picked as successor by his long-ruling predecessor Nursultan Nazarbayev in part because his diplomatic career meant he lacked a significant domestic power base—was seen as beholden to Moscow as a result.[42] Nevertheless, Tokayev said he would comply with the sanctions, explicitly declaring his intent in a June interview with Russia's main state broadcaster.[43] Shortly thereafter, Kazakh media reported Tokayev had rejected a medal Putin sought to award him.[44] Though the Kremlin denied the report, the message was clear. In response, Moscow curtailed Kazakh oil exports via the Caspian Pipeline Consortium.[45] Russia ultimately climbed down without any overt concessions from Kazakhstan—the Ukraine conflict and its sanctions-wrought economy left the Kremlin without the capacity to spar with Tokayev. By November, the balance of power had shifted. Moscow openly pleaded with Kazakhstan to lower its rail tariffs to help it ship its exports, something it would have previously demanded.[46] The Kremlin also subsequently allowed Kazakhstan to replace its sanctions-stricken oil in the Druzhba pipeline to Europe.[47]

Russia's influence was further weakened across other countries in its 'near abroad'. In September, protests broke out in front of the Russian Embassy in Yerevan, Armenia's capital, after Azeri forces moved past Russian peacekeepers placed in the disputed Nagorno-Karabakh region to take positions within Armenia proper, without a response from the Kremlin.[48] Azerbaijan's president, Ilham Aliyev, who had signed a new friendship agreement with Moscow on the eve of the invasion, took to openly belittling Russia's role in Karabakh, stating that Azerbaijan would not deal with Karabakh representatives who, in his view, were 'sent from Moscow, with pockets stuffed with billions stolen from the Russian people'.[49]

Russia was distracted. Putin saw the war over Ukraine as a battle for global influence and openly called on the so-called 'Global South' to endorse his agenda. The Russian press began floating his war aims, including declarations that the war would lead not just Saudi Arabia but Turkey and Egypt to join a would-be BRICS alliance.[50] Putin had used a June summit of BRICS members to announce his intent to create a new 'international reserve currency based on the basket of currencies of our countries'.[51] However, none of the BRICS countries took any serious steps towards doing so. Meanwhile, Beijing may have been buying up Russian commodities and increasing trade, but it continued to refrain from providing the major new financing Moscow needed to replace its loss of access to Western credit markets.[52]

Putin's strategy was misguided. China and Russia could not become the basis for a new international monetary alliance because they both run major capital surpluses and operate capital controls, meaning they lack the ability to export their savings to one another.[53] If trust were as deep as Moscow claims it to be, it would export all of its surplus to China—this would make it even more dependent on Beijing while failing to alleviate the fact that China still needs a market to export its own excess savings. And while MBS's Saudi Arabia may prefer partnering with Moscow to Washington, even if it joined a genuine BRICS alliance this would do little to alleviate its structural challenges as it too runs sizable surpluses. Though Egypt and Turkey do run deficits, they are far too small to balance out the collective surplus. Putin's approach would require markets the size of the United States, the EU, and the UK to invest their surplus. Beijing recognised this, explaining its reluctance to get on board with Putin's efforts. China wants to re-order the global international monetary system, placing itself on top, whereas Moscow has increasingly sought not just to undermine it but to challenge its very fundamentals, a process that began with the Ukrainian Eurobond discussed in Chapter 1 and has escalated ever since.

Russia is misguided in its belief that the BRICS countries could serve as an alternative basis for an international economic order able to compete with the West. The Kremlin's tactics in the economic war also caused substantial ripple effects across non-Western economies, but those states that worked with Russia were largely not partnering with it and instead taking advantage of Russia's weakened position to try and alleviate the costs that they faced. Saudi Arabia was arguably the greatest beneficiary, but as its dispute with Russia in early 2020, discussed in Chapter 11, shows, the two countries are still fundamentally competitors for shares of the international oil markets, and such competition will likely grow as global oil demand is forecast to decrease. But despite Putin's misunderstanding of the structures of the international political and economic order, he does appear to at least understand how short-term economic trends can play to his advantage. He prepared his full-scale invasion of Ukraine as inflation was spiking amid the end of COVID-19 restrictions in most of the world at the end of 2021. He sought to take advantage of the timing because he recognised that any subsequent economic war would be highly inflationary and that the West—which had enjoyed an ultra-low inflation environment for the previous fourteen years, a result of sluggish growth in the aftermath of the 2008 global financial crisis—was unprepared for this challenge.

18

THE INFLATION WEAPON

Liz Truss resigned as British prime minister on 20 October 2022—
after just forty-five days in office. Six days earlier, she had sacked
her confidant, neighbour, and ideological fellow traveller Kwasi
Kwarteng as chancellor. In doing so, she jettisoned the radical
low-tax economic policy their government had announced on 23
September. The crisis of governance should have been foreseen.
Truss had spent the previous years on a series of ministerial
sojourns that she appeared to view with the seriousness of a British
costume or 'fancy dress' party—she was regularly photographed in
outfits miming those worn by her Conservative heroine Margaret
Thatcher. These photo-ops regularly took priority over her policy
agenda.[1] During a Moscow trip while serving as foreign secretary
on the eve of Putin's invasion, Truss fumbled a question about
Rostov and Voronezh, responding, 'the U.K. will never recognize
Russian sovereignty over these regions'—unaware that they had
been undisputed Russian territory for centuries. However, she did
manage to get a photo recreating Thatcher's 1987 visit, donning
a fur cap-and-coat-combo in front of St Basil's Cathedral outside
the Kremlin.[2]

Truss's incompetence led her to misunderstand the basics
of Russia policy—but she did at least seem to recognise that the
Kremlin played a role in making her economic agenda impossible,
albeit at too late a stage to save her administration.

In her final speech in office, Truss made clear that she saw the
Kremlin as partly responsible for her resignation, stating that
Putin's illegal war in Ukraine was the foremost cause of the 'time of
great economic and international instability' in which she stumbled

into power.[3] Truss's resignation was a direct result of her bungled economic policy, as Kwarteng later admitted—but Putin's economic war was indeed a factor.[4] The global inflationary environment caused by Putin's energy weaponisation and energy price hikes had forced central banks to raise interest rates repeatedly throughout 2022 after keeping them at near zero in the thirteen years following the 2008 global financial crisis.

Truss and Kwarteng's agenda was based on using fiscal policy to expand the money supply, yet rising interest rates served to constrain it. IMF Director Kristalina Georgieva had tried to warn them off the plan, declaring that the IMF's 'message to everybody [is] ... fiscal policy should not undermine monetary policy'.[5] The dollar's dominance imposes policy constraints not only on opponents targeted by sanctions such as Russia but also on allies. Because Britain's currency lacks the genuine reserve status of the US dollar, Truss's agenda of expanding UK money supply was a fundamental threat to the value of the pound, which the markets had recognised, sending the currency crashing in the aftermath of Kwarteng's 23 September announcement. Georgieva's comment was intended to highlight how Truss and Kwarteng's agenda was also illogical given the global environment at the time—for it to have any chance of being effective, the UK would have had to halt interest rate increases. Doing so would have further weakened the pound, however, as UK-domiciled capital would likely flee for the relatively higher and safer interest rates on offer in the United States, whose central bank, the Federal Reserve, was signalling further hikes to come.

As the determiners of interest rates and the market's lender of last resort, central banks' actions shape savings policy, exchange rates, and borrowing rates more than any other institution. While governments are responsible for setting the fiscal policy their voters elect them to enact, central banks are responsible for setting monetary policy independent of the government in office at the time.

The pre-eminence of monetary policy over fiscal policy has been demonstrated repeatedly in recent decades, particularly in times of crisis, as shown by Greece's failed attempts to countervail the European central bank's diktats in the wake of the global financial crisis and subsequent Great Recession, or inversely central banks' linchpin role in cushioning the deflationary impact of the COVID-19 pandemic and ensuing lockdowns through record-expansions in their balance sheets. This response was warranted as the pandemic threatened to send economies into a deflationary spiral, but the recovery as restrictions were lifted at the end of 2021 had unleashed inflation as global supply chains struggled to catch up.

Putin's 2022 invasion of Ukraine coincided with this inflationary environment and the restrictions that it would place on central banks' and governments' ability to respond. Russia had also done its part to help fuel the problem, throttling gas supplies to Europe in the last half of 2021 to drive up prices.[6] The Kremlin was prescient in recognising that the development of LNG markets, while a long-term risk to its ability to use gas pipelines as leverage, had helped create a global energy market that meant rising prices in Europe would trickle across the globe.

Britain, however, appeared better prepared than most for the newfound importance of LNG—a market that it had in fact helped birth. The first ever LNG delivery was carried by the *Methane Pioneer*, arriving at Britain's Canvey Island from Louisiana in 1959.[7] Britain became the first country with commercial LNG importation five years later.[8]

British officials were complacent about their insulation from Putin's energy threats—the UK received only 4 per cent of its gas from Russia in 2021.[9] However, over the preceding twenty years, gas markets had become more globalised, with prices in one region increasingly affecting those in others.[10] By the end of 2021, the development of the LNG market, the preference for short-term contracts, and the emergence of financial markets to arbitrage price differences had globalised gas prices.[11] Britain also had the second-largest LNG import capacity of any European country, at 35.5 billion cubic metres per annum as of 2021, just behind Spain's 44.3 billion cubic metres.[12] Although this was enough for some 59 per cent of Britain's total gas demand, it imported far less—thanks to its domestic production in the North Sea and imports from Europe.[13]

Nevertheless, gas prices were even higher in Britain than the rest of Europe through 2021. The reason was straightforward: Britain, unlike most of the rest of Europe, lacked any considerable capacity to store gas. In 2017, Britain's sole gas storage facility was shuttered by its owner, Centrica. British ministers, including Truss, who was serving as Chief Secretary to the Treasury when the decision was made, assessed the impact at the time and raised no objections.[14]

Britain was left in a weak position, and energy price increases were at the core of it. When Kwarteng's successor as chancellor, Jeremy Hunt, finally announced his restructured budget in November, it was accompanied by a report from the Office of Budget Responsibility (OBR), something Kwarteng had refused to do. The bleak picture the report painted when it was finally published was likely a key reason Kwarteng chose not to release it, as it would have made Truss and Kwarteng's aborted economic agenda—which had included an elimination of the highest tax rate and a lift on bankers' bonus limits—look even more regressive.

The OBR report noted that inflation, at a forty-year high of 11 per cent, was driven primarily by energy prices and warned it would have been 2.5 percentage points higher were it not for the government's Energy Price Guarantee. Introduced during Truss's fleeting premiership, the guarantee capped household bills and bailed out the energy industry in return.[15] The guarantee only blunted the pain, however, with the Progressive Economy Foundation warning that the country's poorest faced spending 47 per cent of their disposable income in the winter on energy bills.[16] The OBR warned that 'higher energy prices lower the effective productivity of the economy by reducing the volume of goods and services that it is profitable for firms to supply when the price of an important, and largely imported, input rises'.[17] Cost estimates for the guarantee ran to as much as £150 billion,[18] though this would depend on the long-term price of gas. Centrica's gas storage facility did reopen in time for the winter of 2022 but only at 20 per cent of its previous 120 billion cubic metre capacity.[19]

Britain was by no means alone in suffering from the energy crisis—inflation in the United States peaked at 9.1 per cent in June. Britain's European neighbours may have had more gas storage but faced excruciating bills while trying to fill it ahead of the winter. In the Eurozone, inflation reached an all-time high of 10.6 per cent in October 2022.[20]

The economic impact of the inflation was severe and served as Putin's primary threat to Europe's commitment to the sanctions regime. During European discussions of which sanctions to impose on Russia, jockeying among the EU's members repeatedly led to exclusions for their own industries.[21] European disunity also remained a theme, as the EU struggled to agree on a unified policy to counter the impact, failing to agree on proposals for the creation of a European gas company.[22] Their scramble for gas was, however, not just a short-term strategy—the EU as a whole, with the notable exception of Hungary, began to plan for a new long-term future less dependent on Russian gas.

Germany agreed on and launched its first LNG import facility after the Russian invasion of Ukraine in February 2022. It began operating on 15 November, 200 days after the start of construction. It also planned to launch four more LNG facilities over the following year.[23] The Netherlands, France, Greece, and Poland all stepped up their own efforts to develop import facilities, as did Spain and Italy, which sought further imports from North Africa. Algeria even agreed to begin resupplying to Slovenia, where its gas had been priced out by Russian supplies since 2012.[24]

As with Britain, European politics were subject to fluctuations in gas prices in combating inflation. Central banks' interest rate increases drove down money growth in other sectors by diminishing bank lending and economic growth. Putin's strategy may have failed to break Europe's back on the sanctions strategy and on arms supplies for Kyiv, which steadily grew throughout the year, despite initial reticence from Berlin and Paris in particular. But whereas one of the main impacts in the West's previous major sanctions regime—that imposed against Iran over its nuclear ambitions—had been to stimulate crippling inflation, Putin had turned the 'inflation weapon' back on the West while limiting its ability to stimulate growth to make up for it.[25]

The same high energy prices that underpinned European inflation meanwhile served to alleviate inflation in Russia. Although there was a major initial spike following the central bank and financial sector sanctions imposed on it in February and its subsequent default, by the summer of 2020 inflation in Russia had begun to fall, albeit not to pre-invasion levels. Record balance-of-trade surpluses meant the Kremlin was flush with hard currency, despite sanctions, because it could still bank the oil and gas price increases Russia's war had created. However, Russia was left more dependent on commodity earnings than it had ever been before, and the sanctions left Moscow highly constrained in how it could spend them. Yet, as export earnings fell in line with Russia's declining energy deliveries to Europe in the second half of 2022, Putin refused to acknowledge that his own energy weaponisation was responsible.

Putin felt the blame lay elsewhere. He saw the sanctions imposed over his war as unjust, clear in his longstanding complaint that the global financial system was also unjust—though he always left his own energy weaponisation unmentioned. In March, he declared that '[i]mposing sanctions is the logical continuation and the distillation of the irresponsible and short-sighted policy of the US and EU countries' governments and central banks. They themselves have driven up global inflation.'[26] In a June speech, he stated that 'a direct result of the European politicians' actions and events this year will be the further growth of inequality in these countries, which will, in turn, split their societies still more, and the point at issue is not only the well-being but also the value orientation of various groups in these societies'.[27]

As the economic consequences of the sanctions started to be felt domestically, the Kremlin began to obfuscate its own economic data, and Russia was forced into grinding austerity.[28] It prioritised military spending above all else, even while tacitly acknowledging the failures of its weapons procurement strategy of the previous decade by quietly scrapping its state arms production programme on 10 November.[29] Putin ordered a complete rewrite within four days 'in line with the actual needs' of its armed forces.[30] Yet he was happy to let Russian consumers suffer.

Despite the Russian central bank plunging its interest rates back to pre-February levels, corporate lending cratered, as did the mortgage market and loans for increasingly scarce automobiles.[31] Consumer technologies such as iPhones that Russians clamoured for went up steeply in price and, despite the Kremlin's attempts to enable 'parallel imports', the number of new iPhones registered to Russian accounts fell fourfold in 2022 compared to 2021.[32] Putin was willingly overseeing a transition from an autocratic capitalist system to an autarkic state economy. Some trappings of the markets will remain, but Russian purchasing power was being eviscerated even if not by inflation.

By the winter of 2022, Putin's inflation weapon was failing. Energy and food price increases in the first six months after Russia's February invasion had been at the core of inflation rises.[33] Its decrease was also in large part because the West's efforts to diversify away from Russian hydrocarbons were more successful than initially forecast—and because the impact of Russia's war on global food supplies was curtailed by the Black Sea Grain Initiative that kept Ukrainian grain flowing. Inflation in the United States, the UK, and the Eurozone began to fall in December compared to the previous month's records.

Putin appeared to believe that inflation would help bring about trends in the West that would sap support for the sanctions against Russia. In a speech on 27 October 2022, he described the economic war as the cause of inflation, stating that it was 'the systemic mistakes of [Western] political leaders, the political leadership of [Western] countries in the energy and food sectors and in monetary policy that led to an unprecedented growth of inflation'.[34] He subsequently remarked that 'international politics ... should certainly be based on the opinion of ordinary voters ... [and] that ordinary people should know ... Russia is not the enemy.'[35]

The economic war's inflationary impact was picked up on by politicians on the far right and far left across Europe and the United States to criticise continued support for Ukraine, but public support for sanctions remained high across the West. An October poll of Germans found that although a majority thought they would suffer more economically from their imposition than Russia would, 33 per cent wanted them maintained and another 30 per cent backed tightening the sanctions even further.[36] In the United States' November mid-term elections, sanctions were not a major issue of disagreement between Republicans and Democrats, with the exception of the former's most extreme Trumpian fringe, which called for reducing support for Ukraine—most of whose candidates were defeated.

Putin did not just miscalculate how inflation would affect support for Ukraine and the sanctions strategy but also Russia's ability to counteract the dollar system. In the same October speech, he argued that 'the United States made a huge mistake by using the dollar as a weapon in fighting for its political interests', stating that Russia would lead on creating a new 'supranational global monetary system' and that growing trade with India and China on rouble, rupee, and yuan terms was already paving the way.[37]

The dollar's share of global reserves remained steady, even experiencing a slight uptick following the invasion.[38] While there had been diversification away from the dollar in the Trump years, three-quarters of it was into the currencies of Canada, Australia, Sweden, South Korea, and Singapore.[39] These were not only countries that had joined the sanctions regime against Russia but that also, crucially, had received the US Federal Reserve's blessing for swap lines, meaning that they could effectively draw on dollars in the event of a crisis.[40]

The dollar's continued dominance gave it an outsize role to play in shaping the international response to the crisis. Although US inflation was lower than in Europe, the Fed's interest rate increases meant that the impact of crisis was felt even in markets with relatively low inflation. As South Korea's central bank governor noted in August, his bank was 'independent from the government, but we are not independent from the Fed'[41]—meaning that it would have to keep up with its interest rate increases despite significantly lower inflation. Only Japan resisted following along, keeping its interest rates near-zero. But this was an intentional policy by the Japanese central bank, which had long been actively seeking to increase inflation, because it hoped it would increase consumer demand and lower wage pressures. Although Japan nonetheless remained a rare island of low inflation throughout 2022, the yen fell to decade lows against the US dollar. Contrary to Putin's prognostications, the dollar moved from strength to strength.

The dollar's dominance does give Washington a hugely significant amount of political influence over global markets, but it also gives it a responsibility to ensure international stability. This is where Russia's strategy posts its most lasting threats. The dollar system could be described using the mathematician Nassim Nicholas Taleb's idea of 'anti-fragility'. Taleb argues things that survive a certain level of shock are 'robust', but those that gain from shocks are 'anti-fragile'. The dollar system frequently exhibits this characteristic. Various recent global economic crises have also seen a flight to the dollar or US Treasury bond as a safe haven, including during the post-2008 Great Recession despite its origins in US mortgage markets. Russia's economic war is no different. But while Putin's onslaughts on the international monetary system and on Ukraine continue, Washington will have to ensure that global faith in the dollar is retained.

As 2022 drew to a close, fears began to mount in Europe over the amount of industrial production that was shifting to the United States.[42] These strains and those from secondary impacts could also affect the dollar system. Despite all her other failings, Truss was right to blame Russia for her inability to pursue fiscal expansion— but the UK's policy choices were also constrained by the dollar system, as rising US rates meant Britain had little choice but to follow suit if it did not want the value of the pound to plummet. Every other country faces similar constraints no matter how friendly it is with Washington. One impact of the economic war will be to further drive investment to the United States, with its cheaper energy resources and both Republicans' and Democrats' embrace of neo-mercantilist policies that seek to move production of critical industries to the United States. But if Washington wants to maintain the exorbitant privilege of the dollar system, it will have to ensure that it acts with a sense of responsibility for its allies and make sure they are not left to face the brunt of Russia's economic war while the United States profits.

Russia cannot win the economic war with the tools at its disposal. The West, however, could still lose it. European disunity and tensions between the continent and the United States could once again offer the Kremlin ways to increase its leverage over the continent as it did after the 2014 annexation of Crimea. The United States' willingness to continue to impose sanctions against Russia may wane before Putin gives up on his war in Ukraine, something that he has shown no inclination for. Such an outcome would lead to more attempts by Russia to disrupt the international economic order, not fewer.

CONCLUSION

As of the time of publication, the economic war is not over. It is unlikely to end while Putin remains in the Kremlin. Its outcome will be a decisive factor in determining Ukraine's future. Kyiv may be able to beat back Putin's onslaught, but, if Russia has the economic wherewithal to regroup and attack again, it will. The outcome of the economic war will also shape Russia's own future. Even when it does end, the Western-held debts and shares that have been frozen will be far more significant factors in determining the world's relationship to a post-Putin Russia than they were in shaping its relationship to the post-Soviet one. And while Putin has failed in his attempts to collapse the global economic order, he has wrecked his own economy, sowing seeds of destruction that will continue to sprout even after he is gone.

Putin has used economic levers over other states ever since he assumed the presidency. Since staking his rule on an existential war of destruction against supposedly fraternal Ukraine, he has bet the house of Russia's economy. He shows no signs of folding. Russia's aggression has only hardened the West's resolve in sanctioning and weakening the Russian economy; even non-aligned countries have increasingly shied away from Putin's genocidal and self-destructive mania.

Although the economic war consists of a large coalition, it is powered largely by the United States. The power of the dollar and its central role in global financial and monetary markets gives it the ability to constrain even Russia's would-be allies. In the run-up to his invasion of Ukraine on 24 February 2022, Putin's securing of a 'friendship without limits' declaration from Beijing reportedly included a secret protocol with a mutual defence commitment along the lines of those that underpin the North Atlantic Treaty.[1] But there were limits, and the pledge reportedly included conditions that excluded territories recently annexed during war, a proviso Beijing allegedly insisted upon.[2] Although trade between the two countries rose 29.3 per cent in 2020, exports from China to Russia grew only 12.8 per cent while those from Russia to China surged 43.4 per cent.[3] Beijing lapped up Russia's discounted commodities but offered Putin little of the support that he needed to advance his economic agenda: fewer new loans were agreed in 2022 than in 2014, Beijing offered no overt materiel support for Russia's war in Ukraine, and no progress was made regarding the future of the proposed Power of Siberia 2 pipeline. The economic war has shown there are also limits to China's willingness to support the Russian economy—and Beijing's reticence to support Putin's war indicates it may see the conflict as more of a threat to its attempts to become the world's pre-eminent economic power.

Unlike Russia, China is a serious economic threat to the West and in particular the United States' dollar-derived 'exorbitant privilege'. It has spent years increasing its loans abroad, structured its own arbitration tribunals and bilateral investment treaties independent of the systems of governance the West prefers, and takes a radically different approach to sovereign-to-sovereign lending—evidence of a clear and concerted strategy to try to improve its position in the international monetary and financial hierarchy. However, Beijing has not sought to escalate its trade wars with Washington into an economic war as Russia did. While its holdings of US Treasury bonds fell 17 per cent in 2022, there have been previous similar fluctuations—and it in fact increased holdings of other US government-backed debts that the Federal Reserve has been selling as part of its quantitative tightening policy.[4] On trade and technology, China is undoubtedly increasingly a competitor, but on the macro-level it is in many ways still a partner to the United States.

Beijing may turn into a more hostile actor as tensions between China and the West continue to grow. The relationship could be shattered if Beijing's bellicosity towards Taiwan leads it down a path similar to Putin's towards Ukraine. For now, China still puts a premium on Western economic linkages, from the Hong Kong dollar and its peg to the dollar to access to US capital and consumer markets. As long as Beijing retains capital controls for its own market—which mean that the renminbi and Chinese assets cannot serve as an international reserve currency anywhere near the scale of the dollar—it will remain tomorrow's grave economic threat.

Despite his defeats, Putin remains a threat to the US-led international economic order as well. However, the most immediate threat to the West's advantageous geo-economic position comes from within. The damage from the economic war is affecting Europe far more than the United States, and Washington stands to benefit while Europe suffers more acutely. The higher energy prices Europe faces, both in the short term and in the need to invest substantially in new infrastructure to replace Russian gas sources, will make Europe's economy increasingly uncompetitive. Efforts by Washington aimed at protecting the United States from China's economic threats will also serve to incentivise production in Europe to shift across the Atlantic. This is not just tomorrow's problem. The impacts of the Biden administration's flagship legislation, the 2022 Inflation Reduction Act, are already leading to tensions between the United States and the EU, as the bill effectively serves to subsidise production for strategically important industries like microchips and batteries, which, in turn, will complicate Europe's own attempts to stimulate such production.[5]

Europe faces other strategic and structural issues that make it the West's weak link. European Union sanctions still require annual reaffirmation from the bloc's twenty-seven member states. The threat of war fatigue looms, and Europe's economic challenges offer a renewed opening for populist parties eager to partner with Moscow when they see a strategic benefit. The most immediate threat to Europe's economic war strategy comes from Hungary, whose demand to continue importing Russian gas has left the South Stream and Balkan Stream routes into Europe open for Russian gas. Budapest's gas network is linked to Austria's, where the far-right Freedom Party (FPÖ) remains an electoral force.

The FPÖ's leader, Herbert Kickl, has declared his belief that Austria still 'needs a thriving future association with Russia'.[6] While Vienna was supportive throughout 2022 of abstaining from Russian gas purchases, the FPÖ could grant Russia a route back to Central Europe's main gas hub in the future. Demonstrating Austria's hesitation to abandon the Russian market, its second-largest bank continued lending in Russia, even to Russian soldiers, more than a year after Russia's vastly expanded invasion of Ukraine.[7] A senior executive at the bank told the *Financial Times* that Raiffeisen's Russian subsidiary was even handling '40–50% of all the money flows between Russia and the rest of the world'.[8]

Other threats to Western unity are graver still, and more fundamental. Pro-Putin parties sit at the heart of Italy's ruling coalition, while France's main opposition party, the far-right National Rally, is indebted to a Russian military contractor, a loan it is only due to finish repaying in 2028.[9] But it is Germany—where outright pro-Russian support is relegated to the political fringe—that poses the greatest challenge.

Germany is Europe's undisputed economic leader and should be its political leader too. Yet despite Chancellor Scholz's *Zeitenwende* recognising that business as before with Moscow cannot resume while Putin is in the Kremlin, the elite in Berlin remains reticent in the latter regard. Berlin's elites have failed to own up to their mistakes, which has made addressing them all the more challenging. In a November 2022 interview, ex-Chancellor Merkel claimed that her government's diplomacy had saved Ukraine from an earlier crushing Russian attack, ignoring the fact that Russia gained eight years to build up its military for attacks against Ukraine. She did not acknowledge that her energy policy also fuelled Russia's financial firepower, nor that her support for building up economic interdependencies with Putin's Kremlin had weakened Germany's strategic position.[10] Scholz's government is also unwilling to undertake the more radical changes that Germany's energy industry needs if the country is to remain the bloc's economic engine. There is a clear need for Germany to endorse a change in its approach to Europe as well—explicitly supporting the development of an EU debt issuance would help the bloc finance its energy transition and build up resilience from future geo-economic threats.

First and foremost, Europe must tackle the structural challenges facing its energy industry. Germany's failure to embrace nuclear power and shutter its remaining power plants in 2023 was a crucial mistake. While it is not a panacea to Europe's energy needs— France itself is a case in point, given that its nuclear power plants were affected by severe outages throughout 2022 that caused their output to fall 23 per cent—Germany's decision will make it even more dependent on global gas prices.[11] And despite their challenges, France's plants still produced more than Germany's entire renewables sector at 279 to 256 terawatt hours—although Germany was Europe's leader in the field with renewables contributing 44.6 per cent of its electricity production.[12] Nuclear power is also susceptible to Russia's energy weaponisation threats, given Rosatom's outsize role in the industry and Russia's own influence over uranium resources. While Russia is only the sixth largest producer of uranium, neighbouring Kazakhstan is responsible for 45 per cent.[13] Dependency on nuclear energy should be avoided, but it should be part of the future mix alongside the transition to renewable energies. Although atomic energy should be a key strategic priority for the West going forward, the most significant way to reduce future geo-economic threats to energy production is ensuring diversification and a lack of reliance on any one source.

But the ramifications of the energy war will be felt far outside of Europe as well. Russia still poses a threat to its neighbours outside Ukraine. Arguably the most vulnerable is Kazakhstan. Since the invasion, it has sought to move away from its Russian dependency at an unprecedented pace. Kazakhstan's fellow Central Asian states also face risks from the fallout, as Russia's economic challenges and the sanctions make Central Asia increasingly dependent on China. Europe and the United States have aimed to ramp up their economic diplomacy, including working together to try to find new oil export routes,[14] finally breaking from viewing the region primarily through a security lens. However, the region's geography is unchangeable, and for exports to be re-routed away from Russia they will have to go through either Iran, Afghanistan, or China— none of which is an appealing prospect to Western policymakers— or via the Caspian Sea, which Moscow presently blocks. Yet even some observers in Moscow have begun to acknowledge that Putin's strategy is weakening Russia's influence throughout Eurasia.

The Caspian is likely to be a key point of contention. It already saw a substantial increase in Central Asian countries re-routing key oil- and gas-derived products to Azerbaijan over its waters. However, Russia retains enough influence that regional states are unwilling to explicitly act against its interests—for example by finally endorsing the construction of trans-Caspian gas pipelines. The region's issues are themselves complex, and increasing Europe's strategic dependency on gas shipped from Azerbaijan has its own risks. In 2022, Azerbaijan invaded its neighbour, Armenia, and it is ruled by a regime no less kleptocratic than Moscow's. Baku also lacks the gas resources to fulfil its pledges to Europe without importing Russian gas, undermining its potential as a panacea to Europe's energy woes.[15] Adding Central Asian gas to the mix, however, would alleviate this challenge—and also incentivise Azerbaijan not to further risk its gas relationship with Europe through additional aggression against Armenia. But first and foremost, a more active Western diplomatic role in the region is needed.

The same applies to Western engagement with estranged Turkey. Its recent gas discoveries and control of pipelines from Azerbaijan and Russia mean its vital strategic position cannot be ignored. And while Erdoğan mismanaged the Turkish economy, his political dealings bought his government lifelines in the form of financial support from a wide array of actors including Qatar, Saudi Arabia, China, the UAE, and Russia—almost all the major regional actors except the United States and the European countries he is formally allied to through NATO. Whether Ankara continues to play both sides off of one another or shifts to being a more genuine ally to the West may prove pivotal.

The economic war has also upturned the balance of power in Middle Eastern energy geopolitics. Gas will be far more important than oil for the foreseeable future. The Middle East's largest gas exporter, Qatar, hosted the football World Cup at the end of 2022—an event that symbolised the success of its strategy of placing natural gas at the heart of its economy. Despite criticisms of Qatar's human rights record ahead of and during the event—hundreds of thousands of migrant workers toiled in poor conditions and as many as 6,500 may have died[16]—Qatar is unlikely to face any negative political or economic consequences. Without its gas, the energy crisis in Europe would have been even more devastating. Recognising this, Germany signed a fifteen-year gas supply deal with Qatar in the middle of the World Cup.[17]

Qatar's rise will cause a chain reaction in the region. Rival Saudi Arabia is also seeking to increase its position as a gas player, aiming to raise production levels by 50 per cent by 2030.[18] Riyadh hopes that its energy significance will continue to shield de facto ruler MBS from again being treated as an international pariah, as he was in the aftermath of the Khashoggi murder. There is ample precedent for energy interests to manifest such an about-face in the West's approach. For example, Maduro's Venezuela secured some sanction relief at the end of 2022, given the renewed importance of its energy resources. Yet things are trending in the wrong direction for the West in the region. Despite the US role as Saudi Arabia's and the UAE's key security guarantors, both showed an increasing willingness to act in contravention of US interests throughout 2022.

The West faces other headaches in the Middle East as well. Among these is its relationship with Israel, which produces the world's best missile and drone defence system, the Iron Dome. Despite the Kremlin's antisemitic propaganda targeting Ukraine and President Zelensky, who is Jewish, and crackdowns on Russia's Jewish community throughout 2022, Tel Aviv refused to supply Kyiv with key air defence systems, and it did not join the sanctions regime against Russia. In November 2022, Benjamin Netanyahu, who is known to be an admirer of Putin, returned as prime minister. Netanyahu's return, Israel's recent political instability, and the creeping annexation of Palestinian territory threaten its position as a Western ally. Yet its drones, cyber and other defence technology are increasingly important geopolitical prizes—and the West's rivals could exploit tensions to try and gain more access.

Yet not all is bleak. India has, like China, boosted its commodities purchases from Russia but has been shifting away from its dependency on Russian weaponry and is increasingly positioning itself as a partner, if not quite an ally, of the West given shared concerns over Beijing.[19] Putin's vision of a new economic order is unlikely to be realised; at best, he can hope for a bipolar order between China and the West, but this would leave Russia subservient to Beijing—and his attempts to accelerate divergence in 2022 were a marked failure. The dollar system survived the year unscathed, even strengthened. This supports the economist Peter Bernholz's argument against one of economics' longstanding maxims—that bad money drives out good, known as Gresham's law. Bernholz posited that the inverse is true internationally, where good money drives out bad as states need money that is accepted abroad.[20] And there is no money as good as the dollar.

However, the dollar's position also faces internal threats. Former President Trump may have faced a setback when his favoured candidates underperformed in the 2022 midterms, but, immediately thereafter, he announced he would seek the presidency again. And, while he is the flagbearer for the Republican Party's soft-on-Russia agenda, the rest of the party also risks discarding the international support necessary to maintain the dollar's hegemony. A former Reagan administration aide, who backed impeaching Trump in 2019, even published an op-ed in November 2022 calling for the United States to withdraw from NATO to end the conflict in Ukraine.[21] Trump reportedly considered precisely such a withdrawal from NATO during his time in office and has since openly spoken of allowing Putin to annex parts of Ukraine to achieve peace.[22] Such moves would not halt Putin's agenda, but enflame it, and it would shatter Washington's bedrock security guarantees for Europe and in turn the Atlantic Alliance.

Putin's full-scale invasion of Ukraine and the ensuing economic war should prompt consideration about how to strengthen, not weaken, the United States' security alliances as well as its economic ones. A serious conversation about the threats to the dollar system is sorely lacking, though not quite as absent as healthy debate about how to strengthen it—a challenge present on both sides of the aisle. It is ludicrous—and manifestly as against the US interest as withdrawing from NATO—that regulatory agencies in the United States have even considered supporting cryptocurrencies, as have both leading Democratic and Republican politicians. Not only would this help actors such as Russia evade sanctions but, if their proponents' fantasies of creating a new non-dollar based financial system are realised, it would weaken US geopolitical power far more than even a drastic cut in the US defence budget. The irony is that whereas so many in the West are oblivious to the geopolitical significance of the dollar, Russia very much is not. In a pair of 27 October speeches, Putin referred to the dollar-based international economic order as an 'unfair hegemonic system',[23] while his trusted aide-de-camp Sechin claimed that sanctions imposed on Russia were representative of US efforts to retain its hegemony and that they threaten 'to abolish the sovereign rights of countries to [control] their own resources'.[24]

The Kremlin is right about the power of the dollar. Russia's 2022 invasion of Ukraine and actions in the ensuing economic war aimed to secure its status as a major global power, making it the dominant player in Eurasia and undermining the US-led West's hegemony. This has failed. The United States may no longer have the geopolitical hegemony it enjoyed immediately after the Soviet collapse—even Francis Fukuyama, the oft-misunderstood author of the 'end of history' thesis, which posited that the collapse would precede a future in which liberal democracy and free trade would come to be near universal, has acknowledged he may have been wrong.[25] What hegemony does remain is in the international economic order. The West should strive to protect the dollar system and further develop the economic order built upon it, though there is no guarantee it will, in the future, handle that power justly.

There is a risk that politicians in the United States could abuse the power of the dollar for purposes that are not in the core interests of the United States or its allies, or where they risk causing more backlash than they bring benefit. An over-use of sanctions in cases where they are not warranted or the most effective tool risks undermining the dollar system.[26] And there should be no expectation that Washington will always use its economic weapons prudently. It has certainly acted unjustly in the past. There are also many cases of human rights abuses, war crimes, and malign economic statecraft that Washington does not respond to with sanctions, and it is unlikely to in the future. It is true this is not always equitable, and there are legitimate concerns that it perpetuates inequality. Nonetheless, the US-led economic order and the dollar system also have many benefits, least of all serving as the key engine for global economic growth.

The outcome of Russia's invasion of Ukraine and economic war offers an opportunity to begin addressing some of the criticisms that the dollar system acts to perpetuate inequality and injustices. Calls for an international package to invest in Ukraine's reconstruction and to re-assess its debt offer opportunities to have the US-led economic order act in a manner that benefits those so cruelly affected by an unjust war of aggression. So too will responding to whatever kind of Russia succeeds Putin's, for his failures in the economic war and in invading Ukraine are certain to be the beginning of the end for his regime. How long that process will take to play out is unclear, but, when the time comes, Russia will inevitably be pulled back into the international economic order. International capital will demand it, given the potential returns on offer. That such integration is necessary for Russia to return to growth and invest in its long-term future means the Russian people will demand it as well. The West should ensure that Russia's eventual return to the international economic order is contingent on it honouring its neighbours' sovereignty, the de-politicisation of commodity supplies, and the return of democracy. If these contingencies are met, all sanctions and trade restrictions should be lifted, even if geopolitical differences between the new Russia and the West remain. Failure to do so would risk repeating the path that led to the economic war in the first place.

NOTES

INTRODUCTION

1. Anishchuk (2013).
2. Mackinder (1942), p. 150.
3. See Toal (2017).
4. Short (2022), p. 562.
5. Ibid.
6. Ibid., p. 579; Ingimundarson (2022), pp. 10–11.
7. Prasad (2014), pp. 16–17.
8. Goldberg et al. (2022).
9. Bertaut et al. (2021).

1. BOND OF WAR

1. Nemtsova (2015).
2. Kyiv City Administration (2018).
3. Ibid.
4. *Ukrainska Pravda* (2013).
5. Ibid.
6. Ibid.
7. Sakwa (2022), pp. 210–11.
8. Rosenthal (2004).
9. Olearchyk (15 August 2013).
10. BBC Russian Service (2013).
11. Krasnolutska (2013).
12. Danilova (2013).
13. Ukrainian Presidential Office (2014).
14. Short (2022), p. 577.
15. The medals awarded by Russia's Ministry of Defence for the 'liberation' of Crimea give 20 February 2014 as the start date of the operation. See Cathcart (2015).
16. Office of the President of Russia (17 April 2014).
17. Vanek Smith (2019).
18. Eichengreen et al. (2022).

19. Bullough (2018), pp. 39–43.
20. Tucker (1986).
21. Gulati (2014).
22. Gelpern (27 April 2014).
23. Weidemaier and Gulati (2020).
24. Luhn (10 April 2014).
25. Ostanin (2014).
26. Vesti (2014).
27. Anishchuk (2013).
28. Zhukov (2014).
29. Smart Holding (2014).
30. Burdyga (2022).
31. Olearchyk (18 December 2013).
32. Ivanova and Seddon (2022).
33. Interview with the author, 6 September 2022.
34. Grey et al. (2014).
35. Reuters (10 June 2010).
36. Federal Bureau of Investigation (2014).
37. Kramer (2014).
38. De la Paz (2017).
39. Skorkin (2021).
40. Cullison (2014).
41. Olearchyk (2015).
42. Carroll (2015).
43. Kramer (12 May 2017). Kyiv brought a lawsuit in the UK courts to try and claw back $1.9 billion from Kolomoisky and his business partners, but the case was adjourned in March 2022 when a judge approved their application that Russia's invasion made a fair trial impossible. See: Brick Court Chambers (2022).
44. Erlanger and Herszenhorn (2017).
45. Eristavi (2015).
46. Hess (19 September 2018), p. 25.
47. Ibid., pp. 14–15.
48. Korsunskaya (2015).
49. Ibid., p. 14.
50. IMF News (2015).
51. Ibid.
52. Vzglyad (2016).

2.   THE WEST FIGHTS BACK

1. McDowell (2023), pp. 33–35.

2. Dawisha (2014), pp. 31, 55–6.

3. Short (2022), pp. 130–75.

4. US Department of the Treasury (20 March 2014).

5. Dawisha (2014), pp. 63–70.

6. Dmitriev et al. (2022).

7. US Department of the Treasury (20 March 2014).

8. Hume and Sheppard (2016).

9. US Department of the Treasury (20 March 2014).

10. Farchy (2014).

11. Blas and Farchy (2021), p. 313.

12. Hume and Sheppard (2016).

13. Enerdata (2014).

14. Swint and Shiryaevskaya (2013).

15. *The Moscow Times* (2014).

16. Office of the White House Press Secretary (20 March 2014).

17. US Department of the Treasury (16 July 2014).

18. Joint Investigation Team (2016).

19. Plunkett (2014).

20. Joint Investigation Team (2016).

21. Pawlak (2014).

22. BBC (19 September 2015).

23. Rostec (2014).

24. Prince (2019).

25. Kokorin (2021).

26. Sayari (2020).

27. Zinets (2020).

28. Zinets (2021).

29. RFE/RL (12 March 2021).

30. Office of the Chairman of the Senate Foreign Relations Committee (2017).

31. Office of the White House Press Secretary (2017).

32. Gibbons-Neff (2018).

33. Zengerle (2018).

34. Doff and Galouchko (2018).

35. House of Commons Debate (2018).

36. Ambrose (2018).

37. LeBlanc (2021).

38. Ruiz Loyola (2019).

39. Ibid.

40. Office of the President of Russia (16 July 2018).

41. Hess (16 August 2019).

42. Office of the White House Press Secretary (2021).

43. Ibid.
44. Goodman et al. (2021).
45. Ministry of Foreign Affairs of the Russian Federation (2021).
46. Milchenko (2021).
47. Graff (2023).
48. Ibid.
49. Jack (2022); Office of the President of Russia (17 April 2022).

3. RUSSIA UNDER SANCTIONS

1. Wiśniewska (2012).
2. BP (2013).
3. Weaver (2013).
4. Ambrose (2018).
5. Papchenkova and Starinskaya (2016); Yakoreva (2016).
6. Short (2022), pp. 356–9, 405–6.
7. Chung (2006).
8. Ibid.
9. Kuznetsov (2014).
10. Hirst (2015).
11. Schreck (2014).
12. BOFIT Weekly (2021).
13. Short (2022), p. 127.
14. Ibid., p. 127.
15. Ibid., p. 131.
16. Dawisha (2014), pp. 133–4.
17. Fabrichnaya and Golubkova (2016).
18. Boyes and Kravtsova (2015).
19. Dawisha (2014), pp. 132–3.
20. Ibid., pp. 189–91.
21. Ibid., p. 252.
22. Reuters (26 November 2010).
23. Short (2022), p. 259.
24. Ibid., p. 162.
25. Dawisha (2014), pp. 338–9.
26. Short (2022), p. 242; Petrova (2017).
27. Short (2022), p. 333.
28. Ibid.
29. TASS (2015).
30. Walker (2014).
31. Reuters (2014).
32. Shagina (2021).

33. Korsunskaya et al. (2019).
34. McDowell (2023), p, 81.
35. All banks operating dollar transactions are required to have correspondent banking relations ultimately tying them to a bank with access to the Clearing House Interbank Payments System, for which they have to have operations in the United States. See McDowell (2023), pp. 26–31.
36. Shagina (2021).
37. Kärnfelt (2020)
38. Agentsvo (2022).
39. Vedomosti (2018).
40. Interview with author, 14 September 2022.
41. Götz et al. (2021).
42. Interview with author, 14 September 2022.
43. Burlakova and Boyko (2021); Produkty.by (2022).
44. Bloomberg (5 September 2022).
45. Luhn (26 September 2014).
46. Ibid.
47. Roth (2014).
48. *The Economist* (2017).
49. Kramer (15 December 2017).
50. *The Economist* (2017).
51. The Bell (2018).
52. Turak (2018).
53. Tamkin (2018).
54. US Department of the Treasury (2018).
55. Sulzer (2018).
56. Belton (2012).
57. Abou-Sabe et al. (2022).
58. Croft (2018).
59. Tsui (2022).
60. Office of the President of Russia (7 June 2018).
61. Polyus (2019).
62. Foy (1 April 2019).
63. Hess (25 June 2019), pp. 11–14.
64. Caruana Galizia et al. (2022).
65. Gould-Davies (2020).
66. Hess (29 January 2019).
67. Foy (1 April 2019).
68. Rusal (2019).

4. ˙ GASEOUS INTERDEPENDENCE

1. Wetzel (2014).
2. Frum (2021);Thompson (2022), p. 52.
3. Wetzel (2014).
4. Moody (2022).
5. Ibid.
6. Stern (2005), p. 2.
7. Office of the President of Russia (2017).
8. Ibid.
9. Ibid.
10. Ibid.
11. Asmus (2010), pp. 120–40.
12. Friedman (1996).
13. Luttwak (1990), p. 17.
14. Helleiner (2021), p. 4.
15. Avtonomov and Bruina (2018), p. 210.
16. Drezner (2000), pp. 153–230.
17. Maurer (2008).
18. Deutsche Welle (2008).
19. Bennhold (2022).
20. RFE/RL (2006).
21. Holland (2021).
22. European Commission (2008), p. 4.
23. Ibid., pp. 15–16.
24. Scevola and Zhdannikov (2007).
25. Neukirch (2010).
26. Shikerova and Bedrov (2022).
27. Ibid.
28. Dimitrov (2020); Frolova (2020).
29. Reed (2014).
30. Gardner (2014).
31. Tcherneva (2014).
32. Reuters (2015).
33. German Energy and Economy Ministry (2015).
34. Polish Office of Competition and Consumer Protection (2016).
35. Sytas (2016).
36. Polish Office of Competition and Consumer Protection (2016).
37. OMV Group (2017).
38. Dunai and Grove (2014).
39. Office of the Prime Minister of Hungary (2014).
40. Adkins (2020).

41. Szabó (2022).
42. International Investment Bank (2015).
43. Zalan (2017).
44. Szabó (2017); Oliver and Hirst (2016).
45. Meck (2016).
46. Ibid.
47. Lyrchichkova and Stolyarov (2017).
48. Simakov and Fadeeva (2015)
49. Foy and Chazan (2017).
50. Velkey (2017).
51. Apuzzo and Novak (2019).
52. Hungary Today (2021).
53. RFE/RL (2 June 2021).

5. THE ERDOĞAN FACTOR

1. Intelligence Online (2020).
2. See: https://www.adnansen.com/#energy
3. Ibid.
4. TASS (2018).
5. Şimşek (2020); *Daily Sabah* (2021).
6. Intelligence Online (2020). Turkish President Recep Tayyip Erdoğan's government has frequently imprisoned political and business opponents without revealing evidence. The last that was heard of the Özturk case was in January 2022, when the Turkish Constitutional Court rejected an appeal from Özturk that her arrest was illegal. See O'Byrne (28 July 2022).
7. RFE/RL (2014).
8. Letsch (2013).
9. Schanzer (2018).
10. *The Straits Times* (2014).
11. Bechev (2022), pp. 125–7.
12. Ibid., p. 172.
13. Weiner (2022).
14. Pagliery (2017).
15. Yackley (2021).
16. Deutsche Welle (2015).
17. Ibid.
18. Townsend and Ellehuus (2019).
19. Ibid.
20. BBC (13 August 2016).
21. Mankoff (2016).

22. Ibid.
23. *Daily Sabah* (2016).
24. Ibid.
25. Townsend and Ellehuus (2019).
26. McFadden et al. (2017).
27. Flynn (2016).
28. Townsend and Ellehuus (2019).
29. BBC (2019).
30. Gould and Mehta (2019).
31. Thompson (2022), p. 82.
32. Nikolov (2022).
33. Detsch (2021).

6. EURASIAN ECONOMIC DISUNION

1. Drezner (2000), pp. 153–230.
2. Bagirova and Bousso (2017).
3. Conlin (2020), p. 34.
4. Marriott and Minio-Paluello (2013), p. 44.
5. BP (2021).
6. BBC (2002).
7. Marriott and Minio-Paluello (2013), p. 17.
8. Levine (2017), pp. 238–9.
9. Bagirova and Bousso (2017).
10. Hess (19 May 2022), p. 425.
11. Short (2022), p. 388.
12. Clinton Presidential Library (2017).
13. Steinbeck (2000), p. 144.
14. Earle (2012).
15. Traub (2010).
16. Tully (2008).
17. Pearce (2011), p. 2.
18. Georgian Journal (2012).
19. Chikhladze (2019).
20. BBC (31 May 2015).
21. Higgins (2017).
22. Pertaia (2017).
23. Transparency International Georgia (2022).
24. Hess and Otarashvili (2020), p. 11.
25. Gramer and Mackinnon (2018).
26. Ibid., p. 10.
27. Ibid., p. 13.

28. Ibid., pp. 5–6.
29. Civil.ge (2021).
30. Nazaretyan (2021).
31. Office of the President of Russia (2013).
32. Bedevian (2013).
33. Babayan (2016).
34. Danielyan (2017).
35. Ibid.
36. Karapetyan (2021).
37. Ibid.
38. Abrahamyan (2021).
39. Karapetyan (2021).
40. Abrahamyan (2021).
41. Ibid.
42. Batashvili (2019).
43. Office of the President of Russia (16 July 2018).
44. Kucera (2019).
45. Ibid.
46. Ibid.
47. Abrahamyan (2018); Lomsadze (2015).
48. Badalian (2021).
49. Stempel (2017).
50. Eckel (2019).
51. DeHart (2013).
52. Eckel (2019).
53. BBC (2016).
54. Farchy (2015).
55. Galeotti (2016).
56. Auyezhov (2017).
57. RFE/RL (3 September 2017); bneIntellinews (2017).
58. Sattarov (2017).
59. RFE/RL (21 September 2017).
60. Pannier (2018).
61. Hess (19 May 2022), p. 428.
62. Hess (15 February 2019).
63. RFE/RL (2019).
64. Hashimova (2021).
65. Hess (7 July 2022).
66. Hess and Anceschi (2022).
67. Ibid.
68. Zaugg (2019).
69. Eurasianet (2018).

70. Pannier (2022).
71. Shuster and Gurt (2009).
72. Columbia Harriman Institute (2017).
73. Eurasianet (2016).
74. Putz (2016).
75. Ibid.
76. Eurasianet (16 October 2018).
77. RFE/RL (24 December 2021).

7. VISIONS OF GOLD AND AFRICA

1. Flanagan (2019).
2. Fabricius (2019).
3. Popkov (2019).
4. Sauer (2017).
5. Sauer (26 September 2022).
6. Ibid.
7. Troianovski (2022).
8. Short (2022), p. 544.
9. MacFarquhar (2018).
10. Reuters (14 February 2023).
11. Chesnokov (2019).
12. Office of the President of Russia (2019)
13. Al Jazeera (2019).
14. Cotterill and Walker (2021).
15. Economist Intelligence (2019).
16. Hanlon (2021).
17. Andarko sold its share in the Mozambique LNG project to Total in September 2019.
18. Rosneft (2019).
19. Reuters (26 November 2010).
20. International Energy Agency (2020), p. 11.
21. Reuters (8 October 2018).
22. Africa Intelligence (2021).
23. Marten (2019).
24. Parens (2022).
25. Marten (15 September 2022), p. 2; Seldin (2022).
26. Marten (15 September 2022), pp. 3–11.
27. Ibid., p. 10.
28. Golubovich (2018).
29. Kwarteng (2014), p. 359.
30. Clinch (2014).

31. Ruinformer (2015).
32. Lenta (2017).
33. Ibid.
34. Ibid.
35. Helleiner (2021), p. 91.
36. Hess (25 June 2019), p. 10.
37. TASS (2019).
38. BFM (2021).
39. Finanz.ru (2020).
40. Tkachev (2021).
41. Zygar (2016), pp. 112, 211, 218.
42. Fabrichnaya and Golubkova (2016); Central Bank of Russia (2022).
43. BFM (2021).
44. Johnson (2023).

8.   RUSSIA'S CARACAS CACHE

 1. BBC (2017).
 2. Flanagan and Mendelson Forman (2008).
 3. Zygar (2016), p. 179.
 4. Ibid.
 5. Londoño (2017).
 6. Hausmann (2017).
 7. Sequera (2018).
 8. Vyas and Kurmanaev (2017).
 9. Zygar (2016), p. 179.
10. Hess (30 January 2019), p. 2.
11. Londoño (2017); BBC (2017).
12. Congressional Research Service (2022), p. 2.
13. Hess (30 January 2019), p. 8.
14. Domm (2018).
15. Congressional Research Service (2022), p. 2.
16. Ibid.
17. *The New York Times* (2019).
18. CNBC.
19. Roth (2019).
20. Marten (20 July 2022).
21. US Department of the Treasury (2020).
22. US Department of the Treasury (2019).
23. Ibid.
24. Rosneft (2020).
25. The Bell (2020).

26. Ibid.
27. Rosneft (2020).
28. Hess (30 March 2020).
29. Ulmer and Buitrago (2017).
30. Shuster (2018).
31. Ibid.
32. Ibid.
33. Serkov et al. (2018).
34. Ibid.
35. Interfax (2022).
36. Svoboda (2022), p. 7.
37. World Nuclear News (2021).
38. Hess (29 January 2019).

9.   PUTIN'S PIVOT TO ASIA

1. Office of the President of Russia (24 October 2014).
2. Ibid.
3. Kucera (2014).
4. Maçães (2018), pp. 13–14.
5. Iyer (2017).
6. Reznik (2013).
7. Ibid.
8. Reuters (15 October 2016).
9. Olivero (2022).
10. Parpiani et al. (2021).
11. Kirchberger (2022), pp. 88–95.
12. Grossman (2021).
13. Vietnam Plus (2013); Moreau (2010).
14. Thayer (2013).
15. Astrasheuskaya (2016).
16. Rosneft (2013)
17. Ibid.
18. Rosneft (2015); Oil Capital (2020).
19. Rosneft (2016).
20. Reed (2019).
21. Trickett (2020).
22. Ibid.
23. Afanasiev (2021).
24. Burmistrova (2019).
25. Trickett (2020).
26. Ranada (2019).

27. Gita-Carlos (2019).
28. Crisis Group (2022).
29. Brown (2019), p. 148.
30. Ibid., p. 151.
31. Koshino and Ward (2022), p. 122.
32. Nakano (2019).
33. Shagina (10 January 2020).
34. Simes Jr (2020).
35. James Martin Center for Nonproliferation Studies (2022), pp. 63–4; US Department of the Treasury (31 March 2022).
36. Channel News Asia (2021).
37. Shagina (April 2020), p. 12.
38. Miller (2022), pp. 342–3.

10. BEIJING AS BIG BROTHER

1. Smolchenko and Nedbaeva (2013).
2. Cox (2022).
3. Smolchenko and Nedbaeva (2013).
4. Savic (2016).
5. Office of the President of Russia (1 September 2014).
6. Grivach (2014).
7. Galaktinova and Reiter (2016).
8. Anin et al. (2020).
9. Shamgun and Dmitriev (2022).
10. Lukin (2018), p. 150.
11. Ibid.
12. Fadeeva et al. (2017).
13. Ibid.
14. Mitrokhina (2022).
15. Reuters (8 December 2021).
16. Golubkova and Pinchuk (2015).
17. Leung (2015).
18. Marsh (2018).
19. Ibid.
20. Reuters (28 October 2016).
21. Short (2022), pp. 405–6, 514–55.
22. Farchy and Blas (2021), pp. 301–2.
23. Ibid.
24. Hess (16 May 2018).
25. Lukin (2018), p. 145.
26. Hess (27 July 2022).

27. Ibid.
28. Ng and Yu (2018).
29. AFP (2017).
30. Zhang and Aizhu (2018).
31. Zheng (2019).
32. Reuters (19 November 2018).
33. Trickett (2020).
34. Ibid.
35. Steil and Della Rocca (2022).
36. Nehru (2014).
37. Ibid.
38. Andreoni (2019); World Bank (2019), p. 8. The World Bank reports data on an annual year running from 1 July to 30 June.
39. New Development Bank (2021).
40. Humphrey (2015).
41. Rusal (2017).
42. Spivak (2021).
43. Reuters (1 March 2022); Branigan (2014).
44. Aizhu (2022).
45. Reuters (17 February 2022).
46. Sheppard et al. (2022).
47. China Power Team (2022).
48. Xinhua (2019).

11. MIDDLE EASTERN POWER PLAYS

1. Office of the President of Russia (2016).
2. Ibid.
3. Buckley (2017).
4. Ibid.
5. Foy et al. (2017).
6. Buckley (2017).
7. Hope and Scheck (2020), pp. 72–4, 321.
8. Ibid., pp. 67–9.
9. Ibid., pp. 69–71.
10. Ibid.
11. Hubbard (2020), pp. 122–7.
12. Riedel (2021).
13. Voronova et al. (2018).
14. Wintour (7 June 2017).
15. Voronova et al. (2018).
16. Ibid.

17. Hubbard (2020), pp. 189–96.
18. Barnard and Abi-Habib (2017).
19. Hope and Scheck (2020), p. 71.
20. Spencer (2016).
21. Micklethwait (2016).
22. Reed (2016); Soldatkin (2016).
23. Taylor (2015).
24. Hope and Scheck (2020), pp. 140–58.
25. Riedel (2017).
26. Al Arabiya (2017).
27. Wintour (5 October 2017).
28. Meredith (2018).
29. Al Jazeera (2018).
30. Murtagh et al. (2020).
31. Ibid.
32. Reed (2020).
33. BBC (2020).
34. Raval (2020).
35. International Institute for Strategic Studies (2022).
36. Mackinnon (2021).
37. Krylova (2017), pp. 588–90; Short (2022), pp. 524–30.
38. Salem (2013).
39. Reuters (2012).
40. Zhdannikov and Soldatkin (2017).
41. Goudsouzian and Fatah (2014).
42. Georgy and Rasheed (2017).
43. Ibid.
44. Zhdannikov and Soldatkin (2017).

12. THE ECONOMIC WAR IN UKRAINE

1. Kravcheko (2022).
2. TSN (2022); New Voice of Ukraine (24 February 2022).
3. East Renewable AB (2022), p. 2.
4. Ibid.
5. East Renewable AB (2021), p. 2.
6. Stuckey (2019).
7. Keating (2022).
8. Harrison (2022).
9. Smith Thayer (2022).
10. Plypypiv (2022).
11. Yaffa (2017).

12. Litivinova (2018).
13. Meyer (2021); Martinez and Cathey (2022).
14. Yaffa (2017).
15. Meduza (2019).
16. Mokrushin (2022).
17. Mostovoye Bureau (2016).
18. Ibid.
19. Mokrushin (2022).
20. Media Initiative for Human Rights (2022), p. 12.
21. Byrne et al. (2022), pp. 13–14.
22. Altman (2022).
23. Kyiv School of Economics (2022), p. 3; Singh Sodia (2022).
24. Collier (2022).
25. Gorin (2022).
26. Independent Defence Anti-Corruption Committee (2018).
27. Schwirtz (2022).
28. The Ukrainian authorities had been in the process of building up a new port in Berdyansk west of Mykolaiv, also on the shores of the Azov Sea, before Putin's renewed invasion in 2022.
29. TASS (2023).
30. SCM (2023).
31. Samsung (2022).
32. Ibid.
33. Forbes India (2012).
34. Hyde (2021).
35. Ibid.
36. Olearchyk (2021).
37. Skorkin (2022).
38. Ibid.
39. Coalson (2015).
40. BBC (2023) and Tkach (2022); Maksimchuk (2022).
41. Debtwire (2019), p. 4.
42. Skorkin (2022).
43. BBC Russian Service (2022).
44. Ibid.
45. Ibid.
46. Newsru.co.il (2022).
47. Shevchuk (2022).
48. Roshina (2022); Chirenko (2022).
49. Chirenko (2022).
50. Sky News (2022).
51. BBC (2022).

52. Walker (2022).
53. Zhegulev (2023).
54. Sayari (2020).
55. Reuters (22 October 2022).
56. Maksimchuk (2022).
57. Champion and Krasnolutska (2022).
58. Reuters (27 July 2022).
59. The Insider (2022); Grozev (2022).
60. Rathbone and Hall (2023).
61. Champion and Krasnolutska (2022).
62. Ibid.
63. Ibid.
64. Ibid.
65. Porter (2022).
66. Kiel Institute for the World Economy (2022).
67. Ibid.
68. Congressional Research Service (2023), p. 1.
69. Rudgewick (2022).
70. Wheatley and Chazan (2022).
71. Gulati and Weidemaier (2022).
72. Mosolova and Olearchyk (2023).
73. Steil and Della Rocca (2018).

13. THE WEST'S ECONOMIC WAR AGAINST RUSSIA

1. Office of the White House Press Secretary (2022).
2. Ibid.
3. Fleming et al. (2022).
4. Ibid.
5. Vallée (2022).
6. BBC (4 May 2022).
7. Hess (8 June 2022); Kursiv (2022).
8. Reuters (26 September 2022); Lillis (2022).
9. Nelson (2022).
10. Ziemba (2022).
11. Tooze (2022).
12. US Department of the Treasury (24 February 2022).
13. The UK authorities did sanction Gazprombank in March 2022. However, the UK was far less dependent on Russian hydrocarbons than mainland Europe, and its sanctions do not have extraterritoriality.
14. Guarascio (2022).
15. UK Department for Digital, Culture, Media and Sport (2022).

16. AFP (2021).
17. Ibid.
18. Ibid.
19. BBC (1 November 2022).
20. Tetley and Morpugo (2022).
21. Collard (2022).
22. Alecci (2022).
23. Gauthier-Villars (2022).
24. Alecci (2022).
25. Salama et al. (2022).
26. US Department of the Treasury (2 August 2022); Gauthier-Villars (2022).
27. Reuters. 'Russia's SUEK, EuroChem ask bondholders for debt payment freeze', Reuters, 16 August 2022. https://www.reuters.com/markets/commodities/russian-coal-producer-suek-asks-bondholders-postpone-debt-payments-2022-08-16/
28. US Department of the Treasury (3 March 2022).
29. The broad license he received was revoked on 12 April 2023. See: US Department of the Treasury (2023).
30. BBC (27 October 2022); Ince et al. (2022); Debre and Gambrell (2022).
31. Davis (2022).
32. Sauer (2 June 2022).
33. Tognini (2022).
34. Balmer and Parodi (2022).
35. Krutov et al. (2022).
36. Eccles (2022); Isidore and Liakos (2022).
37. Ibid.
38. Dyson (2022).
39. Jeffrey (2022).
40. Oser (2022).
41. Meade (2022).
42. Dempsey et al. (2022).
43. Abnett et al. (2022).
44. Ibid.
45. Stevis-Gridneff (2022).
46. Hine, Lucy. 'Marinakis swoops on former Sovcomflot aframax quartet,' TradeWinds, 17 May 2022. https://www.tradewindsnews.com/tankers/marinakis-swoops-on-former-sovcomflot-aframax-quartet/2-1-1220115
47. Lowry, Nigel. 'Leading Greek shipowners denounce sanctions "failure,"' Lloyd's List, 07 June 2022, https://lloydslist.maritimeintelligence.

informa.com/LL1141155/Leading-Greek-shipowners-denounce-sanctions-failure. Pappachristou, Harry. 'Zelenskyy rebukes Greek tankers for carrying Russian oil', TradeWinds, 06 July 2022. https://www.tradewindsnews.com/tankers/zelenskyy-rebukes-greek-tankers-for-carrying-russian-oil/2-1-1252985

48. IEA (2022), p. 336.
49. Lawson (2022); Browning et al. (2022); Hess (22 September 2022).
50. The EU agreed to phase out two-thirds of Russian gas purchases by 2023, but Russia's actions played a far greater role in prompting the shift away from Russian gas.
51. International Energy Agency (2022), p. 86.
52. US Department of the Treasury (8 August 2022).
53. Bloomberg (5 September 2022).
54. Ibid.
55. Aminu and Olivares-Caminal (2022).

14. RUSSIA ADRIFT

1. McCauley (2022).
2. Inozemtsev (2022).
3. Ibid; Wong and Ma (2022).
4. Inozemstsev; Tavberidze (2022).
5. Weidemaier and Gulati (2022).
6. Ibid.; Hess (25 June 2019), pp. 14, 17.
7. Inozemtsev (2022).
8. Interfax (2022).
9. Hunder (2022).
10. Aminu and Olivares-Caminal (2022).
11. Hess (21 March 2022).
12. Oosterlinck (2016), pp. 120–1; Malik (2018), p. 198.
13. Oosterlinck (2016), p. 3.
14. Malik (2018), pp. 217–31.
15. Weidemaier and Gulati (2022).
16. Buchheit and Gulati (2022).
17. Español (2022).
18. Ibid.
19. Although Russia's 2022 default is typically referred to as its third sovereign debt default, it is technically the fifth when counting the restructuring of its debts after the Soviet collapse and its bank debts in the years after the 1998 default. A special mention is owed to Paul McNamara, who is always keen to hark on this point. See: Government of the Russian Federation and Central Bank of Russia (1999) and

Baker (1997). For the role of the West and international institutions in responding to Russia's 1998 default, see Gilman (2010), pp. 207–54.

20. Sonnenfeld and Tian (2022).
21. Bennetts (2019); Sauer (26 September 2022).
22. Turak (2022).
23. Reuters (28 November 2022).
24. Reuters (2023).
25. Ivanova and Stognei (2023).
26. McCausland (2022).
27. Ibid.
28. Barns-Graham (2022).
29. Chorzempa and von Daniels (2023).
30. US Bureau of Industry and Security (2022).
31. Kilcrease (2022).
32. US Bureau of Industry and Security (2022).
33. Kilcrease (2022).
34. Devonshire-Ellis (2022).
35. Swanson (2023).
36. Ellyatt (2022).
37. Rozhansky and Romaliyskaya (2022).
38. Van Brugen (2022).
39. Braw (3 October 2022).
40. Office of the President of Russia (27 October 2022).
41. Reuters (28 September 2022).
42. Torbati and Scheyder (2017).
43. RFE/RL (8 October 2022).
44. Mitrova (2022).
45. IEA (2022), p. 336.
46. Ibid.
47. Mitrova (2022); Eddy (2022).
48. Marsha and Chambers (2022). There was little doubt that Putin's recognition of the Russian-backed people's republics was a precursor to Russia's plans to annex them, as Putin similarly recognised Crimea's 'independence' before its annexation in 2014. See Vasovic and Croft (2014).
49. Al Jazeera (12 October 2022); Preussen (19 August 2022).
50. Reuters (2020).
51. Humpert (2022).
52. Chorzempa and von Daniels (2023).

15. RUSSIA'S RIPOSTES AND COMMODITIES CLASHES

1. US Department of Agriculture (2022).
2. Ibid.
3. Eliseev (2022).
4. Özberk (2022).
5. BBC (3 March 2022).
6. Ibid.
7. *Argus* (2022).
8. New Voice of Ukraine (27 December 2022).
9. Ivanova et al. (2022).
10. General Assembly of the United Nations (2022).
11. RFE/RL (30 June 2022).
12. Bachega and Gregory (2022).
13. Reuters (22 October 2022).
14. Inman (2022).
15. TASS (27 April 2022).
16. Weselowsky (2022).
17. Bloomberg (12 May 2022).
18. Gustafson (2020), p. 379.
19. Simon (2019).
20. Reuters (30 May 2022).
21. Reuters (1 October 2022).
22. Ibid.
23. Lawson (2 September 2002).
24. Faulconbridge and Ravidkumar (2022).
25. Volz and Gardner (2018).
26. Shuster and Gurt (2009).
27. Solomon (2023); Siebold and Alkousa (2023).
28. RFE/RL (10 May 2022).
29. Gas Infrastructure Europe (2023).
30. Statistics Norway (2022).
31. Jolly (2022).
32. US Department of Justice (2022).
33. Ibid.
34. Ibid.
35. Ibid.
36. Hurtado (2022).
37. Meduza (2023).
38. Martins Sousa and Pohjanpalo (2022).
39. Environmental Investigation Agency (2022), p. 2.
40. Martins Sousa and Pohjanpalo (2022).

41. Environmental Investigation Agency (2022), p. 2.
42. Ibid., pp. 3–4.
43. Ibid., p. 3.
44. Nardelli et al. (2022).
45. Ibid.
46. Interview with author, 1 November 2022.
47. Interview with author, 21 February 2023; forthcoming analysis by Allen Maggard and the Center for Analytical Defence Studies.
48. US Department of Commerce (2022).
49. Egan (2022).
50. Goodman (2019).
51. Saul (2022).
52. Farchy et al. (2022).
53. Mukherji (2023).
54. Darvas and Martins (2022).
55. Preussen (31 August 2022); Reuters (12 October 2022).
56. Sezer (29 September 2022).
57. Sezer (28 October 2022).
58. Jones (2022).
59. Rosatom (2022).
60. Soylu (2022).
61. Ibid.
62. Ibid.
63. Akman (2023).
64. Reuters (19 October 2022).
65. Kozok (2022).

16. EUROPE ADRIFT

1. ING (2017); Jordan and Thomas (2022).
2. Umwelt Bundesamt (2022).
3. Haddad (2022).
4. BASF (2022).
5. Kohlmann (2022); Oltermann (2022).
6. Hansen and Knolle (2022).
7. Oltermann (2022).
8. Connolly (2022).
9. *The Economist* (22 September 2022); Müller (2001).
10. Rosneft (2017).
11. Reuters (17 November 2021).
12. Venkina (2019).
13. Nasralla and Somasekhar (2022).

14. Wiedemann (2022).

15. Ibid.

16. Sciorilli Borrelli et al. (2022).

17. BBC (19 September 2015).

18. Seddon and Politi (2017).

19. Ebhart and Follain (2019).

20. Sheppard et al. (2023).

21. Zakurdaeva and Maglov (2019).

22. Biesecker et al. (2022).

23. Işık (2022).

24. Hess (21 March 2022).

25. Eurostat (2022).

26. Ibid.

27. Elliott (2021).

28. DutchNews (2022); Schaps (2022); European Commission (2022).

29. European Commission (2022).

30. Cooper (2022).

31. Steitz (2016).

32. Reuters (18 August 2020).

33. Bündner (2022).

34. YLE (2022).

35. Ibid.

36. Storbeck et al. (2022).

37. Meredith (6 September 2022).

38. Storbeck et al. (2022).

39. Reuters (23 September 2022).

40. Mehrer (2022).

41. Gehrke (2021); Scally (2022).

42. Bruegel's calculation of fiscal support also includes measures taken between 1 September 2021 and 24 February 2022, before Putin vastly expanded his invasion of Ukraine but when the Russian throttling of gas supplies had already helped drive up energy prices. Sgaravatti et al. (2023).

43. SwissInfo (2022).

44. Manufacturing.net (2022).

45. See Kaiser (1974).

17. OIL AND GAS WAR GOES GLOBAL

1. Ichord Jr (2020).

2. Mangi and Murtaugh (2018).

3. Stapczynski and Mangi (2022).

  4. Shackle (2018).
  5. BBC (9 April 2022).
  6. Snider (2022).
  7. Ibid.
  8. Stapczynski and Mangi (2022).
  9. Isaad and Reynolds (2022).
 10. Zaman (2022).
 11. *The Express Tribune* (2022); Knight (2021).
 12. US International Trade Administration (2022).
 13. Stapczynski (2022).
 14. Al Jazeera (13 October 2022).
 15. Parfitt and Tang (2022).
 16. Meredith (5 September 2022); Verma (2022).
 17. Sunillkumar (2023).
 18. Kantchev et al. (2023).
 19. Al Jazeera (8 November 2022).
 20. Chaudhury (2022).
 21. Arab News (2022).
 22. Reed (2023).
 23. Holland (2022).
 24. Holland (2022); Sanger (2021).
 25. Kalin et al. (2022).
 26. Office of US Senator Joni Ernst (2022).
 27. Haynes (2022).
 28. Bloomberg (20 October 2022).
 29. Lee and Di Paola (2022); Reuters (15 July 2022).
 30. Hellenic Shipping News (2022).
 31. Parraga and Binnie (2022).
 32. International Energy Agency (2022), p. 52.
 33. Nair (2022).
 34. DiChristopher (2019).
 35. Reuters (25 July 2022).
 36. *The Economist* (15 September 2022).
 37. Macdonald-Smith (2022).
 38. Shiryaevskaya and Koh (2022).
 39. Farmer (2022).
 40. Euronews (2022); TASS (15 September 2022).
 41. Yihe (2022).
 42. Hess (8 June 2022).
 43. Baunov (2022).
 44. Tengrinews (2022).
 45. Putz (2022).

46. Van Leijen (2022).
47. Kumenov (2023)
48. Hess (4 August 2022).
49. Trend.az (2022).
50. Vasilyeva and Baynazarov (2022).
51. TASS (22 June 2022).
52. Hess (27 July 2022).
53. Pettis (2019).

18. THE INFLATION WEAPON

1. Cole and Heale (2022).
2. Silverman (2022).
3. Truss (2022).
4. Newton Dunn and Wright (2022).
5. IMF News (2022).
6. Ambrose (2021).
7. Society of International Gas Tanker and Terminal Operators (2014), pp. 10–11.
8. Ship Technology (2014).
9. Bolton (2022).
10. See Jensen (2004); Tsafos (2018); and Gilbert et al. (2021).
11. Gilbert et al. (2021).
12. Plant and Nance (2021).
13. UK Department for Business, Energy, and Industrial Strategy (2022), p. 5.
14. Duff (2022).
15. Office of Budget Responsibility (2022), p. 9.
16. Progressive Economy Forum (2022).
17. Office of Budgetary Responsibility (2022), p. 25.
18. Jessop (2022).
19. Buli (2022).
20. Reuters (17 November 2022).
21. Stevis-Gridneff (2022).
22. Strasburg and Morenne (2022).
23. Kurmayer (2022).
24. Maček (2022).
25. Batmanghelidj (2022), pp. 7–16.
26. Office of the President of Russia (17 June 2022).
27. Office of the President of Russia (27 October 2022).
28. Trickett (2022).
29. *The Moscow Times* (2022).

30. Ibid.
31. Trickett (2022).
32. Kurasheva (2022).
33. Barrett (2022).
34. Office of the President of Russia (27 October 2022).
35. Ibid.
36. RTL (2022).
37. Office of the President of Russia (27 October 2022).
38. Schmidt (2022).
39. Eichengreen (28 March 2022).
40. Cassetta (2022).
41. Schneider et al. (2022).
42. Bounds et al. (2022).

CONCLUSION

1. Matthews (2022).
2. Ibid.
3. Russia Briefing (2023).
4. Saito and Kawate (2023); Setser (2023).
5. Moens et al. (2022).
6. Perkonig (2022).
7. Jones et al. (2023).
8. Ibid.
9. Dalton (2022).
10. Osang (2022).
11. Alderman (2022); Enerdata (2023).
12. Enerdata (2023); Reuters (28 November 2022).
13. World Nuclear Association (2022).
14. Martyshko (2022).
15. Hess (4 August 2022); O'Byrne (22 November 2022).
16. Pattison and McIntyre (2022).
17. Wintour (2022).
18. Gnana (2022).
19. Lalwani and Jacob (2023).
20. See Bernholz (2015).
21. Fein (2022).
22. Barnes and Cooper (2019); Allen (2023).
23. Office of the President of Russia (27 October 2022).
24. Kolesnikov (2022).
25. Gibson (2022).
26. McDowell (2023), pp. 159–62.

BIBLIOGRAPHY

Abnett, Kate, Jan Strupczewski, and Ingrid Melander, 'EU Agrees Russia Oil Embargo, Gives Hungary Exemptions', Reuters, 31 May 2022, https://www.reuters.com/world/europe/best-we-could-get-eu-bows-hungarian-demands-agree-russian-oil-ban-2022-05-31

Abou-Sabe, Kenzi, Andrew Lehren, Yasmine Salam, and Nancy Ing, 'How a Mysterious Putin Ally, the "Russian Gatsby", Moves His Billions', NBC, 11 April 2022, https://www.nbcnews.com/news/world/mysterious-putin-ally-russian-gatsby-moves-billions-rcna23603

Abrahamyan, Eduard, 'Pashinyan Formulates Armenia's New Iran Strategy', The Jamestown Foundation, 15 October 2018, https://jamestown.org/program/pashinyan-formulates-armenias-new-iran-strategy/

Abrahamayan, Gohar, 'The Nikol Pashinyan Administration: 2018–Present', EVN Report, 24 September 2021, https://evnreport.com/magazine-issues/the-nikol-pashinyan-administration-2018-present/

Adkins, William, 'EU Top Court Rules Hungary's Asylum Policies Unlawful', Politico, 17 December 2020, https://www.politico.eu/article/hungary-failed-eu-obligations-for-asylum-seekers-cjeu/

Adomeit, Hannes, 'Putin's "Greater Russia": Misunderstanding or Mission?', Raam Op Rusland, 27 February 2018, https://www.raamoprusland.nl/dossiers/geopolitiek/878-putin-s-greater-russia-misunderstanding-or-mission

Afanasiev, Vladimir, 'Zarubezhneft to Pick Up Rosneft's Offshore Assets in Vietnam', Upstream Online, 11 May 2021, https://www.upstreamonline.com/production/zarubezhneft-to-pick-up-rosnefts-offshore-assets-in-vietnam/2-1-1007528

AFP, 'Former Hong Kong Home Secretary Patrick Ho Arrested in US over Alleged Africa Bribery Scheme', 21 November 2017, https://www.scmp.com/news/hong-kong/law-crime/article/2120784/us-arrests-former-hong-kong-home-secretary-patrick-ho

BIBLIOGRAPHY

———— 'Arrested Billionaire Banker Tinkov Switches Focus to Cancer Foundation', 15 February 2021, https://www.themoscowtimes.com/2021/02/15/im-retired-arrested-billionaire-tinkov-switches-focus-to-cancer-foundation-a72942

Africa Intelligence, 'Moscow Remains Involved in Cabo Delgado Despite Wagner's Exit', 2 December 2021, https://www.africaintelligence.com/southern-africa-and-islands/2021/12/02/moscow-remains-involved-in-cabo-delgado-despite-wagner-s-exit, 109708624-gra

Aizhu, Chen, 'Russia, China Agree 30-Year Gas Deal via New Pipeline, to Settle in Euros', Reuters, 4 February 2022, https://www.reuters.com/world/asia-pacific/exclusive-russia-china-agree-30-year-gas-deal-using-new-pipeline-source-2022-02-04/

Akman, Beril, 'Mystery Money Financed Half of Turkey's 2022 Current-Account Gap', Bloomberg, 13 February 2023, https://www.bloomberg.com/news/articles/2023-02-13/mystery-money-financed-half-of-turkey-s-2022-current-account-gap

Akman, Beril and Kerim Karakaya, 'Mystery Money Flows Help Turkey Finance Widening Foreign Gap', Bloomberg, 12 September 2022, https://www.bloomberg.com/news/articles/2022-09-12/turkey-current-account-deficit-widens-more-than-expected-in-july

Akshay, K. V. L., 'CCI Approves Rosneft Buyout of Essar Oil', *The Economic Times*, 2 December 2016, https://economictimes.indiatimes.com/industry/energy/oil-gas/cci-approves-rosneft-buyout-of-essar-oil/articleshow/55729047.cms

Al-Serori, Leila, Oliver Das Gupta, Peter Münch, Frederik Obermaier, and Bastian Obermayer, 'Caught in the Trap', *Süddeutsche Zeitung*, 18 May 2019, https://www.sueddeutsche.de/projekte/artikel/politik/caught-in-the-trap-e675751/

Al Arabiya, 'Mohammed bin Salman to Putin: We've Achieved a Lot and Strive for More', 30 May 2017, https://english.alarabiya.net/News/gulf/2017/05/30/Mohammed-Bin-Salman-to-Putin-We-have-achieved-a-lot-and-strive-for-more

Al Jazeera, 'Russia "to Supply S-400 System to Qatar" Despite Saudi Position', 2 June 2018, https://www.aljazeera.com/news/2018/6/2/russia-to-supply-s-400-system-to-qatar-despite-saudi-position

———— 'Mozambique President, Renamo Leader Sign Peace Deal', 1 August 2019, https://www.aljazeera.com/news/2019/8/1/mozambique-president-renamo-leader-sign-peace-deal

BIBLIOGRAPHY

———— 'Putin Offers to Boost Gas Supplies to Europe via Nord Stream 2', 12 October 2022, https://www.aljazeera.com/news/2022/10/12/putin-offers-to-boost-gas-supplies-to-europe-via-nord-stream-2

———— 'UN Condemns Russia's Annexation Move: How Did Countries Vote?', 13 October 2022, https://www.aljazeera.com/news/2022/10/13/un-condemns-russias-annexations-in-ukraine-how-countries-voted

———— 'India to Continue Buying Oil from Russia as Ties Deepen', 8 November 2022, https://www.aljazeera.com/news/2022/11/8/india-to-continue-buying-oil-from-russia-as-ties-deepen

Alderman, Liz, 'As Europe Quits Russian Gas, Half of France's Nuclear Plants Are Off-Line', *The New York Times*, 16 November 2022, https://www.nytimes.com/2022/11/15/business/nuclear-power-france.html

Alecci, Scilla, 'Putin Allies Mordashov and Roldugin Targeted in Latest Round of US Sanctions', International Consortium of Investigative Journalists, 2 June 2022, https://www.icij.org/investigations/russia-archive/putin-allies-mordashov-and-roldugin-targeted-in-latest-round-of-us-sanctions/

Altman, Howard, 'Captured Russian Weapons Are Packed with U.S. Microchips', The Drive, 26 May 2022, https://www.thedrive.com/the-war-zone/captured-russian-weapons-are-packed-with-foreign-microchips

Ambrose, Jillian, 'BP's Bob Dudley: US Is Handing Out Sanctions on Russia "Like Train Tickets"', *The Telegraph*, 24 April 2018, https://www.telegraph.co.uk/business/2018/04/24/bps-bob-dudley-us-handing-sanctions-russia-like-train-tickets/

———— 'Gazprom Profits as Russia Prospers from Europe's Gas Crisis', *The Guardian*, 13 December 2021, https://www.theguardian.com/world/2021/dec/13/gazprom-hits-record-income-as-russia-prospers-from-europes-gas-crisis

Aminu, Nasir and Rodrigo Olivares-Caminal, 'Russian Debt Default: What Does It Mean for Russia and Global Financial Markets?', World Economic Forum, 12 July 2022, https://www.weforum.org/agenda/2022/07/russian-debt-default-russia-global-financial-markets/

Andreoni, Manuela, 'What Happened to the BRICS Bank?', The Third Pole, 18 November 2019, https://www.thethirdpole.net/en/regional-cooperation/new-development-bank/

BIBLIOGRAPHY

Anin, Roman, Alesya Marokhovskaya, and Irina Dolinina, 'Kirill i Katya: Liubov, razluka, ofshory i neogranichenniy resurs; Istoriya samoy taynoy pary Rossii' [Kiril and Katya: Love, separation, offshores, and unlimited resources; The history of Russia's most secret couple], iStories, 7 December 2020, https://istories.media/investigations/2020/12/07/kirill-i-katya-lyubov-razluka-ofshori-i-neogranichennii-resurs-istoriya-samoi-tainoi-pari-rossii/

Apuzzo, Matt and Benjamin Novak, 'Hungary Rolls Out Red Carpet for Obscure Russian Bank, Stoking Spy Fears', *The New York Times*, 18 March 2019, https://www.nytimes.com/2019/03/18/world/europe/hungary-russian-bank-spy-orban-putin.html

Arab News, 'Pakistan to Negotiate with Russia after US Acknowledges Right to Buy Discounted Oil—Finance Minister', 20 October 2022, https://www.arabnews.com/node/2184991/pakistan

Argus, 'Ammonia Most Exposed Fertilizer to Ukraine Conflict', 2 March 2022, https://www.argusmedia.com/en/news/2307380-ammonia-most-exposed-fertilizer-to-ukraine-conflict

Aris, Ben, 'Remembering Russia's 1998 Financial Crisis', *The Moscow Times*, 22 August 2018, https://www.themoscowtimes.com/2018/08/22/remembering-russias-1998-financial-crash-op-ed-a62595

Ash, Timothy, 'It's Costing Peanuts for the US to Defeat Russia', Centre for European Policy Analysis, 18 November 2022, https://cepa.org/article/its-costing-peanuts-for-the-us-to-defeat-russia/

Asmus, Ronald, *A Little War that Shook the World: Georgia, Russia and the Future of the West*, New York: Palgrave Macmillan, 2010.

Astakhova, Olesya, 'Russia's Rosneft Elects Former German Chancellor Schroeder as Chairman', Reuters, 29 September 2017, https://www.reuters.com/article/us-rosneft-egm-schroeder-idUSKCN1C426Q

Astrasheuskaya, Nastassia, 'Russia, Vietnam Expand Energy Cooperation with New Oil, Gas Deals', S&P Global, 16 May 2016, https://www.spglobal.com/commodityinsights/pt/market-insights/latest-news/natural-gas/051716-russia-vietnam-expand-energy-cooperation-with-new-oil-gas-deals

Auyezhov, Olzhas, 'Uzbek President Sidelines Member of Ruling Triumvirate', Reuters, 26 April 2017, https://www.reuters.com/article/us-uzbekistan-politics-idUSKBN17S1LS

Avtonomov, Vladimir and Elizaveta Bruina, 'List and Russia', in Harald Hagemann, Stephan Seiter, and Eugen Wendler (eds), *The Economic Thought of Fredrich List*, New York: Routledge, 2018, pp. 198–212.

Babayan, Nelli, 'Armenia's Everlasting Protest and Its Resonance in Post-Soviet States', Foreign Policy Research Institute, 18 August 2016, https://www.fpri.org/article/2016/08/armenias-everlasting-protest-resonance-post-soviet-states/

Bachega, Hugo and James Gregory, '"Massive" Drone Attack on Black Sea Fleet—Russia', BBC, 31 October 2022, https://www.bbc.co.uk/news/world-europe-63437212

Badalian, Naira, 'Armenia, Russia Agree on Gas Price for Next 10 Years', Arm Info, 23 December 2021, https://finport.am/full_news.php?id=45269&lang=3

Bagirova, Nailia and Ron Bousso, 'BP-Led Group Extends Azeri Oil "Contract of the Century"', Reuters, 14 September 2017, https://www.reuters.com/article/uk-bp-azerbaijan-agreement-idUKKCN1BP0G3

Baker, Stephanie, 'Russia: Landmark Debt Restructuring Deal Signed', RFE/RL, 9 October 1997, https://www.rferl.org/a/1086755.html

Balmer, Crispian and Emilio Parodi, 'Italy Impounds Luxury Yacht Linked to Russian President', Reuters, 6 May 2022, https://www.reuters.com/world/europe/italy-orders-seizure-yacht-linked-by-media-russian-president-2022-05-06/

Barns-Graham, William, 'Russian Consumer Spending Drops by a Tenth Post-sanctions, But Ukraine's Economy Predicted to Halve', Institute of Export & International Trade, 11 April 2022, https://www.export.org.uk/news/601875/Russian-consumer-spending-drops-by-a-tenth-post-sanctions-but-Ukraines-economy-predicted-to-halve-.htm

BASF, 'Ludwigshafen Site 2021 in Figures', 30 January 2022, https://www.basf.com/global/de/documents/Ludwigshafen/standort-in-zahlen-2022/2022_BASF_Ludwigshafen%20site%20in%20figures_2021_en.pdf

Batashvili, David, 'Nikol Pashinyan's Russian Problem', Rondeli Foundation, 1 December 2019, https://gfsis.org.ge/publications/view/2684

Batmanghelidj, Esfandyar, 'The Inflation Weapon: How American Sanctions Harm Iranian Households', Sanctions & Security Research Project, January 2022, https://sanctionsandsecurity.org/wp-content/uploads/2022/01/2022-January-Iran-Case_Batmanghelidj.pdf

BIBLIOGRAPHY

Baunov, Peter, 'Tokayev Tells Russian TV Kazakhstan Won't Break Western Sanctions', bneIntellinews, 16 June 2022, https://www.intellinews.com/tokayev-tells-russian-tv-kazakhstan-won-t-break-western-sanctions-247682/

BBC, 'Caspian Pipeline Dream Becomes Reality', BBC, 17 September 2002, http://news.bbc.co.uk/1/hi/world/europe/2263611.stm

——— 'Georgian ex-President Saakashvili Named Ukraine Regional Governor', 31 May 2015, https://www.bbc.co.uk/news/world-europe-32943701

——— 'Mistral Warships: Russia and France Agree Compensation Deal', 5 August 2015, https://www.bbc.co.uk/news/world-europe-33798102

——— 'Putin and Berlusconi in Crimea Wine Row', 19 September 2015, https://www.bbc.co.uk/news/world-europe-34297545

——— 'Turkey Coup Attempt: Nearly 82,000 Sacked or Suspended', 13 August 2016, https://www.bbc.co.uk/news/world-europe-37070731

——— 'Uzbekistan PM Mirziyoyev Named Interim President', 8 September 2016, https://www.bbc.co.uk/news/world-asia-37310718

——— 'Russia's Rosneft Wins Gas Licences in Venezuela', 18 December 2017, https://www.bbc.co.uk/news/business-42388488

——— 'Turkey Defies US as Russian S-400 Missile Defence Arrives', 12 July 2019, https://www.bbc.co.uk/news/world-europe-48962885

——— 'US Oil Prices Turn Negative as Demand Dries Up', 21 April 2020, https://www.bbc.co.uk/news/business-52350082

——— 'Estonian Cargo Ship Sinks after Blast in Black Sea', 3 March 2022, https://www.bbc.com/news/world-europe-60606515

——— 'Fugitive Putin Ally Medvedchuk Arrested—Security Service', 13 April 2022, https://www.bbc.co.uk/news/world-europe-61089039

——— 'Imran Khan: What Led to Charismatic Pakistan PM's Downfall?', 9 April 2022, https://www.bbc.co.uk/news/world-asia-61047736

——— 'What Is Swift and Why Is Banning Russia so Significant?', 4 May 2022, https://www.bbc.co.uk/news/business-60521822

——— 'South Africa Row over Russian Superyacht's Arrival', 27 October 2022, https://www.bbc.co.uk/news/world-africa-63395322

———— 'Banker Oleg Tinkov Renounces Russian Citizenship over Ukraine', 1 November 2022, https://www.bbc.com/news/world-europe-63466138

———— 'Ukraine Billionaire Ihor Kolomoisky Targeted in New Anti-corruption Swoop', 1 February 2023, https://www.bbc.co.uk/news/world-europe-64482072

BBC Russian Service, 'Putin namponil Ukraine pro dengi i gaz' [Putin reminded Ukraine about money and gas], 27 November 2013, https://www.bbc.com/russian/international/2013/11/131127_ukraine_eu_russia_economy

———— 'Factcheck BBC: Raketniy udar po torgovomu tsenru Kremenchuga' [BBC Fact Check: Missile attack on the Kremenchug shopping centre], 28 June 2022, https://www.bbc.com/russian/features-61961234

Bechev, Dimitar, 'Russia's Influence in Bulgaria', New Direction, 2018, https://newdirection.online/2018-publications-pdf/ND-report-RussiasInfluenceInBulgaria-preview-lo-res.pdf

———— Turkey under Erdoğan: How a Country Turned from Democracy and the West, New Haven: Yale University Press, 2022.

Bedevian, Asthik, 'New Details of Russian–Armenian Gas Deal Emerge', Azatutyun, 17 December 2013, https://www.azatutyun.am/a/25204160.html

Beioley, Kate and Polina Ivanova, 'Russian Tycoon Tinkov Claims He Was Forced to Sell Bank Stake after Denouncing "Crazy War"', The Financial Times, 2 May 2022, https://www.ft.com/content/41b887c4-ed52-4cf0-8a6f-394d578ea6a2

The Bell, 'Sechin prislal korzinki s kolvasoj chinovnikam pravitseltsva' [Sechin sent baskets with sausages to state officials], 25 December 2018, https://thebell.io/sechin-prislal-korzinki-s-kolbasami-chinovnikam-pravitelstva

———— 'Russia Gives Up Controlling Stake in Rosneft', 8 April 2020, https://thebell.io/en/3347-2/

Belton, Catherine, 'Suleiman Kerimov, the Secret Oligarch', The Financial Times, 10 February 2012, https://www.ft.com/content/ad4e8816-52d0-11e1-ae2c-00144feabdc0

———— Putin's People: How the KGB Took Back Russia and Then Took On the West, London: HarperCollins, 2020.

Bennetts, Mark, 'Pro-Putin Rapper Sets Record for Unpopularity on Russian YouTube', The Guardian, 10 September 2019, https://www.

theguardian.com/world/2019/sep/10/pro-putin-rapper-sets-record-for-unpopularity-on-russian-youtube

————— 'Cold War Looms for Ukrainians Facing a Winter without Power', *The Times*, 6 November 2022, https://www.thetimes.co.uk/article/cold-war-looms-for-ukrainians-facing-a-winter-without-power-fqs2zw08h

Bennhold, Katrin, 'The Former Chancellor Who Became Putin's Man in Germany', *The New York Times*, 23 April 2022, https://www.nytimes.com/2022/04/23/world/europe/schroder-germany-russia-gas-ukraine-war-energy.html

Bernholz, Peter, *Monetary Regimes and Inflation: History, Economic and Political Relationships*, Cheltenham: Edward Elgar, 2015 [2003].

BFM, 'V Gosdume zaintersovalis rossiiskim zolotom' [Russian gold is considered in the Duma], 21 December 2021, https://www.bfm.ru/news/489035

Biesecker, Mikhail, Sarah El Deeb, and Beatrice Dupuy, 'Russia Smuggling Ukrainian Grain to Help Pay for Putin's War', Associated Press, 3 October 2022, https://apnews.com/article/russia-ukraine-putin-business-lebanon-syria-87c3b6fea3f4c326003123b21aa78099

Blackwill, Robert and Jennifer Harris, *War by Other Means: Geoeconomics and Statecraft*, Cambridge: Belknap Press of Harvard University Press, 2017.

Blas, Javier and Jack Farchy, *The World for Sale: Money, Power and the Traders Who Barter the Earth's Resources*, London: Penguin Random House, 2021.

Bloomberg, 'Russia Bans Gas Flows to Europe through Key Yamal Pipeline', 12 May 2022, https://www.bloomberg.com/news/articles/2022-05-12/russia-bans-gas-flows-to-europe-through-key-yamal-pipeline

————— 'Russia Privately Warns of Deep and Prolonged Economic Damage', 5 September 2022, https://www.bloomberg.com/news/articles/2022-09-05/russia-risks-bigger-longer-sanctions-hit-internal-report-warns

————— 'Russia's Elite Flocking to the Gulf Bring in New Business', 20 October 2022, https://www.bloomberg.com/news/articles/2022-10-20/wealth-hotspot-in-gulf-gets-boost-from-russian-millionaires

bneIntellinews, 'Uzbekistan Lifts Currency Controls, Driving Hopes of Investment Renaissance', 5 September 2017, https://www.

intellinews.com/uzbekistan-lifts-currency-controls-driving-hopes-of-investment-renaissance-128332

BOFIT Weekly, 'Covid Crisis Reduces Russian Real Incomes to Lowest Level in a Decade', The Bank of Finland Institute for Emerging Economies, 14 May 2021, https://www.bofit.fi/en/monitoring/weekly/2021/vw202119_1/

Bolton, Paul, 'Import of Fossil Fuels from Russia', House of Commons Library, 11 November 2022, https://commonslibrary.parliament.uk/research-briefings/cbp-9523/

Bounds, Andy, Sam Fleming, Richard Milne, Sarah White, Guy Chasan, and Barney Jopson, 'European Industry Pivots to US as Biden Subsidy Sends "Dangerous Signal"', The Financial Times, 20 November 2022, https://www.ft.com/content/59a8d135-3477-4d0a-8d12-20c7ef94be07

Boyes, Roger and Katerina Kravtsova, 'Path to Power: How Putin's Band of Brothers Became Billionaires', The Times, 15 July 2015, https://www.thetimes.co.uk/article/path-to-power-how-putins-band-of-brothers-became-billionaires-8qjmrwkrzzg

BP, 'Rosneft and BP Complete TNK-BP Sale and Purchase Transaction', 20 March 2013, https://www.bp.com/en/global/corporate/news-and-insights/press-releases/rosneft-and-bp-complete-tnk-bp-sale-and-purchase-transaction.html

———— 'Baku-Supsa Loaded 1000th Tanker at Supsa Terminal on the Black Sea', 29 November 2021, https://www.bp.com/content/dam/bp/country-sites/en_ge/georgia/home/images-2021/Baku-Supsa-1000th-Tanker-press%20release.pdf

Branigan, Tania, 'Booming Chinese Frontier Town Reveals Growing Russian Ties—and Old Divide', The Guardian, 13 October 2014, https://www.theguardian.com/world/2014/oct/13/booming-chinese-frontier-town-reveals-growing-russian-ties--age-old-divide

Braw, Elisabeth, 'Putin's Mobilization Will Further Upend the Russian Economy', Politico, 3 October 2022, https://www.politico.eu/article/putins-mobilization-will-further-upend-the-russian-economy/

———— 'How Greek Companies and Ghost Ships Are Helping Russia', Foreign Policy, 23 November 2022, https://foreignpolicy.com/2022/11/23/how-greek-companies-and-ghost-ships-are-helping-russia/

Brick Court Chambers, 'War in Ukraine Makes Fair Trial Impossible in Privatbank Dispute', Brick Court Chambers, 31 March 2022, https://www.brickcourt.co.uk/news/detail/war-in-ukraine-makes-fair-trial-impossible-in-privatbank-dispute

Brown, James, 'Abe's Russia Policy', *Asia Policy* 14, no. 1 (January 2019), pp. 148–55, https://www.jstor.org/stable/26642268

Browning, Noah, Dmitry Zhdannikov, and Jonathan Saul, 'Russia Poised to Largely Skirt New G7 Oil Price Cap', Reuters, 21 October 2022, https://www.reuters.com/business/energy/russia-poised-largely-skirt-new-g7-oil-price-cap-2022-10-21/

Buchheit, Lee and Mitu Gulati, 'The Fate of Ukraine's Debts', *The Financial Times*, 14 March 2022, https://www.ft.com/content/27f279e6-d3b2-497f-b61e-195808201091

Buckley, Neil, 'Glencore–QIA Deal for Rosneft Stake Starts to Lose Its Lustre', *The Financial Times*, 18 January 2017, https://www.ft.com/content/c735dc00-dccf-11e6-86ac-f253db7791c6

Buli, Nora, 'Centrica Reopens UK's Rough Gas Storage Site in Time for Winter', Reuters, 28 October 2022, https://www.reuters.com/business/energy/british-gas-owner-centrica-reopens-rough-gas-storage-site-2022-10-28/

Bullough, Oliver, *Moneyland: Why Thieves and Crooks Now Rule the World and How to Take it Back*, London: Profile Books, 2018.

———— *Butler to the World: How Britain Helps the World's Worst People Launder Money, Commit Crimes, and Get Away with Anything*, New York: St. Martin's Press, 2022.

Burdyga, Igor, 'The Rise and Fall of Putin's Man in Ukraine', Open Democracy, 26 July 2022, https://www.opendemocracy.net/en/odr/medvedchuk-putin-poroshenko-treason-ukraine-russia/

Burgis, Tom, *Kleptopia: How Dirty Money Is Conquering the World*, London: William Collins, 2020.

Burlakova, Ekjaterina and Anastasia Boyko, 'Rossia mozhet razreshit besposhlinniy voz godyaviny i svininy' [Russia may allow the duty-free import of beef and pork], *Vedomosti*, 7 November 2021, https://www.vedomosti.ru/business/articles/2021/11/07/894759-rossiya-govyadini

Burmistrova, Svetlana, 'Popavshie pod sanktysii "Silovye mashiny" podali v sud v Vietnam' [Sanctioned 'power machines' sues Vietnam], RBC, 30 October 2019, https://www.rbc.ru/business/30/10/2019/5db8261c9a7947dc86f80c4f

Bündner, Helmut, 'Uniper hält Erdgas in den Speichern zurück' [Uniper holds natural gas in reserve], *Frankfurter Allgemenie Zeuting*, 28 April

2022, https://www.faz.net/aktuell/wirtschaft/unternehmen/uniper-warum-der-gazprom-kunde-erdgas-in-den-speichern-zurueckhaelt-17987938.html

Byrne, James, Gary Somerville, Joe Byrne, Jack Watling, Nick Reynolds, and Joe Baker, 'Silicon Lifeline', Royal United Services Institute, 8 August 2022, https://static.rusi.org/RUSI-Silicon-Lifeline-final-web.pdf

Cassetta, John Michael, 'The Geopolitics of Swap Lines', Harvard Kennedy School M-RCBG Associate Working Paper Series, no. 181, April 2022, https://www.hks.harvard.edu/sites/default/files/centers/mrcbg/files/181_AWP_final.pdf

Carroll, Oliver, 'Star Wars in Ukraine: Poroshenko vs Kolomoisky', Politico, 12 December 2015, https://www.politico.eu/article/star-wars-in-ukraine-poroshenko-vs-kolomoisky/

Caruana Galizia, Paul, Matt Russel, and Katie Gunning, 'Greg Barker: The Lord's Work', Tortoise, 11 April 2022, https://www.tortoisemedia.com/audio/greg-barker-the-lords-work/

Cathcart, Will, 'Putin's Crimean Medal of Honor, Forged before the War Even Began', The Daily Beast, 25 April 2015 [Updated 17 July 2017], https://www.thedailybeast.com/putins-crimean-medal-of-honor-forged-before-the-war-even-began

Central Bank of Russia, 'Statement by Bank of Russia Governor Elvira Nabiullina', 24 April 2022, https://www.cbr.ru/eng/press/event/?id=6676

Champion, Marc and Daryna Krasnolutska, 'One Missile Shook Ukraine's Grain Trade; Another Might Kill It', Bloomberg, 25 October 2022, https://www.bloomberg.com/news/articles/2022-10-25/one-missile-shook-ukraine-s-grain-trade-another-might-kill-it?sref=nScyySLq

Channel News Asia, 'Eurasian Economic Union–Singapore FTA Will Make "Positive Contribution" to Economic Relations', 17 December 2021, https://www.channelnewsasia.com/singapore/eaeu-singapore-fta-positive-contribution-economic-relations-russia-singapore-2387171

Chaudhury, Dipanjan Roy, 'EAM Jaishankar Defends India's Long-Standing Ties with Russia', The Economic Times, 11 October 2022, https://economictimes.indiatimes.com/news/india/eam-jaishankar-defends-indias-long-standing-ties-with-russia/articleshow/94769879.cms

BIBLIOGRAPHY

Chazan, Guy, 'Crude Awakening: The German Town on the Front Line of Russian Sanctions', *The Financial Times*, 21 August 2022, https://www.ft.com/content/0c5d883b-e282-436f-85d9-08b6f3ba2abf

Chellaney, Brahma, 'Putin's War and the Mirage of the Rules-Based Order', Project Syndicate, 22 March 2022, https://www.project-syndicate.org/commentary/ukraine-war-destroys-rules-based-order-benefits-china-by-brahma-chellaney-2022-03

Chesnokov, Edvard, 'President Mozambika: Rossiya spisala 90% nashego dolga, my tsenim takix partnyorov' [President of Mozambique: Russia has written off 90 per cent of our debt, we value such partners], *Komsomolskaya Pravda*, 21 August 2019, https://www.kp.ru/daily/27019.4/4081204/

Chikhladze, Tamar, 'The Oligarch's Hometown: The Founding Legend of the Georgian Dream', JAM News, 14 March 2019, https://jam-news.net/the-oligarchs-hometown-the-legend-of-the-georgian-dream/

China Power Team, 'How Has the China–Russia Relationship Evolved?', China Power, 12 May 2022, https://chinapower.csis.org/history-china-russia-relations/

Chirenko, Maria, 'Rada lishila plomochiy nardepa ot "Oppobloka"' [The Rada removed the authority of a deputy from the 'Opposition Bloc'], DS News, 21 September 2022, https://www.dsnews.ua/politics/rada-pozbavila-povnovazhen-nardepa-vid-opobloku-21092022-466507

Chung, Joanna, 'Bankers to Reap $120m on Rosneft IPO', *The Financial Times*, 27 June 2006, https://www.ft.com/content/6d5a6cb8-0603-11db-9dde-0000779e2340

Civil.ge, 'Pandora Papers: Ivanishvili's Purported Secret Stakes', 6 October 2021, https://civil.ge/archives/446317

Clinch, Matt, 'Could Russia Back Its Currency with Gold?', CNBC, 24 December 2014, https://www.cnbc.com/2014/12/23/could-russia-back-its-currency-with-gold.html

CNBC, 'National Security Advisor John Bolton on Venezuela Protests', 30 April 2019, https://www.cnbc.com/video/2019/04/30/national-security-advisor-john-bolton-on-venezuela-protests.html

Coalson, Robert, 'Ukrainian Oligarch Tears into RFE/RL Journalist', RFE/RL, 20 March 2015, https://www.rferl.org/a/ukraine-kolomoysky-rfe-journalist/26912164.html

Cohen, Benjamin, *Currency Statecraft: Monetary Rivalry and Geopolitical Ambition*, Chicago: University of Chicago Press, 2019.

BIBLIOGRAPHY

Cole, Harry and James Heale, 'On Tour with Team Truss: Diva Demands and a Lot of Selfies', *The Times*, 29 October 2022, https://www.thetimes.co.uk/article/liz-truss-team-tour-book-extract-r7jj8rs6s

Collard, George, 'Severstal Unsure if Investors Are Chasing Coupon Payment', Global Capital, 28 March 2022, https://www.globalcapital.com/article/29w6vdnsl5glvpf8csagw/emerging-markets/severstal-unsure-if-investors-are-chasing-coupon-payment

Collier, Ian, 'Vladimir Putin Says Missile Strikes across Ukraine Are in Retaliation for Crimea Bridge "Terrorist" Blast', Sky News, 10 October 2022, https://news.sky.com/story/putin-says-missile-strikes-across-ukraine-retaliation-for-crimea-bridge-blast-12717302

Columbia Harriman Institute, 'The Reminiscences of Alexander Cooley', 20 March 2017, https://oralhistory.harriman.columbia.edu/interview/5

Congressional Research Service, 'Venezuela: Overview of U.S. Sanctions', 31 May 2022, https://crsreports.congress.gov/product/pdf/IF/IF10715

———— 'U.S. Security Assistance to Ukraine', 26 January 2023, https://crsreports.congress.gov/product/pdf/IF/IF12040

Conlin, Jonathan, *Mr. Five Per Cent: The Many Lives of Calouste Gulbenkian, the World's Richest Man*, Princeton: Princeton University Press, 2020.

Connolly, Kate, 'Germany to Delay Phase-Out of Nuclear Plants to Shore Up Energy Security', *The Guardian*, 5 September 2022, https://www.theguardian.com/world/2022/sep/05/germany-to-delay-phase-out-of-nuclear-plants-to-shore-up-energy-security

Cooke, Brian, *The Grand Crimean Railway: The Railway That Won a War*, Knutsford: Cavalier House, 1990.

Cooper, Charlie, 'The Russian Gas Habit Europe Can't Quit: LNG', Politico, 6 November 2022, https://www.politico.eu/article/russia-gas-europe-lng-putin/

Cotterill, Joseph and Owen Walker, 'Mozambique Reels from Credit Suisse "Tuna Bond" Scandal', *The Financial Times*, 25 October 2021, https://www.ft.com/content/f8288871-6a21-447c-8031-f69aa8ee80fa

Cox, Michael, 'Axis of Inconvenience: China, Russia and the Crisis in Ukraine', LSE Blog, 2 February 2022, https://blogs.lse.ac.uk/cff/2022/02/02/axis-of-inconvenience-china-russia-and-the-crisis-in-ukraine/

Crisis Group, 'Coming to Terms with Myanmar's Russia Embrace', Crisis Group, 4 August 2022, https://www.crisisgroup.org/asia/south-east-asia/myanmar-russia-internal/coming-terms-myanmars-russia-embrace

Croft, Jane, 'Oleg Deripaska Takes Stand to Determine Control of Norilsk Nickel', *The Financial Times*, 14 May 2018, https://www.ft.com/content/9e699632-5793-11e8-b8b2-d6ceb45fa9d0

Cullison, Alan, 'Ukraine's Secret Weapon: Feisty Oligarch Ihor Kolomoisky', *The Wall Street Journal*, 27 June 2014, https://www.wsj.com/articles/ukraines-secret-weapon-feisty-oligarch-ihor-kolomoisky-1403886665

Daily Sabah, 'Erdoğan, Putin Sign Agreement on Turkish Stream Gas Pipeline Project', 10 October 2016, https://www.dailysabah.com/energy/2016/10/10/erdogan-putin-sign-agreement-on-turkish-stream-gas-pipeline-project

———— 'Turkish Counterespionage Ops Shield Dissidents', 26 October 2021, https://www.dailysabah.com/politics/news-analysis/turkish-counterespionage-ops-shield-dissidents

Dale Davidson, James and William Rees-Mogg, *The Sovereign Individual*, London: Macmillan, 1997.

Dalton, Matthew, 'Marine Le Pen's Far-Right French Party to Pay Nearly $13 Million to Russian Military Contractor', *The Wall Street Journal*, 22 April 2022, https://www.wsj.com/articles/marine-le-pens-far-right-french-party-to-pay-nearly-13-million-to-russian-military-contractor-11650644840

Danielyan, Emil, 'Russian-Armenian Tycoon Expanding Influence in Armenia', Eurasianet, 2 November 2017, https://eurasianet.org/russian-armenian-tycoon-expanding-influence-in-armenia

Danilova, Maria, 'Putin: Russia to Buy $15 Billion in Ukraine Bonds', Associated Press, 17 December 2013, https://apnews.com/article/3e84daaa74a041f9a76632e6a4eaedfe

Davis, Julia, Twitter Post, 27 February 2022, 20:35 UTC, https://twitter.com/JuliaDavisNews/status/1574860347697205262

Dawisha, Karen, *Putin's Kleptocracy*, New York: Simon & Schuster, 2014.

De la Paz, Fabian Deigo Miguel, 'Metinvest Ceases Operations in Disputed Ukraine Regions', S&P Global, 16 March 2017, https://www.spglobal.com/marketintelligence/en/news-insights/trending/32fzcp7pbdd6arveradfjq2

Debre, Isabel and John Gambrell, 'Sanctioned Russian Oligarch's Megayacht Hides in a UAE Creek', AP News, 1 June 2022, https://

apnews.com/article/russia-ukraine-politics-technology-middle-east-c6592eb5a483c7d95e47cc9bd8f77bde

Debtwire, 'Shareholder Profile: Ihor Kolomoisky, Riding Political Victory, Sets Sights on PrivatBank', 30 May 2019, https://www.mergermarket.com/assets/Shareholder%20Profile.pdf

DeHart, Jonathan, 'Inside Uzbekistan's First Family Feud', The Diplomat, 27 September 2013, https://thediplomat.com/2013/09/inside-uzbekistans-first-family-feud/

Dempsey, Harry, Neil Hume, and Oliver Telling, 'Russia's Largest Shipping Group Sells Part of Fleet to Repay Debts', The Financial Times, 23 May 2022, https://www.ft.com/content/31b80bbb-59f3-4d7a-b901-329867797d41

Detsch, Jack, 'The U.S. Army Goes to School on Nagorno-Karabakh Conflict', Foreign Policy, 30 March 2021, https://foreignpolicy.com/2021/03/30/army-pentagon-nagorno-karabakh-drones/

Deutsche Welle, 'Nord Stream Pipeline Firm Hires Former Finnish Premier', 15 August 2008, https://www.dw.com/en/nord-stream-pipeline-firm-hires-former-finnish-premier/a-3566969

———— 'Russia Suspends TurkStream Talks', 12 March 2015, https://www.dw.com/en/russia-suspends-gas-pipeline-talks-with-turkey/a-18892887

———— 'Germany Extends Lifetime of Remaining Nuclear Plants', 17 October 2022, https://www.dw.com/en/germany-extends-lifetime-of-all-3-remaining-nuclear-plants/a-63466196

DiChristopher, Tom, 'US to Become a Net Energy Exporter in 2020 for First Time in Nearly 70 years, Energy Dept Says', CNBC, 24 January 2019, https://www.cnbc.com/2019/01/24/us-becomes-a-net-energy-exporter-in-2020-energy-dept-says.html

Dimitrov, Martin, 'How a Bizarre Beach Plot Landed Bulgaria's Longtime PM in Hot Water', The Guardian, 20 August 2020, https://www.theguardian.com/world/2020/aug/20/political-storm-threatens-to-engulf-bulgarias-longtime-pm

Dmitriev, Denis, Ilya Lozovsky, Miranda Patrucic, and Olesya Shmagun, 'Mysterious Group of Companies Tied to Bank Rossiya Unites Billions of Dollars in Assets Connected to Vladimir Putin', OCCRP, 20 June 2022, https://www.occrp.org/en/asset-tracker/mysterious-group-of-companies-tied-to-bank-rossiya-unites-billions-of-dollars-in-assets-connected-to-vladimir-putin

Doff, Natasha and Ksenia Galouchko, 'As U.K. Condemns Russia, Investors Pile into Gazprom Bond Sale', Bloomberg, 15 March

2018, https://www.bloomberg.com/news/articles/2018-03-15/
as-u-k-condemns-russia-investors-pile-into-gazprom-bond-
sale?sref=B0Y81EZP

Domm, Patti, 'Trump Security Pick John Bolton Likely to Turn Up Heat
on Iran and Boost Oil Prices', CNBC, 23 March 2018, https://
www.cnbc.com/2018/03/23/bolton-likely-to-turn-up-heat-on-
iran-and-boost-oil-prices.html

Drezner, Daniel, *The Sanctions Paradox: Economic Statecraft and International
Relations*, New York: Cambridge University Press, 2000.

Dunai, Marton and Thomas Grove, 'Russia to Increase Hungary's Nuclear
Power', Reuters, 14 January 2014, https://www.reuters.com/
article/russia-hungary-idUKL6N0KO28L20140114

Duff, Ryan, 'Liz Truss Questioned over Closure of Rough Gas Storage
Facility', Energy Voice, 19 August 2022, https://www.energyvoice.
com/oilandgas/437044/liz-truss-questioned-over-closure-of-
rough-gas-storage-facility/

DutchNews, 'Energy Bills to be Partly Capped from November
in Government U-Turn', 20 September 2022, https://www.
dutchnews.nl/news/2022/09/energy-bills-to-be-partly-capped-
from-november-in-government-u-turn/

Dutkiewicz, Piotr, 'Missing in Translation', Russia in Global Affairs, 20
December 2009, https://eng.globalaffairs.ru/articles/missing-in-
translation/

Duxbury, Charlie, 'Nord Stream Investigation Tests EU Intelligence
Sharing around the Baltic', Politico, 28 October 2022, https://
www.politico.eu/article/sweden-denmark-germany-nord-stream-
investigation-tests-eu-intelligence-sharing-around-the-baltic/

Dyson, Bob, 'Insurers' $15B Russia Aviation Puzzle Will Take Years
to Solve', S&P Global, 12 April 2022, https://www.spglobal.
com/marketintelligence/en/news-insights/latest-news-
headlines/insurers-15b-russia-aviation-puzzle-will-take-years-to-
solve-69640586

Earle, Jonathan, 'Georgian Organized Clashes, Investigators Say', *The
Moscow Times*, 12 December 2012, https://www.themoscowtimes.
com/2012/12/13/georgian-organized-clashes-investigators-
say-a20183

East Renewable AB, 'Report for the Third Quarter of 2020', 21 January
2021, https://emergy.com/wp-content/uploads/2021/01/East-
Renewable-AB-Report-for-the-third-quarter-of-2020.pdf

BIBLIOGRAPHY

———— 'Syvash Wind Farm Construction Update', 1 March 2022, https://feed.stamdata.com/documents/NO0011160368_ IB_01_20220302.pdf

Ebhart, Tommaso and John Follain, 'Italy Can't Stop Talking about Salvini's Russia Tape Scandal', Bloomberg, 15 July 2019, https:// www.bloomberg.com/news/articles/2019-07-15/italy-can-t-stop-talking-about-salvini-s-russia-tape-scandal

Eccles, Mari, 'Russia Scrambles to Save Aviation as Sanctions Begin to Bite', Politico, 6 May 2022, https://www.politico.eu/article/ russia-scrambles-to-save-aviation-as-sanctions-begin-to-bite/

Eckel, Mike, 'Russia's MTS to Pay $850 Million to Settle Uzbek Bribery Case', RFE/RL, 6 May 2019, https://www.rferl.org/a/russia-s-mts-to-pay-850-million-to-settle-uzbek-bribery-case/29809370. html

The Economist, 'Russian Oligarch Vladimir Yevtushenkov Falls from Grace, Again', 6 July 2017, https://www.economist.com/ business/2017/07/06/russian-oligarch-vladimir-yevtushenkov-falls-from-grace-again

———— 'China's Plunging Energy Imports Confound Expectations', 15 September 2022, https://www.economist.com/finance-and-economics/2022/09/15/chinas-plunging-energy-imports-confound-expectations

———— 'Germany's Government Seizes Russian Energy Assets', 22 September 2022, https://www.economist.com/business/2022/ 09/22/germanys-government-seizes-russian-energy-assets

Economist Intelligence Unit, 'Eurobond Restructuring Accepted by Bondholders', 13 September 2019, https://country.eiu.com/ article.aspx?articleid=698436453&Country=Mozambique&topic =Economy&subtopic_3

Eddy, Melissa, 'Three Inquiries, But No Answers to Who Blew Holes in Nord Stream Pipelines', *The New York Times*, 25 October 2022.

Egan, Matt, 'Russian Oil Tankers Are Vanishing off the Map', CNN, 30 March 2022, https://edition.cnn.com/2022/03/30/business/ russia-sanctions-oil/index.html

Eichengreen, Barry, 'Ukraine War Accelerates the Stealth Erosion of Dollar Dominance', *The Financial Times*, 28 March 2022, https:// www.ft.com/content/5f13270f-9293-42f9-a4f0-13290109ea02

Eichengreen, Barry, Ricardo Hausmann, and Ugo Panizza, 'Original Sin: The Pain, the Mystery, and the Road to Redemption', Paper presented at Currency and Maturity Matchmaking: Redeeming Debt from Original Sin, Inter-American Development Bank, Washington, DC, 21–2 November 2002, https://repository.graduateinstitute.ch/record/286974/files/hausmann2002.pdf

Eliseev, Andriy, 'Odessa popala pod obstrel rossiyan' [Odessa came under Russian shelling], Nikvesti, 24 February 2022, https://nikvesti.com/news/incidents/241679

Elliott, Stuart, 'Netherlands Rules Out Change to Groningen Gas Field Policy Despite High Prices', S&P Global, 16 September 2021, https://www.spglobal.com/commodityinsights/en/market-insights/latest-news/natural-gas/091621-netherlands-rules-out-change-to-groningen-gas-field-policy-despite-high-prices

Ellyatt, Holly, 'Putin Mobilizes 300,000 Troops for War in Ukraine and Warns He's Not Bluffing with Nuclear Threat', CNBC, 21 September 2022, https://www.cnbc.com/2022/09/21/russia-ukraine-war-putin-announces-partial-military-mobilization.html

Enerdata, 'How Is Gazprom Adapting to Changing Market Conditions?', 7 May 2014, https://www.enerdata.net/publications/executive-briefing/how-gazprom-adapting-changing-market-conditions.html

Environmental Investigation Agency, 'How Russian Conflict Birch Makes Its Way to American Consumers', 30 September 2022, https://us.eia.org/wp-content/uploads/2022/09/russian-birch-report.pdf

Eristavi, Maxim, 'The Woman Who's Trying to Save Ukraine', Politico, 28 August 2015, https://www.politico.eu/article/ukraine-natalie-jaresko-debt-deal-russia-crimea-war-donetsk-hryvnia-inflation-crisis/

Erlanger, Steven and David Herszenhorn, 'I.M.F. Prepares $18 Billion in Loans for Ukraine', *The New York Times*, 28 March 2017, https://www.nytimes.com/2014/03/28/world/europe/ukraine-bailout.html

Español, Marc, 'Western Creditors Suspend Debt Relief to Sudan over Coup as Country's Economy Sinks', Al-Monitor, 26 June 2022, https://www.al-monitor.com/originals/2022/06/western-creditors-suspend-debt-relief-sudan-over-coup-countrys-economy-sinks

Eurasianet, 'China Figures Reveal Cheapness of Turkmenistan Gas', 31 October 2016, https://eurasianet.org/china-figures-reveal-cheapness-turkmenistan-gas

————— 'Turkmenistan: After Us, the Flood Will Come', 22 May 2018, https://eurasianet.org/turkmenistan-after-us-the-flood-will-come

————— 'Turkmenistan: Back in the Gazprom Groove?', 16 October 2018, https://eurasianet.org/turkmenistan-back-in-the-gazprom-groove

Euronews, 'Moscow Says Power of Siberia 2 Pipeline to China Will "Replace" Nord Stream 2', 15 September 2022, https://www.euronews.com/2022/09/15/moscow-says-power-of-siberia-2-pipeline-to-china-will-replace-nord-stream-2

European Commission, 'Second Strategic Energy Review (Council Document 15944/08)', Council of the European Union, 19 November 2008, https://data.consilium.europa.eu/doc/document/ST-15944-2008-INIT/en/pdf

————— 'State Aid: Commission Approves Dutch Scheme to Support the Filling of the Gas Storage Facility Bergermeer in Context of Russia's Invasion of Ukraine', 12 July 2022, https://ec.europa.eu/commission/presscorner/detail/en/IP_22_4324

Eurostat, 'Gross Domestic Product (GDP) at Current Market Prices by NUTS 3 Regions', 18 April 2022, http://appsso.eurostat.ec.europa.eu/nui/show.do?lang=en&dataset=nama_10r_3gdp

Evans, Damon, 'Zarubezhneft to Create New "Gas Cluster" in Southeast Asia after Asset Deals', Energy Voice, 23 June 2021, https://www.energyvoice.com/oilandgas/asia/331924/zarubezhneft-to-create-new-gas-cluster-in-southeast-asia-after-asset-deals/

The Express Tribune, 'Govt Plans 14,000MW Solar Power through Incentives', 10 August 2022, https://tribune.com.pk/story/2370408/govt-plans-14000mw-solar-power-through-incentives

Fabrichnaya, Elena and Katya Golubkova, 'How Russia's Central Bank Chief Held the Line', Reuters, 26 September 2016, https://www.reuters.com/article/us-russia-cenbank-nabiullina-insight-idUSKCN11W166

Fabricius, Peter, 'Wagner Private Military Force Licks Wounds in Northern Mozambique', The Daily Maverick, 29 November 2019, https://www.dailymaverick.co.za/article/2019-11-29-wagner-private-military-force-licks-wounds-in-northern-mozambique/

Fadeeva, Alina, Ludmila Podobedova, and Timofey Dzyadko, 'Stroitelstvom Amurskogo GPZ zaimetsya podryadchik "Transefti" i NOVATEKa' [Construction of the Amur Petrochemical Complex will be carried out by the contractor of Transneft and Novatek], RBC, 6 July 2017, https://www.rbc.ru/business/06/07/2017/595e09b39a794783e2b52e11

Farchy, Jack, 'Sanctioned Timchenko Sells Gunvor Stake', *The Financial Times*, 20 March 2014, https://www.ft.com/content/72ac6954-b06a-11e3-8efc-00144feab7de

———— 'Central Asia: After the Strongmen', *The Financial Times*, 13 May 2015, https://www.ft.com/content/1938344c-ed87-11e4-987e-00144feab7de

Farchy, Jack, Ben Bartenstein, and Archie Hunter, 'The Latest Russia Oil Mystery: Vostok Sale Announced Then Denied', Bloomberg, 4 November 2022, https://www.bloomberg.com/news/articles/2022-11-04/the-latest-russia-oil-mystery-vostok-sale-announced-then-denied

Farell, Henry and Abraham Newman, 'Weak Links in Finance and Supply Chains Are Easily Weaponized', *Nature*, 9 May 2022, https://www.nature.com/articles/d41586-022-01254-5

Farmer, Ben, 'British Ship Brings First Gas Exports from Mozambique to Europe', *The Telegraph*, 14 November 2022, https://www.telegraph.co.uk/business/2022/11/14/british-ship-brings-first-gas-exports-mozambique-europe/

Faulconbridge, Guy and Sachin Ravidkumar, 'Russia Says UK Navy Blew Up Nord Stream, London Denies Involvement', Reuters, 29 October 2022, https://www.reuters.com/world/europe/russia-says-british-navy-personnel-blew-up-nord-stream-gas-pipelines-2022-10-29/

Fein, Bruce, 'Congress Should End the War in Ukraine by Withdrawing from NATO', The Hill, 25 November 2022, https://thehill.com/opinion/national-security/3750203-congress-should-end-the-war-in-ukraine-by-withdrawing-from-nato/

Fenske, Christiane, 'PCK Raffinerie in Schwedt: Der Stolz der jungen DDR' [PCK refinery in Schwedt: The pride of the young DDR], SUPERillu, 9 July 2022, https://www.superillu.de/magazin/heimat/ddr/geschichte/die-raffinerie-schwedt-1838

Finanz.ru, 'Minfin nachal gotovitsya k arestu valiutnikh rezervov Rossii' [MinFin began to prepare for the seizure of Russia's currency reserves], 13 October 2020, https://www.finanz.ru/novosti/valyuty/minfin-nachal-gotovitsya-k-arestu-valyutnykh-rezervov-rossii-1029801100

Flanagan, Jane, 'Bloodshed and Retreat from Mozambique for Putin's private Army the Wagner Group', *The Times*, 25 November 2019, https://www.thetimes.co.uk/article/bloodshed-and-retreat-from-mozambique-for-putin-s-private-army-the-wagner-group-696tnpzqh

Flanagan, Stephen and Johanna Mendelson Forman, 'Russia's Reengagement in the Western Hemisphere', Center for Strategic and International Studies, 25 November 2008, https://www.csis.org/analysis/russias-reengagement-western-hemisphere.

Fleming, Sam, James Politi, and Valentina Pop, 'Weaponisation of Finance: How the West Unleashed "Shock and Awe" on Russia', *The Financial Times*, 6 April 2022, https://www.ft.com/content/5b397d6b-bde4-4a8c-b9a4-080485d6c64a

Flynn, Michael, 'Our Ally Turkey Is in Crisis and Needs Our Support', The Hill, 8 November 2016, https://thehill.com/blogs/pundits-blog/foreign-policy/305021-our-ally-turkey-is-in-crisis-and-needs-our-support/

Forbes India, 'Europe's Top 20 Billionaires', 26 March 2012, https://www.forbesindia.com/article/worlds-billionaires-2012/europes-top-20-billionaires/32578/1

Foy, Henry, '"We Need to Talk about Igor": The Rise of Russia's Most Powerful Oligarch', *The Financial Times*, 1 March 2018, https://www.ft.com/content/dc7d48f8-1c13-11e8-aaca-4574d7dabfb6

———— 'Russian Rail Freight Operator Rustranscom Seeks London IPO', *The Financial Times*, 1 April 2019, https://www.ft.com/content/39daacca-549e-11e9-a3db-1fe89bedc16e

———— 'The UK Executives Helping Burnish Russia's Image', *The Financial Times*, 4 April 2019, https://www.ft.com/content/0d58751a-5566-11e9-91f9-b6515a54c5b1

Foy, Henry and Guy Chazan, 'Gerhard Schröder Appointed Chairman of Rosneft', *The Financial Times*, 29 September 2017, https://www.ft.com/content/100db270-a518-11e7-9e4f-7f5e6a7c98a2

Foy, Henry, Rachel Sanderson, and James Politi, 'The Ties That Bind Italy and Russia', *The Financial Times*, 29 October 2017, https://www.ft.com/content/ffbe03c0-b976-11e7-8c12-5661783e5589

France24, 'Norway, Poland Open New Gas Pipeline amid Nord Stream Leaks', 27 September 2022, https://www.france24.com/en/tv-shows/business-daily/20220927-norway-poland-open-new-gas-pipeline-as-nord-stream-leaks

Friedman, Thomas, 'Foreign Affairs Big Mac I', *The New York Times*, 8 December 1996, https://www.nytimes.com/1996/12/08/opinion/foreign-affairs-big-mac-i.html

Frolova, Natalya, 'A "Friendly" Deal: How Russian Money Supports Corrupted Bulgarian Politicians', The Insider, 29 May 2020, https://theins.ru/en/uncategorized/221767

Frum, David, 'The West's Nuclear Mistake', *The Atlantic*, 8 December 2021, https://www.theatlantic.com/ideas/archive/2021/12/germany-california-nuclear-power-climate/620888/

Galaktinova, Aleksandra and Svetlana Reiter, 'Stroit "Silu Sibiri" budet blizkaya k vladeltsu TRC "RIO" kompaniya' [Construction of 'Power of Siberia' will be a company close to the owner of the RIO shopping centre], RBC, 1 March 2016, http://rbc.ru/business/01/03/2016/56d5a3809a7947fe606e76e4

Galeotti, Mark, '"RepressIntern": Russia's Security Cooperation with Fellow Authoritarians', Open Democracy, 22 November 2016, https://www.opendemocracy.net/en/odr/repressintern-russian-security-cooperation-with-fellow-authoritarians/

Gardner, Andrew, 'South Stream Battle Brings Down Bulgarian Government', Politico, 12 June 2014, https://www.politico.eu/article/south-stream-battle-brings-down-bulgarian-government/

Gas Infrastructure Europe, 'Aggregated Gas Storage Inventory—EU', 8 March 2023, https://agsi.gie.eu/data-overview/eu

Gauthier-Villars, David, 'Wife of Russian Billionaire Melnichenko Contests EU Sanctions', Reuters, 4 June 2022, https://www.reuters.com/article/us-ukraine-crisis-melnichenko-idAFKBN2NL0DK

Gehrke, Laurenz, 'Germany's Scholz Calls for EU Ostpolitik', Politico, 11 August 2021, https://www.politico.eu/article/youre-so-vague-germanys-scholz-calls-for-new-russia-policy/

Gelpern, Anna, 'Ukraine's Russian Bonds: A Gazprom Clause?', Credit Slips, 27 April 2014, https://www.creditslips.org/creditslips/2014/04/ukraines-russian-bonds-another-pesky-clause-makes-you-wonder.html%20

——— 'Russia's Contract Arbitrage', *Capital Markets Law Journal* 9, no. 3 (July 2014), pp. 308–26.

General Assembly of the United Nations, 'H.E. Mr. Nana Addo Dankwa Akufo-Addo, President', 21 September 2022, https://gadebate.un.org/en/77/ghana

Georgian Journal, 'Investment Fund Triggers Speculations', 29 November 2012, https://georgianjournal.ge/business/21189-investment-fund-triggers-speculations.html

Georgy, Michael and Ahmed Rasheed, 'Iranian Commander Issued Stark Warning to Iraqi Kurds over Kirkuk', Reuters, 20 October 2017, https://www.reuters.com/article/cnews-us-mideast-crisis-iraq-kirkuk-fall-idCAKBN1CP2CW-OCATP

German Energy and Economy Ministry, 'Bundestag: Druchsache 18/6349', 22 October 2015, https://dejure.org/Drucksachen/Bundestag/BT-Drs._18/6349

Gibbons-Neff, Thomas, 'How a 4-Hour Battle between Russian Mercenaries and U.S. Commandos Unfolded in Syria', *The New York Times*, 24 May 2018, https://www.nytimes.com/2018/05/24/world/middleeast/american-commandos-russian-mercenaries-syria.html

Gibson, Megan, 'Francis Fukuyama: We Could Be Facing the End of "the End of History"', *The New Statesman*, 30 March 2022, https://www.newstatesman.com/encounter/2022/03/francis-fukuyama-on-the-end-of-the-end-of-history

Gilbert, Alex, Morgan Bazilian, and Samantha Gross, 'The Emerging Global Natural Gas Market and the Energy Crisis of 2021–2022', Brookings, 9 December 2021, https://www.brookings.edu/wp-content/uploads/2021/12/FP_20211214_global_energy_crisis_gilbert_bazilian_gross.pdf

Gillespie, Todd and Kitty Donaldson, 'UK Unveils £40 Billion Winter Energy Bill Bailout for Businesses', Bloomberg, 21 September 2022, https://www.bloomberg.com/news/articles/2022-09-21/uk-energy-bill-bailout-for-businesses-may-cost-40-billion

Gilman, Martin, *No Precedent, No Plan: Inside Russia's 1998 Default*, Cambridge, MA: MIT University Press, 2010.

Gita-Carlos, Ruth Abbey, 'Russian Oil Firm Needs to Re-enter Deal with PH Gov't: Palace', PNA, 17 October 2019, https://www.pna.gov.ph/articles/1083478

Glauber, Joseph and Joseph Laborde, 'The Russia–Ukraine Grain Agreement: What Is at Stake?', International Food Policy Research Institute, 27 July 2022, https://www.ifpri.org/blog/russia-ukraine-grain-agreement-what-stake

Gnana, Jennifer, 'Saudi Drilling Company Eyes Fast Growth in Oil, Gas Production', S&P Global, 18 September 2022, https://www.spglobal.com/commodityinsights/en/market-insights/latest-news/oil/091822-saudi-drilling-company-eyes-fast-growth-in-oil-gas-production

BIBLIOGRAPHY

Goetzmann, William, *Money Changes Everything: How Finance Made Civilization Possible*, Princeton: Princeton University Press, 2017.

Golubkova, Katya and Denis Pinchuk, 'Kremlin Pivot to China Slowed as Projects Delayed', Reuters, 27 August 2015, https://www.reuters.com/article/uk-russia-china-projects-idUKKCN0QW15T20150827

Golubovich, Alexei, 'Mozhno li naiti zamenu dollaru v odnom otdelno vyatom Tamozhennom soyuze' [Is it possible to find a replacement for the dollar in the unified customs union?], *Vedomosti*, 14 April 2018, https://www.vedomosti.ru/finance/articles/2014/04/14/mozhno-li-najti-zamenu-dollaru-v-odnom-otdelno-vzyatom

Goodman, Joshua, 'Oil Tankers "Go Dark" off Venezuela to Evade US Sanctions', Associated Press, 14 November 2019, https://apnews.com/article/84cabe36652c4194ae2db852e8bab2c4

Goodman, Peter, Jack Ewing, and Matt Phillips, 'Sanctions on Russian Debt Are Called a "First Salvo" That Sends a Message', *The New York Times*, 15 April 2021, https://www.nytimes.com/2021/04/15/business/biden-russia-sanctions-debt.html

Gorin, Nazar, 'Soviet Economic Integration or Industrial Colonialism?', Heinrich Böll Stiftung, 1 September 2022, https://ua.boell.org/en/2022/09/01/soviet-economic-integration-or-industrial-colonialism

Goudsouzian, Tanya and Lara Fatah, 'The Kurds Take Kirkuk, Now What?', Al Jazeera, 16 June 2014, https://www.aljazeera.com/news/2014/6/16/analysis-the-kurds-take-kirkuk-now-what

Gould, Joe and Aaron Mehta, 'Lawmakers Say Trump Is Locked into Turkey Sanctions', Defense News, 16 July 2019, https://www.defensenews.com/congress/2019/07/16/trump-cuts-off-f-35-for-turkey-and-lawmakers-say-sanctions-are-coming/

Gould-Davies, Nigel, 'The Russia Report: Key Points and Implications', International Institute for Strategic Studies, 21 July 2020, https://www.iiss.org/blogs/analysis/2020/07/isc-russia-report-key-points-and-implications

Government of the Russian Federation and Central Bank of Russia, 'Statement of the Government of the Russian Federation and Central Bank of Russia on Economic Policies', 13 July 1999, https://www.imf.org/external/np/loi/1999/071399.htm

Graeber, David, *Debt; The First 5,000 Years*, New York: Melville House Printing, 2011.

BIBLIOGRAPHY

Graff, Garett, '"Something Was Badly Wrong": When Washington Realized Russia Was Actually Invading Ukraine', Politico, 24 February 2023, https://www.politico.com/news/magazine/2023/02/24/russia-ukraine-war-oral-history-00083757

Grigas, Agnia, *Beyond Crimea: The New Russian Empire*, New Haven: Yale University Press, 2016.

Grivach, Alexey, 'A Window to Asia', Russia in Global Affairs, 23 September 2014, https://eng.globalaffairs.ru/articles/a-window-to-asia/

Grossman, Derek, 'How US–Vietnam Ties Might Go Off the Rails', *The Diplomat*, 1 February 2021, https://thediplomat.com/2021/02/how-us-vietnam-ties-might-go-off-the-rails/

Grozev, Christo, 'The Remote Control Killers behind Russia's Cruise Missile Strikes on Ukraine', Bellingcat, 24 October 2022, https://www.bellingcat.com/news/uk-and-europe/2022/10/24/the-remote-control-killers-behind-russias-cruise-missile-strikes-on-ukraine/

Guarascio, Francesco, 'EU's Full Ban on Russian Coal to Be Pushed Back to mid-August', Reuters, 7 April 2022, https://www.reuters.com/business/energy/eus-full-ban-russian-coal-be-pushed-back-mid-august-source-2022-04-07/

Gul, Ayzal, 'Khan after Putin Visit: Pakistan to Import Wheat, Gas from Russia', VOA, 2022, https://www.voanews.com/a/khan-after-putin-visit-pakistan-to-import-wheat-gas-from-russia-/6463734.html

Gulati, Mitu, 'Mr. Putin's Clever Bond Issue', *The Financial Times*, 10 March 2014, https://www.ft.com/content/bad26105-ad34-3281-8649-acca1f0cad47

Gulati, Mitu and Mark Weidemaier, 'Why Did the Dog Not Bark (or Why Did the Creditors Consent so Readily (Podcast))', Clauses & Controversies, 23 October 2022, https://soundcloud.com/clauses-controversies/ep-86-ft-mitu-mark

Gustafson, Thane, *The Bridge: National Gas in a Redivided Europe*, Cambridge, MA: Harvard University Press, 2020.

Götz, Linde, Maximilian Heigermoser, and Tinoush Jaghdani, 'Russia's Food Security and Impact on Agri-Food Trade', in Stephen Wegren and Frode Nilssen (eds), *Russia's Role in the Contemporary International Agri-Food Trade System*, Palgrave Advances in Bioeconomy: Economics and Policies, Cham: Palgrave Macmillan, 2021, https://doi.org/10.1007/978-3-030-77451-6_5

BIBLIOGRAPHY

Haddad, Mohammed, 'How Much of Europe's Energy Comes from Gas?', Al Jazeera, 6 September 2022, https://www.aljazeera.com/news/2022/9/6/infographic-how-much-of-europes-energy-gas

Hanlon, Joseph, 'Mozambique Palma Attack: Why IS Involvement Is Exaggerated', BBC, 17 April 2021, https://www.bbc.co.uk/news/world-africa-56773012

Hansen, Holger and Kirsti Knolle, 'Germany Agrees 200 bln Euro Package to Shield against Surging Energy Prices', Reuters, 29 September 2022, https://www.reuters.com/business/energy/german-govt-agrees-relief-package-response-soaring-energy-prices-sources-2022-09-29/

Harrison, Luke, 'London PV Market Facing Potential EUR200m Syvash Wind Farm Loss in Ukraine', Insurance Insider, 15 March 2022, https://www.insuranceinsider.com/article/29u6br0uppsc1i627ka9s/london-pv-market-facing-potential-eur200mn-syvash-wind-farm-loss-in-ukraine

Hashimova, Umida, 'Not So Fast: Will Uzbekistan Join the Eurasian Economic Union?', *The Diplomat*, 7 October 2021, https://thediplomat.com/2019/10/not-so-fast-will-uzbekistan-join-the-eurasian-economic-union/

Hausmann, Ricardo, 'The Hunger Bonds', Project Syndicate, 26 May 2017, https://www.project-syndicate.org/commentary/maduro-venezuela-hunger-bonds-by-ricardo-hausmann-2017-05

Haynes, Deborah, 'Russia Flew €140m in Cash and Captured Western Weapons to Iran in Return for Deadly Drones, Source Claims', Sky News, 8 November 2022, https://news.sky.com/story/russia-gave-eur140m-and-captured-western-weapons-to-iran-in-return-for-deadly-drones-source-claims-12741742

Helleiner, Eric, *The Neomercantilists: A Global Intellectual History*, Ithaca, NY: Cornell University Press, 2021.

Hellenic Shipping News, 'US Crude Oil Exports to Europe Have Risen by 52.2% So Far This Year', 29 October 2022, https://www.hellenicshippingnews.com/us-crude-oil-exports-to-europe-have-risen-by-52-2-so-far-this-year/

Hess, Maximilian, 'China Has Decided Russia Is Too Risky an Investment', *Foreign Policy*, 16 May 2018, https://foreignpolicy.com/2018/05/16/china-has-decided-russia-is-too-risky-an-investment/

———'Bond of War: Russian Geo-economics in Ukraine's Sovereign Debt Restructuring', Foreign Policy Research Institute, 19 September

2018, https://www.fpri.org/article/2018/09/bond-of-war-russian-geo-economics-in-ukraines-sovereign-debt-restructuring/

———— 'Sechin's Folly', Riddle, 29 January 2019, https://ridl.io/sechin-s-folly/

———— 'Russia in Venezuela: Geopolitical Boon or Economic Misadventure?', Foreign Policy Research Institute, 30 January 2019, https://www.fpri.org/article/2019/01/russia-in-venezuela-geopolitical-boon-or-economic-misadventure/

———— 'Lessons Learned from Deripaska's Sanctions Deal', *The Moscow Times*, 1 February 2019, https://www.themoscowtimes.com/2019/02/01/lessons-learned-from-deripaskas-sanctions-deal-op-ed-a64352

————'Uzbekistan Asks Bond-Buyers to Be Its Valentine with $1 Billion Sale', Eurasianet, 15 February 2019, https://eurasianet.org/uzbekistan-asks-bond-buyers-to-be-its-valentine-with-1-billion-sale

———— 'Geopolitics, Sanctions, and Russian Sovereign Debt since the Annexation of Crimea', Foreign Policy Research Institute, 25 June 2019, https://www.fpri.org/article/2019/06/geopolitics-sanctions-and-russian-sovereign-debt-since-the-annexation-of-crimea/

————'Explaining Trump's Belated Russia Sanctions', Riddle, 16 August 2019, https://ridl.io/explaining-trump-s-belated-russia-sanctions/

————'Another Sechin Trick in Venezuela', Riddle, 30 March 2020, https://ridl.io/another-sechin-trick-in-venezuela/

———— 'Russia and Central Asia: Putin's Most Stable Region?', *Orbis* 64, no. 3 (May 2020), pp. 421–33, https://doi.org/10.1016/j.orbis.2020.05.005

————'Economic Crisis Helped Putin Rise to Power: It Could Also Be His Downfall', *The New Statesman*, 21 March 2022, https://www.newstatesman.com/world/europe/2022/03/economic-crisis-helped-putin-rise-to-power-it-could-also-be-his-downfall

————'Going Dutch Could Help Break Europe's Addiction to Russian Gas', *The New Statesman*, 19 May 2022, https://www.newstatesman.com/international-politics/2022/05/going-dutch-could-help-break-europes-addiction-to-russian-gas

————'How Russia's Invasion of Ukraine Has Affected Kazakh Politics', Foreign Policy Research Institute, 8 June 2022, https://www.fpri.org/article/2022/06/how-russias-invasion-of-ukraine-has-affected-kazakh-politics/

———— 'Why the World Should Pay Attention to Unrest in Karakalpakstan', Al Jazeera, 7 July 2022, https://www.aljazeera.com/opinions/2022/7/7/why-unrest-in-a-remote-region-of-uzbekistan-matters

———— 'Putin Doesn't Fit with China's Plans for an Alternative Global Financial Order', bneIntellinews, 27 July 2022, https://intellinews.com/hess-putin-doesn-t-fit-with-china-s-plans-for-an-alternative-global-financial-order-251778

———— 'Will a New War Crash Europe's Azerbaijani Gas Dreams?', *Foreign Policy*, 4 August 2022, https://foreignpolicy.com/2022/08/04/azerbaijan-nagorno-karabakh-armenia-gas-oil-europe-russia-pipelines-war/

———— 'Russia Can't Protect Its Allies Anymore', *Foreign Policy*, 22 September 2022, https://foreignpolicy.com/2022/09/22/russia-armenia-azerbaijan-war-nagorno-karabakh/

———— 'Putin's Plan to Take On the World Economic Order Hits a Wall', Al Jazeera, 13 December 2022, https://www.aljazeera.com/opinions/2022/12/13/putins-plan-to-take-on-the-world-economic-order-hits-a-wall

Hess, Maximilian and Luca Anceschi, 'Turkmenistan Is All about the Berdimuhamedovs', *Foreign Policy*, 9 March 2022, https://foreignpolicy.com/2022/03/09/turkmenistan-election-berdimuhamedov-dynasty/

Hess, Maximilian and Maia Otarashvili, 'Georgia's Doomed Deep-Sea Port Ambitions: Geopolitics of the Cancelled Anaklia Project', Foreign Policy Research Institute, 2 October 2020, fpri.org/wp-content/uploads/2020/10/georgias-doomed-deep-sea-port-ambitions.pdf

Higgins, Andrew, 'Mikheil Saakashvili, Ex-president of Georgia, Arrested in Ukraine, Again', *The New York Times*, 8 December 2017, https://www.nytimes.com/2017/12/08/world/europe/saakashvili-arrest-ukraine.html

Hirst, Tomas, 'Russian Central Bank Admits Massive Rosneft Bond Sale Fuelled the Ruble Crash', Insider, 3 February 2015, https://www.businessinsider.com/russian-central-bank-chief-admits-rosneft-bond-sale-was-opaque-2015-2

Holland, Emily, 'Poisoned by Gas: Institutional Failure, Energy Dependency, and Security', PhD diss., Columbia University, 17 July 2017, https://doi.org/10.7916/D8W387KP

————— 'Europe's Energy Security Problem Leaves It in the Cold', War on the Rocks, 30 November 2021, https://warontherocks. com/2021/11/europes-energy-security-problem-leaves-it-in-the-cold/

Holland, Steve, 'Biden Vows Consequences for Saudi Arabia after OPEC+ Decision', Reuters, 13 October 2022, https://www.reuters.com/world/us-president-biden-re-evaluating-relationship-with-saudi-after-opec-decision-2022-10-11/

Hope, Bradley and Justin Scheck, *Blood and Oil: Mohammed bin Salman's Ruthless Quest for Global Power*, London: John Murray, 2020.

House of Commons Debate, 'National Security and Russia', Hansard, vol. 638, col. 531, 26 March 2018, https://hansard.parliament.uk/commons/2018-03-26/debates/B5EF4CEE-D0E9-4613-81C4-DDD9F03015EE/NationalSecurityAndRussia

Hubbard, Ben, *MBS: The Rise to Power of Mohammed Bin Salman*, London: William Collins, 2020.

Hume, Neil and David Sheppard, 'Gunvor Boss Used $1bn Payout to Sever Ties with Russian Oligarch', *The Financial Times*, 31 May 2016, https://www.ft.com/content/dfa7da28-236a-11e6-aa98-db1e01fabc0c

Humpert, Matle, 'Russian LNG to Europe Flies under Radar; France's TotalEnergies Continues Imports from Arctic', High North News, 14 October 2022, https://www.highnorthnews.com/en/russian-lng-europe-flies-under-radar-frances-totalenergies-continues-imports-arctic

Humphrey, Chris, 'China's AIIB Bank Set to Become Major Player While New BRICS Bank Lags Behind', Overseas Development Institute, 1 December 2015, https://odi.org/en/insights/chinas-aiib-bank-set-to-become-major-player-while-new-brics-bank-lags-behind/

Hunder, Max, 'Ukraine's Northern Regions Say Russian Troops Have Mostly Withdrawn', Reuters, 4 April 2022, https://www.reuters.com/world/europe/ukraines-northern-regions-say-russian-troops-have-mostly-withdrawn-2022-04-04/

Hurtado, Patricia, 'Russians Arrested for Smuggling US Military Tech, PDVSA Oil', Bloomberg, 19 October 2022, https://www.bloomberg.com/news/articles/2022-10-19/five-russians-charged-in-scheme-to-obtain-us-military-technology

Hungary Today, 'Finance Minister Inaugurates HQ of International Investment Bank', 19 February 2021, https://hungarytoday.hu/finance-minister-inaugurates-hq-of-international-investment-bank/

BIBLIOGRAPHY

Hyde, Lily, 'Ukraine's President Alleges Coup Attempt Involving Country's Richest Man', Politico, 27 November 2021, https://www.politico.eu/article/ukraine-zelenskiy-coup-akhmetov-russia/

Ichord Jr, Robert, 'Transforming the Power Sector in Developing Countries: Geopolitics, Poverty, and Climate Change in Pakistan', Atlantic Council, 9 January 2020, https://www.atlanticcouncil.org/in-depth-research-reports/issue-brief/transforming-the-power-sector-in-developing-countries-geopolitics-poverty-and-climate-change-in-pakistan/

IMF News, 'IMF Adjusts Its Policy on Arrears to Official Creditors', 10 December 2015, https://www.imf.org/en/News/Articles/2015/09/28/04/53/sopol120815a

———— 'Transcript of October 2022 MD Kristalina Georgieva Press Briefing on GPA', 13 October 2022, https://www.imf.org/en/News/Articles/2022/10/13/tr101322-transcript-of-md-press-briefing-annual-meetings

Ince, Elif, Michael Forsythe, and Carlotta Gall, 'Russian Superyachts Find Safe Haven in Turkey, Raising Concerns in Washington', *The New York Times*, 23 October 2022, https://www.nytimes.com/2022/10/23/world/europe/russian-superyachts-find-safe-haven-in-turkey-raising-concerns-in-washington.html

Independent Defence Anti-Corruption Committee, 'Crossing the Line: How the Illegal Trade with Occupied Donbas Undermines Defence Integrity', 8 October 2018, https://nako.org.ua/en/news/crossing-the-line-how-the-illegal-trade-with-occupied-donbas-has-undermined-defence-integrity

ING, 'There's No Denying It Anymore, the Eurozone Is in Recession', 6 October 2017, https://think.ing.com/articles/no-denying-it-anymore-the-eurozone-is-in-recession/

Inman, Phillip, 'Why Is Vladimir Putin Demanding Russian Gas Is Paid for in Roubles?', *The Guardian*, 31 March 2022, https://www.theguardian.com/business/2022/mar/31/why-is-vladimir-putin-demanding-russian-gas-is-paid-for-in-roubles

Inozemtsev, Vladislav, 'Russia's Default: Believe It or Not', Riddle, 18 March 2022, https://ridl.io/russia-s-default-believe-it-or-not/

The Insider, 'Ubiity na udalyonke: Kto i kak navodit upravlyayemyye rakety na ukrainskiye grazhdanskiye obyekty' [Assasination by remote-control: Who directs guided missiles at Ukrainian civilian targets and how], 22 October 2022, https://theins.ru/politika/255158

BIBLIOGRAPHY

Intelligence Online, 'Gazprom Spying Affair: The Collapse of Ali Sen's Network', 10 November 2020, https://www.intelligenceonline.com/international-dealmaking/2020/11/10/gazprom-spying-affair-the-collapse-of-ali-sen-s-network,109620310-art

Interfax, 'Proizvodstvo avtomatov Kalshnikov v Venesuelye ne smogut zapustit v 2022 godu' [It will not be possible to launch the production of Kalashnikovs in Venezuela in 2022], 27 May 2022, https://www.interfax.ru/world/843231

International Energy Agency, 'Gas 2020', International Energy Agency, June 2020, https://iea.blob.core.windows.net/assets/555b268e-5dff-4471-ac1d-9d6bfc71a9dd/Gas_2020.pdf

———— 'World Energy Outlook', International Energy Agency, 27 October 2022, http://www.iea.org/reports/world-energy-outlook-2022

International Institute for Strategic Studies, 'Russia and Sanctions Evasion', 27 July 2022, https://doi.org/10.1080/13567888.2022.2096344

International Investment Bank, 'Hungary Regains Full Membership in Russia-Based International Investment Bank', International Investment Bank, 28 May 2015, https://iib.int/en/articles/hungary-regains-full-membership-in-russia-based-international-investment-bank

Isaad, Haneea and Sam Reynolds, 'Finding the Right Way Forward in Pakistan's Energy Crisis', *The Diplomat*, 22 July 2022, https://thediplomat.com/2022/07/finding-the-right-way-forward-in-pakistans-energy-crisis

Isidorde, Chris and Chris Liakos, 'Russia Moves to Seize Hundreds of Planes from Foreign Owners', CNN, 17 March 2022, https://edition.cnn.com/2022/03/16/business/russia-aircraft-seizure/index.html

Ivanova, Polina, Chris Cook, and Laura Pitel, 'How Russia Secretly Takes Grain from Occupied Ukraine', *The Financial Times*, 30 October 2022, https://www.ft.com/content/89b06fc0-91ad-456f-aa58-71673f43067b

Ivanova, Polina, and Max Seddon, 'Russia's Melancholy Oligarchs', *The Financial Times*, 7 September 2022, https://www.ft.com/content/daee2387-6d96-4f2e-9a80-5cc70cd8cc67

Iyer, Vijay, 'To Us the Rosneft Deal Signifies Our Ability to Build Assets: Prashant Ruia', *The Economic Times*, 23 August 2017, https://

economictimes.indiatimes.com/markets/expert-view/to-us-the-rosneft-deal-signifies-our-ability-to-build-assets-prashant-ruia-essar-group/articleshow/60174891.cms?from=mdr

Işık, Yörük, Twitter Post, 11 August 2022, 19:11 UTC, https://twitter.com/YorukIsik/status/1557791866460012546

———— Twitter Post, 13 October 2022, 11:45 UTC, https://twitter.com/YorukIsik/status/1580509940447207426

Jakes, Lara, Michael Crowley, and David Sanger, 'Biden Chooses Antony Blinken, Defender of Global Alliances, as Secretary of State', *The New York Times*, 22 November 2020, https://www.nytimes.com/2020/11/22/us/politics/biden-antony-blinken-secretary-of-state.html

James Martin Center for Nonproliferation Studies, 'Export Controls in an Era of Strategic Competition', September 2022, https://www.tradecompliance.io/sites/default/files/2022-09/sectoral%20guidance%20as%20posted%209%20sept_0.pdf

Jensen, James, 'The Development of a Global LNG Market', Oxford Institute for Energy Studies, 2004, https://www.oxfordenergy.org/wpcms/wp-content/uploads/2010/11/NG5-TheDevelopmentofAGlobalLNGMarketIsItLikelyIfSoWhen-JamesJensen-2004.pdf

Jeffrey, Rebecca, 'Antonov Factory Hit as Ukraine Conflict Continues', Air Cargo News, 15 March 2022, https://www.aircargonews.net/airlines/freighter-operator/antonov-factory-hit-as-ukraine-conflict-continue/

Jessop, Julian, 'The Energy Price Guarantee May Cost Much Less than Is Feared', *The Spectator*, 24 September 2022, https://www.spectator.co.uk/article/the-energy-price-guarantee-may-cost-much-less-than-is-feared/

Johnson, Juliet, 'Forbidden Fruit: Russia's Uneasy Relationship with the Dollar', *Review of International Political Economy* 15, no. 3 (August 2008), pp. 378–98, https://www.jstor.org/stable/25261975

Johnson, Miles, 'Wagner Leader Generated $250mn from Sanctioned Empire', *The Financial Times*, 21 February 2023, https://www.ft.com/content/98e478b5-c0d4-48a3-bcf7-e334a4ea0aca

Joint Investigation Team, 'JIT Presentation of First Results of the MH17 Criminal Investigation', Netherlands Public Prosecution Service, 28 September 2016, https://www.prosecutionservice.nl/topics/mh17-plane-crash/criminal-investigation-jit-mh17/jit-presentation-first-results-mh17-criminal-investigation-28-9-2016

Jolly, Jasper, 'European Gas Prices Fall to Pre-Ukraine War Level', *The Guardian*, 29 December 2022, https://www.theguardian.com/environment/2022/dec/29/european-gas-prices-fall-to-pre-ukraine-war-level

Jones, Marc, 'Turkey's Recurring Currency Nightmare Strikes Again', Reuters, 30 May 2022, https://www.reuters.com/markets/europe/turkeys-recurring-currency-nightmare-strikes-again-2022-05-30/

Jones, Sam, 'Ukrainian Billionaire Dmitry Firtash: "Putin Will Go Further; What Will Europe Do Then?"', *The Financial Times*, 29 July 2022, https://www.ft.com/content/18184ed1-d96f-4c4b-a5e9-8e22e10a2890

Jones, Sam, Owen Walker, and Anastasia Stognei, 'How Austria's Raiffeisen Got Stuck in Russia—While Making Record Profits', *The Financial Times*, 25 February 2023, https://www.ft.com/content/1cea1f08-83ac-4471-9fa4-1cdfcc86fcb0

Jordan, Dearbail and Daniel Thomas, 'Bank of England Expects UK to Fall into Longest Ever Recession', BBC, 4 November 2022, https://www.bbc.co.uk/news/business-63471725

Joshi, Manoj, 'The Rules-Based Order', Observer Research Foundation, 21 March 2021, https://www.orfonline.org/research/the-rules-based-order/

Kalin, Stephen, Summer Said, and Dion Nissenbaum, 'U.S.–Saudi Relations Buckle, Driven by Animosity between Biden and Mohammed bin Salman', *The Wall Street Journal*, 24 October 2022, https://www.wsj.com/articles/u-s-saudi-relations-biden-mbs-animosity-11666623661

Karapetyan, Astghik, 'The Serzh Sargsyan Administration: 2008–2018', EVN Report, 23 September 2021, https://evnreport.com/magazine-issues/the-serzh-sargsyan-administration-2008-2018/

Kaiser, Robert, *Cold Winter, Cold War*, London: Weidenfeld & Nicolson, 1974.

Kantchev, Georgi, Andrew Duehren, and Joe Wallace, 'Russian Oil Is Still Flowing, and That Is What the West Wants', *The Wall Street Journal*, 23 February 2023, https://www.wsj.com/articles/russian-oil-is-still-flowing-and-that-is-what-the-west-wants-41cc3256

Keating, Sean, 'DFI Cooperation: A Future Casualty of War?', Uxolo, 2 March 2022, https://www.uxolo.com/articles/7103/DFI-cooperation-a-future-casualty-of-war

Kiel Institute for the World Economy, 'Ukraine Support Tracker', 25 October 2022, https://www.ifw-kiel.de/topics/war-against-ukraine/ukraine-support-tracker/

Kirchberger, Sarah, 'Russian–Chinese Military–Technological Cooperation and the Ukrainian Factor', in Sarah Kirchberger, Svennja Sinjen, and Nils Wörmer (eds), *Russia–China Relations*, Cham: Springer, 2022, pp. 75–100.

Klein, Zvika, 'Russia Orders Jewish Agency to Stop All Operations in Country', *The Jerusalem Post*, 5 July 2022, https://www.jpost.com/diaspora/article-711227

Knight, Oliver, 'Huge Potential for Solar and Wind in Pakistan', World Bank Blogs, 22 February 2021, https://blogs.worldbank.org/energy/huge-potential-solar-and-wind-pakistan

Kohlmann, Thomas, 'Can German Industry Get Off Gas?', Deutsche Welle, 8 January 2022, https://www.dw.com/en/how-german-industry-plans-to-cut-its-gas-consumption/a-62654811

Kokorin, Sergei, 'O chyom Andrei Boginskiy ne rasskazal presidentu' [What Andrei Boginskiy did not explain to the president], Versia, 10 November 2021, https://versia.ru/kak-vertolyoty-rossii-osvaivali-byudzhet-na-proekte-ka-62

Kolesnikov, Roman, 'Otkroveniya Sechina' [Sechin's Revelations], Biznes Online, 27 October 2022, https://www.business-gazeta.ru/article/569207

Kolkhatkar, Sheelah, 'Will Sanctions against Russia End the War in Ukraine', *The New Yorker*, 24 October 2022, https://www.newyorker.com/magazine/2022/10/31/will-sanctions-against-russia-end-the-war-in-ukraine

Kollewe, Julia, 'EDF Cuts Output at Nuclear Power Plants as French Rivers Get Too Warm', *The Guardian*, 3 August 2022, https://www.theguardian.com/business/2022/aug/03/edf-to-reduce-nuclear-power-output-as-french-river-temperatures-rise

Korsunskaya, Darya, 'Russia Says Ready to Ease Some Ukraine Debt Terms, Reiterates Debt Not Commercial', Reuters, 18 November 2015, https://www.reuters.com/article/us-ukraine-crisis-russia-eurobonds-idUKKCN0T736N20151118

Koshino, Yuka and Robert Ward, *Japan's Effectiveness a Geo-economic Actor: Navigating Great Power Competition*, Abingdon: Routledge, 2022.

Kowalcze, Kamil, Petra Sorge, and Vanesa Dezem, 'Germany Ready to Up Uniper Aid to €60 Billion in Worst Case', Bloomberg, 26 October

2022, https://www.bloomberg.com/news/articles/2022-10-26/germany-ready-to-double-uniper-aid-to-60-billion-in-worst-case?leadSource=uverify%20wall

Kozok, Firat, 'Erdogan Hints at Possible Gas Reserve Revision in Black Sea', Bloomberg, 2 November 2022, https://www.bloomberg.com/news/articles/2022-11-02/erdogan-hints-at-possible-gas-reserve-revision-in-black-sea-la02z2gy

Kramer, Andrew, 'Workers Seize City in Eastern Ukraine From Separatists', *The New York Times*, 15 May 2014, https://www.nytimes.com/2014/05/16/world/europe/ukraine-workers-take-to-streets-to-calm-Mariupol.html

——— 'Questions Surround Ukraine's Bailouts as Banking Chief Steps Down', *The New York Times*, 12 May 2017, https://www.nytimes.com/2017/05/12/world/europe/ukraine-central-bank-valeria-gontareva.html

——— 'Fancy Sausages and a $2 Million Bribe: A Trial Uncovers Kremlin Infighting', *The New York Times*, 15 December 2017, https://www.nytimes.com/2017/12/15/world/europe/russia-ulyukayev-bribery.html

Krasnolutska, Daryna, 'Ukraine CDS Jump to Three-Year High after Moody's Downgrade', Bloomberg, 24 September 2013, https://www.bloomberg.com/news/articles/2013-09-24/ukraine-cds-jump-to-three-year-high-after-moody-s-downgrade

Kravcheko, Olga, 'V Genichesk voshli voiska RF—mer' [Russian forces enter Henichesk—mayor], Segodnya.ua, 24 February 2022, https://www.segodnya.ua/regions/others/v-genichesk-voshli-voyska-rf-mer-1605069.html

Krutov, Mark, Sergei Dobrynin, and Carl Schreck, 'Yakhty dlya Putina, katery dlya Minoborony: Kto rulit "Sheherazadoi"' [Yachts for Putin, cutters for the Ministry of Defence: Who controls 'Scheherezade'?], Radio Svoboda, 24 March 2022, https://www.asvoboda.org/a/yahta-dlya-putina-katera-dlya-minoborony-kro-rulit-sheherezadoj/31766887.html

Krylova, Yulia, 'Lock-in Effect in the Russian–Libyan Economic Relations in the post-Arab Spring Period', *The Journal of North African Studies* 22, no. 4 (28 February 2017), pp. 578–94, https://doi.org/10.1080/13629387.2017.1296359

Kucera, Joshua, 'Putin Signals Russia's Shift to Asia', *The Diplomat*, 31 October 2014, https://thediplomat.com/2014/10/putin-signals-russian-shift-to-asia/

————— 'Russia Raises Gas Prices for Armenia in the New Year', Eurasianet, 3 January 2019, https://eurasianet.org/russia-raises-gas-prices-for-armenia-in-the-new-year

Kumenov, Almaz, 'Kazakhstan to Send Oil to Germany via Russian Pipeline', Eurasianet, 13 January 2023, https://eurasianet.org/kazakhstan-to-send-oil-to-germany-via-russian-pipeline

Kurasheva, Anastasiya, 'Prodazhi novyx iPhone obrushilis v 4 raza po sravneniyu c proshlym godom' [Sales of new iPhones fell four times in comparison with last year], *Vedomosti*, 13 October 2022, https://www.vedomosti.ru/technology/articles/2022/10/14/945478-prodazhi-novih-iphone-obrushilis

Kurkowska, Ewa, Alberto Nardelli, and John Ainger, 'EU Warns That Price Cap on Gas for Power Needs UK, Swiss Involvement', Bloomberg, 24 October 2022, https://www.bloomberg.com/news/articles/2022-10-24/eu-warns-that-cap-on-gas-for-power-needs-uk-swiss-involvement

Kurmayer, Nichoals, 'Germany Inaugurates First New LNG Terminal', Euractiv, 15 November 2022, https://www.euractiv.com/section/energy/news/germany-inaugurates-first-new-lng-terminal/

Kursiv, 'Kazakhstan Reports Freezing Banking Assets', Kursiv, 24 May 2022, https://kz.kursiv.media/en/2022-05-24/kazakhstan-reports-freezing-banking-assets/

Kuznetsov, Vladimir, 'Rosneft Gets Central Bank Help Refinancing $7 Billion Loan', Bloomberg, 12 December 2014, https://www.bloomberg.com/news/articles/2014-12-12/rosneft-s-10-8-billion-refinancing-driven-by-central-bank-cash

Kwarteng, Kwasi, *War and Gold: A Five-Hundred-Year History of Empires, Adventures and Debt*, London: Bloomsbury, 2014.

Kyiv City Administration, 'Mazurenko, Pavlo Antoliivich', 30 September 2018, https://ato.kyivcity.gov.ua/content/mazurenko-pavlo-anatoliyovych.html

Kyiv School of Economics, 'Assessment of Damages in Ukraine Due to Russia's Military Aggression as of September 1, 2022', 1 September 2022, https://kse.ua/wp-content/uploads/2022/10/ENG_Sep22_FINAL_Sep1_Damages_Report-1.pdf

Lavrov, Seyon, 'VKS Rossii unichtozhili tsekh po sborke zaviadvigatelyei na predpriyatii "Motor Sich" v Zaporozhye' [Russian airforce destroyed Motor Sich's aircraft engine assembly factory in Zaporozhye], Zvezda,

20 November 2022, https://tvzvezda.ru/news/202211201413-Vsfzi.html

Lawson, Alex, 'G7 Countries Agree Plan to Impose Price Cap on Russian Oil', *The Guardian*, 2 September 2022, https://www.theguardian.com/business/2022/sep/02/g7-poised-to-agree-plan-to-impose-price-cap-on-russian-oil

——— 'Nord Stream 1: Gazprom Announces Indefinite Shutdown of Pipeline', *The Guardian*, 2 September 2022, https://www.theguardian.com/business/2022/sep/02/nord-stream-1-gazprom-announces-indefinite-shutdown-of-pipeline

Lebedenko, Svitlana, 'The Rise of Sino-Russian Biotech Cooperation', The Foreign Policy Research Institute, 9 May 2022, https://www.fpri.org/article/2022/05/the-rise-of-sino-russian-biotech-cooperation/

LeBlanc, Paul, 'Fiona Hill Reflects on "Terrible Spectacle" of Trump–Putin Summit ahead of Biden's Meeting with Russian President', CNN, 16 June 2021, https://edition.cnn.com/2021/06/15/politics/fiona-hill-trump-biden-putin-cnntv/index.html

Lee, Julian and Anthony Di Paola, 'Russia Delivers First Crude Cargo to UAE's Ruwais Refinery', Bloomberg, 14 November 2022, https://www.bloomberg.com/news/articles/2022-11-14/russia-delivers-first-crude-cargo-to-uae-s-ruwais-refinery

Lenta, 'Ulitsiya stabilnosti: Moizno li vernut zolotoi standart' [An ounce of stability: Could the gold standard return?], 23 April 2017, https://lenta.ru/articles/2017/04/23/gold_standard/

Letsch, Constanze, 'Turkish Ministers' Sons Arrested in Corruption and Bribery Investigation', *The Guardian*, 17 December 2013, https://www.theguardian.com/world/2013/dec/17/turkish-ministers-sons-arrested-corruption-investigation

Leung, James, 'Xi's Corruption Crackdown', *Foreign Affairs*, May/June 2015, https://www.foreignaffairs.com/china/xis-corruption-crackdown

Levine, Steve, *The Oil and the Glory: The Pursuit of Empire and Fortune on the Caspian Sea*, New York: Random House, 2017.

Lillis, Joanna, *Dark Shadows: Inside the Secret World of Kazakhstan*, London: I.B. Tauris, 2019.

——— 'Central Asia to Suffer as Remittances from Russia Nosedive', Eurasianet, 11 March 2022, https://eurasianet.org/central-asia-to-suffer-as-remittances-from-russia-nosedive

Litivinova, Daria, 'A Bridge Too Far for Russia's Propagandists', Coda, 13 November 2018, https://www.codastory.com/disinformation/bridge-too-far-russia-propagandists/

Lo, Bobo. *Russia and the New World Disorder*. London: Chatham House, 2015.

Lomsadze, Girogi, 'Gazprom to Take Over Iranian–Armenian Pipeline', Eurasianet, 4 June 2015, https://eurasianet.org/gazprom-to-take-over-iranian-armenian-pipeline

Londoño, Ernesto, 'Tired of Regional Critics, Venezuela Looks to Russia and China', *The New York Times*, 27 December 2017, https://www.nytimes.com/2017/12/27/world/americas/venezuela-maduro-brazil-canada.html

Luhn, Alec, 'Pro-Russian Occupiers of Ukrainian Service Building Voice Defiance', *The Guardian*, 10 April 2014, https://www.theguardian.com/world/2014/apr/10/luhansk-protesters-occupy-security-headquarters

——— 'Moscow Court Orders Seizure of Russian Oligarch's Stake in Bashneft Oil', *The Guardian*, 26 September 2014, https://www.theguardian.com/business/2014/sep/26/russian-oligarch-vladimir-yevtushenkov-stake-bashneft-oil-seized

Lukin, Alexander, *China and Russia: The New Rapprochement*, Cambridge: Polity Press, 2018.

Luttwak, Edward, 'From Geopolitics to Geo-economics: Logic of Conflict, Grammar of Commerce', *The National Interest* 20 (Summer 1990), pp. 17–23, https://www.jstor.org/stable/42894676

Kilian, Lutz and Michael Plante, 'The Russian Oil Supply Shock of 2022', Federal Reserve Bank of Dallas, 22 March 2022, https://www.dallasfed.org/research/economics/2022/0322

Lyrchichkova, Anastasia and Gleb Stolyarov, 'Russia Sought Siemens Turbines for Crimean Plants—Document', Reuters, 16 June 2017, https://www.reuters.com/article/ukraine-crisis-crimea-power-idUSL8N1JD45W

Macdonald-Smith, Angela, 'Woodside Steps Up as Putin Cuts Gas to Europe', *Australian Financial Review*, 6 September 2022, https://www.afr.com/companies/energy/putin-s-gas-threat-pushes-uniper-to-woodside-lng-20220906-p5bfpw

MacFarquhar, Neil, 'Russia's Troll Factory', *The New York Times*, 18 February 2018, https://www.nytimes.com/2018/02/18/world/europe/russia-troll-factory.html

Macias, Amanda, 'Biden Signs Bill That Aims to Streamline U.S. Military Aid to Ukraine', CNBC, 9 May 2022, https://www.cnbc.com/2022/05/09/biden-signs-ukraine-lend-lease-military-aid-bill-amid-russia-invasion.html

Mackinder, Halford James, 'The Geographical Pivot of History', *The Geographical Journal* 23, no. 4 (April 1904), pp. 421–37, https://doi.org/10.2307/1775498

———— *Democratic Ideals and Reality*. Washington, DC: National Defense University Press, 1942 [1919].

Mackinnon, Amy. 'Putin's Shadow Warriors Stake Claim to Syria's Oil', *Foreign Policy*, 17 May 2021, https://foreignpolicy.com/2021/05/17/putin-shadow-warriors-stake-claim-syria-oil-energy-wagner-prigozhin-libya-middle-east/

Maksimchuk, Nikolai, '"Ukrnafta", "Motor Sich" i drugie predpriyatiya perekhodit v sobstvennost gosudarstva' [Ukrnafta, Motor Sich, and other enterprises become state property], *Ekomomichna Pravda*, 7 November 2022, https://www.epravda.com.ua/rus/news/2022/11/7/693528/

Malik, Hassan, *Bankers and Bolsheviks: International Finance and the Russian Revolution*, Princeton: Princeton University Press, 2018.

Mance, Henry, 'Sabine Weyand: "The EU found out we are dependent on Russia. We can't afford that"', *The Financial Times*, 12 September 2022, https://www.ft.com/content/b6a67923-fd14-4fab-8fc1-c1fed175c85c

Mangi, Faseeh and Murtaugh, Dan, 'Playing Gas Firms Off Each Other Saved Pakistan $600 Million', Bloomberg, 9 September 2018, https://www.bloomberg.com/news/articles/2018-09-09/playing-gas-giants-off-each-other-saved-pakistan-600-million

Mankoff, Jeff, 'A Friend in Need? Russia and Turkey after the Coup', Center for Strategic and International Studies, 29 July 2016, https://www.csis.org/analysis/friend-need-russia-and-turkey-after-coup

Manufacturing.net, 'BASF Bringing Specialty Chemical Production to U.S.', 5 August 2022, https://www.manufacturing.net/chemical-processing/news/22366796/basf-bringing-specialty-chemical-production-to-us

Marriott, James and Minio-Paluello, Mika, *The Oil Road: Journeys from the Caspian Sea to the City of London*, London: Verso, 2013.

Marsh, Sarah and Madeline Chambers, 'Germany Freezes Nord Stream 2 Gas Project as Ukraine Crisis Deepens', Reuters, 22 February 2022, https://www.reuters.com/business/energy/germanys-scholz-halts-nord-stream-2-certification-2022-02-22/

Marten, Kimberly, 'Russia's Use of Semi-state Security Forces: The Case of the Wagner Group', *Post-Soviet Affairs* 35, no. 3 (26 March 2019), pp. 181–204, https://doi.org/10.1080/1060586X.2019.1591142

———— 'Russian Military and Economic Interests and Influence in Latin America and the Caribbean: Threats, Limits, and U.S. Policy Recommendations', Testimony before the Committee on Foreign Affairs Subcommittee on the Western Hemisphere, Civilian Security, Migration, and International Economic Policy United States House of Representatives, 20 July 2022, https://docs.house.gov/meetings/FA/FA07/20220720/115002/HHRG-117-FA07-Wstate-MartenK-20220720.pdf

———— 'Russia's Use of the Wagner Group: Definitions, Strategic Objectives, and Accountability', Testimony before the Committee on Oversight and Reform Subcommittee on National Security United States House of Representatives, 15 September 2022, https://oversight.house.gov/sites/democrats.oversight.house.gov/files/Marten%20Testimony.pdf

Marsh, Jenni, 'The Rise and Fall of a Belt and Road Billionaire', CNN, 12 December 2018, https://www.cnn.com/interactive/2018/12/asia/patrick-ho-ye-jianming-cefc-trial-intl/

Martinez, Luis and Libby Cathey, 'Pentagon Says Enough Russian Forces to Move on Ukraine's Cities', ABC, 28 January 2022, https://abcnews.go.com/Politics/pentagon-russian-forces-move-ukraines-cities/story?id=82534587

Martins Sousa, Dayanne and Kati Pohjanpalo, 'Toilet Paper Is Going to Get Costlier: Blame Russia', Bloomberg, 12 October 2022, https://www.bloomberg.com/news/articles/2022-10-12/suppy-chain-crisis-ensnarls-toilet-paper-producers-as-russia-ban-roils-market

Matthews, Owen, 'The Red Line: Biden and Xi's Secret Ukraine Talks Revealed', *The Spectator*, 26 November 2022, https://www.spectator.co.uk/article/the-red-line-biden-and-xis-secret-ukraine-talks-revealed/

Maurer, Noel, 'Who Cares about Georgia? Not the Markets', The Power and the Money Blog, 5 September 2008, https://noelmaurer.typepad.com/aab/2008/09/who-cares-about.html

Mazower, Mark, *Governing the World: The History of an Idea*, London: Penguin, 2013.

Maçães, Bruno, *The Dawn of Eurasia*, London: Allen Lane, 2018.

Maček, Sebastijan, 'Slovenia Secures Algerian Gas to Cover Third of Its Needs', Euractiv, 16 November 2022, https://www.euractiv.com/section/politics/news/slovenia-secures-algerian-gas-to-cover-third-of-its-needs/

Martyshko, Nikito, 'Amerikanskiy posol: SrShA aktivno obsuzhdayut s pravitelstvom novye kanaly eksporta kazakhstanskoj nefti' [American ambassador: The United States is actively working with the government to find new routes for the export of Kazakh oil], Informburo, 25 November 2022, https://informburo.kz/novosti/amerikanskij-posol-ssha-aktivno-obsuzhdayut-s-pravitelstvom-novye-kanaly-eksporta-kazahstanskoj-nefti

McCausland, Phil, 'Sanctions Force Russia to Produce Popular Car without Air Bags, Other Safety Features', NBC, 14 June 2022, https://www.nbcnews.com/news/world/sanctions-force-russia-produce-popular-car-safety-features-even-kremli-rcna32863

McCauley, Robert, 'What Russia's Fortress Balance Sheet Can Tell Us about the Dollar's Future', *The Financial Times*, 23 June 2022, https://www.ft.com/content/523e4fcc-71d1-4eaf-b7d2-30a876540389

McFadden, Cynthia, William Arikin, and Tim Uehlinger, 'How the Trump Team's First Military Raid in Yemen Went Wrong', NBC, 1 October 2017, https://www.nbcnews.com/news/us-news/how-trump-team-s-first-military-raid-went-wrong-n806246

McGreal, Chris, 'Trump's Endorsement Hurt Republicans in Midterms—Aside from JD Vance', *The Guardian*, 9 November 2022, https://www.theguardian.com/us-news/2022/nov/09/trump-endorsed-candidates-republicans-midterm-performance

Meade, Richard, 'Banks Start Selling Sovcomflot Fleet as Sanctions Deadlines Loom', *Lloyd's List*, 12 May 2022, https://lloydslist.maritimeintelligence.informa.com/LL1140801/Banks-start-selling-Sovcomflot-fleet-as-sanctions-deadlines-loom

Meck, Georg, 'Mister Russland der deutschen Wirtschaft' [Mr Russia of the German economy], *Frankfurt Allgemeine Zeitung*, 7 February 2016, https://www.faz.net/aktuell/wirtschaft/menschen-wirtschaft/klaus-mangold-mister-russland-der-deutschen-wirtschaft-14056422.html

Media Initiative for Human Rights, 'Crimean Sanctions: Violations, Monitoring and Enforcement', 8 October 2022, https://

euromaidanpress.com/wp-content/uploads/2022/Sanctions_
Crimea_Platform_Shandra_engl_A4_edited.pdf

Meduza, 'The Company Owned by Arkady Rotenberg That Built Russia's
Crimean Bridge Says It Didn't Make a Profit on the Project', 12
November 2019, https://meduza.io/en/news/2019/11/12/the-
company-owned-by-arkady-rotenberg-that-built-russia-s-crimean-
bridge-says-it-didn-t-make-a-profit-on-the-project

Mehrer, Angela, 'Turn of Phrase: Germany's Zeitenwende', European
Council on Foreign Relations, 15 August 2022, https://ecfr.eu/
article/turn-of-phrase-germanys-zeitenwende/

Meredith, Sam, 'Qatar Quitting OPEC Means the Oil Cartel Is Now
Just a "Two-Member Organization", Oil Analyst Says', CNBC, 3
December 2018, https://www.cnbc.com/2018/12/03/qatar-
quitting-opec-leaves-oil-cartel-a-two-member-organization.html

——— 'India Says It Will Look Carefully at Russian Oil Price Cap,
Rejects Moral Duty to Boycott Moscow', CNBC, 5 September
2022, https://www.cnbc.com/2022/09/05/india-says-it-will-
look-carefully-at-russian-oil-price-cap.html

——— 'German Gas Giant Uniper Says the Worst Is Still to Come after
Russia Halts Flows to Europe', CNBC, 6 September 2022, https://
www.cnbc.com/2022/09/06/uniper-says-worst-is-still-to-come-
as-russia-halts-gas-flows-to-europe.html

Meyer, Henry, 'Russia Moving Forces to Crimea in Ukraine Build-Up,
Analysts Say', Bloomberg, 24 November 2021, https://www.
bloomberg.com/news/articles/2021-11-24/russia-moving-forces-
to-crimea-in-ukraine-build-up-analysts-say

Micklethwait, John, 'Vladimir Putin Just Wants to Be Friends',
Bloomberg, 8 September 2016, https://www.bloomberg.com/
features/2016-vladimir-putin-interview/

Mihm, Andreas, 'Schröder, Setschin und Putins Öl' [Schröder, Sechin,
and Putin's Oil], Frankfurter Allgemeine Zeitung, 29 January 2018,
https://www.faz.net/aktuell/wirtschaft/unternehmen/rosneft-
chef-igor-setschin-uebers-geschaeft-15422926.html

Milchenko, Angelina, 'Na Rukax, no ne v rezervax: Chto budet s dollarom
v Rossii' [On hand, but not in reserves: What will happen with the
dollar in Russia?], Gazeta.ru, 5 June 2021, https://www.gazeta.ru/
business/2021/06/05/13621754.shtml

Miller, Chris, Putinomics: Power and Money in Resurgent Russia, Chapel Hill:
UNC Press, 2018.

———— *Chip War: The Fight for The World's Most Critical Technology*, London: Simon & Schuster, 2022.

Miller, Edward, *Bankrupting the Enemy: The U.S. Financial Siege of Japan before Pearl Harbor*, Annapolis: Naval Institute Press, 2007.

Ministry of Foreign Affairs of the Russian Federation, 'Foreign Minister Sergey Lavrov's Statement and Answers to Media Questions at a Joint News Conference with Foreign Minister of the Republic of Serbia Nikola Selakovic', Ministry of Foreign Affairs of the Russian Federation, 16 April 2021, https://www.mid.ru/en/press_service/minister_speeches/1419942/

Mitrokhina, Ekaterina, 'SK zaderzhal 11 uchastnikov pogromov na amurskom zavode "Gazproma"' [Investigative committee arrests eleven participants in riots at Gazprom's Amur plant], RBC, 20 July 2022, https://www.rbc.ru/rbcfreenews/5f15c8ec9a7947484c36d357

Mitrova, Tatiana, 'Understanding the Impact of Sanctions on the Russian Oil and Gas Sector with Limited Data', Columbia Center on Global Energy Policy, 29 September 2022, https://www.energypolicy.columbia.edu/research/qa/qa-understanding-impact-sanctions-russian-oil-and-gas-sector-limited-data

Moens, Barbara, Jakov Hanke Vela, and Jacopo Barigazzi, 'Europe Accuses US of Profiting from War', Politico, 24 November 2022, https://www.politico.eu/article/vladimir-putin-war-europe-ukraine-gas-inflation-reduction-act-ira-joe-biden-rift-west-eu-accuses-us-of-profiting-from-war/

Mokrushin, Sergei, 'Voina i sanktsii: Kak evropeiskiy biznes «pomog» Rossii podgotovit krymskiy platsdarm' [War and sanctions: How European business 'helps' Russia prepare its Crimean foothold], RFE/RL, 18 March 2022, https://ru.krymr.com/amp/31759702.html

Moody, Oliver, '"Merkel's Toxic Legacy": Germany Nears a Reckoning over Ties to Russia', *The Times*, 6 April 2022, https://www.thetimes.co.uk/article/merkels-toxic-legacy-germany-nears-a-reckoning-over-ties-to-russia-7lgms9vz8

Moreau, Ron, 'Can Buried Treasure Save Afghanistan?', *Newsweek*, 13 June 2010, https://www.newsweek.com/can-buried-treasure-save-afghanistan-214492

Moscow Times, '$650Bln of Corporate Debt Intertwines Russia and the West', 12 March 2014, https://www.themoscowtimes.com/2014/03/12/650bln-of-corporate-debt-intertwines-russia-and-the-west-a32901

———— '20 trillionov na veter' [20 trillion thrown to the wind], 11 November 2022, https://www.moscowtimes.ru/2022/11/11/20-trillionov-na-veter-krupneishaya-v-rossiiskoi-istorii-gosprogramma-proizvodstva-oruzhiya-ostanovlena-posle-provalov-v-ukraine-a26303

Mostovoye Bureau, 'Vnedrenie i primenenie tekhnologii PDR, OOO "Mostovoye Byuro"' [Implementation and application of PDR technology for OOO Mostovoe Bureau], Mostovoe Byuro, 6 December 2016, https://mb-spb.com/vnedrenie-i-primenenie-tehnologii-pdr-ooo-mostovoe-byuro

Mulder, Nicholas, *Economic Weapon: The Rise of Sanctions as a Tool of Modern War*, New Haven: Yale University Press, 2022.

Murtagh, Dan, Alex Longley, and Jackie Davalos, 'Oil Plunges Most since 1991 after Producers Embark on Price War', Bloomberg, 8 March 2020, https://www.bloomberg.com/news/articles/2020-03-08/oil-in-freefall-after-saudis-slash-prices-in-all-out-crude-war

Müller, Uwe, 'Schwedt feiert die Privatisierung seiner Raffinerie: Schwedt feiert die Privatisierung seiner Raffinerie' [Schwedt commemorates the privatisation of its refinery], *Die Welt*, 4 September 2001, https://www.welt.de/print-welt/article460985/Schwedt-feiert-die-Privatisierung-seiner-Raffinerie.html

Nair, Dinesh, 'Saudi Arabia Money Muscles into Old Enemy Territory in Deals Hunt', Bloomberg, 8 November 2022, https://www.bloomberg.com/news/newsletters/2022-11-08/saudi-arabia-money-muscles-into-old-enemy-territory-in-deals-hunt

Nakano, Jane, 'Japan to Invest in the Latest Russian LNG Project', Center for Strategic and International Studies, 12 July 2019, https://www.csis.org/analysis/japan-invest-latest-russian-lng-project

Nardelli, Alberto, Bryce Baschuk, and Marc Champion, 'Putin Stirs European Worry on Home Appliance Imports Stripped for Arms', Bloomberg, 29 October 2022, https://www.bloomberg.com/news/articles/2022-10-29/putin-stirs-european-worry-on-home-appliance-imports-stripped-for-arms

Nasralla, Shadia and Arathy Somasekhar, 'U.S. Sour Crude Cargo Sails to Germany as Russia Sanctions Bite', Reuters, 9 August 2022, https://www.reuters.com/business/energy/us-sour-crude-cargo-sails-germany-russia-sanctions-bite-2022-08-08/

Nazaretyan, Hovhannes, 'Russia's Increasing Military Presence in Armenia', EVN Report, 4 March 2021, https://evnreport.com/politics/russia-s-increasing-military-presence-in-armenia/

BIBLIOGRAPHY

Neagu, Bogdan, 'Romania to Cover Moldova's Electricity Deficit Caused by Russia Bombing', Euractiv, 14 October 2022, https://www.euractiv.com/section/energy/news/romania-to-cover-moldovas-electricity-deficit-caused-by-russia-bombing/

Nehru, Vikram, 'The BRICS Bank: Now Comes the Hard Part', Carnegie Endowment for International Peace, 17 July 2014, https://carnegieendowment.org/2014/07/17/brics-bank-now-comes-hard-part-pub-56189

Nelson, Eshe, 'Russia's Stock Index Reopens and Rises with Government Intervention', *The New York Times*, 24 March 2022, https://www.nytimes.com/2022/03/24/business/russian-stock-exchange-moex.html

Nemtsova, Anna, 'Father of Ukraine Revolution Speaks Out', The Daily Beast, 17 October 2015 [Updated 13 April 2017], https://www.thedailybeast.com/father-of-ukraine-revolution-speaks-out

Neukirch, Ralf, 'The Eternal Rivalry of Joschka Fischer and Gerhard Schröder', *Der Spiegel*, 15 February 2010, https://www.spiegel.de/international/germany/who-has-the-longer-pipeline-the-eternal-rivalry-of-joschka-fischer-and-gerhard-schroeder-a-677853.html

New Development Bank, 'NDB Board of Directors Approved USD 1 Billion Equivalent Covid-19 Emergency Program Loan to Russia for Supporting Frontline Health Workers', 29 March 2021, https://www.ndb.int/press_release/ndb-board-of-directors-approved-usd-1-billion-equivalent-covid-19-emergency-program-loan-to-russia-for-supporting-frontline-health-workers/

The New York Times, 'W. Wood Prince, 83, of Chicago; Businessman Adopted by Cousin', 30 January 1998, https://www.nytimes.com/1998/01/30/business/w-wood-prince-83-of-chicago-businessman-adopted-by-cousin.html

———— 'Venezuela Crisis: Guaidó Calls for Uprising as Clashes Erupt', 30 April 2019, https://www.nytimes.com/2019/04/30/world/americas/venezuela-coup-guaido-military.html

New Voice of Ukraine, 'In Henichesk, Woman Chased Away Russian Soldiers', 24 February 2022, https://nv.ua/ukraine/events/v-genicheske-zhenshchina-progonyala-rossiyskih-soldat-50219744.html

———— 'Russian Forces Destroy Azot Chemical Plant in Severodonetsk', 27 December 2022, https://english.nv.ua/business/russia-destroys-

azot-chemical-plant-in-severodonetsk-ukraine-news-50293595.
html

Newnham, Randall, *Deutsche Mark Diplomacy: Positive Economic Sanctions in German–Russian Relations*, University Park, PA: Penn State Press, 2002.

Newsru.co.il, 'Raketniy obstrel Kremenchuga: Zavodu "Kredmash byl prichinyon ushcherb, no versiya minoborony RF lozhnaya"' [Rocket shelling of Kremenchug, the Kredmash plant was damaged, but the version of the Russian Defence Ministry is false], 29 June 2022, https://www.newsru.co.il/world/29jun2022/kremenchug_104.html

Newton Dunn, Tom and Olivia Wright, 'Kwasi Kwarteng: I Warned Liz Truss over Her Radical Reforms', *The Times*, 10 November 2022, https://www.thetimes.co.uk/article/kwasi-kwarteng-talk-tv-interview-liz-truss-z0zg5fgpk

Ng, Eric and Xie Yu, 'China Detains CEFC's Founder Ye Jianming, Wiping Out US$153 Million in Value off Stocks', *South China Morning Post*, 1 March 2018, https://www.scmp.com/business/companies/article/2135238/china-detain-cefc-founder-ye-jianming-stocks

Nikolov, Krassen, 'Bulgaria Launches Full Investigation into Turkish Stream', Euractiv, 13 May 2022, https://www.euractiv.com/section/energy-environment/news/bulgaria-launches-full-investigation-into-turkish-stream/

Office of the Chairman of the Senate Foreign Relations Committee, '10 Bipartisan Senators Introduce Comprehensive Russia Sanctions Legislation', 10 January 2017, https://www.foreign.senate.gov/press/dem/release/10-bipartisan-senators-introduce-comprehensive-russia-sanctions-legislation

Office of the President of Russia, 'Intervu ispanskim sredstvam massovoi informatsii' [Interview with Spanish media], 7 February 2006, https://web.archive.org/web/20090817065003/http://www.kremlin.ru/appears/2006/02/07/1759_type63379_101129.shtml

———— 'Annual Address to the Federal Assembly', 10 May 2006, www.en.kremlin.ru/events/president/transcripts/23577

———— 'Speech and the Following Discussion at the Munich Conference on Security Policy', 10 February 2007, http://en.kremlin.ru/events/president/transcripts/copy/24034

———— 'Speech at Meeting of the Russian–Armenian Interregional Forum', 2 December 2013.

BIBLIOGRAPHY

———— 'Vladimir Putin Answered Journalists' Questions on the Situation in Ukraine', 4 March 2014, http://en.kremlin.ru/events/president/news/20366

———— 'Direct Line with Vladimir Putin', 17 April 2014, http://en.kremlin.ru/events/president/news/20796

———— 'Speech at a Ceremony to Mark the Joining of Power of Siberia Gas Pipeline's First Section', 1 September 2014, http://en.kremlin.ru/events/president/transcripts/46529

———— 'Meeting of the Valdai International Discussion Club', 24 October 2014, http://en.kremlin.ru/events/president/news/46860

———— 'Meeting with Rosneft CEO Igor Sechin', 7 December 2016, http://en.kremlin.ru/events/president/transcripts/53431

———— 'Direct Line with Vladimir Putin', 7 June 2018, http://en.kremlin.ru/events/president/news/57692

———— 'Transcript of Eurasian Economic Council Expanded Meeting', 14 May 2018, http://en.kremlin.ru/events/president/transcripts/57468

———— 'News Conference following Talks between the Presidents of Russia and the United States', 16 July 2018, http://en.kremlin.ru/events/president/news/58017

———— 'Interview to Tass News Agency', 21 October 2019, http://en.kremlin.ru/events/president/news/61858/print

———— 'Article by Vladimir Putin "On the Historical Unity of Russians and Ukrainians"', 12 July 2021, http://en.kremlin.ru/events/president/news/66181

———— 'Meeting on Socioeconomic Support for Regions', 16 March 2022, http://en.kremlin.ru/events/president/news/67996

———— 'St Petersburg International Economic Forum Plenary Session', 17 June 2022, http://en.kremlin.ru/events/president/news/68669

———— 'Valdai International Discussion Club Meeting', 27 October 2022, http://en.kremlin.ru/events/president/transcripts/69695

Office of the Prime Minister of Hungary, 'Prime Minister Viktor Orbán's Speech at the 25th Bálványos Summer Free University and Student Camp', 30 July 2014, https://2010-2015.miniszterelnok.hu/in_english_article/_prime_minister_viktor_orban_s_speech_at_the_25th_balvanyos_summer_free_university_and_student_camp

Office of US Senator Joni Ernst, 'Ernst Urges White House to Maintain Bipartisan-Supported Security Cooperation with Middle East

BIBLIOGRAPHY

Partners', 12 October 2022, https://www.ernst.senate.gov/news/press-releases/ernst-urges-white-house-to-maintain-bipartisan-supported-security-cooperation-with-middle-east-partners

Office of the White House Press Secretary, 'Statement by the President on Ukraine', 20 March 2014, https://obamawhitehouse.archives.gov/the-press-office/2014/03/20/statement-president-ukraine

———— 'Press Conference with President Obama and Prime Minister Rutte of the Netherlands', 25 March 2014, https://obamawhitehouse.archives.gov/the-press-office/2014/03/25/press-conference-president-obama-and-prime-minister-rutte-netherlands

———— 'Statement by President Donald J. Trump on Signing the "Countering America's Adversaries through Sanctions Act"', 2 August 2017, https://trumpwhitehouse.archives.gov/briefings-statements/statement-president-donald-j-trump-signing-countering-americas-adversaries-sanctions-act/

———— 'Imposing Costs for Harmful Foreign Activities by the Russian Government', 15 April 2021, https://www.whitehouse.gov/briefing-room/statements-releases/2021/04/15/fact-sheet-imposing-costs-for-harmful-foreign-activities-by-the-russian-government/

———— 'Remarks by President Biden on the United Efforts of the Free World to Support the People of Ukraine', 26 March 2022, https://www.whitehouse.gov/briefing-room/speeches-remarks/2022/03/26/remarks-by-president-biden-on-the-united-efforts-of-the-free-world-to-support-the-people-of-ukraine/

Oil Capital, '"Rosneft" otkazalas ot bureniya v spornykh ofshornykh vodakh Vyetnama' [Rosneft refuses to drill in disputed offshore waters of Vietnam], 11 August 2020, https://oilcapital.ru/news/2020-08-11/rosneft-otkazalas-ot-bureniya-v-spornyh-ofshornyh-vodah-vietnama-smi-1039843

Olearchyk, Roman, 'Russia Accused of Triggering Trade War with Ukraine', *The Financial Times*, 15 August 2013, https://www.ft.com/content/99068c0e-0595-11e3-8ed5-00144feab7de

———— 'Ukraine's Yanukovich Returns from Moscow on Akhmetov's Plane—and on a Tight Leash', *The Financial Times*, 18 December 2013, https://www.ft.com/content/5ea517e4-a08e-30aa-8492-710ef8dc94d9

———— 'Poroshenko Warns Rival over "Pocket Army"', *The Financial Times*, 23 March 2015, https://www.ft.com/content/c4fda6b4-d184-11e4-ad3a-00144feab7de

———— 'Ukraine President Fights Oligarch on Home Front as Russia Threat Looms', *The Financial Times*, 19 December 2021, https://www.ft.com/content/8e5e09fc-e49b-49bb-8635-93752d207cfe

Oliver, Christian and Nicholas Hirst, 'EU Approves Hungary Nuclear Deal amid Oettinger Controversy', Politico, 17 November 2016, https://www.politico.eu/article/eu-approves-hungary-nuclear-deal-amid-oettinger-controversy/

Olivero, Tina, 'India Account for Nearly Half of Upcoming Crude Oil Refinery Projects', Global Data, 24 June 2022, https://www.globaldata.com/media/oil-gas/india-account-nearly-half-upcoming-crude-oil-refinery-projects-asia-2026-reveals-globaldata/

Oltermann, Philip, 'How Gas Rationing at Germany's BASF Plant Could Plunge Europe into Crisis', *The Guardian*, 15 September 2022, https://www.theguardian.com/business/2022/sep/15/gas-rationing-germany-basf-plant-europe-crisis

OMV Group, 'Nord Stream 2 AG and European Energy Companies Sign Financing Agreements', 24 April 2017, https://www.omv.com/en/news/nord-stream-2-ag-and-european-energy-companies-sign-financing-agreements

Osang, Alexander, '"Das Gefühl war ganz klar: Machtpolitisch bist du durch"' ['The feeling was clear: In terms of political power, you are through'], *Der Spiegel*, 24 November 2022, https://www.spiegel.de/panorama/ein-jahr-mit-ex-kanzlerin-angela-merkel-das-gefuehl-war-ganz-klar-machtpolitisch-bist-du-durch-a-d9799382-909e-49c7-9255-a8aec106ce9c

Ostrovsky, Arkady, *The Invention of Russia: The Journey from Gorbachev's Freedom to Putin's War*, London: Atlantic Books, 2015.

O'Byrne, David, 'Turkey, Russia Gas Ties Grow Contentious amid Ukraine War', Al-Monitor, 28 July 2022, https://www.al-monitor.com/originals/2022/07/turkey-russia-gas-ties-grow-contentious-amid-ukraine-war#ixzz7fRP4pDUQ

———— 'Azerbaijan's Russian Gas Deal Raises Uncomfortable Questions for Europe', Eurasianet, 22 November 2022, https://eurasianet.org/azerbaijans-russian-gas-deal-raises-uncomfortable-questions-for-europe

Obermaier, Frederik and Bastian Obermayer, *Die Ibiza Affäre* [The Ibiza affair], Cologne: Kiepenheuer & Witsch, 2019.

Oosterlinck, Kim, *Hope Springs Eternal: French Bondholders and the Repudiation of the Russian Debt*, trans. Anthony Bulger, New Haven: Yale University Press, 2016.

Oser, David, 'Sovcomflot Added to UK's Russian Sanctions List', *Lloyd's List*, 25 March 2022, https://lloydslist.maritimeintelligence.informa.com/LL1140300/Sovcomflot-added-to-UKs-Russian-sanctions-list

Ostanin, Iggy, 'Revealed: Around 40 Russian Troops from Pskov Died in the Ukraine, Reinforcements Sent In', Bellingcat, 27 August 2014, https://www.bellingcat.com/news/mena/2014/08/27/revealed-around-40-russian-troops-from-pskov-died-in-the-ukraine-reinforcement-sent-in/

Özberk, Tayfun, 'Russia–Ukraine Conflict: What Happened in the Black Sea So Far?', *Naval News*, 27 February 2022, https://www.navalnews.com/naval-news/2022/02/russia-ukraine-conflict-what-happened-in-the-black-sea-so-far/

Pagliery, Jose, 'Turkey's Erdogan Helped Iran Evade US Sanctions, Witness Claims', CNN, 1 December 2017, https://edition.cnn.com/2017/11/30/middleeast/reza-zarrab-us-trial-erdogan/index.html

Pannier, Bruce, 'Rustam & Rustam's Fish and Chicken Emporium', RFE/RL, 21 April 2018, https://www.rferl.org/a/uzbekistan-rustam-rustam-s-fish-and-chicken-emporium/29183819.html

——— 'Europe's Wait for Turkmen Natural Gas Continues', Foreign Policy Research Institute, 13 September 2022, https://www.fpri.org/article/2022/09/europes-wait-for-turkmen-natural-gas-continues /

Pantucci, Rafaello and Alexandros Petersen, *Sinostan: China's Inadvertent Empire*, London: Oxford University Press, 2022.

Papchenkova, Margarita and Galina Starinskaya, 'Poluchit doxody ot "Rosneftegaza" v byudzhet, vozmozhno, ne poluchit' [Receiving dividends from Rosneftegaz to the state budget may not be possible], *Vedomosti*, 25 October 2016, https://www.vedomosti.ru/economics/articles/2016/10/25/662262-dohodi-rosneftegaza

Parens, Raphael, 'The Wagner Group's Playbook in Africa: Mali', Foreign Policy Research Institute, 18 March 2022, https://www.fpri.org/article/2022/03/the-wagner-groups-playbook-in-africa-mali/

Parfitt, Tom and Didi Tang, 'Now Is Not the Time for War, Narendra Modi Tells Putin', *The Times*, 16 September 2022, https://www.thetimes.co.uk/article/now-is-not-the-time-for-war-narendra-modi-tells-putin-qs9xvkp00

Parpiani, Kashish, Nivedita Kapoor, and Angad Singh, 'India's Purchase of the S-300: Understanding the CAATSA Conundrum', Observer

Research Foundation, 25 February 2021, https://www.orfonline.org/research/india-purchase-s400-understanding-caatsa-conundrum/

Parraga, Marianna and Isla Binnie, 'Guyana Oil Producers Ramp Up Exports to Thirsty European Refiners', Reuters, 8 September 2022, https://www.reuters.com/business/energy/guyana-oil-producers-ramp-up-exports-thirsty-european-refiners-2022-09-08/

Pattison, Pete and Niamh McIntyre, 'Revealed: 6,500 Migrant Workers Have Died in Qatar since World Cup Awarded', *The Guardian*, 23 February 2022, https://www.theguardian.com/global-development/2021/feb/23/revealed-migrant-worker-deaths-qatar-fifa-world-cup-2022

Pawlak, Justyna, 'Grieving Dutch Minister Made Europe Re-think Russia Sanctions', Reuters, 25 July 2014, https://www.reuters.com/article/uk-ukraine-crisis-eu-insight-idUKKBN0FU1M020140725

Pearce, Katy, 'Poverty in the South Caucasus', *Caucasus Analytical Digest* 34 (21 December 2011), pp. 2–12, https://css.ethz.ch/content/dam/ethz/special-interest/gess/cis/center-for-securities-studies/pdfs/CAD-34.pdf

Perkonig, Angela, 'Kickl: "Brauchen gedeihliche Zukunft mit Russland"' [Kickl: 'Need a thriving future with Russia], Puls24, 28 July 2022, https://www.puls24.at/news/politik/fpoe-chef-herbert-kickl-brauchen-gedeihliche-zukunft-mit-russland/271473

Pertaia, Luke, 'How and Why a Piece of Central Tbilisi Was Sold for ₾1', OC-Media, 13 October 2017, https://oc-media.org/features/how-and-why-a-piece-of-central-tbilisi-was-sold-for-1/

Petrova, Svetlana, 'Kak rukovodityel predybornogo shtaba Putina stal milliarderom' [How Putin's campaign chief became a billionaire], *Vedomosti*, 24 July 2017, https://www.vedomosti.ru/business/articles/2017/07/24/725454-dohod

Phillips-Fein, Kim, 'The Bitter Origins of the Fight over Big Government', *The Atlantic*, March 2019, https://www.theatlantic.com/magazine/archive/2019/03/fdr-herbert-hoover-big-government/580456/

Plunkett, John, 'Russia Today Reporter Resigns in Protest at MH17 Coverage', *The Guardian*, 18 July 2014, https://www.theguardian.com/media/2014/jul/18/mh17-russia-today-reporter-resigns-sara-firth-kremlin-malaysia

Plypypiv, Ihor, 'Ukraine Has Lost 90% of Wind Energy', *Ukrainska Pravda*, 23 October 2022, https://www.pravda.com.ua/eng/news/2022/10/23/7373137/

Polish Office of Competition and Consumer Protection, 'Nord Stream 2: Application Withdrawn', 12 August 2016, https://uokik.gov.pl/news.php?news_id=12511

Polyus, 'Results of the Share Issuance', 27 December 2019, https://polyus.com/en/media/press-releases/results-of-the-share-issuance/

Popkov, Roman, 'Neudachniy pokhod ambitsioznyx muzhchin: "ChVK Vagnera" teryaet goloby v Mozambikye' [Ambitious men's unsuccessful campaign: 'PMC Wagner' lose their heads in Mozambique], MBX Media, 28 November 2019, https://mbk-news.appspot.com/sences/neudachnyj-poxod-ambicio/

Porter, Richard, 'EBRD Commits up to €3 Billion to Ukraine', European Bank for Reconstruction and Development, 24 October 2022, https://www.ebrd.com/news/2022/ebrd-commits-up-to-3-billion-to-ukraine.html

Posaner, Joshua, 'Lagarde: "Sick" Putin behind Europe's Inflation Crisis', Politico, 29 October 2022, https://www.politico.eu/article/vladimir-putin-inflation-crisis-christine-lagard-ecb/

Preussen, Wilhemine, 'Activate Nord Stream 2 ASAP, Says German Parliament Vice President', Politico, 19 August 2022, https://www.politico.eu/article/vice-president-of-the-german-parliament-calls-for-activation-of-nord-stream-2/

———— 'Hungary Signs New Gas Deal with Gazprom', Politico, 31 August 2022, https://www.politico.eu/article/hungary-signs-deal-with-gazprom-over-additional-gas/

Prince, Todd, 'Up In Arms: Ukrainian Aircraft-Engine Plant Caught Up in U.S.–China Rivalry', RFE/RL, 27 August 2019, https://www.arferl.org/a/ukrainian-aircraft-motor-sich-u-s--china-rivalry/30132082.html

Produkty.by, 'Aktualnye dannye po rossiiskomu rynku myasnoi produktsii' [Up-to-date data on the Russian meat market], 4 March 2022, https://produkt.by/news/aktualnye-dannye-po-rossiyskomu-rynku-myasnoy-produkcii

Progressive Economy Forum, 'New PEF Research Shows Energy Price Guarantee Failure', 22 September 2022, https://progressiveeconomyforum.com/blog/new-pef-research-shows-energy-price-guarantee-failure/

Putz, Catherine, 'Russia's Gazprom Stops Buying Gas from Turkmenistan', The Diplomat, 6 January 2016, https://thediplomat.com/2016/01/russias-gazprom-stops-buying-gas-from-turkmenistan/

———— 'More Difficulties for the Caspian Pipeline Consortium', *The Diplomat*, 23 August 2022, https://thediplomat.com/2022/08/more-difficulties-for-the-caspian-pipeline-consortium/

Ranada, Pia, 'Duterte Fires Gov't Oil Exploration Corporation Chief', Rappler, 15 October 2019, https://www.rappler.com/nation/242582-duterte-fires-government-oil-exploration-corporation-chief-pedro-aquino/

Raval, Anjli, 'Saudi Arabia Will Make Further Oil Supply Cut to "Encourage" Peers', *The Financial Times*, 11 May 2020, https://www.ft.com/content/4981aab1-b9cf-45f0-b72a-1c289a5a99b6

Reed, Ed, 'Yellen Encourages Africa to Take Advantage of Cheap Russian Fuel', Energy Voice, 20 January 2023, https://www.energyvoice.com/oilandgas/africa/477226/african-energy-cap-russian/

Reed, John, 'US Accuses China of "Coercion" over Vietnam Offshore Oil', *The Financial Times*, 23 August 2019, https://www.ft.com/content/b26ac618-c553-11e9-a8e9-296ca66511c9

Reed, Stanley, 'A Conduit for Russian Gas, Tangled in Europe's Conflicts', *The New York Times*, 30 June 2014, https://www.nytimes.com/2014/07/01/business/international/south-stream-pipeline-project-in-bulgaria-is-delayed.html

———— 'Russia and Others Join OPEC in Rare, Coordinated Push to Cut Oil Output', *The New York Times*, 10 December 2016, https://www.nytimes.com/2016/12/10/business/russia-opec-saudi-arabia-cut-oil-output.html

———— 'OPEC and Russia Agree to Cut Oil Production', *The New York Times*, 9 April 2020, https://www.nytimes.com/2020/04/09/business/energy-environment/opec-saudiarabia-russia-oil-coronavirus.html

Reuters, 'Russia's Energy Tsar: Who Is Igor Sechin?', 10 June 2010, https://www.reuters.com/article/idINIndia-49470420100620

———— 'Russia's Putin Calls for Moving Away from Dollar', 26 November 2010, https://www.reuters.com/article/russia-putin-dollar-idUSLDE6AP15020101126

———— 'Gazprom Neft Signs Production Sharing Deals with Kurdistan', 1 August 2012, https://www.reuters.com/article/russia-gazpromneft-iraq-idUSL6E8J1L9220120801

———— 'Gazprom, European Partners Sign Shareholders Agreement on Nord Stream-2', 4 September 2015, https://www.reuters.com/article/russia-forum-nord-stream-idUKL5N11A04B20150904

———— 'Rosneft–Essar Deal Not Subject to Sanctions: Russia's VTB Head', 15 October 2016, https://www.reuters.com/article/us-essar-oil-m-a-rosneft-oil-sanctions-idUKKBN12F0JN

———— 'Russia to Order 19.5 pct Rosneft Stake Sale Next Week—Source', 28 October 2016, https://www.reuters.com/article/russia-rosneft-privatisation-idUSL8N1CY3FM

———— 'Mozambique Signs Oil Exploration Agreements with Exxon, Rosneft', 8 October 2018, https://www.reuters.com/article/us-mozambique-oil-idUSKCN1MI1YJ

———— 'China's CEFC Paid Out Compensation after Rosneft Stake Deal Fell Through', 19 November 2018, https://www.reuters.com/article/us-rosneft-privatisation-cefc-idUSKCN1NO1RU

———— 'Bulgaria Can Boost Balkan Stream Capacity to Ship Non-Russian Gas', 6 March 2020, https://www.reuters.com/article/bulgaria-gas-turkstream-idAFL8N2AZ355

———— 'Fortnum Raises Stake in Uniper to More than 75%', 18 August 2020, https://www.reuters.com/article/uniper-ma-fortum-oyj-idUSL8N2FK2OR

———— 'Russia's Rosneft Acquires Shell's 37.5% Stake in German Refinery PCK Schwedt', 17 November 2021, https://www.reuters.com/business/russias-rosneft-acquires-shells-375-stake-german-refinery-pck-schwedt-2021-11-17/

———— 'Russia's Amur Gas Chemical Complex Secures $9.1 bln in Loans', 8 December 2021, https://www.reuters.com/business/energy/russias-amur-gas-chemical-complex-secures-91-bln-loans-2021-12-08/

———— 'Russian Gas Pipeline Exports to Europe', 17 February 2022, https://www.reuters.com/business/energy/russian-gas-pipeline-exports-europe-2022-02-17/

———— 'China–Russia Trade Has Surged as Countries Grow Closer', 1 March 2022, https://www.reuters.com/markets/europe/china-russia-trade-has-surged-countries-grow-closer-2022-03-01/

———— 'Poland Could Build Second Unit to Receive LNG amid Czech, Slovak Interest', 30 May 2022, https://www.reuters.com/business/energy/poland-could-build-second-unit-receive-lng-amid-czech-slovak-interest-2022-05-30/

———— 'Who Is Buying Russian Crude Oil and Who Has Stopped', 31 May 2022, https://www.reuters.com/business/energy/who-is-still-buying-russian-crude-oil-2022-03-21/

BIBLIOGRAPHY

———— 'Saudi Arabia Doubles Second-Quarter Russian Fuel Oil Imports for Power Generation', 15 July 2022, https://www.reuters.com/business/energy/exclusive-saudi-arabia-doubles-q2-russian-fuel-oil-imports-power-generation-2022-07-14/

———— 'U.S. Becomes Top LNG Exporter in First Half of 2022—EIA', 25 July 2022, https://www.reuters.com/business/energy/us-becomes-top-lng-exporter-first-half-2022-eia-2022-07-25/

———— 'Bridge Closed in Russia-Held Kherson after HIMARS Shelling, Official Says', 27 July 2022, https://www.reuters.com/world/europe/bridge-closed-russia-held-kherson-after-himars-shelling-reports-2022-07-27/

———— 'Russia to Spend $600 Billion on Defence and Security by 2025', 23 September 2022, https://www.reuters.com/business/aerospace-defense/russia-spend-600-bln-defence-security-by-2025-source-2022-09-23/

———— 'Major Tajik Bank Halts Use of Russia's Mir Cards', 26 September 2022, https://www.reuters.com/article/ukraine-crisis-mir-tajikistan-idUSL1N30X0T6

———— 'Oil Output Seen Halved at Sakhalin-1 in 2022—RIA Cites Regional Governor', 28 September 2022, https://www.reuters.com/business/energy/oil-output-seen-halved-sakhalin-1-2022-ria-cites-regional-governor-2022-09-28/

———— 'Gas Starts Flowing to Poland through New Baltic Pipe Pipeline', 1 October 2022, https://www.reuters.com/markets/europe/gas-starts-flowing-poland-through-new-baltic-pipe-pipeline-2022-10-01/

———— 'Hungary Finalises Deferred Payments Deal with Gazprom—Minister', 12 October 2022, https://www.reuters.com/business/energy/hungary-finalises-deferred-payments-deal-with-gazprom-minister-2022-10-12/

———— 'Erdogan Says He Agreed with Putin to Form Natural Gas Hub in Turkey', 19 October 2022, https://www.reuters.com/business/energy/erdogan-says-he-agreed-with-putin-form-natural-gas-hub-turkey-2022-10-19/

———— 'Ukraine Plane Engine Builder Head Held on Treason Charges, Media Report', 22 October 2022, https://www.reuters.com/world/europe/ukraine-plane-engine-builder-head-held-treason-charges-media-2022-10-22/

———— 'Russia Seeks Sanctions Exemptions for State Bank in Ukraine Grain Deal Talks—Sources', 4 November 2022, https://www.reuters.com/business/finance/exclusive-russia-seeks-sanctions-exemptions-state-bank-ukraine-grain-deal-talks-2022-11-04/

———— 'Eurozone Oct Y/Y Inflation Revised Marginally Lower, Still Record High', 17 November 2022, https://www.reuters.com/markets/europe/euro-zone-oct-yy-inflation-revised-marginally-lower-still-record-high-2022-11-17/

———— 'Russian McDonald's Successor Solves Franchise Problem as More Outlets Join', 28 November 2022, https://www.reuters.com/business/retail-consumer/russian-mcdonalds-successor-solves-franchise-problem-more-outlets-join-2022-11-28/

———— 'Russia's Prigozhin Admits Links to What U.S. Says Was Election-Meddling Troll Farm', 14 February 2023, https://www.reuters.com/world/europe/russias-prigozhin-admits-links-what-us-says-was-election-meddling-troll-farm-2023-02-14/

Reznik, Irina, 'Fish Link Kremlin to New Owner of Facebook's Russian Nemesis', Bloomberg, 26 June 2013, https://www.bloomberg.com/news/articles/2013-06-25/fish-tie-kremlin-to-new-owner-of-facebook-s-russian-rival

RFE/RL, 'EU Criticizes Poland's Nazi Pipeline Comment', 2 May 2006, https://www.rferl.org/a/1068083.html

———— 'Crimean Tatar Leader Receives Turkey's Highest State Order', 16 April 2014, https://www.rferl.org/a/crimean-tatar-leader-receives-turkeys-highest-state-order/25335329.html

———— 'Uzbekistan to Liberalize Currency Regulations Starting September 5', 3 September 2017, https://www.rferl.org/a/uzbekistan-currency-sum-dollar-convertible-liberalization-exchange/28714017.html

———— 'Uzbek President Flies Oligarch Airways to UN General Assembly', 21 September 2017, https://www.rferl.org/a/uzbekistan-mirziyoev-usmanov-un-assembly/28749030.html

———— 'U.S. Lifts Uzbek Cotton Ban, Saying Forced Child Labor "Significantly Reduced"', 27 March 2019, https://www.rferl.org/a/u-s-lifts-uzbek-cotton-ban-child-labor-educed-/29845439.html

———— 'Ukraine Plans to Nationalize Jet Engine Producer Motor Sich from Chinese Investors', 12 March 2021, https://www.rferl.org/a/ukraine-motor-sich-nationalization-china-/31146649.html

———— 'Austrian Ex-Foreign Minister Kneissl Becomes Rosneft Board Member', 2 June 2021, https://www.rferl.org/a/karin-kneissl-rosneft-austria/31286880.html

———— 'Russia Doubled Imports of Natural Gas from Turkmenistan in 2021, Envoy Says', 24 December 2021, https://www.rferl.org/a/russia-doubles-gas-imports-turkmenistan/31625051.html

———— 'Ukraine Suspends Some Russian Gas Flow, Blaming Interference of Occupying Forces', 10 May 2022, https://www.rferl.org/a/russia-gas-ukraine-suspend-force-majeure/31843451.html

———— 'Ukraine Says It Has Retaken Infamous Snake Island; Russia Says It Withdrew for "Goodwill"', 30 June 2022, https://www.rferl.org/a/ukraine-snake-island-retaken-russia/31922826.html

———— 'Putin Orders Seizure of Sakhalin-1 Oil-and-Gas Project, Leaving U.S., Japanese, Indian Investors at Risk', 8 October 2022, https://www.rferl.org/a/putin-orders-seizure-sakhalin-1-oil-and-gas-project/32071061.html

Riedel, Bruce, 'The $110 Billion Arms Deal to Saudi Arabia Is Fake News', Brookings, 5 June 2017, https://www.brookings.edu/blog/markaz/2017/06/05/the-110-billion-arms-deal-to-saudi-arabia-is-fake-news/

———— 'The Case of Saudi Arabia's Mohammed bin Nayef', Brookings, 12 February 2021, https://www.brookings.edu/blog/order-from-chaos/2021/02/12/the-case-of-saudi-arabias-mohammed-bin-nayef/

Rosatom, 'Dopolnitelnoe Soglashenie k Kreditomu soglasheniyu ob otkrytii kreditnoj linii No 122/22-b ot 02 Avgusta 2022 goda; [Supplementary Agreement with regards to the loan agreement on opening a credit line No. 122/22-b of 02 August 2022], Rosatom, 03 August 2022, https://zakupki.rosatom.ru/file.ashx?oid=6524417

Rosenthal, Elizabeth, 'Liberal Leader from Ukraine Was Poisoned', *The New York Times*, 12 December 2004, https://www.nytimes.com/2004/12/12/world/europe/liberal-leader-from-ukraine-was-poisoned.html

Roshina, Elena, 'Novinsky otkazalsya ot mandata nardepa' [Novinsky resigned his mandate as a state deputy], *Ukrainska Pravda*, 6 July 2022, https://www.pravda.com.ua/rus/news/2022/07/6/7356623/

Rosneft, 'Rosneft and Vietnam Oil and Gas Group PetroVietnam Sign Agreements for Offshore Projects Development', Rosneft,

12 November 2013, https://www.rosneft.com/press/releases/item/6249/

——— 'Rosneft and PetroVietnam Agree upon Creation of JV for Work on the Pechora Sea Shelf', 5 September 2014, https://www.rosneft.com/press/news/item/153694/

——— 'Rosneft and Japan Drilling Co., Ltd. Signed an Agreement for Drilling Exploration Wells Offshore Vietnam', 4 September 2015, https://www.rosneft.com/press/releases/item/176083/

——— 'Rosneft Commences Exploratory Drilling Offshore Vietnam as a Project Operator', 9 March 2016, https://www.rosneft.com/press/releases/item/180809/

——— 'Rosneft, INP and ENH Expand Cooperation in Mozambique', 22 August 2019, https://www.rosneft.com/press/releases/item/196635/

——— 'Rosneft Sells Its Venezuelan Assets and Becomes an Owner of 9.6% of Its Share Capital', 28 March 2020, https://www.rosneft.com/press/releases/item/200275/

Rostec, 'Russia Increases Its Share in the Helicopter Market', 14 May 2014, https://rostec.ru/en/news/4513399/

Roth, Andrew, 'Billionaire Placed under House Arrest in Russia', *The New York Times*, 17 September 2014, https://www.nytimes.com/2014/09/18/world/europe/russia-oligarch-vladimir-evtushenkov-house-arrest.html

——— 'Russia denies US claim it told Maduro not to flee Venezuela', *The Guardian*, 1 May 2019. https://www.theguardian.com/world/2019/may/01/russia-denies-us-claim-it-told-maduro-not-to-flee-venezuela

Rozhansky, Timofey and Irina Romaliyskaya, 'Pohemu eksperty ne veryat v okanchanie "chastinchnoi mobilizatsii"' [Why experts do not believe in the end of the partial mobilisation], Current Time, 29 October 2022, http://currenttime.tv/a/rossiyskaya-armiya-dovolno-bystro-teryaet-soldat-i-budut-nuzhny-novye-pochemu-eksperty-ne-veryat-v-okonchanie-chastichnoy-mobilizatsii-/32106078.html

RTL, 'Mehrheit der Deutschen überzeugt: Sanktionen schaden Deutschland mehr als Russland' [Majority of Germans convinced: Sanctions hurt Germany more than Russia], 13 October 2022, https://www.rtl.de/cms/umfrage-zu-sanktionen-deutsche-finden-schaden-uns-mehr-als-russland-5010721.html

Rudgewick, Oliver, 'Paris Club Agrees Ukraine Debt Suspension', Public Finance Focus, 20 July 2022, https://www.publicfinancefocus.org/pfm-news/2022/07/paris-club-agrees-ukraine-debt-suspension

Ruinformer, 'Russia gotovitsya vvesti zolotoj rubl' [Russian prepares itself for introduction of gold rouble], 23 January 2015, https://ruinformer.com/page/rossija-gotovitsja-vvesti-zolotoj-rubl

Ruiz Loyola, Benjamín, 'Salisbury, Novichok and the OPCW', *Lupine Online Journal of Pharmacology & Clinical Research* 1, no. 4 (13 August 2019), http://dx.doi.org/10.32474/LOJPCR.2019.01.000118

Rusal, 'UC RUSAL Prices the First Tranche of the Panda Bonds', 16 March 2017, https://rusal.ru/en/press-center/press-releases/uc_rusal_prices_the_first_tranche_of_the_panda_bonds/

——— 'RUSAL Signed the First Sustainability-Linked Syndicated Pre-export Finance Facility in Russia for over USD1 bln', 28 October 2019, https://rusal.ru/en/press-center/press-releases/rusal_signed_the_first_sustainability_linked_syndicated_pre_export_finance_facility_in_russia_for_ov/

Sakwa, Richrad, *Frontline Ukraine: Crisis in the Borderlands*, London: Bloomsbury, 2022 [2016].

Salama, Vivian, Justin Scheck, and Max Colchester, 'Ukrainian President Asked Biden Not to Sanction Abramovich, to Facilitate Peace Talks', *The Wall Street Journal*, 23 March 2022, https://www.wsj.com/articles/ukrainian-president-asked-biden-not-to-sanction-abramovich-to-facilitate-peace-talks-11648053860

Salem, Paul, 'Iraq's Tangled Foreign Interests and Relations', Carnegie Endowment for International Peace, 24 December 2013, https://carnegie-mec.org/2013/12/24/iraq-s-tangled-foreign-interests-and-relations-pub-54010

Sampson, Paul, 'Trafigura Sells Stake in Russian Arctic Oil Venture', Energy Intelligence, 13 July 2022, https://www.energyintel.com/00000181-f925-dfcc-a7eb-fba5ec4c0000

Samsung, 'A Missile May Have Hit Samsung's Ukraine R&D Office in Europe', 10 October 2022, https://www.sammobile.com/news/breaking-missile-hit-samsungs-ukraine-rd-office-europe/

Sarotte, Mary Elise, *Not One Inch: America, Russia and the Making of Post-Cold War Stalemate*, New Haven: Yale University Press, 2021.

Sattarov, Rafael, 'Alisher Usmanov: Uzbekistan's Oligarch of Choice', Carnegie Endowment for International Peace, 16 November 2017, https://carnegiemoscow.org/commentary/74756

Sauer, Pjotr, 'In Push for Africa, Russia's Wagner Mercenaries Are "Out of Their Depth" in Mozambique', *The Moscow Times*, 19 November 2019, https://www.themoscowtimes.com/2019/11/19/in-push-for-africa-russias-wagner-mercenaries-are-out-of-their-depth-in-mozambique-a68220

————— 'US Imposes Sanctions on Luxury Yacht Firm Linked to Putin', *The Guardian*, 2 June 2022, https://www.theguardian.com/world/2022/jun/02/us-imposes-sanctions-on-luxury-yacht-firm-linked-to-putin

————— 'Pro-Putin Rapper Reopens Former Starbucks Coffee Shops in Russia', *The Guardian*, 18 August 2022, https://www.theguardian.com/world/2022/aug/18/pro-putin-rapper-reopens-former-starbucks-coffee-shops-in-russia

————— 'Putin Ally Yevgeny Prigozhin Admits Founding Wagner Mercenary Group', *The Guardian*, 26 September 2022, https://www.theguardian.com/world/2022/sep/26/putin-ally-yevgeny-prigozhin-admits-founding-wagner-mercenary-group

Saul, Jonathan, 'Russia's State-Owned RNRC to Reinsure Russian Oil Shipments, Sources Say', Reuters, 10 June 2022, https://www.reuters.com/business/energy/exclusive-russias-state-owned-rnrc-reinsure-russian-oil-shipments-sources-say-2022-06-10/

Savic, Bob, 'Behind Russia and China's "Special Relationship"', *The Diplomat*, 7 December 2016, https://thediplomat.com/2016/12/behind-china-and-russias-special-relationship/

Sayari, 'Trading with the Enemy: Motor Sich's Bosnian Arrangement with the Russian Defense Sector', 11 May 2020, https://sayari.com/resources/trading-with-the-enemy-motor-sich/

Scally, Derek, 'Scholz Suggests He Saw Putin's Energy Cuts Coming', *The Irish Times*, 12 October 2022, https://www.irishtimes.com/world/europe/2022/10/12/scholz-suggests-he-saw-putins-energy-cuts-coming/

Scevola, Nila and Dmity Zhdannikov, 'Gazprom, Eni Plan Big Gas Pipeline Bypassing Turkey', Reuters, 23 June 2007, https://www.reuters.com/article/us-eni-gazprom-idUSL2328219820070623

Schanzer, Jonathan, 'The Biggest Sanctions-Evasion Scheme in Recent History', *The Atlantic*, 4 January 2018, https://www.theatlantic.com/international/archive/2018/01/iran-turkey-gold-sanctions-nuclear-zarrab-atilla/549665/

Schmidt, Felix, 'The Dollar's Dominance Remains Virtually Unchallenged', KfW Research, 1 November 2022, https://www.

kfw.de/PDF/Download-Center/Konzernthemen/Research/PDF-Dokumente-Fokus-Volkswirtschaft/Fokus-englische-Dateien/Fokus-2022-EN/Focus-No.-406-November-2022-US-dollar.pdf

Schneider, Howard, Ann Saphir, and Cynthia Kim, 'Bank of Korea's Rhee Says Policy Tightening Unlikely to End before Fed', Reuters, 29 August 2022, https://www.reuters.com/markets/asia/bank-koreas-rhee-says-rates-rise-until-inflation-defeated-2022-08-28/

Sciorilli Borrelli, Silvia, James Fontanella-Khan, and David Sheppard, 'Lukoil Rejects US Buyout Group's Offer for Sicily Refinery', The Financial Times, 4 November 2022, https://www.ft.com/content/f63cc4c0-7766-4a9c-bfe5-242a129aa990

Schaps, Karolin, 'Dutch Floating LNG Facility Gets EUR 160m Guarantee', Montel, 27 April 2022, https://www.montelnews.com/news/1315870/dutch-floating-lng-facility-gets-eur-160m-guarantee

Schreck, Carl, 'Crash Course: The Ruble's Volatile Two Decades', RFE/RL, 2 December 2014, https://www.rferl.org/a/ruble-history-crashes-russia-economy/26720846.html

Schwirtz, Michael, 'Last Stand at Azovstal: Inside the Siege that Shaped the Ukraine War', The New York Times, 24 July 2022, https://www.nytimes.com/2022/07/24/world/europe/ukraine-war-mariupol-azovstal.html

Seddon, Max and James Politi, 'Putin's Party Signs Deal with Italy's Far-Right Lega Nord', The Financial Times, 6 March 2017, https://www.ft.com/content/0d33d22c-0280-11e7-ace0-1ce02ef0def9

Seldin, Jeff, 'US Aware of Allegations of Russian Links to Burkinabe Coup', VOA, 27 January 2022, https://www.voanews.com/a/us-aware-of-allegations-of-russian-links-to-burkinabe-coup-/6415668.html

Sequera, Vivian, 'Venezuelans Report Big Weight Losses in 2017 as Hunger Hits', Reuters, 21 February 2018, https://uk.reuters.com/article/us-venezuela-food/venezuelans-report-big-weight-losses-in-2017-as-hunger-hitsidUKKCN1G52HA

Serkov, Dmitry, Inna Sidorkova, and Maksim Solopov, 'Kak raskhishchalis millardy dlya stroitelstva patronnogo zavoda v Venesuelye' [How billions were stolen for the construction of an ammunition factory in Venezuela], RBC, 3 August 2018, https://www.rbc.ru/society/03/08/2018/5b62c2ec9a79473bd5833af8

Sezer, Can, 'Turkey's State Banks Suspend Use of Russian Mir Payment System—Finance Minister', Reuters, 29 September 2022, https://

www.reuters.com/business/finance/turkeys-ziraat-bank-suspends-use-russian-mir-payment-system-ceo-2022-09-29/

———— 'Turkey's Baykar to Complete Plant in Ukraine in Two Years—CEO', Reuters, 28 October 2022, https://www.reuters.com/world/turkeys-baykar-complete-plant-ukraine-two-years-ceo-2022-10-28/

Sgaravatti, Giovanni, Simone Tagliapietra, Cecilia Trasi, and Giorgi Zachmann, 'National Fiscal Responses to the Energy Crisis', Bruegel, 13 February 2023, https://www.bruegel.org/dataset/national-policies-shield-consumers-rising-energy-prices

Shackle, Samira, 'Imran Khan Has Won Over Pakistan; But Real Power Still Lies with the Army', *The Guardian*, 27 July 2018, https://www.theguardian.com/commentisfree/2018/jul/27/imran-khan-won-pakistan-power-army-military-election

Shagina, Maria, 'Has Russia's Pivot to Asia Worked?', *The Diplomat*, 10 January 2020, https://thediplomat.com/2020/01/has-russias-pivot-to-asia-worked/

———— 'Drifting East: Russia's Import Substitution and Its Pivot to Asia', CEES Working Paper, Center for Eastern European Studies, University of Zurich, April 2020, https://www.researchgate.net/publication/340979612_Drifting_East_Russia's_Import_Substitution_and_Its_Pivot_to_Asia

———— 'Technology Controls Can Strangle Russia—Just Like the Soviet Union', *Foreign Policy*, 22 August 2022, https://foreignpolicy.com/2022/08/22/russia-ukraine-war-sanctions-export-controls-technology-transfer-semiconductors-defense-industry-military-espionage/

Shamgun, Olesya and Denis Dmitriev, '"We Cannot Use It": Leaked E-Mails Show How Russian Petrochemical Giant Sibur Paid for Villa Linked to Putin', OCCRP, 20 June 2022, https://www.occrp.org/en/asset-tracker/we-cannot-use-it-leaked-emails-show-how-russian-petrochemical-giant-sibur-paid-for-villa-linked-to-putin

Sheppard, David, Neil Hume, and Tom Mitchell, 'Mongolia Says Russia–China Gas Pipeline Will Break Ground in 2024', *The Financial Times*, 18 July 2022, https://www.ft.com/content/f0080bf6-5e7d-44be-871f-a5d44dccf5c5

Sheppard, David, Silvia Sciorilli Borrelli, and James Fontanella-Khan, 'Russia's Lukoil Sells Italian Refinery to Israeli-Backed Private Equity Fund', *The Financial Times*, 9 January 2023, https://www.ft.com/content/bef2163a-e730-4967-990b-6b325cab5c76

Shevchuk, Maria, "'Rossii net opravdaniya": Novinsky zayavil, chto ne uedet iz Ukrainy i prodlozhit pomogat' naseleniu' ['There is no excuse for Russia': Novinsky states that he will not leave Ukraine and will support the population], Obrozovatel, 8 March 2022, https://news.obozrevatel.com/politics/rossii-net-opravdaniya-novinskij-zayavil-chto-ne-uedet-iz-ukrainyi-i-prodolzhit-pomogat-naseleniyu.htm

Shikerova, Genka and Ivan Bedrov, 'How Russian Energy Giant LUKoil Makes Millions in Bulgaria But Pays Almost No Tax', RFE/RL, 9 February 2022, https://www.rferl.org/a/bulgaria-lukoil-taxes-millions-russsia/31695145.html

Ship Technology, 'Methane Princess LNG Carrier', 25 June 2014, https://www.ship-technology.com/projects/methane-princess-lng-carrier/

Shiryaevskaya, Anna and Anna Koh, 'UK to Import Rare Australian Gas Cargo in Latest Sign of Desperation', Bloomberg, 16 August 2022, https://www.bloomberg.com/news/articles/2022-08-16/uk-to-import-rare-australian-gas-cargo-as-energy-crisis-builds?sref=B0Y81EZP

Shuster, Simon, 'Russia Secretly Helped Venezuela Launch a Cryptocurrency to Evade U.S. Sanctions', Time, 20 March 2018, https://time.com/5206835/exclusive-russia-petro-venezuela-cryptocurrency/

Shuster, Simon and Marat Gurt, 'Turkmen May Sue Russia for "Vacuum-Bomb" Pipe Blast', Reuters, 29 May 2009, https://www.reuters.com/article/us-russia-turkmenistan-gas-sb-idUSTRE54S4TG20090529

Short, Philip, *Putin: His Life and Times*, London: The Bodley Head, 2022.

Siebold, Sabine and Riham Alkousaa, 'West Cautious on Nord Stream Blasts, Germany Confirms Raiding Suspect Ship', Reuters, 8 March 2023, https://www.reuters.com/world/europe/germany-says-nord-stream-attacks-may-be-false-flag-smear-ukraine-2023-03-08/

Silverman, Rosa, 'Liz Truss and the Photos That Show Her Margaret Thatcher Makeover', *The Telegraph*, 11 February 2022, https://www.telegraph.co.uk/women/life/liz-truss-photos-show-margaret-thatcher-makeover/

Simakov, Dmitry and Anna Fadeeva, 'Siemens postavit turbiny dlya krymskikh eletrostantsii' [Siemens to deliver turbines for Crimean power plants], *Vedomosti*, 30 June 2015, https://www.vedomosti.

ru/business/articles/2015/06/30/598584-tehnopromeksport-nashel-turbini-dlya-krimskih-elektrostantsii

Simes Jr, Dimitri, 'Singapore: Russia's New Gateway to Southeast Asia', OZY, 31 May 2020, https://www.ozy.com/the-new-and-the-next/singapore-russia-new-gateway-southeast-asia/285201/

Simon, Frédéric, '"Freedom Gas": US Opens LNG Floodgates to Europe', Euractiv, 2 May 2019, https://www.euractiv.com/section/energy/news/freedom-gas-us-opens-lng-floodgates-to-europe/

Singh Sodia, Chatheti, 'Russian Invasion Has Caused $1 Trillion Worth of Damage to Ukraine', WION, 22 September 2022, https://www.wionews.com/world/russian-invasion-has-caused-1-trillion-worth-of-damage-to-ukraine-report-518716

Skorkin, Konstantin, 'All Change: Donbas Republics Get New Russian Business Boss', Carnegie Endowment for International Peace, 29 June 2021, https://carnegiemoscow.org/commentary/84859

———— 'Ukraine's Oligarchs Are a Dying Breed: The Country Will Never Be the Same', Carnegie Endowment for International Peace, 14 September 2022, https://carnegieendowment.org/politika/87914

Sky News, 'Severodonetsk Now under Russian Control following Weeks-Long Battle', 25 June 2022, https://news.sky.com/story/ukraine-war-severodonetsk-now-under-russian-control-following-weeks-long-battle-12640364

Sliepcevich, C. M. 'Liquefied Natural Gas: A New Source of Energy; Part I, Ship Transportation', *American Scientist* 53, no. 2 (June 1965), pp. 260–97, https://www.jstor.org/stable/27836010

Smith, Elliot, 'Europe's Plans to Replace Russian Gas Are Deemed "Wildly Optimistic"—and Could Hammer Its Economy', CNBC, 29 June 2022, https://www.cnbc.com/2022/06/29/europes-plans-to-replace-russian-gas-are-deemed-wildly-optimistic-and-could-hammer-its-economy.html

Smart Holding, 'SCM and Smart-Holding Announce Completion of the Merger of Their Metals and Mining Assets under Metinvest B.V', 14 July 2014, https://smart-holding.com/en/press-centre/news/2067/

Smith Thayer, Sandra, 'Russia–Ukraine Crisis Raises Political Risk Insurance Profile', Bloomberg Law, 10 May 2022, https://news.bloomberglaw.com/us-law-week/russia-ukraine-crisis-raises-political-risk-insurance-profile

Smolchenko, Anna and Olga Nedbaeva, 'Chinese leader Xi, Putin Agree Key Energy Deals', AFP, 22 March 2013, https://sg.news.yahoo.com/putin-welcomes-chinas-xi-landmark-talks-024906416.html

Snider, Ted, 'Why Imran Khan's Coup Theory Is so Popular in Pakistan', Institute for Responsible Statecraft, 10 May 2022, https://responsiblestatecraft.org/2022/05/10/why-imran-khans-coup-theory-is-so-popular-in-pakistan

Society of International Gas Tanker and Terminal Operators, 'Methane Pioneer Sets the Scene'. LNG Shipping at 50, Society of International Gas Tanker and Terminal Operators, 2014, pp. 10–11, https://www.sigtto.org/media/2905/lng-shipping-at-50compressed.pdf

Soldatkin, Vladimir, 'Say Goodbye to OPEC, Powerful Putin Pal Predicts', Reuters, 10 May 2016, https://www.reuters.com/article/us-russia-opec-sechin-idUSKCN0Y1104

Sonnenfeld, Jeffrey and Steven Tian, 'Some of the Biggest Brands Are Leaving Russia; Others Just Can't Quit Putin: Here's a List', The New York Times, 7 April 2022, https://www.nytimes.com/interactive/2022/04/07/opinion/companies-ukraine-boycott.html

Soylu, Ragıp, 'Russian State Firm Signs $9.1bn Loan Deal to Fund Nuclear Plant in Turkey', Middle East Eye, 19 September 2022, https://www.middleeasteye.net/news/russia-turkey-gazprombank-akkuyu-plant-loan-fund

Spencer, Richard, 'Prince Buys £300m Boat as Austerity Hits Home', The Times, 18 October 2016, https://www.thetimes.co.uk/article/prince-buys-300m-boat-as-austerity-bites-at-home-wwt829d5w

Spivak, Vita, 'Can the Yuan Ever Replace the Dollar for Russia?', Carnegie Endowment for International Peace, 2 August 2021, https://carnegiemoscow.org/commentary/85069

Srivastava, Mehul and Roman Olearchyk, 'Ukraine: The $10bln Steel Plant at the Heart of Russia's Economic Warfare', The Financial Times, 26 August 2022, https://www.ft.com/content/5835e60f-d5b2-4096-b5be-c1ce4f34560c

Stapczynski, Stephen, 'India Grapples with LNG Glut as Customers Balk at High Gas Prices', Bloomberg, 10 November 2022, https://www.bloomberg.com/news/articles/2022-11-10/india-grapples-with-lng-glut-as-consumers-balk-at-high-gas-rates

Stapczynski, Stephen and Faseeh Mangi, 'Europe's Plan to Quit Russian Fuel Plunges Pakistan into Darkness', Bloomberg, 13 June 2022, https://www.bloomberg.com/news/articles/2022-06-13/energy-prices-in-europe-are-creating-power-outages-in-pakistan

Statistics Norway, 'Substantial Strengthening of the Trade Balance in the Third Quarter of 2022', 7 December 2022, https://www.ssb.no/en/utenriksokonomi/utenriksregnskap/statistikk/utenriksregnskap/articles/substantial-strengthening-of-the-trade-balance-in-the-third-quarter-of-2022

Steil, Benn and Benjamin Della Rocca, 'Belt and Road Tracker', Council on Foreign Relations, 1 June 2022, https://www.cfr.org/article/belt-and-road-tracker

Steinbeck, John, *A Russian Journal*. London: Penguin Classics, 2000 [1948].

Steitz, Christoph, 'Uniper's $4.4 Billion Listing Unveils Huge Valuation Gap', Reuters, 12 September 2016, https://www.reuters.com/article/uk-rwe-innogy-ipo-idUKKCN11I0OC

Stempel, Jonathan, 'Telia Settles U.S., European Bribery Probes for $965.8 Million', Reuters, 21 September 2017, https://www.reuters.com/article/us-telia-settlement-idUSKCN1BW1XL

Stepanian, Ruzanna, 'Yerevan Mayor Resigns Over Assault', Azatutyn, 9 December 2010, https://www.azatutyun.am/a/2242752.html

Stern, Jonathan, 'Gas Pipeline Co-operation between Political Adversaries: Examples from Europe', Chatham House, January 2005, https://www.chathamhouse.org/sites/default/files/public/Research/Energy,%20Environment%20and%20Development/jsjan05.pdf

Stevis-Gridneff, Matina, 'As Europe Piles Sanctions on Russia, Some Sacred Cows Are Spared', *The New York Times*, 18 October 2022, https://www.nytimes.com/2022/10/18/world/europe/eu-sanctions-russia-ukraine.html?smid=nytcore-ios-share&referringSource=articleShare

Stoner, Kathryn, *Russia Resurrected: Its Power and Purpose in a New Global Order*, New York: Oxford University Press, 2021.

Storbeck, Olaf, Madelein Speed, Richard Milne, and Sarah Provan, 'Germany Nationalises Struggling Utility Uniper in €29bn Bailout', *The Financial Times*, 21 September 2022, https://www.ft.com/content/2190babb-1cb8-49f1-a9d5-2c9d98539de9

The Straits Times, 'Erdogan Denounces "Judicial Coup" against Turkey', 5 January 2014, https://www.straitstimes.com/world/erdogan-denounces-judicial-coup-against-turkey

BIBLIOGRAPHY

Strange, Susan, *States and Markets*, London: Bloomsbury Revelations, 2015 [1988].

Strasburg, Jenny and Benoît Morenne, 'Race to Secure Gas for Europe's Future Winters Has Already Begun', *The Wall Street Journal*, 20 November 2022, https://www.wsj.com/articles/race-to-secure-gas-for-europes-future-winters-has-already-begun-11668945601

Stuckey, David, 'Inside Out: Framework Financing Agreement for Syvash Wind Farm Ukraine', CEE Legal Matters, 8 November 2019, https://www.ceelegalmatters.com/interviews/11771-inside-out-framework-financing-agreement-for-syvash-wind-farm-ukraine

Sulzer, 'Transfer of Shares Completed—Renova Ownership below 50%—Sulzer Free from US Sanctions', 12 April 2018, https://www.sulzer.com/en/shared/news/sulzer-free-from-us-sanctions

SupChina, 'China in Infographics', 26 July 2017, https://thechinaproject.com/2017/07/26/china-in-infographics/

Svoboda, Karel, 'Russia's Loans as a Means of Geoeconomic Competition in Africa and Latin America', *Problems of Post-Communism*, 14 July 2022, https://doi.org/10.1080/10758216.2022.2094808

Swint, Brian and Anna Shiryaevskaya, 'Rosneft Tops Exxon with 5% of World Oil in Soviet-Era Wells', Bloomberg, 22 March 2013, https://www.bloomberg.com/news/articles/2013-03-22/rosneft-overtakes-exxon-with-5-of-world-oil-in-soviet-era-wells

SwissInfo, 'Swiss Parliament Approves Bailout for Electricity Providers', 13 September 2022, https://www.swissinfo.ch/eng/swiss-parliament-approves-bailout-for-electricity-providers/47896672

Sykes, Patrick, 'Iran Revives LNG Export Plan as World Scrambles for Natural Gas', Bloomberg, 15 March 2022, https://www.bloomberg.com/news/articles/2022-03-15/iran-revives-lng-export-plan-as-world-scrambles-for-natural-gas

Sytas, Andrus, 'EU Leaders Sign Letter Objecting to Nord Stream-2 Gas Link', Reuters, 16 March 2016, https://www.reuters.com/article/uk-eu-energy-nordstream-idUKKCN0WI1YV

Szabó, András, 'The Mysterious German behind Viktor Orban's Russian Deals', Direct36, 17 October 2017, https://www.direkt36.hu/en/a-rejtelyes-nemet-aki-orban-orosz-manovereit-egyengeti/

————— 'Inside the Internal Government Conflict over the Permit for the Controversial Paks 2 Nuclear Power Plant', Direkt36, 31 January 2022, https://wwwa.direkt36.hu/en/igy-vivtak-meg-a-legujabb-csatat-a-kormanyban-az-egyre-problemasabb-paks-ii-korul/

BIBLIOGRAPHY

Şimşek, Abdurrahman, 'Energy Company Deputy Manager, 5 Others Arrested over Espionage in Turkey', *Daily Sabah*, 21 October 2020, https://www.dailysabah.com/business/energy/energy-company-deputy-manager-5-others-arrested-over-espionage-in-turkey

Taleb, Nasiim Nicholas, *Anti-fragile: Things that Gain from Disorder*, London: Allen Lane, 2012.

Tamkin, Emily, 'Trump Administration Says No to New Russia Sanctions, Yes to Cribbing from Forbes', *Foreign Policy*, 30 January 2018, https://foreignpolicy.com/2018/01/30/trump-administration-says-no-to-new-sanctions-yes-to-cribbing-from-forbes-kremlin-russia-state-treasury/

TASS, 'Russia's Urals Blend Average Oil Price down 9.5% in 2014 to $97.6 Per Barrel', 12 January 2015, https://tass.com/economy/770707

———— '"Gazprom" prodal turketskuyu Bosphorus Gaz' [Gazprom sells Turkish Bosphorus Gaz], 1 October 2018, https://tass.ru/ekonomika/5622846

———— 'Bank of Russia May Consider Gold-Backed Cryptocurrency', 23 May 2019, https://tass.com/economy/1059727

———— 'Gazprom Fully Suspends Gas Supplies to Bulgaria, Poland Due to Failure to Pay in Rubles', 27 April 2022, https://tass.com/economy/1443811

———— 'BRICS Basket-Based International Reserve Currency under Consideration—Putin', 22 June 2022, https://tass.com/economy/1469823

———— 'Power of Siberia 2 Can Become Replacement of Nord Stream 2—Russian Deputy PM', 15 September 2022, https://tass.com/economy/1508229

———— '"Roskapstroi" zayavil, chto zavod "Azovstal" v Mariupole vosstanavlivatsya ne budet' [Roskapstroi announced that Azovstal in Mariupol will not be rebuilt], TASS, 24 January 2023, https://tass.ru/ekonomika/16871883

Tatarski, Michael, 'How Russian Timber Bypasses U.S. Sanctions by Way of Vietnam', *The Washington Post*, 1 October 2022, https://www.washingtonpost.com/world/2022/10/01/russia-sanctions-birch-wood-vietnam-china/

Tavberidze, Vazha, 'This Is Not Just "Putin's War" and Russians Should "100 Percent" Feel Guilty: A Veteran Russian Analyst Pulls No Punches',

RFE/RL, 20 May 2022, https://www.rferl.org/a/russia-putin-analysis-ukraine-inozemtsev-collective-guilt/31859680.html

Taylor, Jessica, 'Trump Calls for "Total and Complete Shutdown of Muslims Entering" U.S.', NPR, 7 December 2015, https://www.npr.org/2015/12/07/458836388/trump-calls-for-total-and-complete-shutdown-of-muslims-entering-u-s

Tcherneva, Vessela, 'South Stream: When the Periphery Becomes the Frontline', European Council on Foreign Relations, 5 December 2014, https://ecfr.eu/article/commentary_south_stream_when_the_periphery_becomes_the_frontline373/

Tengrinews, 'Prezident Tokayev otkazalsya ot ordenov' [President Tokayev refuses medals], 18 June 2022, https://tengrinews.kz/sng/prezident-tokaev-otkazalsya-ot-ordenov-471256/

Tetley, Liza and Giulia Morpugo, 'Investors Fume at UK Treasury's License Delays for Russian Firms', Bloomberg, 13 September 2022, https://www.bloomberg.com/news/articles/2022-09-13/investors-fume-at-uk-treasury-s-license-delays-for-russian-firms

Thayer, Carl, 'The Bear Is Back: Russia Returns to Vietnam', *The Diplomat*, 26 November 2013, https://thediplomat.com/2013/11/the-bear-is-back-russia-returns-to-vietnam/

Thompson, Helen, *Disorder: Hard Times in the 21st Century*, Oxford: Oxford University Press, 2022.

Tkach, Mikhail, 'Kolomoisky posetil NABU' [Kolomoisky visited the NABU], *Ukrainska Pravda*, 3 November 2022, https://www.pravda.com.ua/rus/news/2022/11/3/7374850/

Tkachev, Ivan, 'Zoloto vpervye oboshlo dollar v reservax Rossii' [Gold surpassed the share of dollars in Russian reserves for the first time], RBC, 11 January 2021, https://www.rbc.ru/economics/11/01/2021/5ffc6e4d9a79471b76da7381

Toal, Gerard, *Near Abroad: Putin, the West and the Contest over Ukraine and the Caucasus*, New York: Oxford University Press, 2017.

Tognini, Giacomo, 'Vladimir Putin's Superyacht Graceful Has A New Name: "Killer Whale"', *Forbes*, 4 October 2022, https://www.forbes.com/sites/giacomotognini/2022/10/04/vladimir-putins-superyacht-graceful-has-a-new-name-killer-whale/?sh=4a96ee5c26fd

Tooze, Adam, 'About Those Sanctions: SWIFT, Correspondent Banking, and the GL 8 Energy Carve-Out', Chartbook, 24 February 2022, https://adamtooze.substack.com/p/chartbook-86-about-those-sanctions

Torbati, Yeganeh and Ernest Scheyder, 'U.S. Will Not Give Exxon Permission to Drill in Russia', Reuters, 21 April 2017, https://www.reuters.com/article/us-exxon-mobil-sanctions-russia-usa-idUSKBN17N2B5

Townsend, Jim and Rachel Ellehuus, 'The Tale of Turkey and the Patriots', War on the Rocks, 22 July 2019, https://warontherocks.com/2019/07/the-tale-of-turkey-and-the-patriots/

Transparency International Georgia, 'Georgia's Economic Dependence on Russia: Impact of the Russia–Ukraine War', 3 August 2022, https://transparency.ge/en/post/georgias-economic-dependence-russia-impact-russia-ukraine-war

Traub, James, 'The Georgia Syndrome', *Foreign Policy*, 13 August 2010, https://foreignpolicy.com/2010/08/13/the-georgia-syndrome/

Trend.az, 'Prezident Ilham Aliyev: My gotovy govorit s prozhivayushchimi v Karabaxe armyanami, no ne s takimi lyudmi, kak zaslanniy Moskvoi Vardanyan' [President Ilham Aliyev: We are ready to talk with Armenians living in Karabakh but not with those sent by Moscow like Vardanyan], 17 November 2022, https://www.trend.az/azerbaijan/politics/3670302.html

Trickett, Nick, 'Rosneft's Vietnam Exit Hints at Russia Inc.'s Future in Asia', *The Diplomat*, 28 August 2020, https://thediplomat.com/2020/08/rosnefts-vietnam-exit-hints-at-russia-inc-s-future-in-asia/

——— 'Further to Fall: Russia's Grinding Mobilization', Riddle, 10 November 2022, https://ridl.io/further-to-fall-russia-s-grinding-mobilization/

Troianovski, Anton, 'Wagner Founder Has Putin's Support, But the Kremlin's Side-Eye', *The New York Times*, 11 February 2022, https://www.nytimes.com/2023/02/11/world/europe/russia-wagner-group-prigozhin-putin.html

Truss, Mary Elizabeth, 'Liz Truss' Resignation Speech in Full', *The Guardian*, 20 October 2022, https://www.theguardian.com/politics/2022/oct/20/liz-truss-resignation-speech-in-full

Tsafos, Nikos, 'Is Gas Global Yet?', Center for Strategic and International Studies, 23 March 2018, https://www.csis.org/analysis/gas-global-yet

TSN, '25-letniy morpekh vzorvalsya na Henicheskom mostu i ostanovil rossiiskie tanki' [Twenty-five-year-old marine detonates on Henichesk bridge and stopped Russian tanks], 25 February 2022, https://tsn.ua/ru/video/video-novini/25-letniy-morpeh-vzorvalsya-na-genicheskom-mostu-i-ostanovil-rossiyskie-tanki.html

Tsui, Enid, 'Abramovich Buys Norilsk Stake to End Row', CNN, 4 December 2022, https://edition.cnn.com/2012/12/04/business/abramovich-norilsk/index.html

Tucker, Elizabeth, 'Soviet Union Joins the World of Capitalism', *The Washington Post*, 14 August 1986, https://www.washingtonpost.com/archive/business/1986/08/14/soviet-union-joins-the-world-of-capitalism/7d904cbc-ca3b-4fef-8119-ca8765acb23b/

Tully, Andrew, 'U.S. to Provide $1 Billion in Economic Aid to Georgia', RFE/RL, 4 September 2008, https://www.rferl.org/a/US_Providing_1_Billion_In_Economic_Aid_To_Georgia/1196233.html

Turak, Natasha, 'US Treasury Releases List of Russian Oligarchs Linked to Putin', CNBC, 30 January 2018, https://www.cnbc.com/2018/01/30/us-treasury-releases-list-of-russian-oligarchs-linked-to-putin.html

———— 'Goodbye, American Soft Power: McDonald's Exiting Russia after 32 Years Is the End of an Era', CNBC, 20 May 2022, https://www.cnbc.com/2022/05/20/mcdonalds-exiting-russia-after-32-years-is-the-end-of-an-era.html

Uehling, Greta Lynn, *Beyond Memory: The Crimean Tatars' Deportation and Return*, New York: Palgrave Macmillan, 2004.

UK Department for Digital, Culture, Media and Sport, 'Unilateral Declaration regarding the Sale of Chelsea Football Club', 30 May 2022, https://www.gov.uk/government/publications/unilateral-declaration-regarding-the-sale-of-chelsea-football-club/unilateral-declaration-regarding-the-sale-of-chelsea-football-club

UK Office of Budget Responsibility, 'Economic and Fiscal Outlook—November 2022', 17 November 2022, https://obr.uk/docs/dlm_uploads/CCS0822661240-002_SECURE_OBR_EFO_November_2022_WEB_ACCESSIBLE.pdf

Ukrainian Presidential Office, 'Ukaz Prezidenta Ukraini Pro Prisvoennya Zvannya Heroi Ukraini' [Decree of the president of Ukraine on the awarding of the title Hero of Ukraine], Ukrainian Presidential Office, 21 November 2014, https://zakon.rada.gov.ua/laws/show/890/2014

Ukrainska Pravda, 'Pravooxraniteli izbili muzhchinu za Maidan; On umer' [The security services beat a man because of Maidan; He died], 24 December 2013, https://www.pravda.com.ua/rus/news/2013/12/24/7008248/

——— 'Ukraine's Flagship Hetman Sahaidachny Was Sunk to Avoid Capture by Russian Troops', 4 March 2022, https://www.pravda.com.ua/eng/news/2022/03/4/7328077/

Ulmer, Alexandra and Deisy Buitrago, 'Enter the "Petro": Venezuela to Launch Oil-Backed Cryptocurrency', Reuters, 3 December 2017, https://www.reuters.com/article/us-venezuela-economy-idUSKBN1DX0SQ

Umwelt Bundesamt, 'Primärenergieverbracuh' [Primary energy usage], 25 March 2022, https://www.umweltbundesamt.de/daten/energie/primaerenergieverbrauch#definition-und-einflussfaktoren

University of Aberdeen, 'Brief History of the UK North Sea Oil and Gas Industry', Lives in the Oil Industry: Oral History of the UK North Sea Oil and Gas Industry, 12 June 2006, https://www.abdn.ac.uk/oillives/about/nsoghist.shtml

US Department of Agriculture, 'Ukraine Agricultural Production and Trade', 22 April 2022, https://www.fas.usda.gov/sites/default/files/2022-04/Ukraine-Factsheet-April2022.pdf

US Department of Commerce, 'Commerce Takes Further Actions to Target Russian Strategic Industries and Punish Enablers of Aggression', 4 March 2022, https://www.commerce.gov/news/press-releases/2022/03/commerce-takes-further-actions-target-russian-strategic-industries-and

US Department of Justice, 'Five Russian Nationals and Two Oil Traders Charged in Global Sanctions Evasion and Money Laundering Scheme', 19 October 2022, https://www.justice.gov/usao-edny/pr/five-russian-nationals-and-two-oil-traders-charged-global-sanctions-evasion-and-money

US Department of State, 'Secretary Antony J. Blinken with Kiratikorn Naksompop Blauw of Thai PBS', Naksompop Blauw, Kiratikorn, 11 July 2022, https://www.state.gov/secretary-antony-j-blinken-with-kiratikorn-naksompop-blauw-of-thai-pbs/

US Department of the Treasury, 'Treasury Sanctions Russian Officials, Members of the Russian Leadership's Inner Circle, and an Entity for Involvement in the Situation in Ukraine', 20 March 2014, https://home.treasury.gov/news/press-releases/jl23331

——— 'Ukraine-Related Sanctions; Publication of Executive Order 13662 Sectoral Sanctions Identifications List', 16 July 2014, https://home.treasury.gov/policy-issues/financial-sanctions/recent-actions/20140716

——— 'Treasury Designates Russian Oligarchs, Officials, and Entities in Response to Worldwide Malign Activity', 6 April 2018, https://home.treasury.gov/news/press-releases/sm0338

——— 'Treasury Targets Russian Oil Brokerage Firm for Supporting Illegitimate Maduro Regime', 18 February 2020, https://home.treasury.gov/news/press-releases/sm909

——— 'Treasury Targets Additional Russian Oil Brokerage Firm for Continued Support of Maduro Regime', 12 March 2020, https://home.treasury.gov/news/press-releases/sm937

——— 'Treasury Targets Russian Oil Brokerage Firm for Supporting Illegitimate Maduro Regime', 18 February 2020, https://home.treasury.gov/news/press-releases/sm909

——— 'U.S. Treasury Announces Unprecedented & Expansive Sanctions against Russia, Imposing Swift and Severe Economic Costs', 24 February 2022, https://home.treasury.gov/news/press-releases/jy0608

——— 'General License No. 15: Authorizing Transactions Involving Certain Blocked Entities Owned by Alisher Burhanovich Usmanov', 3 March 2022, https://home.treasury.gov/system/files/126/russia_gl15.pdf

——— 'Treasury Targets Sanctions Evasion Networks and Russian Technology Companies Enabling Putin's War', 31 March 2022, https://home.treasury.gov/news/press-releases/jy0692

——— 'Frequently Asked Question: 1074', 2 August 2022, https://home.treasury.gov/policy-issues/financial-sanctions/faqs/topic/6626

——— 'U.S. Treasury Sanctions Notorious Virtual Currency Mixer Tornado Cash', 8 August 2022, https://home.treasury.gov/news/press-releases/jy0916

US International Trade Administration, 'India: Country Commercial Guide', 8 September 2022, http://trade.gov/country-commercial-guides/india-energy

Vallée, Shahin, 'Reserves Freeze Sends Shivers through Moscow', Official Monetary and Financial Institutions Forum, 8 March 2022, https://www.omfif.org/2022/03/reserves-freeze-sends-shivers-through-moscow/

BIBLIOGRAPHY

Van Brugen, Isabel, 'Putin's Mobilization Backfires as 370,000 Flee Russia in Two Weeks', *Newsweek*, 4 October 2022, https://www.newsweek.com/putin-mobilization-backfires-russians-flee-kazakhstan-georgia-eu-1748771

Van Leijen, Marjorie, 'Russian Railways Asks Kazakhstan for Lower Transit Tariff', RailFreight, 15 July 2022, https://www.railfreight.com/beltandroad/2022/11/15/russian-railways-asks-kazakhstan-for-lower-transit-tariffs/t

Van Severen, Sebastiaan, 'Lavrov's Lament: A Russian Take on the Rules-Based Global Order', Blog of the European Journal of International Law, 16 July 2021, https://www.ejiltalk.org/lavrovs-lament-a-russian-take-on-the-rules-based-global-order/

Vanek Smith, Stacey, 'A Bond Is Born', NPR, 29 January 2019, https://www.npr.org/sections/money/2019/01/29/689781231/a-bond-is-born

Vasilyeva, Maria and Elnar Baynazarov, 'Popolnit rady: Egipet, Saudovskaya Aravia i Turtsiya mogut vstupit v BRIKS' [Filling-up with happiness: Egypt, Saudi Arabia, and Turkey may join BRICS], *Izvestia*, 14 July 2022, https://iz.ru/1364353/mariia-vasileva-elnar-bainazarov/popolnit-rady-egipet-saudovskaia-araviia-i-turtciia-mogut-vstupit-v-briks

Vasovic, Aleksandar and Adrian Croft, 'U.S., EU Set Sanctions as Putin Recognizes Crimea "Sovereignty"', Reuters, 17 March 2014, https://www.reuters.com/article/us-ukraine-crisis-idUSBREA1Q1E820140317

Vedomosti, 'Lukashenko rasskazal o proizvodstvye chernoi i krasnoi ikry v Belorussii' [Lukashenko spoke about the production of red and black caviar in Belarus], 30 January 2018, https://www.vedomosti.ru/politics/news/2018/01/30/749401-lukashenko-rasskazal-o-proizvodstve-chernoi-i-krasnoi-ikri

Velkey, Robert, 'Hungary to Enter Long Term Gas Delivery Agreement with Russia from 2021', Hungary Today, 5 October 2017, https://hungarytoday.hu/szijjarto-hungary-enter-long-term-gas-delivery-agreement-russia-2021/

Venkina, Ekaterina, 'Wie man das Druschba Desaster am ende der Pipeline wahrnimmet' [How the Druzhba disaster is seen at this end], Deutsche Welle, 2 July 2019, https://m.dw.com/de/wie-man-das-druschba-desaster-am-ende-der-pipeline-wahrnimmt/a-49440013

BIBLIOGRAPHY

Verma, Nidhi, 'India's Russian Oil Binge Sends Middle East Imports to 19-mth Low—Trade', Reuters, 28 October 2022, https://www.reuters.com/business/energy/indias-russian-oil-binge-sends-middle-east-imports-19-mth-low-trade-2022-10-27/

Vesti, 'Turchynov obyavil o nachalye antiterroristicheskoi operatsii na yugo-vostoke Ukrainy' [Turchynov announced the start of the anti-terrorist operation in the south-east of Ukraine], 7 April 2014, https://vesti.ua/strana/46250-turchinov-objavil-o-nachale-antiterroristicheskoj-operacii-na-jugo-vostoke-ukrainy

Vietnam Plus, 'Once upon a Time: The Russian Village in Vietnam', 13 November 2013, https://en.vietnamplus.vn/once-upon-a-time-the-russian-village-in-vietnam/52077.vnp

Volz, Dustin and Timothy Gardner, 'In a First, U.S. Blames Russia for Cyber Attacks on Energy Grid', Reuters, 15 March 2018, https://www.reuters.com/article/us-usa-russia-sanctions-energygrid-idUSKCN1GR2G3

Voronova, Tatiana, Oksana Kobzeva, and Dmitry Zhdannikov, 'Russian State Bank Secretly Financed Rosneft Sale after Foreign Buyers Balked', Reuters, 9 November 2018, https://www.reuters.com/article/us-rosneft-privatisation-exclusive-idUSKCN1NE132

Vyas, Kejal and Anatoly Kurmanaev, 'Goldman Sachs Bought Venezuela's State Oil Company's Bonds Last Week', *The Wall Street Journal*, 28 May 2017, https://www.wsj.com/articles/goldman-sachs-bought-venezuelan-oil-co-bonds-last-week-1496020176

Vzglyad, 'Medvedev: MVF v sluchaye vydeleniya Ukrainye kredita otkroyet "yashchik Pandory"' [Medvedev: By allocating credit to Ukraine, the IMF will open 'Pandora's Box'], 12 February 2016, https://vz.ru/news/2016/2/12/793878.html

Walsh, Declan, '"From Russia with Love': A Putin Ally Mines Gold and Plays Favorites in Sudan', *The New York Times*, 5 June 2022, https://www.nytimes.com/2022/06/05/world/africa/wagner-russia-sudan-gold-putin.html

Warsaw Institute, 'Rosneft's German Subsidiary Expands Its Activities', Warsaw Institute, 26 August 2019, https://warsawinstitute.org/rosnefts-german-subsidiary-expands-activities/

Wong, Wailin and Adrian Ma, 'Russia Could Default on Its Foreign Debt for the First Time in a Century', NPR, 22 April 2022, https://www.npr.org/2022/04/22/1094240449/russia-could-default-on-its-foreign-debt-for-the-first-time-in-a-century

Walker, Shaun, 'Everything's Fine, Says Putin in Press Conference—Including in My Love Life', *The Guardian*, 18 December 2014, https://www.theguardian.com/world/2014/dec/18/putin-press-conference-sketch-love-life-ukraine-rouble

—— 'Russia Trades Azov Fighters for Putin Ally in Biggest Prisoner Swap of Ukraine War', *The Guardian*, 22 September 2022, https://www.theguardian.com/world/2022/sep/22/ukrainian-putin-ally-viktor-medvedchuk-exchanged-for-200-azov-battalion-fighters-zelenskiy-says

Wallace, Joe and Anna Hirtenstein, 'Russia Confounds the West by Recapturing its Oil Riches', *The Wall Street Journal*, 29 August 2022, https://www.wsj.com/articles/russia-confounds-the-west-by-recapturing-its-oil-riches-11661781928

Waxman, Simon, 'What Rule-Based International Order?', *Boston Review*, 2 March 2022, https://bostonreview.net/articles/what-rule-based-international-order/

Weaver, Courtney, 'Cash-Laden Oligarchs Hunt Pastures New', *The Financial Times*, 5 April 2013, https://www.ft.com/content/25bf411a-9e01-11e2-bea1-00144feabdc0

Weidemaier, Mark and Mitu Gulati, 'A Cautionary Tale: Argentina's Pari Passu Debt Debacle', Credit Slips, 5 January 2020, https://www.creditslips.org/creditslips/2020/01/a-cautionary-tale-argentinas-pari-passu-debt-debacle.html

—— 'A Silver Lining to Russia's Sanctions-Busting Clause?', *The Financial Times*, 19 October 2022, https://www.ft.com/content/36119b6d-770d-4466-8fe5-06728db7fe07

Weiner, Rachel, 'If Anyone Was a Turkish Agent, It Was Michael Flynn, Not Business Partner, Judge Says', *The Washington Post*, 25 March 2022, https://www.washingtonpost.com/dc-md-va/2022/03/25/flynn-turkey-rafiekian-trial/

Weselowsky, Tony, 'Despite Doomsday Predictions, Bulgaria Proves There Is Life after Russian Gas', RFE/RL, 20 May 2022, https://www.rferl.org/a/bulgaria-life-after-russian-gas/31860510.html

Wetzel, Daniel, 'Russen bieten Deutschland Atomstrom an' [Russians offer Germany nuclear power], Welt, 24 June 2014, https://www.welt.de/wirtschaft/energie/article129387616/Russen-bieten-Deutschland-Atomstrom-an.html

Weyer, Eva-Martina, 'Angst um Schwedt ist weiter spürbar' [Fear for Schwedt is still felt], *Nordkurier*, 22 September 2022, https://

www.nordkurier.de/uckermark/angst-um-schwedt-ist-weiter-spuerbar-2249720309.html

Wheatley, Jonathan and Guy Chazan, 'Ukraine Secures Preliminary Deal to Suspend Debt Repayments', *The Financial Times*, 20 July 2022, https://www.ft.com/content/22b32749-c723-4cdc-ad89-0264fadc505a

Wiedemann, Karsten, 'Federal Government Places Rosneft Germany in Trusteeship', Energate, 16 September 2022, https://www.energate-messenger.com/news/226547/federal-government-places-rosneft-germany-in-trusteeship

Wintour, Patrick, 'Russian Hackers to Blame for Sparking Qatar Crisis, FBI Inquiry Finds', *The Guardian*, 7 June 2017, https://www.theguardian.com/world/2017/jun/07/russian-hackers-qatar-crisis-fbi-inquiry-saudi-arabia-uae

————— 'Saudi King's Visit to Russia Heralds Shift in Global Power Structures', *The Guardian*, 5 October 2017, https://www.theguardian.com/world/2017/oct/05/saudi-russia-visit-putin-oil-middle-east

————— 'Germany Agrees 15-Year Liquid Gas Supply Deal with Qatar', *The Guardian*, 29 November 2022, https://www.theguardian.com/world/2022/nov/29/germany-agrees-15-year-liquid-gas-supply-deal-with-qatar

Wiśniewska, Iwona, 'Russia: Speculation on Changes in Ownership within TNK-BP', Centre for Eastern Studies, 13 June 2012, https://www.osw.waw.pl/en/publikacje/analyses/2012-06-13/russia-speculation-changes-ownership-within-tnk-bp

Wood, Mackenzie, 'China's LNG Imports to See Unprecedented Decline in 2022', Wood Mackenzie, 19 July 2022, https://www.woodmac.com/press-releases/chinas-lng-imports-to-see-unprecedented-decline-in-2022/

World Bank, 'Annual Report 2019: Lending Data', World Bank, 19 October 2019, https://thedocs.worldbank.org/en/doc/724041569960954210-0090022019/original/WBAR19LendingData.pdf

World Nuclear Association, 'World Uranium Mining Production', 15 July 2022, https://www.world-nuclear.org/information-library/nuclear-fuel-cycle/mining-of-uranium/world-uranium-mining-production.aspx

BIBLIOGRAPHY

World Nuclear News, 'Construction Starts on Bolivian Research Reactor Complex', 27 July 2021, https://www.world-nuclear-news.org/Articles/Construction-starts-on-Bolivian-research-reactor-c

Xinhua, 'China, Russia Commemorate 70th Anniversary of Diplomatic Ties', 6 July 2019, www.xinhuanet.com/english/2019-06/06/c_138121400.htm

Yackley, Ayla Jean, 'Head of Istanbul Stock Exchange Steps Down', *The Financial Times*, 8 March 2021, https://www.ft.com/content/69eb4968-966c-4060-a02b-cbd8362fbe2e

Yaffa, Joshua, 'Putin's Shadow Cabinet and the Bridge to Crimea', *The New Yorker*, 22 May 2017, https://www.newyorker.com/magazine/2017/05/29/putins-shadow-cabinet-and-the-bridge-to-crimea

Yakoreva, Anastasia, 'Rosneftegaz: Chernaya dyra s polovinoi trilliona' [Rosneftegaz: A black hole with half a trillion], Republic, 1 November 2016, https://republic.ru/posts/75518

Yihe, Xu, 'PipeChina Begins Building Pipeline to Import Gas from Central Asia', UpstreamOnline, 30 September 2022, https://www.upstreamonline.com/lng/pipechina-begins-building-pipeline-to-import-gas-from-central-asia/2-1-1322604

YLE, 'Fortum: Germany to Acquire 30% of Uniper', 22 July 2022, https://yle.fi/news/3-12547290

Zakurdaeva, Kristina and Mihail Maglov, 'The Crimea Circumvention: How EU Firms Are Sidestepping Sanctions and Making Money on the Peninsula', RFE/RL, 3 December 2019, https://www.rferl.org/a/crimea-how-eu-firms-sidestepping-sanctions-making-money-on-peninsula/30303687.html

Zalan, Eszter, 'EU Gives Green Light to Hungary's Nuclear Plant', EU Observer, 6 March 2017, https://euobserver.com/news/137122

Zaman, Sarah, 'Cash-Strapped Pakistan Gets Much-Needed IMF Bailout', VOA, 29 August 2022, https://www.voanews.com/a/cash-strapped-pakistan-gets-much-needed-imf-bailout-/6721636.html

Zarate, Juan, *Treasury's War: The Unleashing of a New Era of Financial Warfare*, New York: PublicAffairs, 2015 [2013].

Zaugg, Julie, 'A Hermit Nation Ruled by an Egomaniac: Is Turkmenistan on the Brink of Collapse?', CNN, 11 August 2019, https://edition.cnn.com/2019/08/10/asia/turkmenistan-caspian-sea-intl-hnk/index.html

Zengerle, Patricia, 'U.S. Senators Introduce Russia Sanctions "Bill from Hell"', Reuters, 2 August 2018, https://www.reuters.com/article/us-usa-russia-sanctions-idUSKBN1KN22Q

Ziemba, Rachel, 'Russia's Economy Has Adjusted to Sanctions; That Doesn't Mean Moscow Is Winning the Financial War', Barron's, 11 April 2022, https://www.barrons.com/articles/russia-strong-ruble-cut-interest-rate-winning-sanctions-war-51649610606

Zinets, Natalia, 'Ukraine Court Rejects Chinese Appeal in Aerospace Deal Opposed by Washington', Reuters, 17 April 2020, https://www.reuters.com/article/us-ukraine-motorsich-idUSKBN21Z1AY

————— 'Ukraine President Approves Sanctions against China's Skyrizon', Reuters, 29 January 2021, https://www.reuters.com/article/ukraine-china-sanctions-idUSL1N2K411U

Zhang, Shu and Chen Aizhu, 'China's CEFC Founder Ye Named in Corruption Case—State Media', Reuters, 12 October 2018, https://www.reuters.com/article/china-corruption-cefc/chinas-cefc-founder-ye-named-in-corruption-case-state-media-idUSL4N1WS26I

Zhdannikov, Dmitry and Vladimir Soldatkin, 'Russia's Rosneft to Take Control of Iraqi Kurdish Pipeline amid Crisis', Reuters, 20 October 2017, https://www.reuters.com/article/us-mideast-crisis-iraq-kurds-rosneft-idUSKBN1CP16L

Zhegulov, Ilya, 'Kak Putin Voznenavidel Ukrainu (How Putin Came To Hate Ukraine)'. Verstka, 25 April 2023. https://verstka.media/kak-putin-pridumal-voynu

Zheng, William, 'Corrupt Chinese "King" Who Took US$10 Million in Bribes Jailed for 12 Years', *South China Morning Post*, 12 April 2019, https://www.scmp.com/news/china/politics/article/3005926/corrupt-chinese-king-who-took-us10-million-bribes-jailed-12

Zhukov, Yevgeny, 'V dvukh gorodakh Donbassa zakhvachyony gorsovyety' [City councils captured in two cities of Donbass], Deutsche Welle, 13 April 2014, https://www.dw.com/ru/в-двух-городах-донбасса-захвачены-горсоветы/a-17564121

Zubok, Vladislav, *Collapse: The Fall of the Soviet Union*, New Haven: Yale University Press, 2021.

Zygar, Mikhail, *All the Kremlin's Men: Inside the Court of Vladimir Putin*, New York: PublicAffairs, 2017 [2016].

ACKNOWLEDGEMENTS

My first and foremost thanks goes to my family, I love you more than you could ever know, even if I have made you gluttons for punishment. To my mother, thank you for never giving up and setting such a high bar. To my father, thank you for your patience and inspiration. To my brother, thank you for always pushing me on. To my baby sister, thank you for always being the person that I look up to most in the world and still finding time to keep a watchful eye over me. And to my step-mother and step-father, thank you for all the joy you bring and for your unwavering support.

The list of academics, journalists, and analysts who have shaped this work is too long to list here, but I am particularly indebted to the team at the Foreign Policy Research Institute, Michael Dwyer at Hurst, my editor Ben Noble, Katharine Khamhaengwong for her many thorough reviews, Tim Page for all of his incredible work in seeing this book come to fruition, Arnold Platon for crafting the map, and Vilnis 'Vilnissimo' Vesma for creating the cartoons.

Finally, if we are shaped by anything, then surely it is the gravitational pull of friendship, which so determines our orbit. With that in mind I would like to extend my most sincere appreciation to Mansoor Ahmad MBE, Ghada Amer, Aanandi Aquino, Annie Auchincloss, E.B, Benton Bair, Anton Barbashin, Oto Berishvili, Karl Bilimoria, Nick Birman-Trickett, Irakli Burchuladze, Dan Cafiero, Justin Campbell, Mike Chanos, Giorgi Chichinadze, Jono Cottingham, Cameron Cowie, Stephen Dizard, Roberta Einer, Sarah Einstein, Liisa Ennuste, Sean Farinaccio, Mikey Freedman, Hussein El Gaafary, Alex Gesswein, Ayesha Ghafoor, Josh Gomez, Dmitry Goryukhin, Bernie de Haldevang, Farah Hamzaoui, Charlotte Jacob, Loona Järvloo, Anna Jeglinska, Abigail Ledes-Åkesson, Lauri Lepik, Andrew Lindsey, Rosanna Lockwood, Isabelle Marino, Akshay Mehra, Jonas Meynert, Richard Mitchelson, Taylor-Chloe Mythen,

319

ACKNOWLEDGEMENTS

Harish Natarajan, Vadim Nazarenko, Alyna Orecharova, Bob O'Toole, Dmytro Potekhin, Aditya Ramachandran, Leonard Rauch, Jake Reingold, Will Rockefeller, Adam Rosen, Artem Satalkin, Zach Schreiber, Max Schwartzapfel, Russell Sechzer, Rayaan Shah, Fraser Simpson, Fred Spencer, Manny Tartaglione, Nikoloz Tevdoradze, Thaniil Theoharis, Irena Timofeeva, Aniket Trivedi, Tarish Trivedi, Tato Tsintsadze, Natasha Turak, Deniz Varol, Sam Van Daele, Ralph Ward-Jackson, Will Weldon, Conor Wolchesky, and Sam Woodcock.

INDEX

321

INDEX